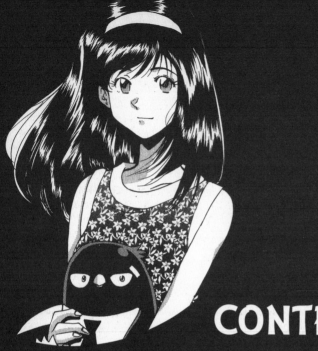

CONTENTS

Ginji Kusanagi is 17 years old and on top of the world. He just made his debut as a pro boxer and he's about to go on a first date with the girl of his dreams, Minako Sasebo. But on the eve of his date, Ginji gets into an "accident" and dies. An odd guardian angel (or perhaps its more of a Buddhist spirit) tells Ginji about a loophole in the cycle of life, death, and reincarnation – all he has to do is live out the life of a penguin, and then he can come back to life in his former body.

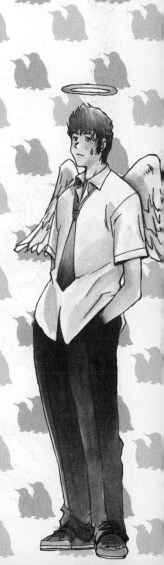

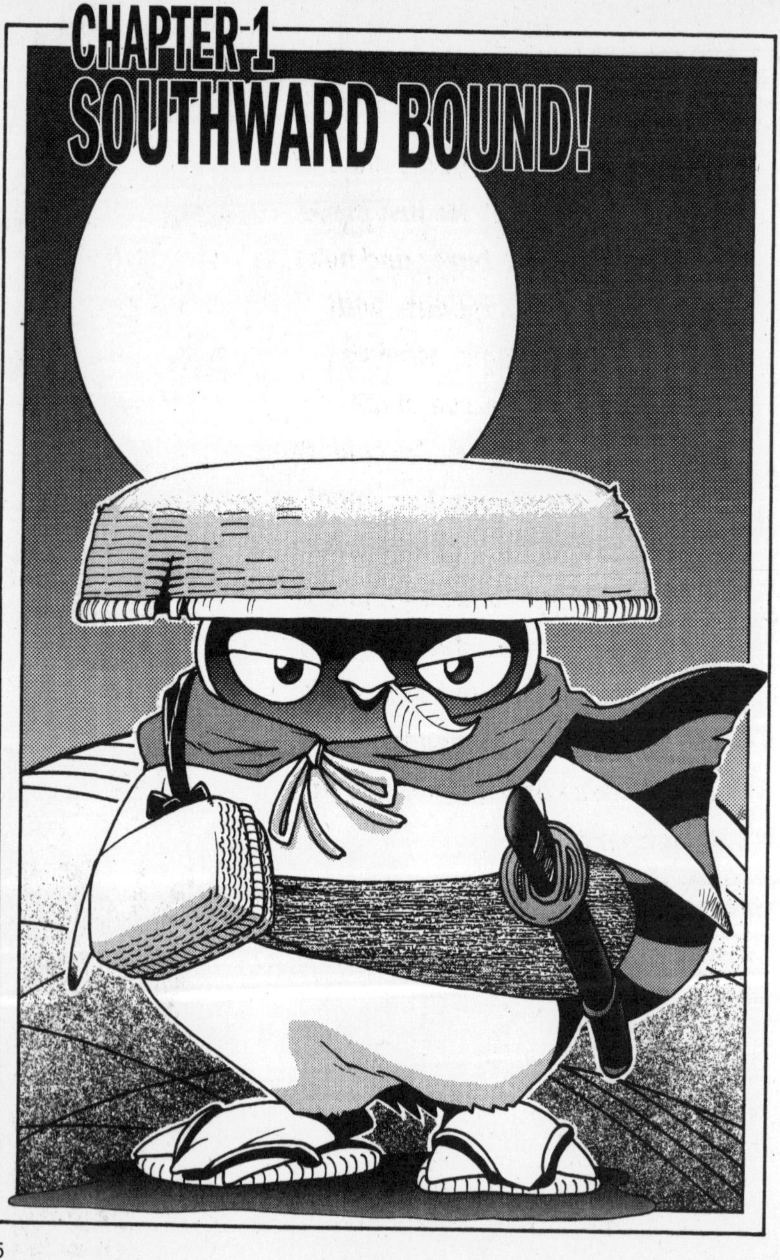
CHAPTER-1
SOUTHWARD BOUND!

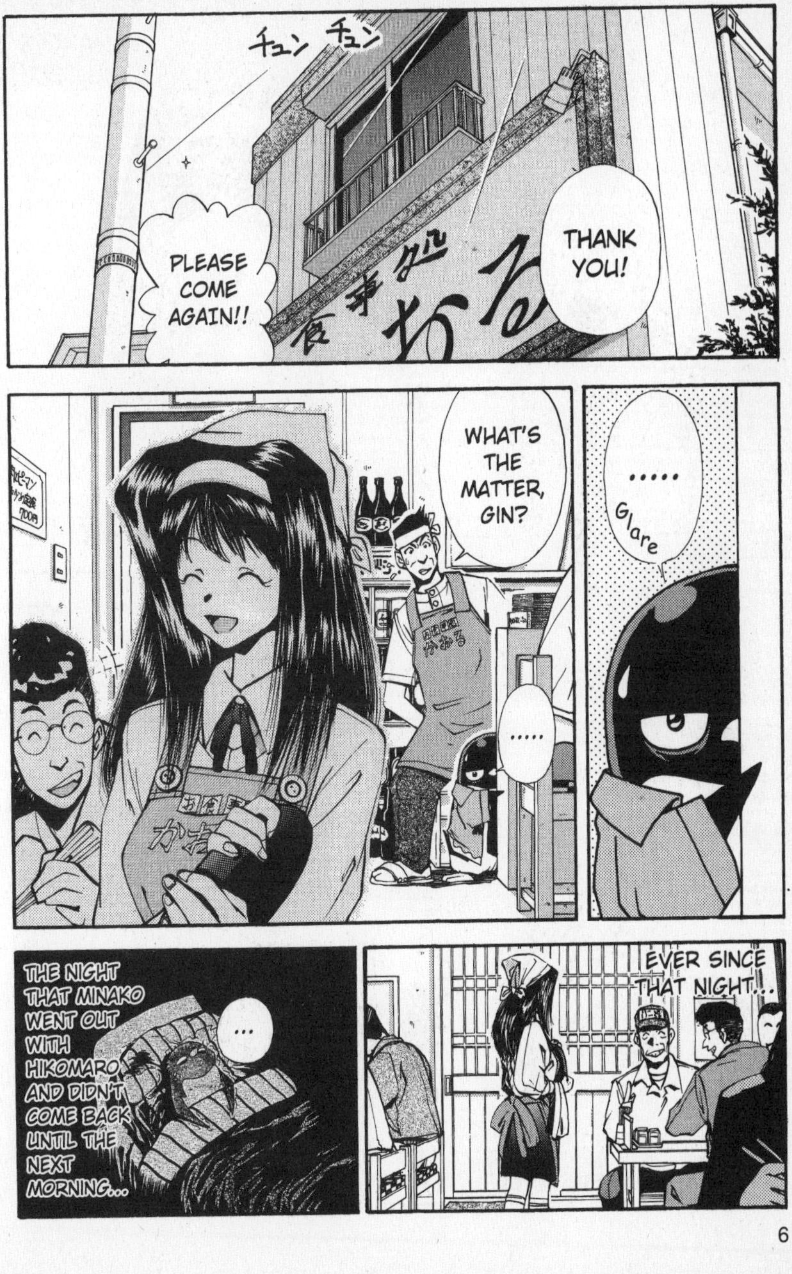
チュン チュン
THANK YOU!
PLEASE COME AGAIN!!
.....
Glare
WHAT'S THE MATTER, GIN?
.....
EVER SINCE THAT NIGHT...
THE NIGHT THAT MINAKO WENT OUT WITH HIKOMARO AND DIDN'T COME BACK UNTIL THE NEXT MORNING...
...

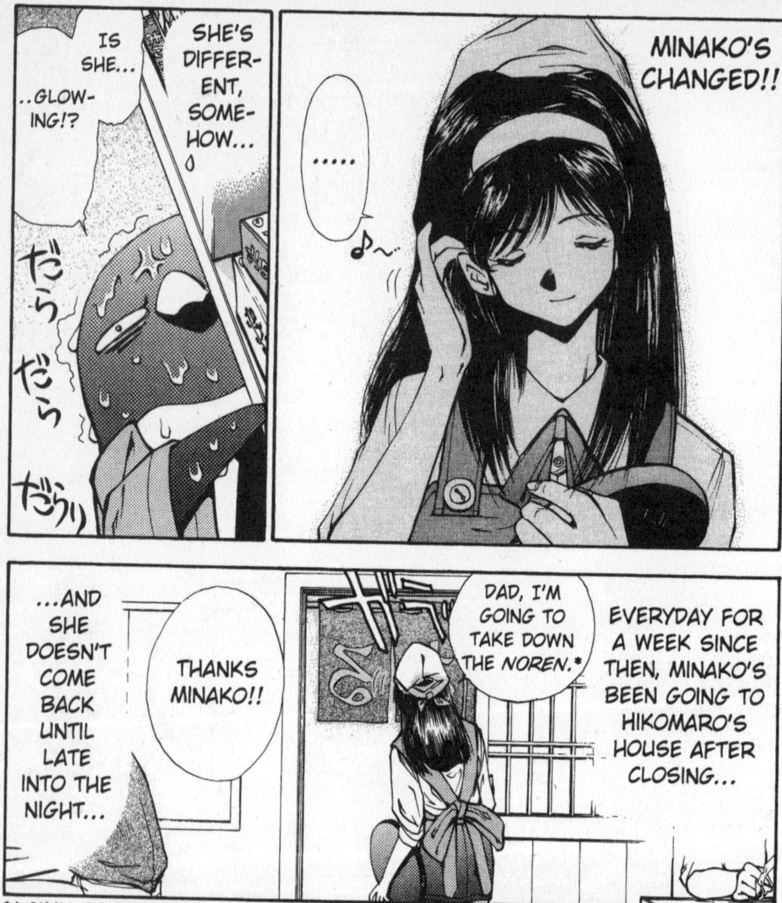
MINAKO'S CHANGED!!
.....
♪~
SHE'S DIFFERENT, SOMEHOW...
IS SHE... ..GLOWING!?
だら
だら
だらり
EVERYDAY FOR A WEEK SINCE THEN, MINAKO'S BEEN GOING TO HIKOMARO'S HOUSE AFTER CLOSING...
DAD, I'M GOING TO TAKE DOWN THE *NOREN.**
THANKS MINAKO!!
...AND SHE DOESN'T COME BACK UNTIL LATE INTO THE NIGHT...

*A SMALL DOORWAY CURTAIN WHICH INDICATES THAT A SHOP IS OPEN FOR BUSINESS.

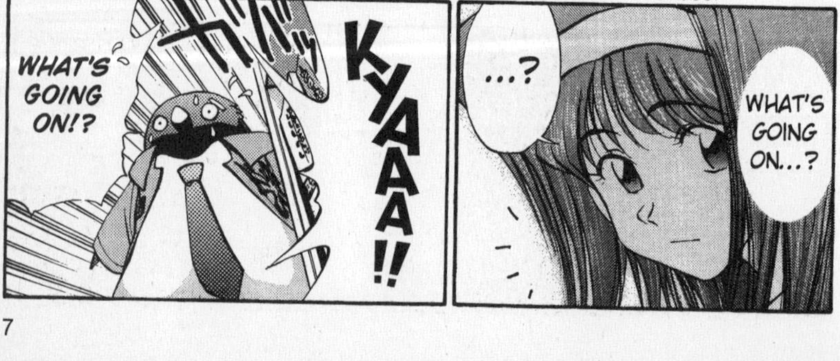
...?
WHAT'S GOING ON...?
KYAAA!!
WHAT'S GOING ON!?

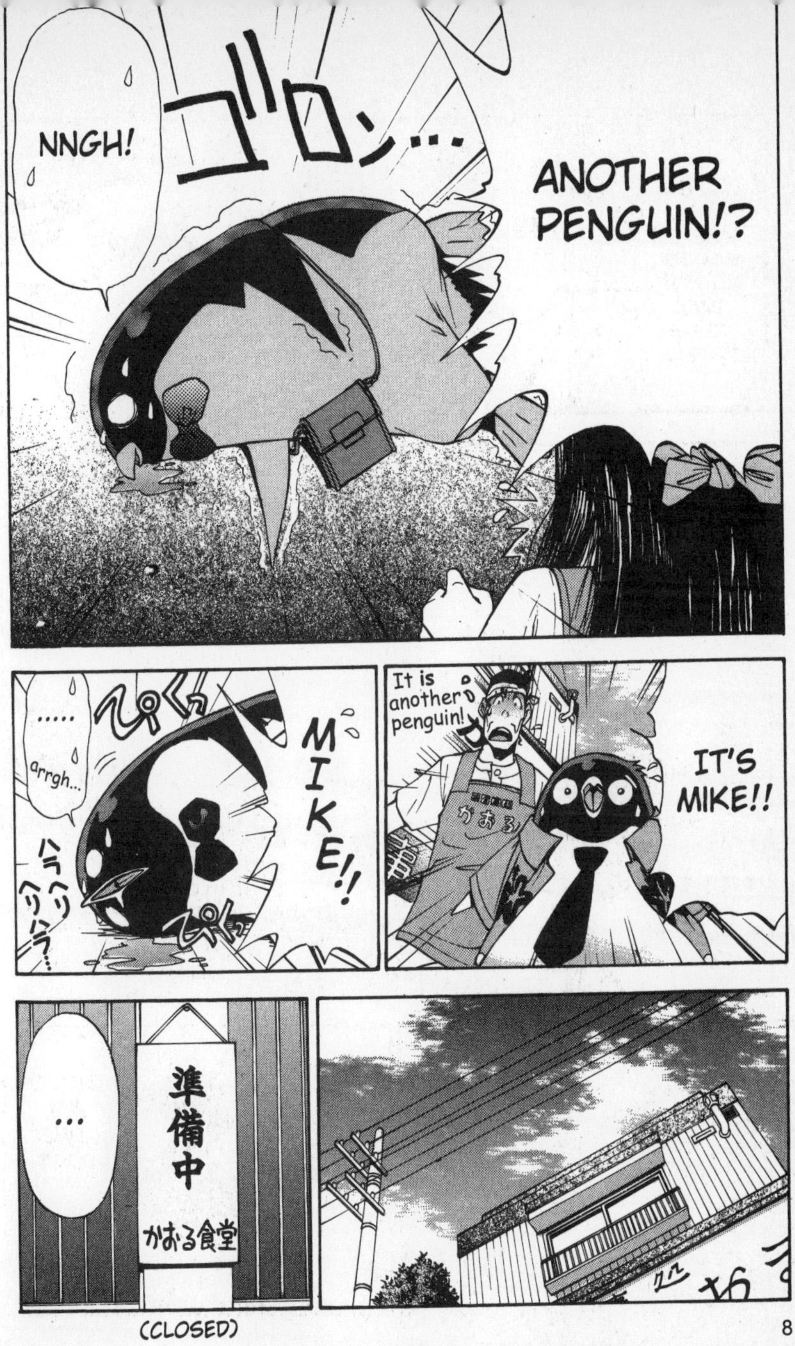
ANOTHER PENGUIN!?
ゴロン…
NNGH!
IT'S MIKE!!
It is another penguin!
かおる
MIKE!!
ぴくっ
.....
arrgh...
ハラヘリヘリハラ…
ぴくっ
準備中
かおる食堂
...

(CLOSED)

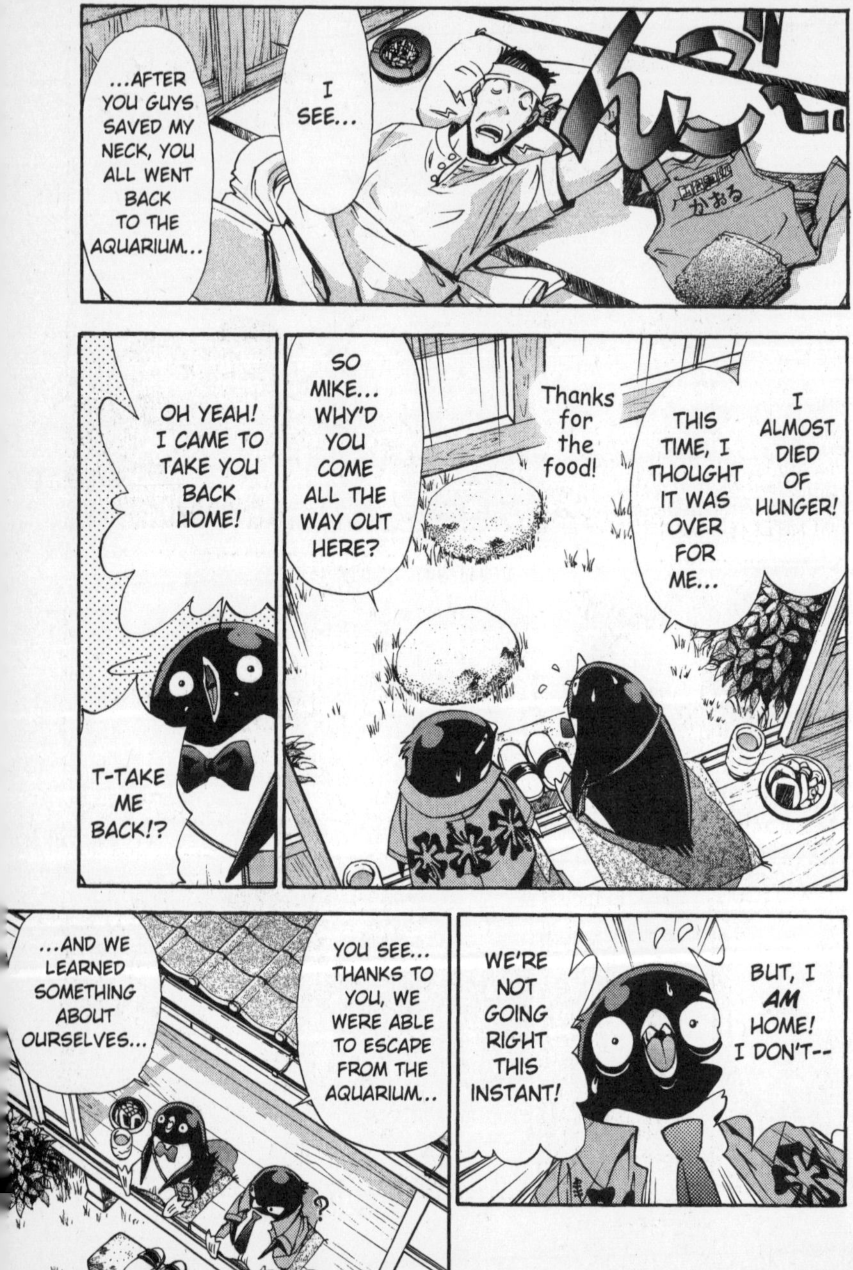
I SEE...
...AFTER YOU GUYS SAVED MY NECK, YOU ALL WENT BACK TO THE AQUARIUM...
かおる
I ALMOST DIED OF HUNGER!
THIS TIME, I THOUGHT IT WAS OVER FOR ME...
Thanks for the food!
SO MIKE... WHY'D YOU COME ALL THE WAY OUT HERE?
OH YEAH! I CAME TO TAKE YOU BACK HOME!
T-TAKE ME BACK!?
BUT, I *AM* HOME! I DON'T--
WE'RE NOT GOING RIGHT THIS INSTANT!
YOU SEE... THANKS TO YOU, WE WERE ABLE TO ESCAPE FROM THE AQUARIUM...
...AND WE LEARNED SOMETHING ABOUT OURSELVES...

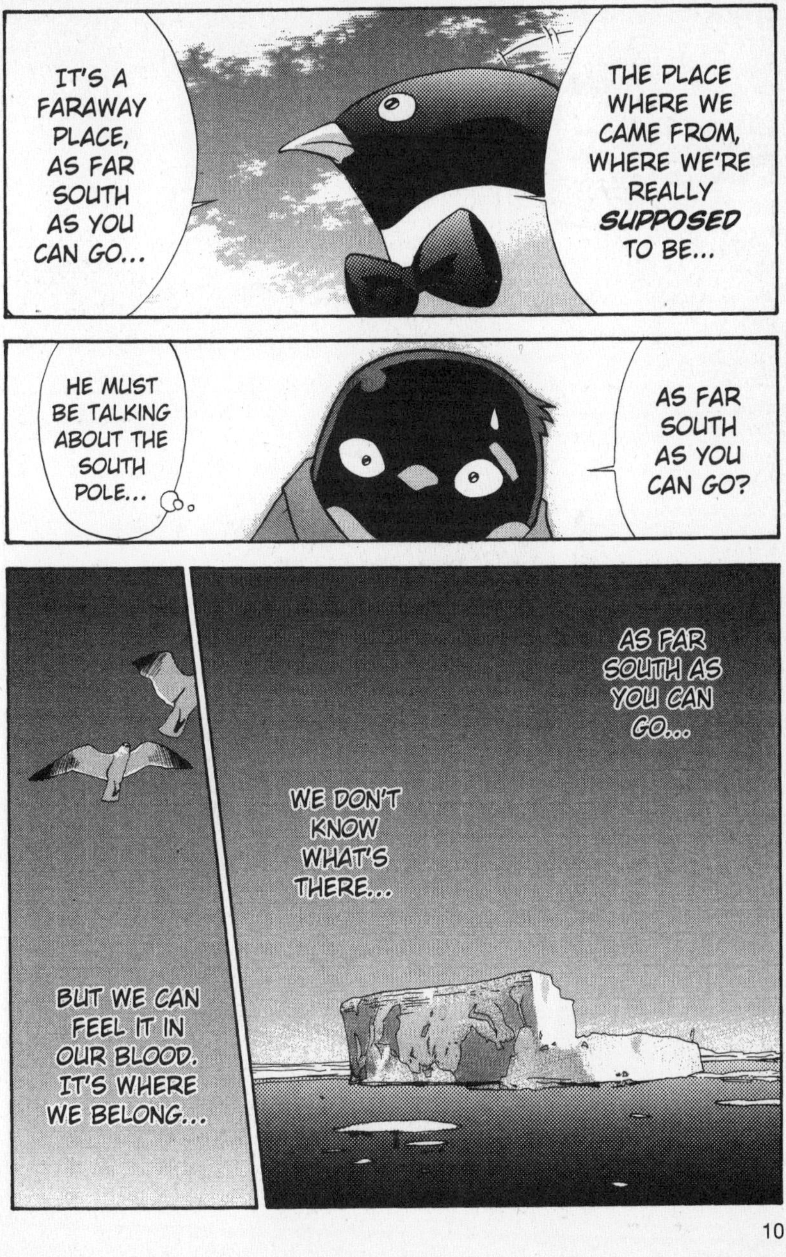
THE PLACE WHERE WE CAME FROM, WHERE WE'RE REALLY **SUPPOSED** TO BE...
IT'S A FARAWAY PLACE, AS FAR SOUTH AS YOU CAN GO...
AS FAR SOUTH AS YOU CAN GO?
HE MUST BE TALKING ABOUT THE SOUTH POLE...
AS FAR SOUTH AS YOU CAN GO...
WE DON'T KNOW WHAT'S THERE...
BUT WE CAN FEEL IT IN OUR BLOOD. IT'S WHERE WE BELONG...

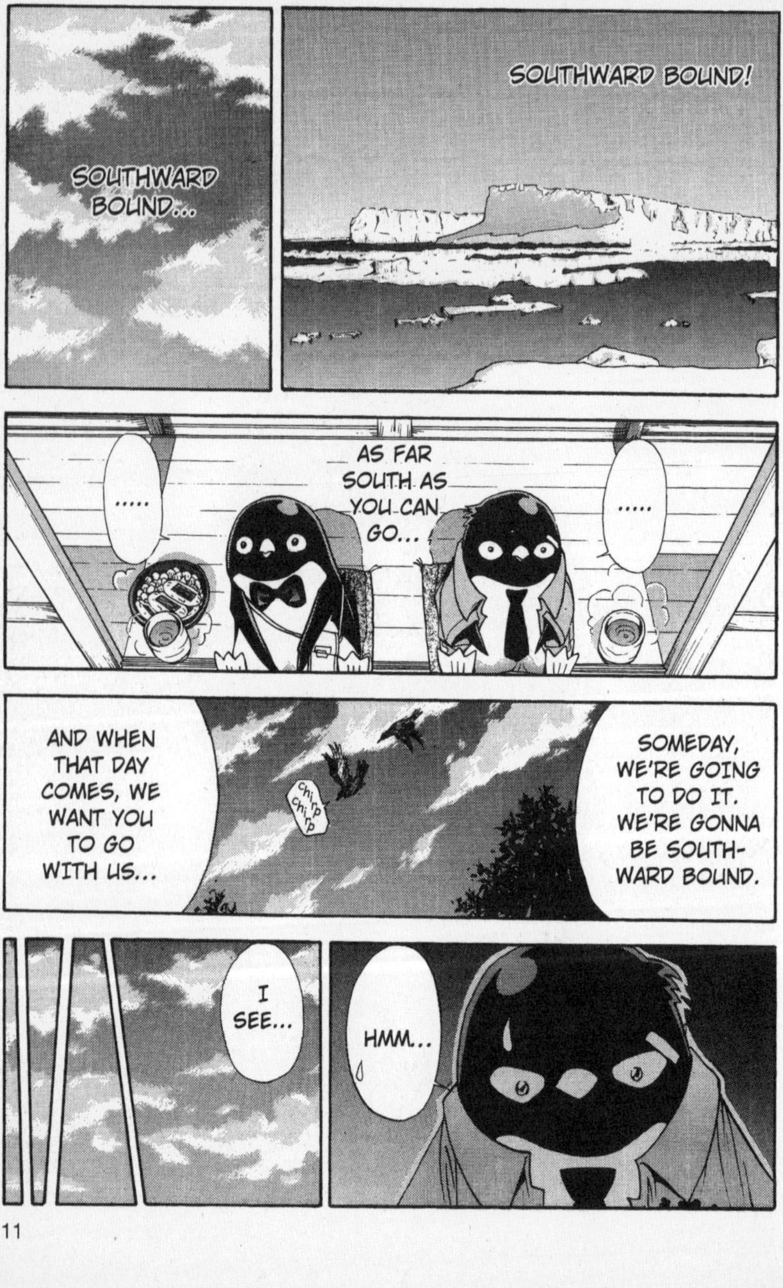
SOUTHWARD BOUND!
SOUTHWARD BOUND...
.....
AS FAR SOUTH AS YOU CAN GO...
.....
SOMEDAY, WE'RE GOING TO DO IT. WE'RE GONNA BE SOUTH-WARD BOUND.
chirp chirp
AND WHEN THAT DAY COMES, WE WANT YOU TO GO WITH US...
HMM...
I SEE...

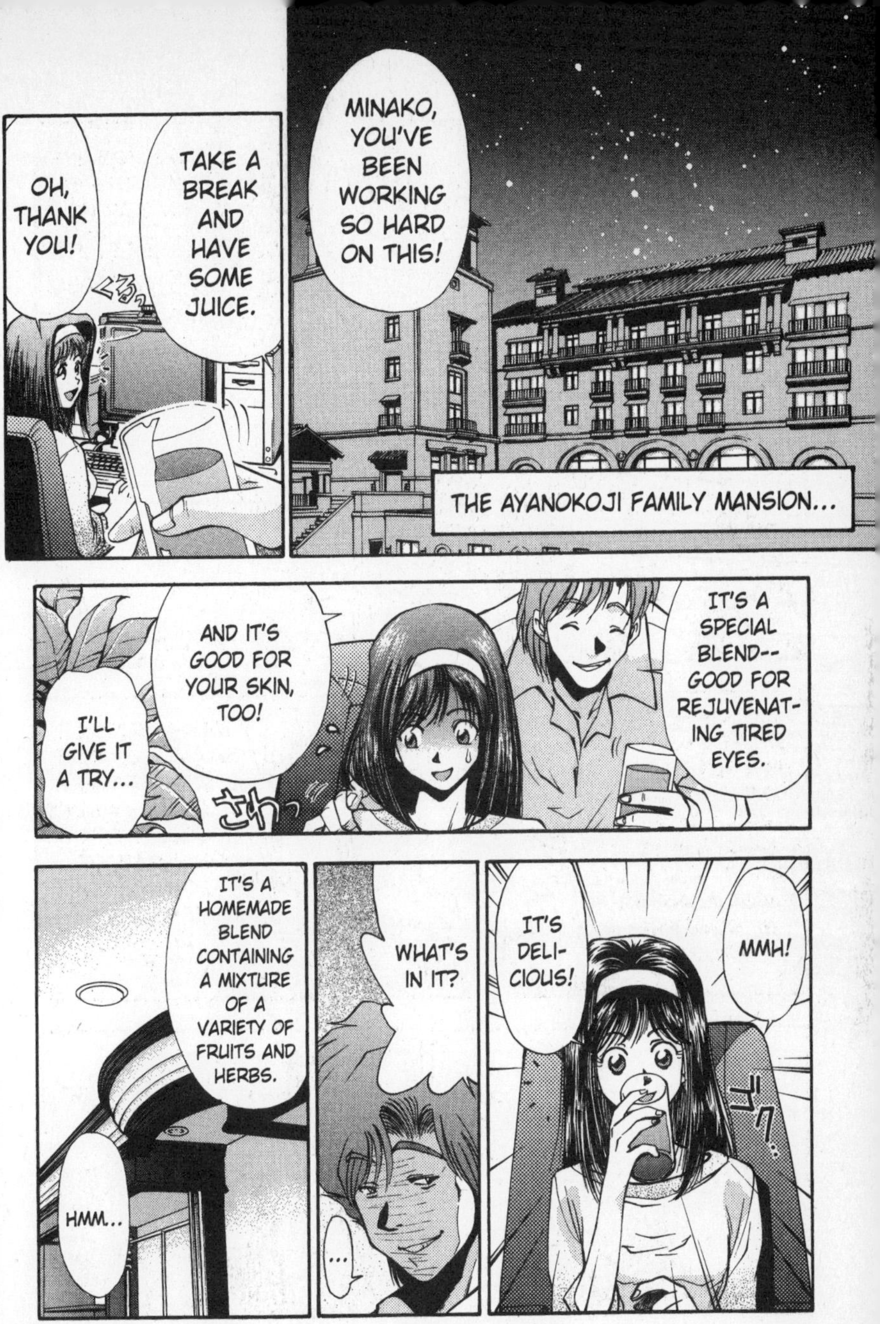
MINAKO, YOU'VE BEEN WORKING SO HARD ON THIS!
THE AYANOKOJI FAMILY MANSION...
TAKE A BREAK AND HAVE SOME JUICE.
OH, THANK YOU!
IT'S A SPECIAL BLEND-- GOOD FOR REJUVENATING TIRED EYES.
AND IT'S GOOD FOR YOUR SKIN, TOO!
I'LL GIVE IT A TRY...
MMH!
IT'S DELICIOUS!
WHAT'S IN IT?
...
IT'S A HOMEMADE BLEND CONTAINING A MIXTURE OF A VARIETY OF FRUITS AND HERBS.
HMM...

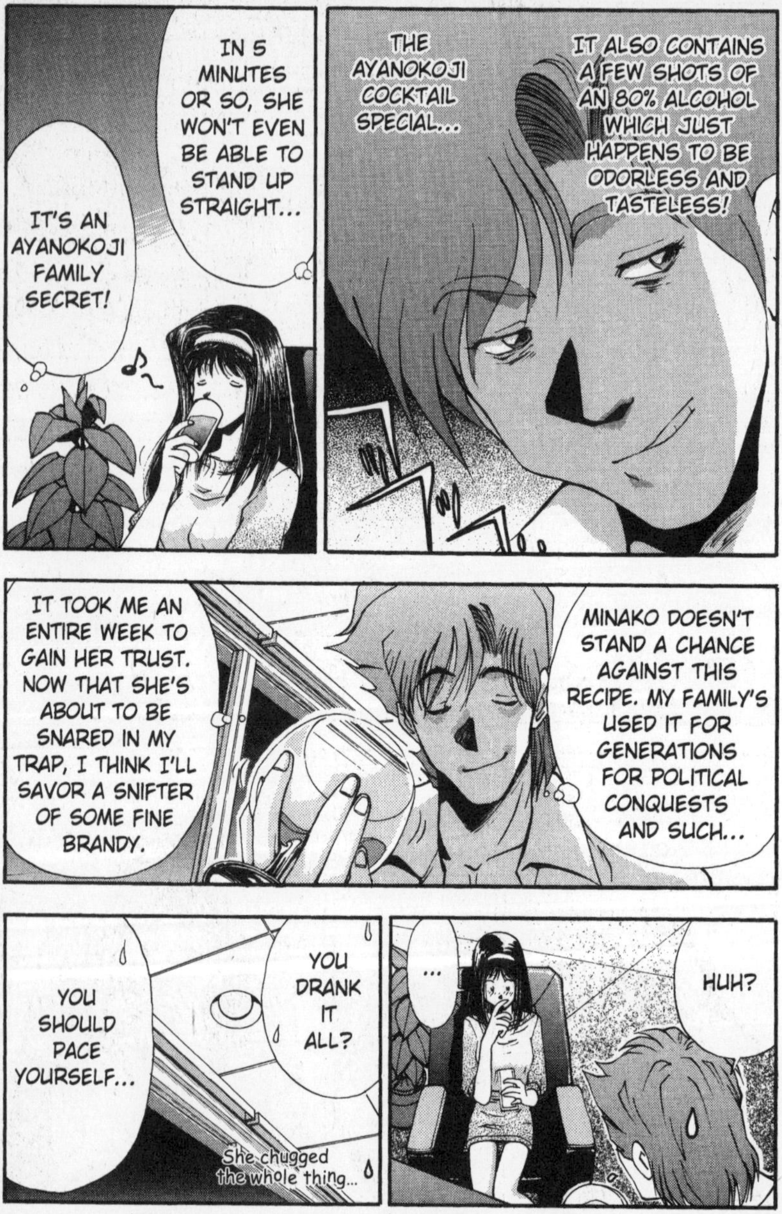

IT ALSO CONTAINS A FEW SHOTS OF AN 80% ALCOHOL WHICH JUST HAPPENS TO BE ODORLESS AND TASTELESS!
THE AYANOKOJI COCKTAIL SPECIAL...
IN 5 MINUTES OR SO, SHE WON'T EVEN BE ABLE TO STAND UP STRAIGHT...
IT'S AN AYANOKOJI FAMILY SECRET!
MINAKO DOESN'T STAND A CHANCE AGAINST THIS RECIPE. MY FAMILY'S USED IT FOR GENERATIONS FOR POLITICAL CONQUESTS AND SUCH...
IT TOOK ME AN ENTIRE WEEK TO GAIN HER TRUST. NOW THAT SHE'S ABOUT TO BE SNARED IN MY TRAP, I THINK I'LL SAVOR A SNIFTER OF SOME FINE BRANDY.
HUH?
...
YOU DRANK IT ALL?
YOU SHOULD PACE YOURSELF...
She chugged the whole thing...

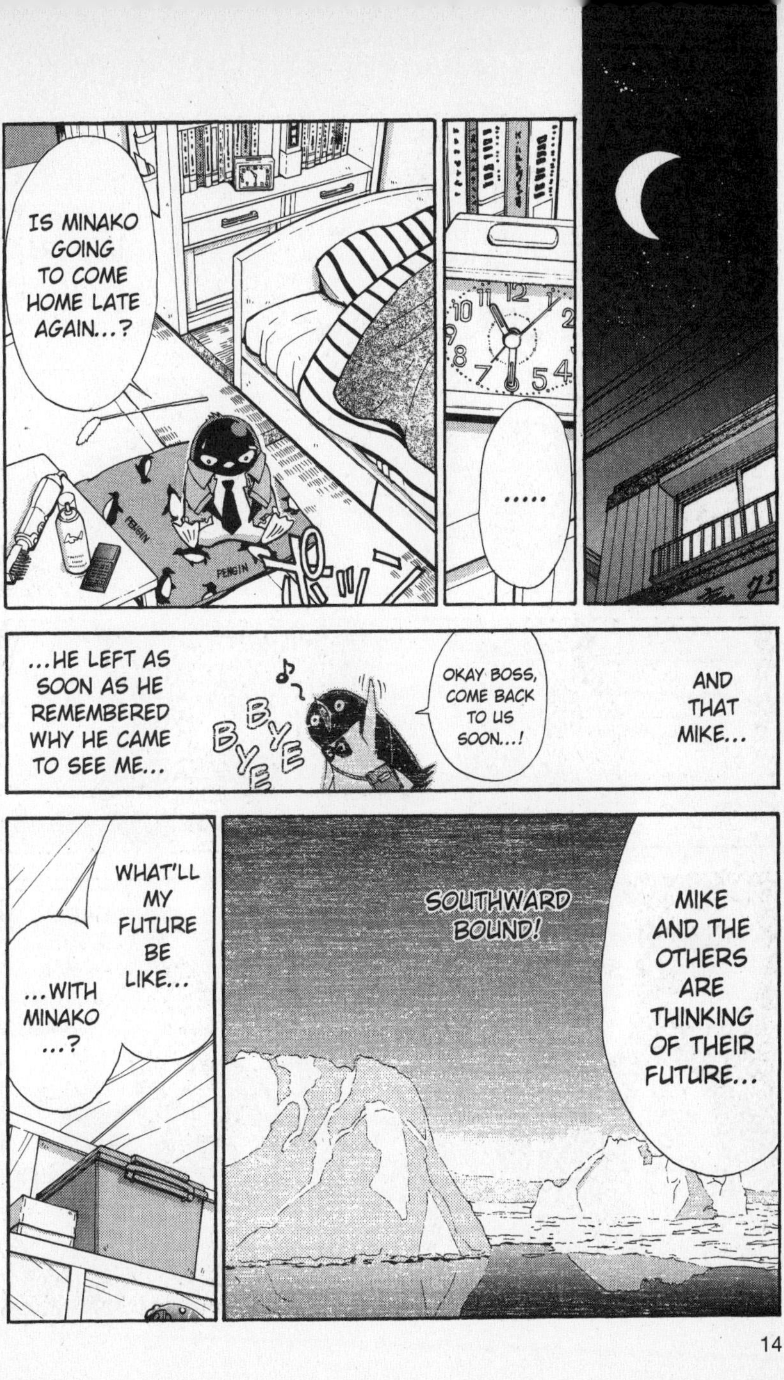
.....
IS MINAKO GOING TO COME HOME LATE AGAIN...?
AND THAT MIKE...
OKAY BOSS, COME BACK TO US SOON...!
BYE BYE
...HE LEFT AS SOON AS HE REMEMBERED WHY HE CAME TO SEE ME...
MIKE AND THE OTHERS ARE THINKING OF THEIR FUTURE...
SOUTHWARD BOUND!
WHAT'LL MY FUTURE BE LIKE...
...WITH MINAKO...?

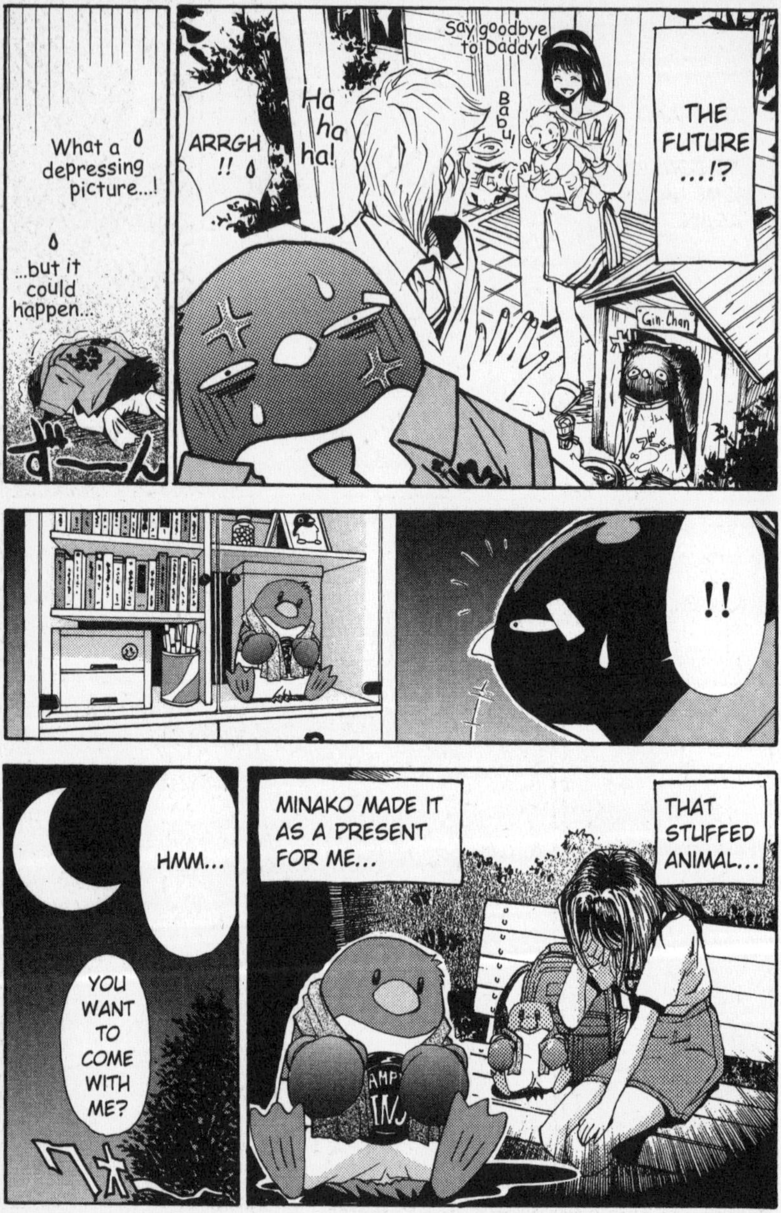
THE FUTURE ...!?
Say goodbye to Daddy!
Babu!
Ha ha ha!
ARRGH !!
What a depressing picture...!
...but it could happen...
!!
THAT STUFFED ANIMAL...
MINAKO MADE IT AS A PRESENT FOR ME...
HMM...
YOU WANT TO COME WITH ME?

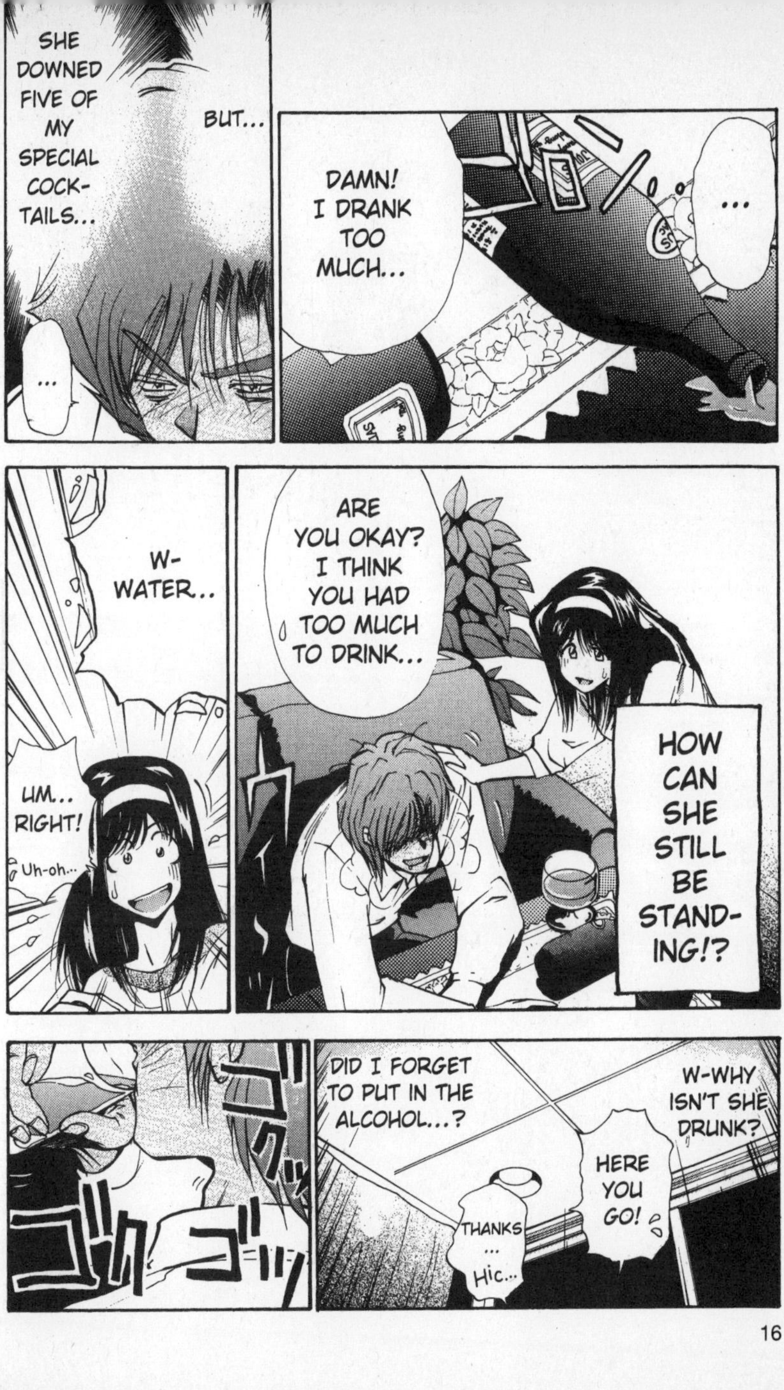
...
DAMN! I DRANK TOO MUCH...
BUT...
SHE DOWNED FIVE OF MY SPECIAL COCK- TAILS...
...
ARE YOU OKAY? I THINK YOU HAD TOO MUCH TO DRINK...
HOW CAN SHE STILL BE STAND- ING!?
W- WATER...
UM... RIGHT!
Uh-oh...
W-WHY ISN'T SHE DRUNK?
DID I FORGET TO PUT IN THE ALCOHOL...?
HERE YOU GO!
THANKS ... Hic...

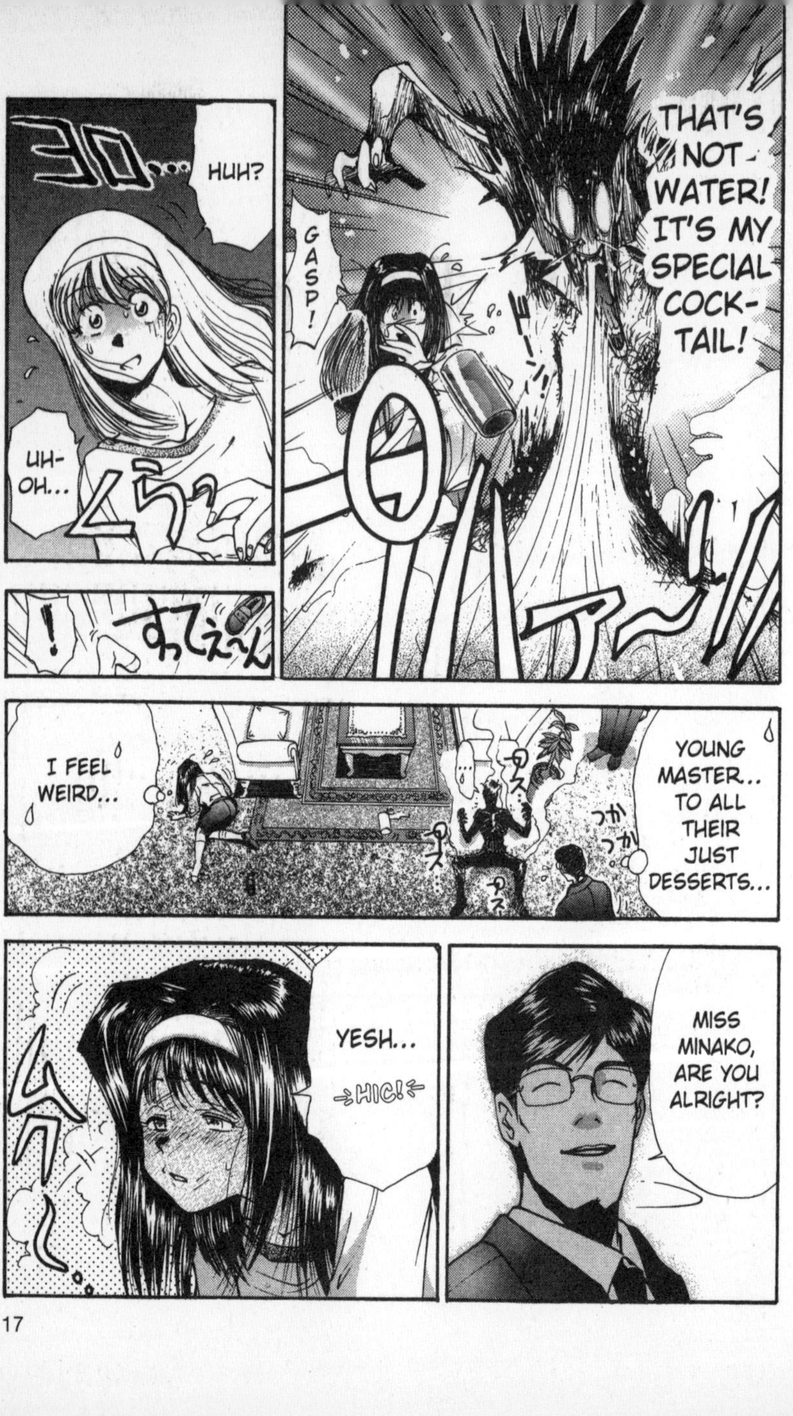
THAT'S NOT-WATER! IT'S MY SPECIAL COCK-TAIL!
GASP!
HUH?
UH-OH...
!
YOUNG MASTER... TO ALL THEIR JUST DESSERTS...
I FEEL WEIRD...
MISS MINAKO, ARE YOU ALRIGHT?
YESH...
HIC!

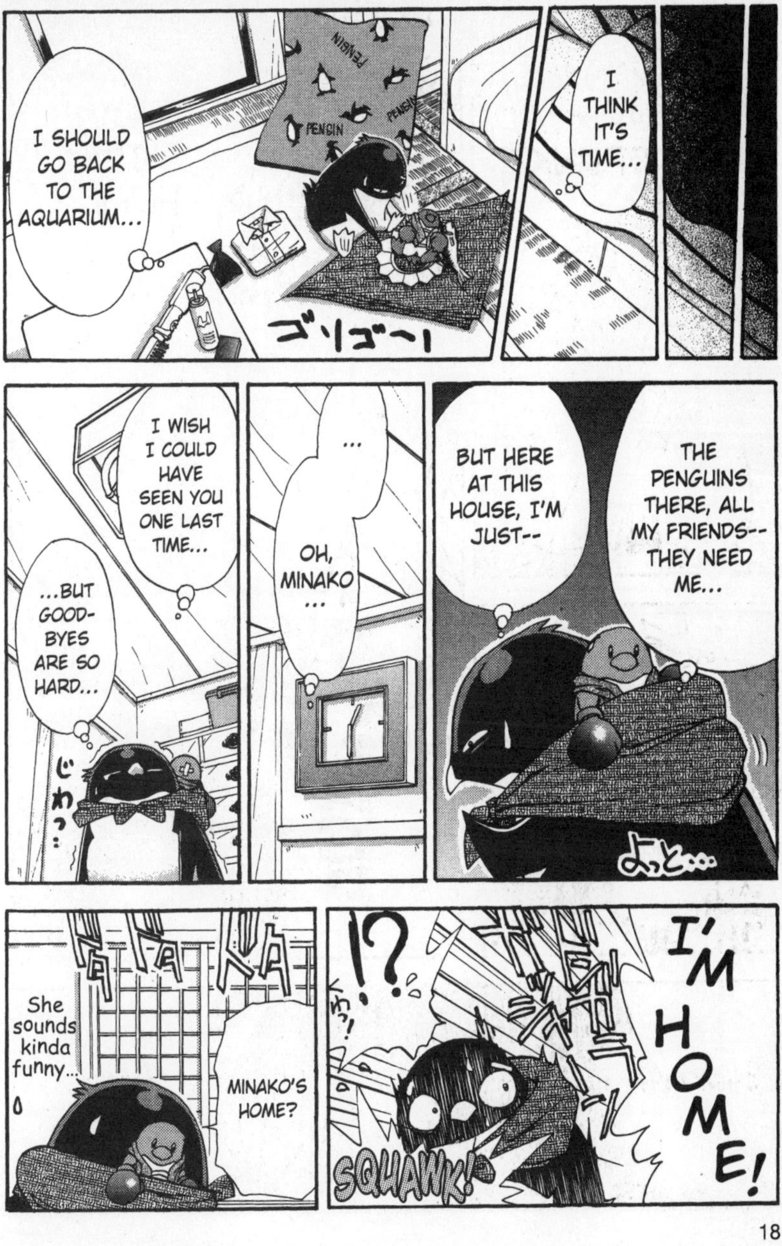
I THINK IT'S TIME...
I SHOULD GO BACK TO THE AQUARIUM...
ゴリゴ〜ー
THE PENGUINS THERE, ALL MY FRIENDS-- THEY NEED ME...
BUT HERE AT THIS HOUSE, I'M JUST--
よっと...
...
OH, MINAKO...
I WISH I COULD HAVE SEEN YOU ONE LAST TIME...
...BUT GOOD-BYES ARE SO HARD...
じわっ...
I'M HOME!
!?
SQUAWK!
MINAKO'S HOME?
She sounds kinda funny...

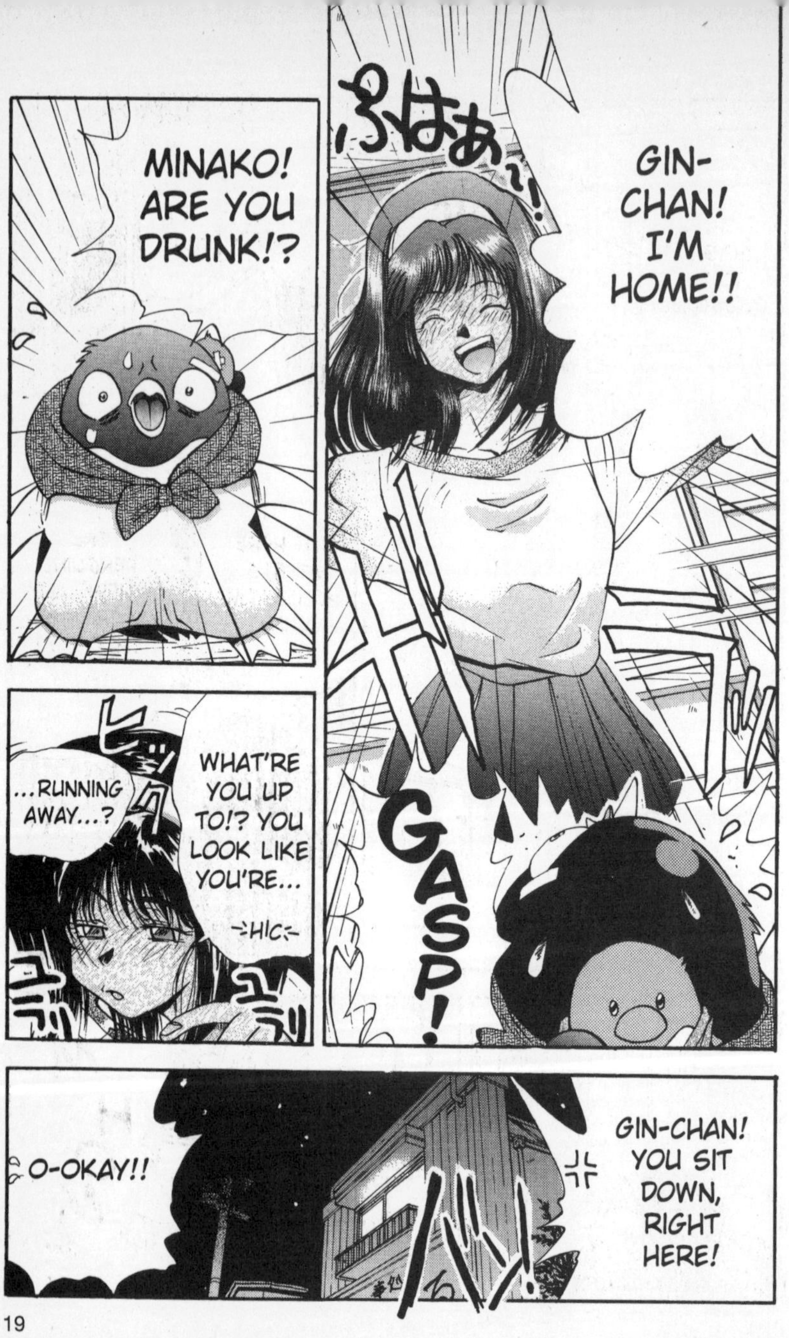
ふはぁ~!!
GIN-CHAN! I'M HOME!!
GASP!
MINAKO! ARE YOU DRUNK!?
WHAT'RE YOU UP TO!? YOU LOOK LIKE YOU'RE...
-HIC-
...RUNNING AWAY...?
GIN-CHAN! YOU SIT DOWN, RIGHT HERE!
O-OKAY!!

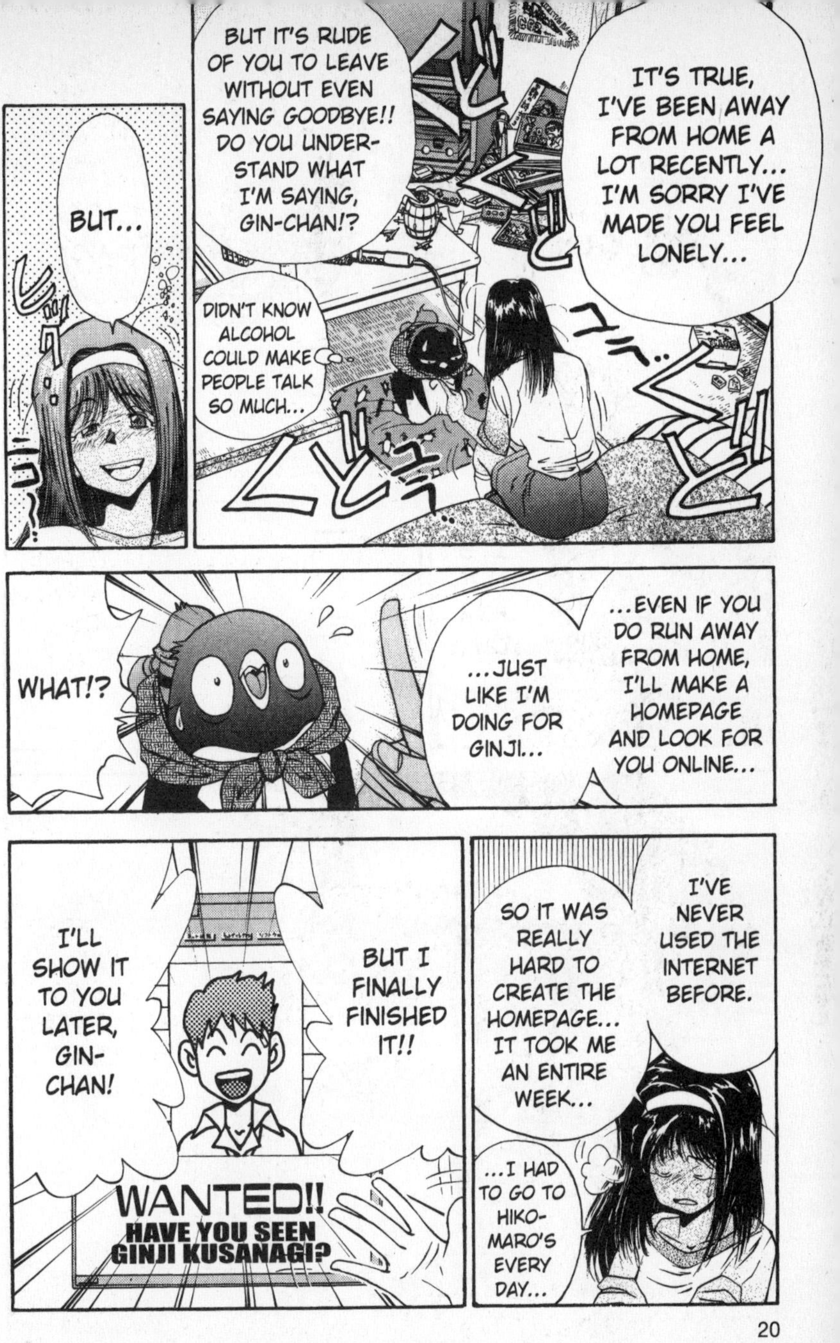
IT'S TRUE, I'VE BEEN AWAY FROM HOME A LOT RECENTLY... I'M SORRY I'VE MADE YOU FEEL LONELY...
BUT IT'S RUDE OF YOU TO LEAVE WITHOUT EVEN SAYING GOODBYE!! DO YOU UNDER-STAND WHAT I'M SAYING, GIN-CHAN!?
DIDN'T KNOW ALCOHOL COULD MAKE PEOPLE TALK SO MUCH...
BUT...
...EVEN IF YOU DO RUN AWAY FROM HOME, I'LL MAKE A HOMEPAGE AND LOOK FOR YOU ONLINE...
...JUST LIKE I'M DOING FOR GINJI...
WHAT!?
I'VE NEVER USED THE INTERNET BEFORE.
SO IT WAS REALLY HARD TO CREATE THE HOMEPAGE... IT TOOK ME AN ENTIRE WEEK...
...I HAD TO GO TO HIKO-MARO'S EVERY DAY...
BUT I FINALLY FINISHED IT!!
I'LL SHOW IT TO YOU LATER, GIN-CHAN!
WANTED!!
HAVE YOU SEEN GINJI KUSANAGI?

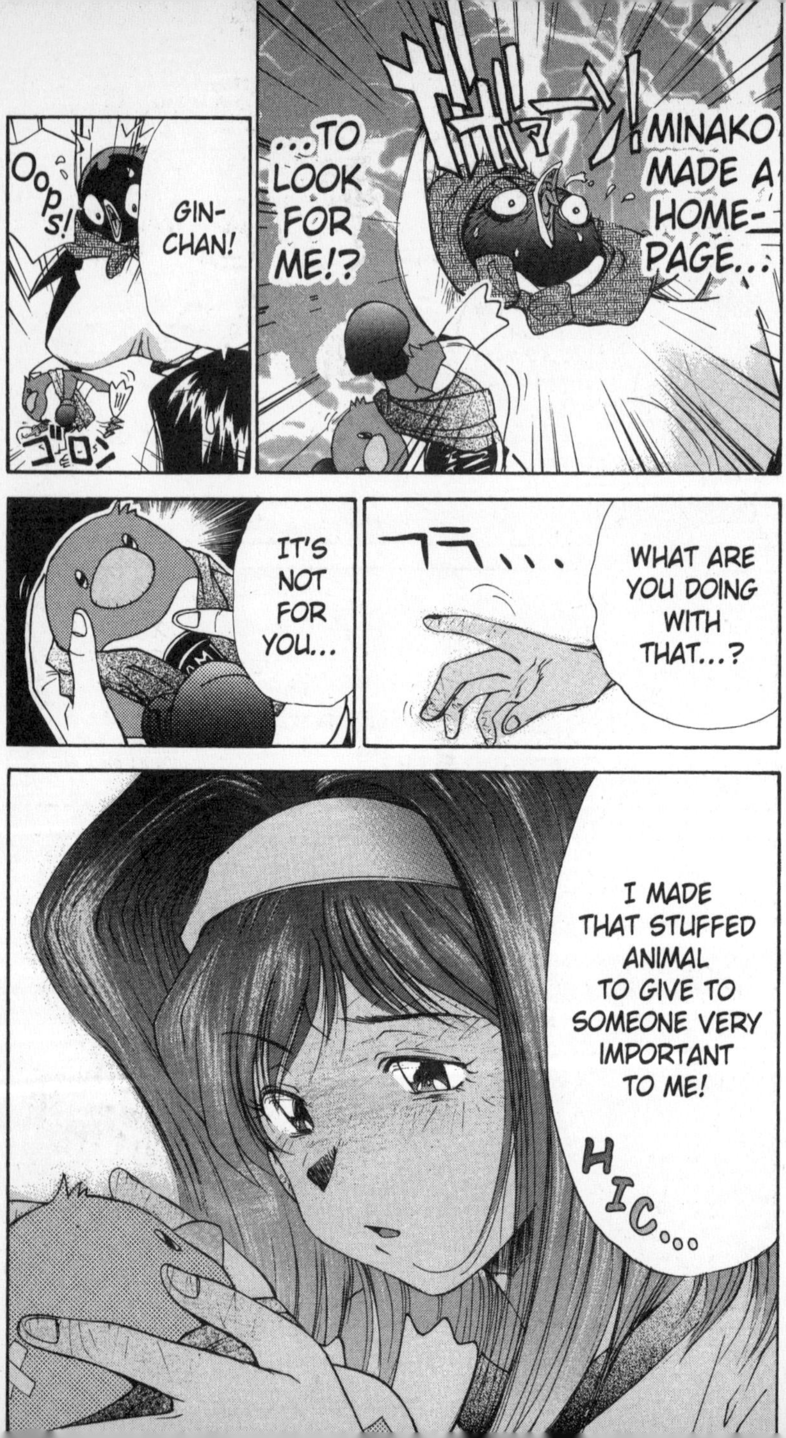
MINAKO MADE A HOME-PAGE...
...TO LOOK FOR ME!?
GIN-CHAN!
Oops!
ゴロン
WHAT ARE YOU DOING WITH THAT...?
フラ...
IT'S NOT FOR YOU...
I MADE THAT STUFFED ANIMAL TO GIVE TO SOMEONE VERY IMPORTANT TO ME!
HIC...

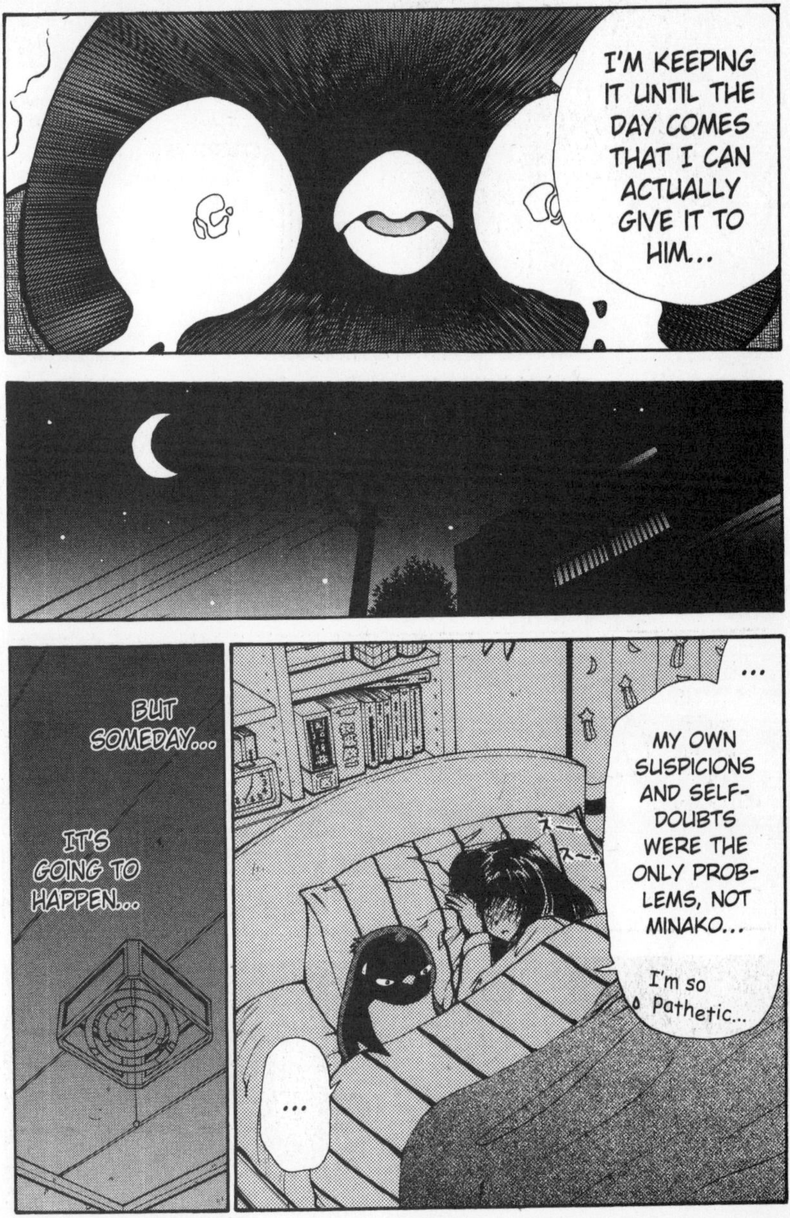
I'M KEEPING IT UNTIL THE DAY COMES THAT I CAN ACTUALLY GIVE IT TO HIM...
...
MY OWN SUSPICIONS AND SELF-DOUBTS WERE THE ONLY PROBLEMS, NOT MINAKO...
I'm so Pathetic...
...
BUT SOMEDAY...
IT'S GOING TO HAPPEN...

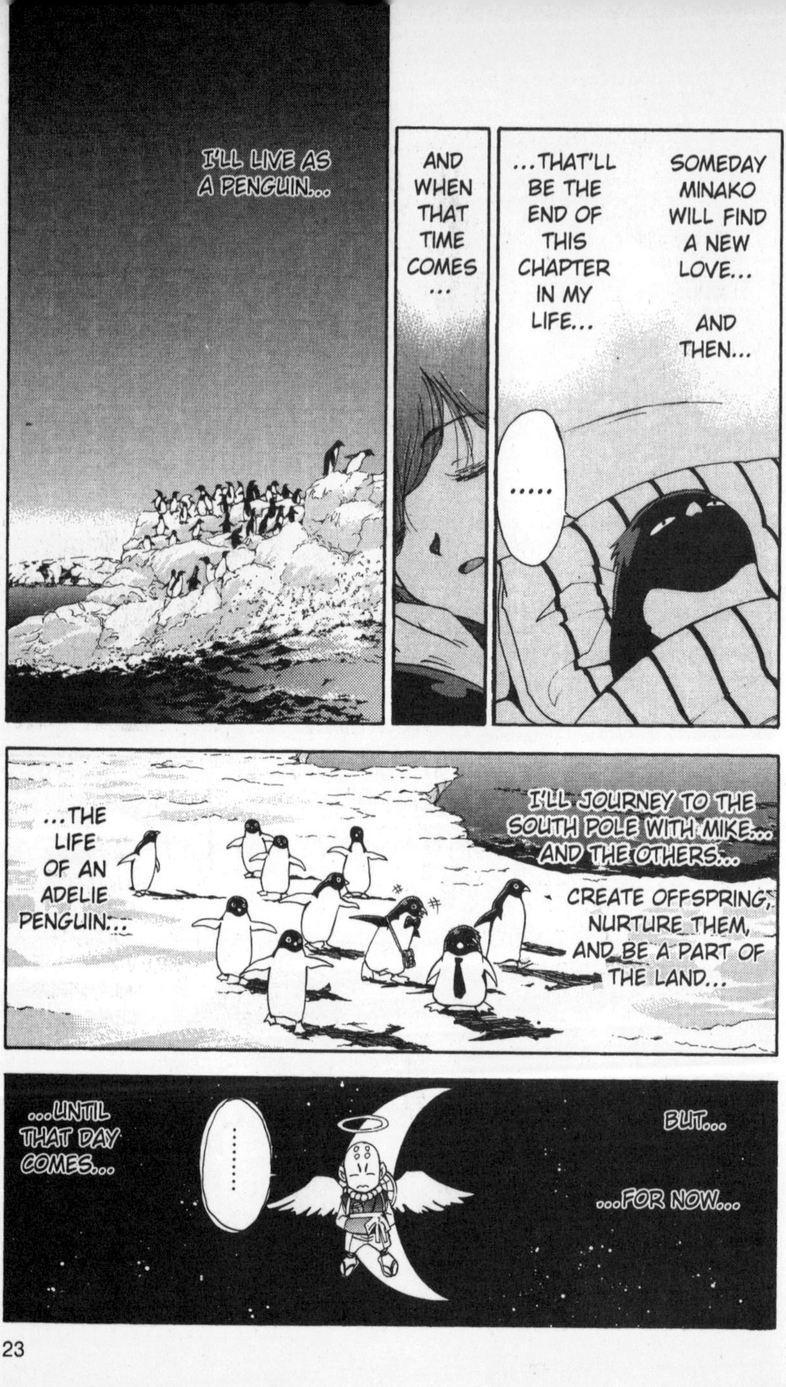
SOMEDAY MINAKO WILL FIND A NEW LOVE...
AND THEN...
...THAT'LL BE THE END OF THIS CHAPTER IN MY LIFE...
.....
AND WHEN THAT TIME COMES...
I'LL LIVE AS A PENGUIN...
I'LL JOURNEY TO THE SOUTH POLE WITH MIKE... AND THE OTHERS...
CREATE OFFSPRING, NURTURE THEM, AND BE A PART OF THE LAND...
...THE LIFE OF AN ADELIE PENGUIN...
BUT...
...FOR NOW...
....
...UNTIL THAT DAY COMES...

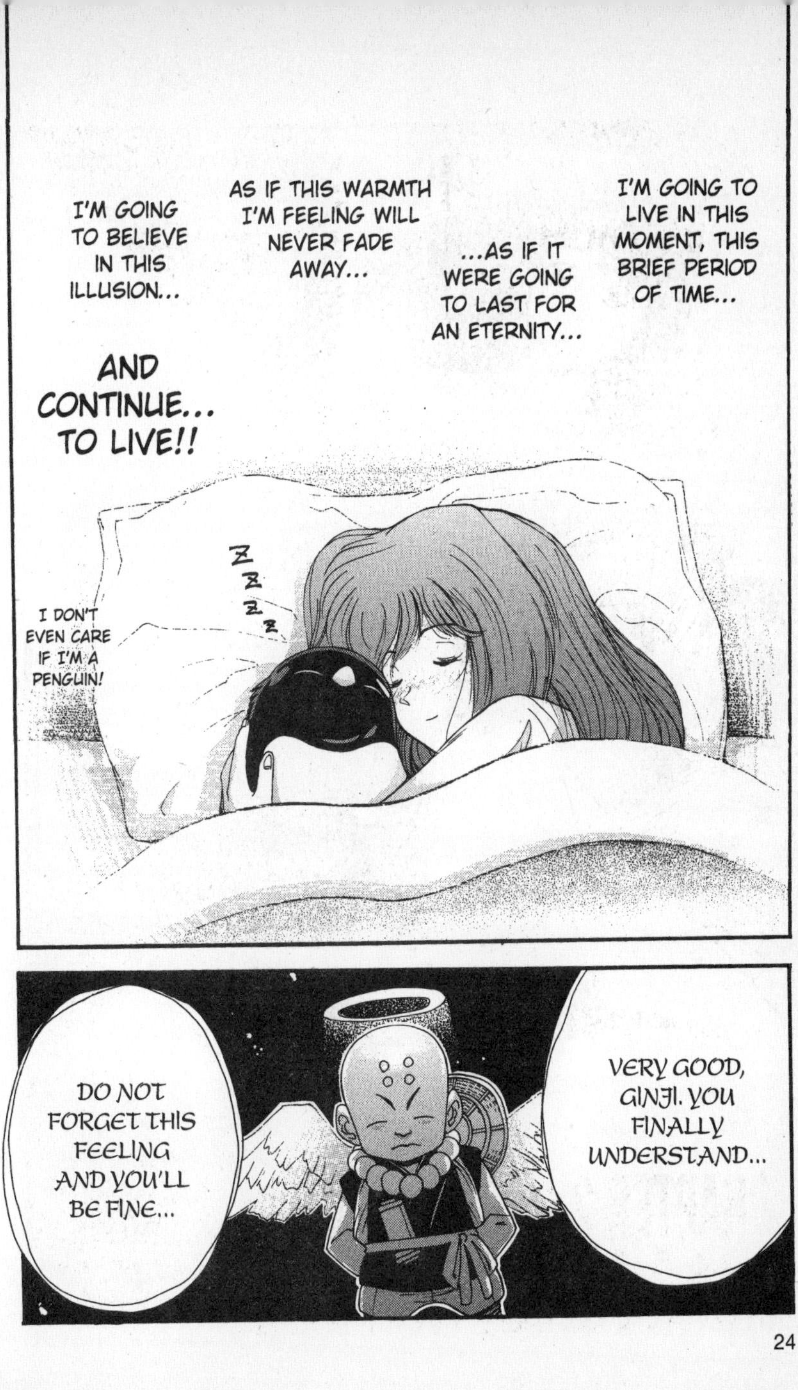
I'M GOING TO LIVE IN THIS MOMENT, THIS BRIEF PERIOD OF TIME...
...AS IF IT WERE GOING TO LAST FOR AN ETERNITY...
AS IF THIS WARMTH I'M FEELING WILL NEVER FADE AWAY...
I'M GOING TO BELIEVE IN THIS ILLUSION...
AND CONTINUE... TO LIVE!!
ZZZZ
I DON'T EVEN CARE IF I'M A PENGUIN!
VERY GOOD, GINJI. YOU FINALLY UNDERSTAND...
DO NOT FORGET THIS FEELING AND YOU'LL BE FINE...

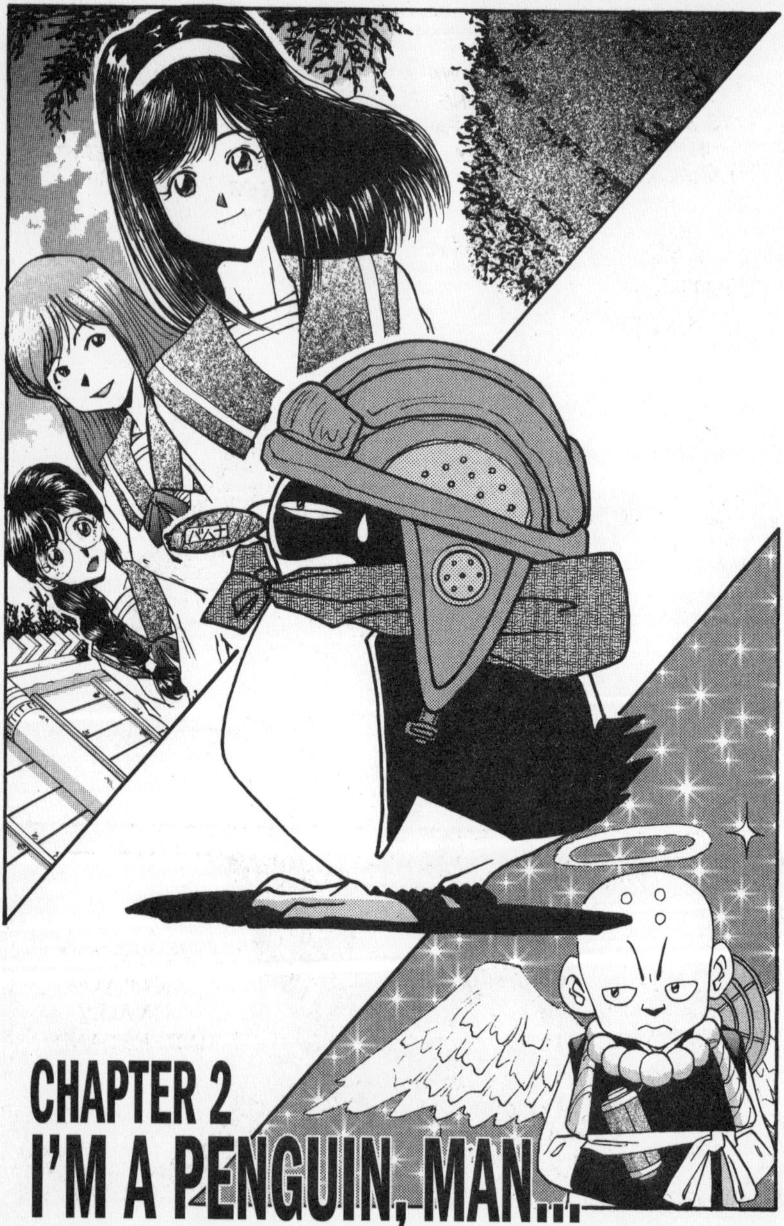

CHAPTER 2
I'M A PENGUIN, MAN...

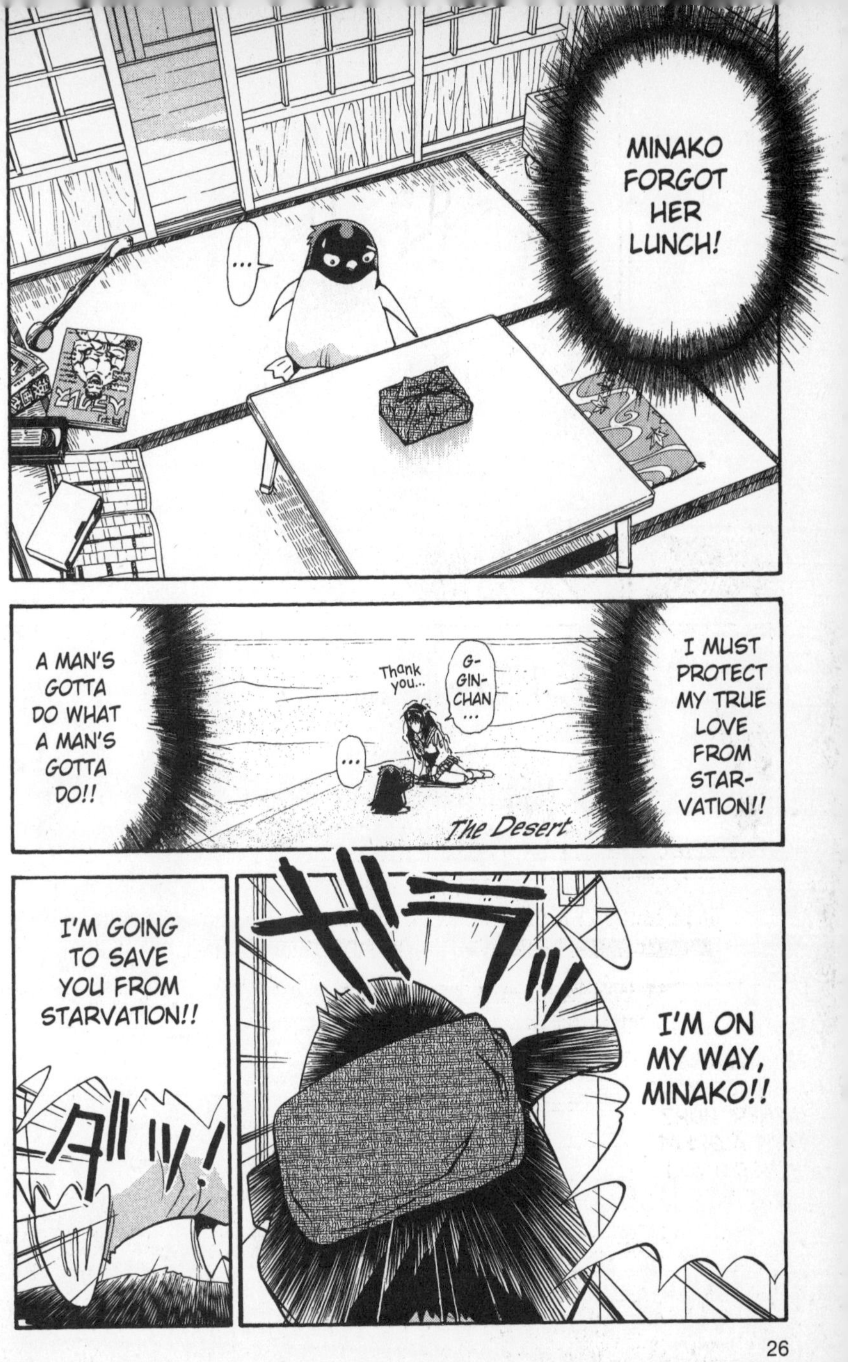
MINAKO FORGOT HER LUNCH!
...
I MUST PROTECT MY TRUE LOVE FROM STAR-VATION!!
G-GIN-CHAN...
Thank you...
...
A MAN'S GOTTA DO WHAT A MAN'S GOTTA DO!!
The Desert
ガラッ
I'M ON MY WAY, MINAKO!!
I'M GOING TO SAVE YOU FROM STARVATION!!
ダッ!

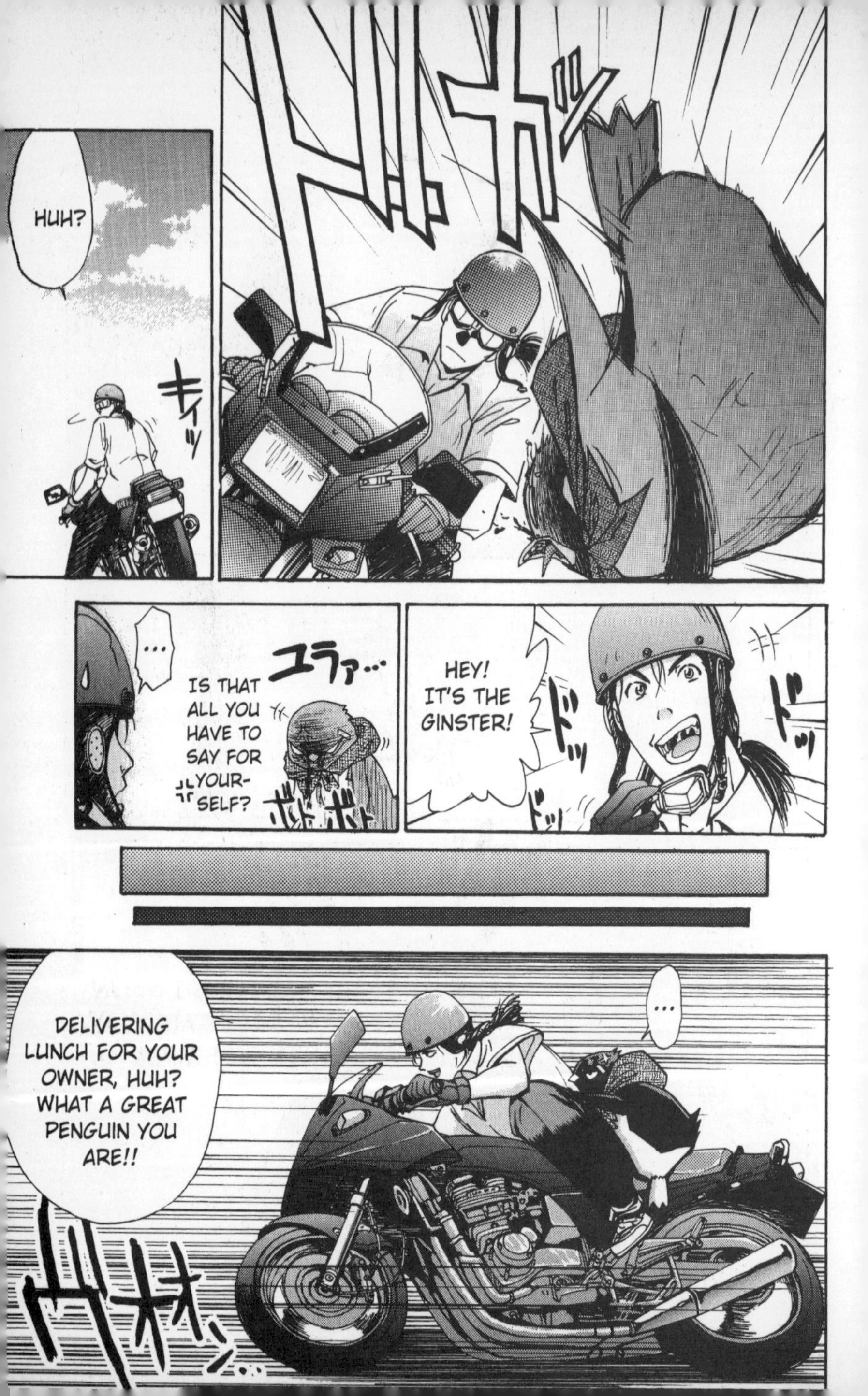
HUH?
HEY! IT'S THE GINSTER!
コラァ…
IS THAT ALL YOU HAVE TO SAY FOR YOURSELF?
...
...
DELIVERING LUNCH FOR YOUR OWNER, HUH? WHAT A GREAT PENGUIN YOU ARE!!

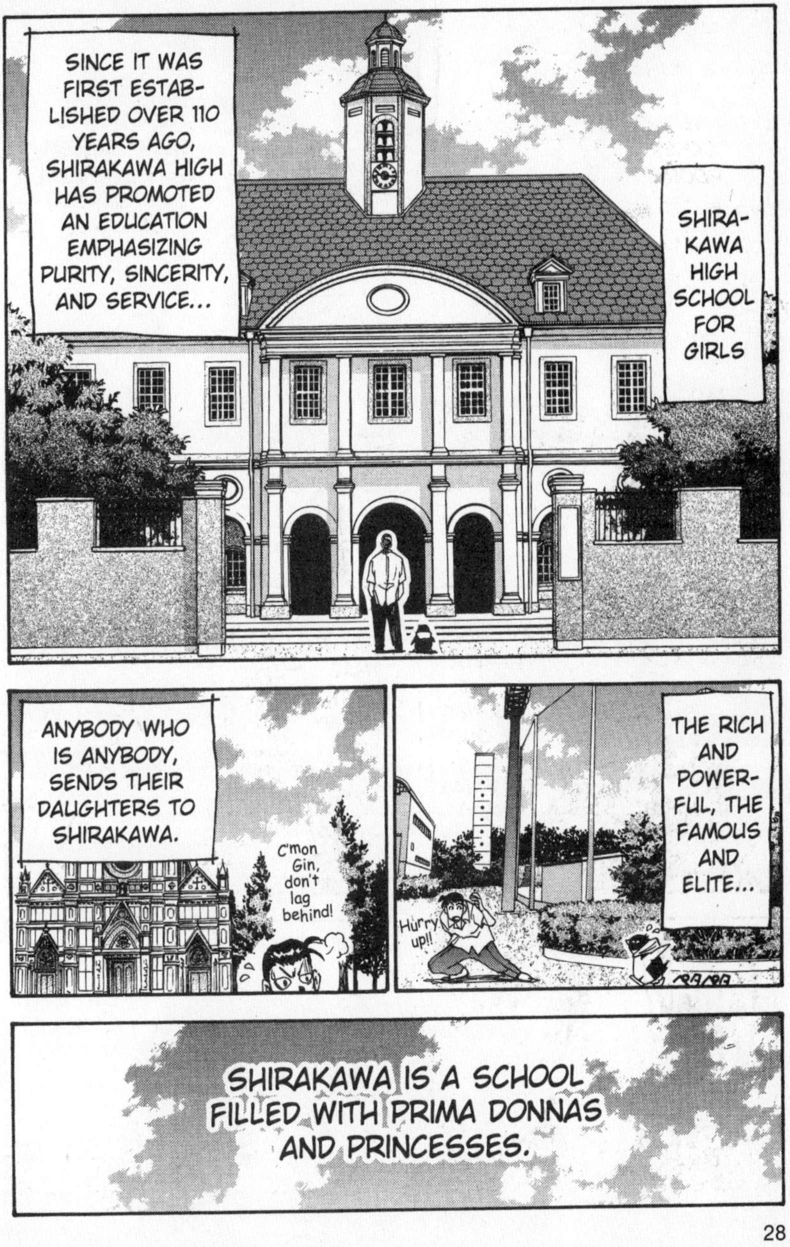
SHIRAKAWA HIGH SCHOOL FOR GIRLS
SINCE IT WAS FIRST ESTABLISHED OVER 110 YEARS AGO, SHIRAKAWA HIGH HAS PROMOTED AN EDUCATION EMPHASIZING PURITY, SINCERITY, AND SERVICE...
THE RICH AND POWERFUL, THE FAMOUS AND ELITE...
Hurry up!!
ANYBODY WHO IS ANYBODY, SENDS THEIR DAUGHTERS TO SHIRAKAWA.
C'mon Gin, don't lag behind!
SHIRAKAWA IS A SCHOOL FILLED WITH PRIMA DONNAS AND PRINCESSES.

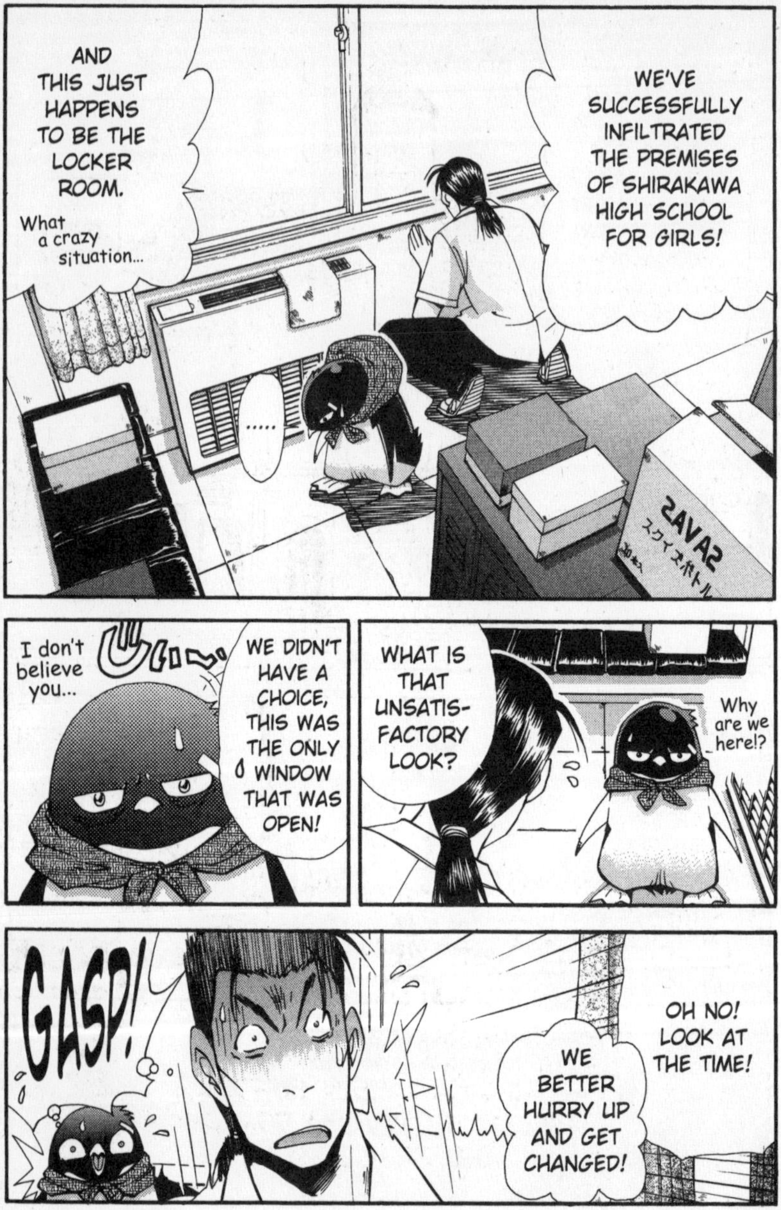
WE'VE SUCCESSFULLY INFILTRATED THE PREMISES OF SHIRAKAWA HIGH SCHOOL FOR GIRLS!
AND THIS JUST HAPPENS TO BE THE LOCKER ROOM.
What a crazy situation...
......
Why are we here!?
WHAT IS THAT UNSATIS-FACTORY LOOK?
WE DIDN'T HAVE A CHOICE, THIS WAS THE ONLY WINDOW THAT WAS OPEN!
I don't believe you...
OH NO! LOOK AT THE TIME!
WE BETTER HURRY UP AND GET CHANGED!
GASP!

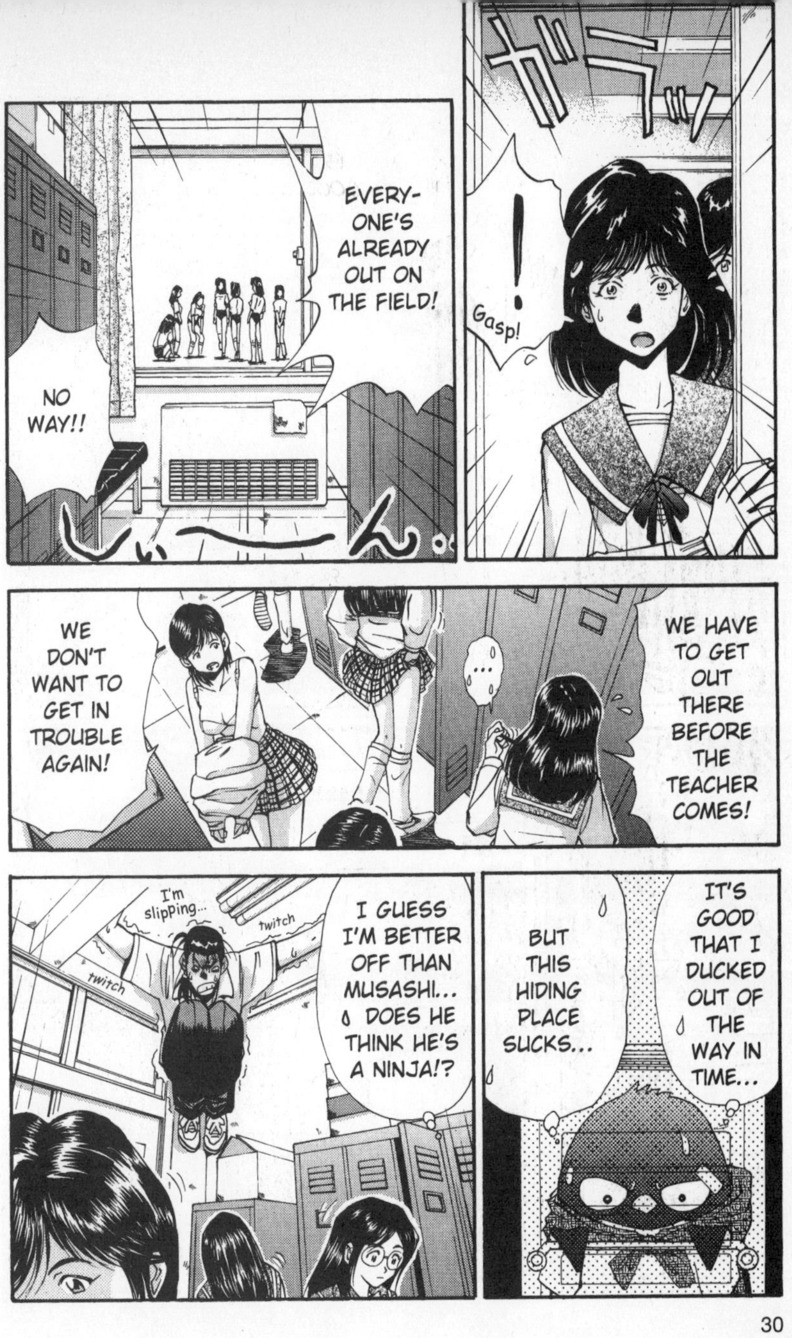
!
Gasp!
EVERYONE'S ALREADY OUT ON THE FIELD!
NO WAY!!
WE HAVE TO GET OUT THERE BEFORE THE TEACHER COMES!
...
WE DON'T WANT TO GET IN TROUBLE AGAIN!
IT'S GOOD THAT I DUCKED OUT OF THE WAY IN TIME...
BUT THIS HIDING PLACE SUCKS...
I GUESS I'M BETTER OFF THAN MUSASHI... DOES HE THINK HE'S A NINJA!?
I'm slipping...
twitch
twitch

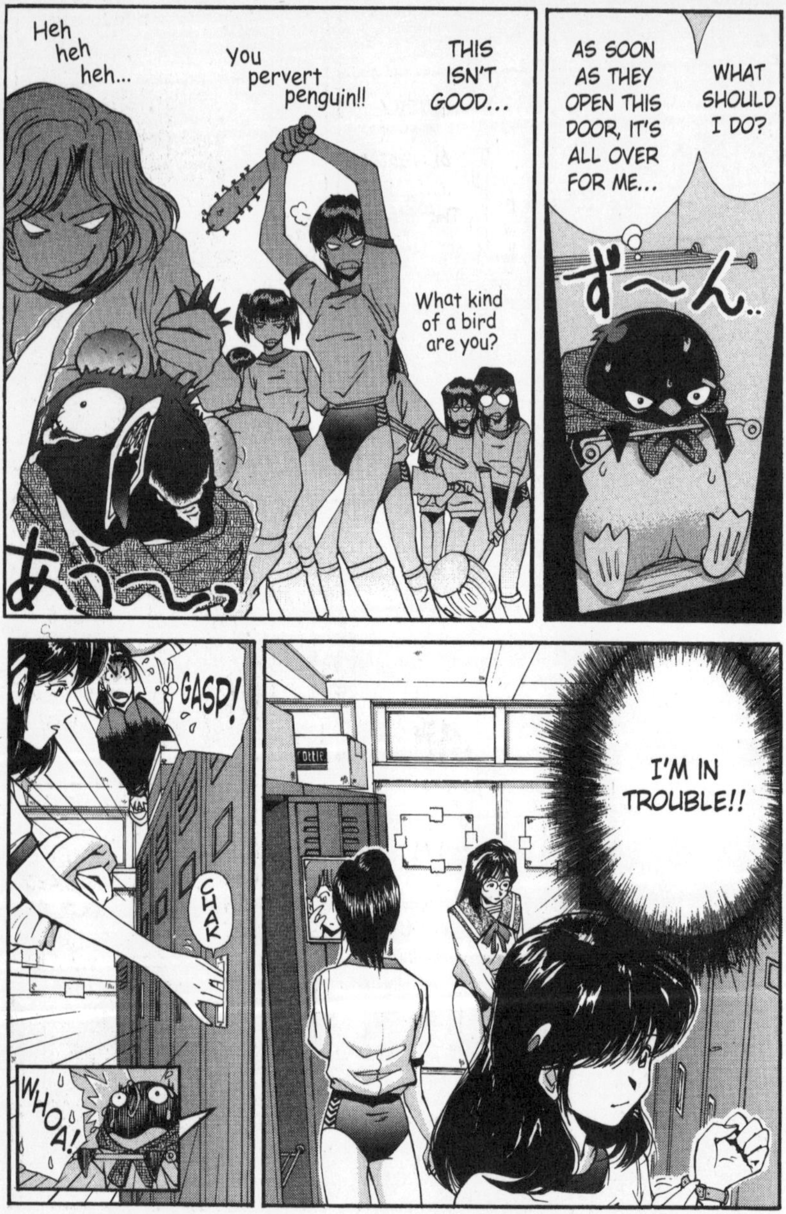
WHAT SHOULD I DO?
AS SOON AS THEY OPEN THIS DOOR, IT'S ALL OVER FOR ME...
ず〜ん..
THIS ISN'T GOOD...
You pervert penguin!!
Heh heh heh...
What kind of a bird are you?
あう〜っ
I'M IN TROUBLE!!
GASP!
CHAK
WHOA!

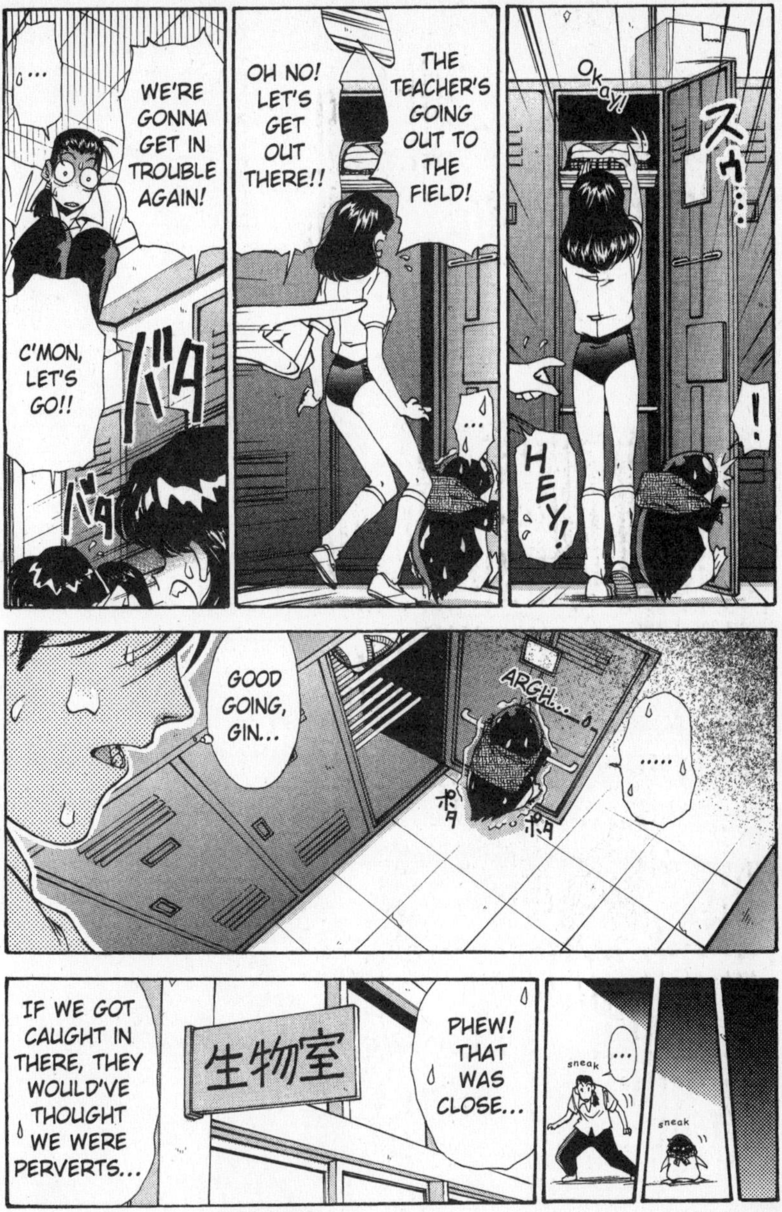
Okay!
スゥ…
!
HEY!
THE TEACHER'S GOING OUT TO THE FIELD!
OH NO! LET'S GET OUT THERE!!
...
...
WE'RE GONNA GET IN TROUBLE AGAIN!
C'MON, LET'S GO!!
バタ
バタ
.....
ARGH...
ポタ
ポタ
GOOD GOING, GIN...
...
sneak
sneak
PHEW! THAT WAS CLOSE...
生物室
IF WE GOT CAUGHT IN THERE, THEY WOULD'VE THOUGHT WE WERE PERVERTS...

(BIOLOGY)

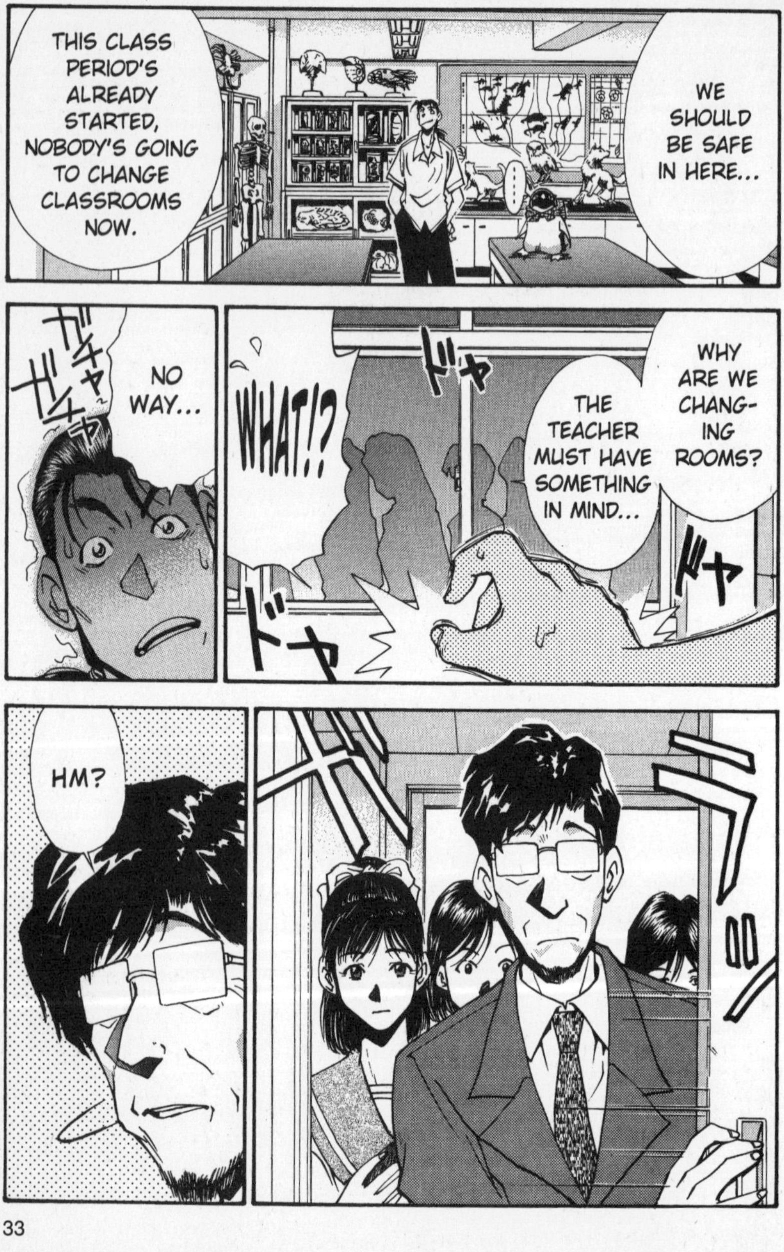
WE SHOULD BE SAFE IN HERE...
THIS CLASS PERIOD'S ALREADY STARTED, NOBODY'S GOING TO CHANGE CLASSROOMS NOW.
...
WHY ARE WE CHANG-ING ROOMS?
ドヤ
THE TEACHER MUST HAVE SOMETHING IN MIND...
ドヤ
WHAT!?
ドヤ
ガチャ
ガチャ
NO WAY...
HM?

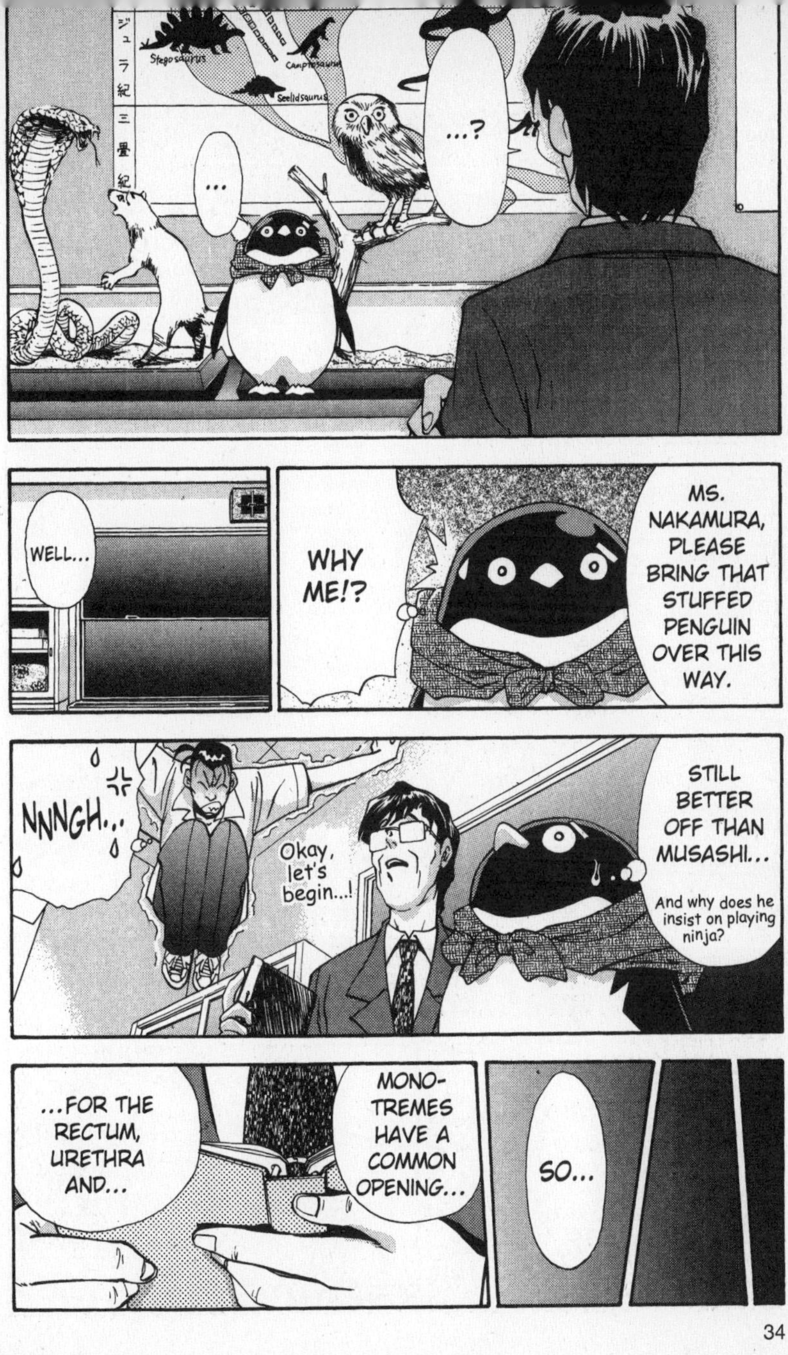
ジュラ紀
三畳紀
Stegosaurus
...?
...
MS. NAKAMURA, PLEASE BRING THAT STUFFED PENGUIN OVER THIS WAY.
WHY ME!?
WELL...
STILL BETTER OFF THAN MUSASHI...
And why does he insist on playing ninja?
Okay, let's begin...!
NNNGH...
SO...
MONO-TREMES HAVE A COMMON OPENING...
...FOR THE RECTUM, URETHRA AND...

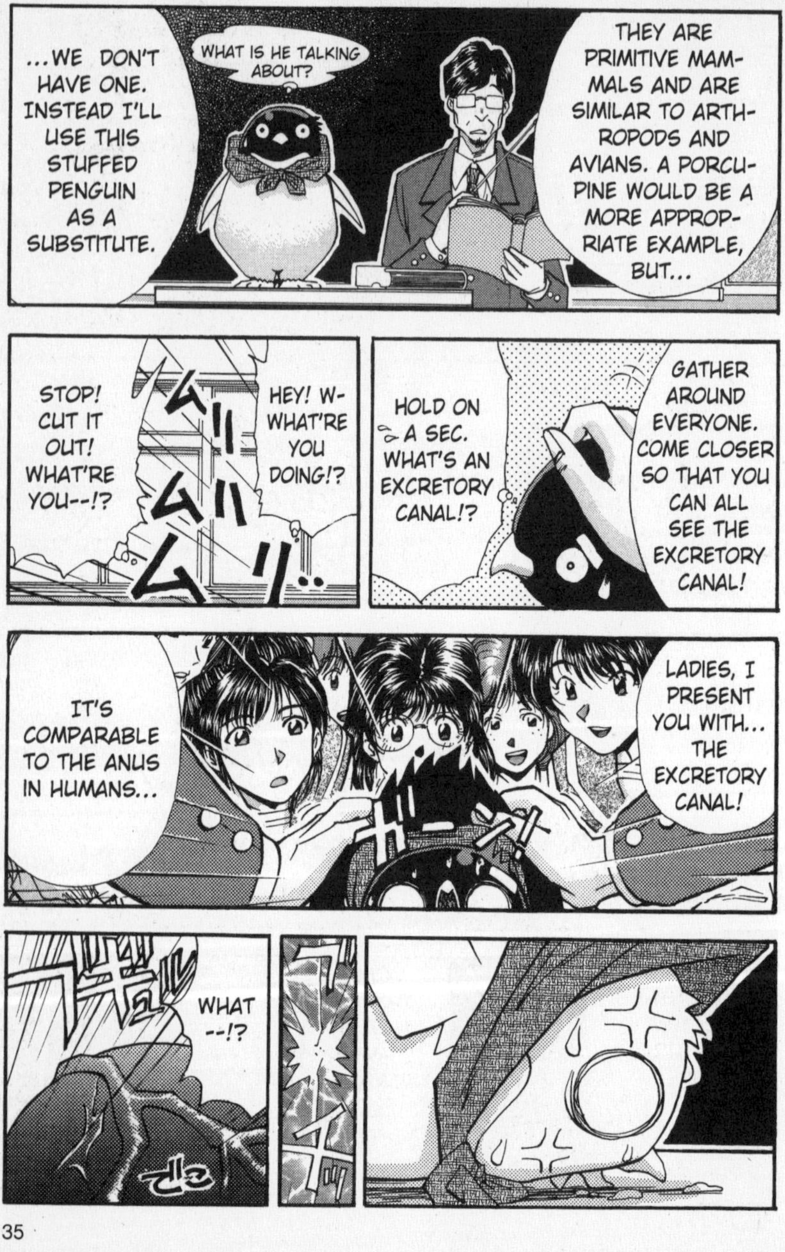
THEY ARE PRIMITIVE MAMMALS AND ARE SIMILAR TO ARTHROPODS AND AVIANS. A PORCUPINE WOULD BE A MORE APPROPRIATE EXAMPLE, BUT...
WHAT IS HE TALKING ABOUT?
...WE DON'T HAVE ONE. INSTEAD I'LL USE THIS STUFFED PENGUIN AS A SUBSTITUTE.
GATHER AROUND EVERYONE. COME CLOSER SO THAT YOU CAN ALL SEE THE EXCRETORY CANAL!
HOLD ON A SEC. WHAT'S AN EXCRETORY CANAL!?
HEY! W-WHAT'RE YOU DOING!?
STOP! CUT IT OUT! WHAT'RE YOU--!?
LADIES, I PRESENT YOU WITH... THE EXCRETORY CANAL!
IT'S COMPARABLE TO THE ANUS IN HUMANS...
WHAT --!?

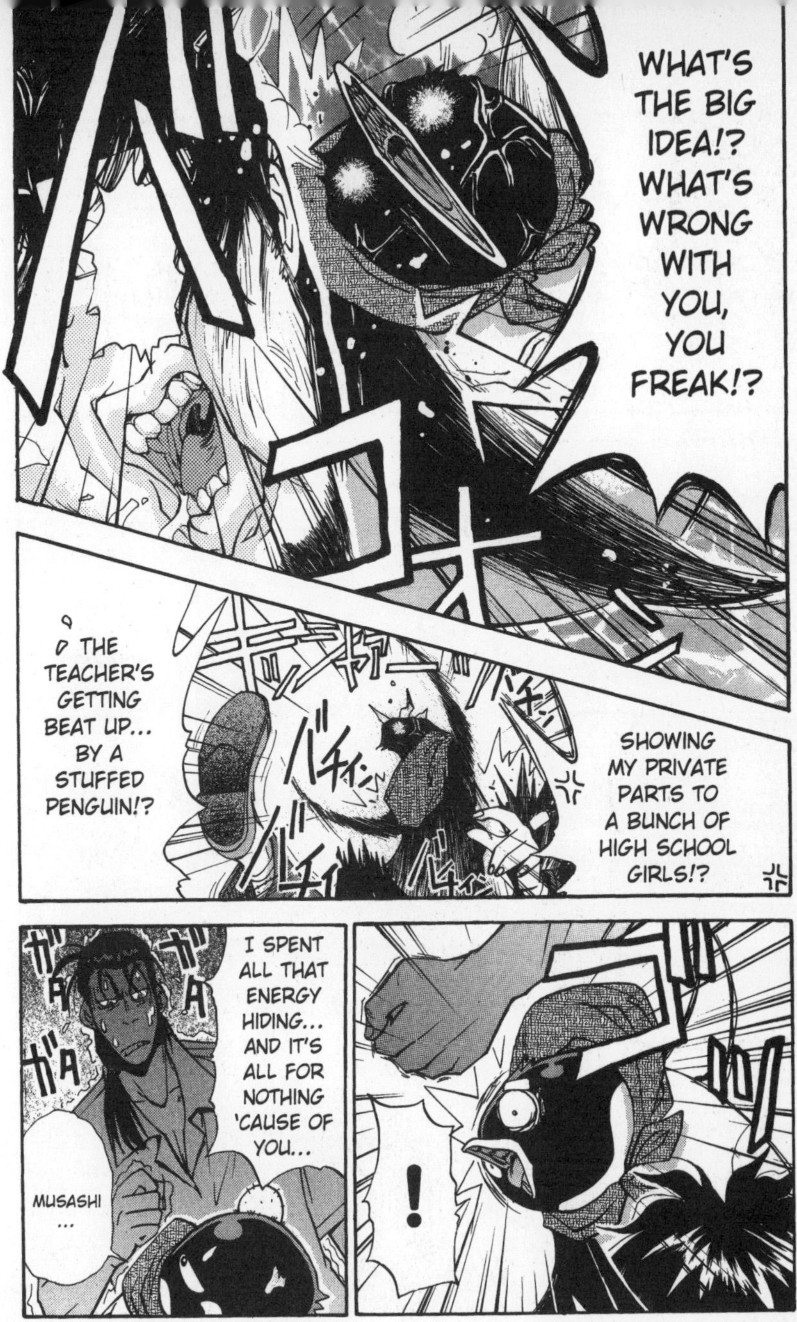
WHAT'S THE BIG IDEA!? WHAT'S WRONG WITH YOU, YOU FREAK!?
SHOWING MY PRIVATE PARTS TO A BUNCH OF HIGH SCHOOL GIRLS!?
THE TEACHER'S GETTING BEAT UP... BY A STUFFED PENGUIN!?
!
I SPENT ALL THAT ENERGY HIDING... AND IT'S ALL FOR NOTHING 'CAUSE OF YOU...
MUSASHI ...

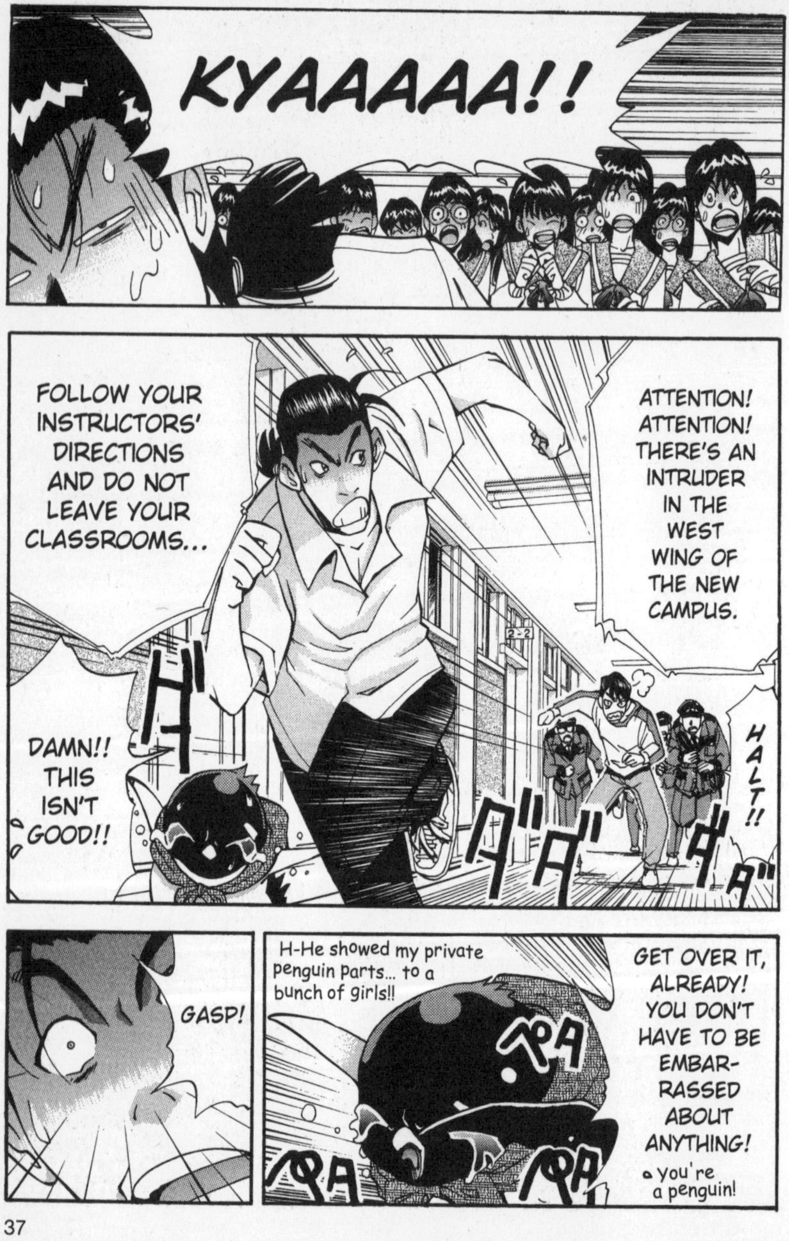
KYAAAAAA!!
ATTENTION! ATTENTION! THERE'S AN INTRUDER IN THE WEST WING OF THE NEW CAMPUS.
FOLLOW YOUR INSTRUCTORS' DIRECTIONS AND DO NOT LEAVE YOUR CLASSROOMS...
HALT!!
DAMN!! THIS ISN'T GOOD!!
GET OVER IT, ALREADY! YOU DON'T HAVE TO BE EMBARRASSED ABOUT ANYTHING!
you're a penguin!
H-He showed my private penguin parts... to a bunch of girls!!
GASP!

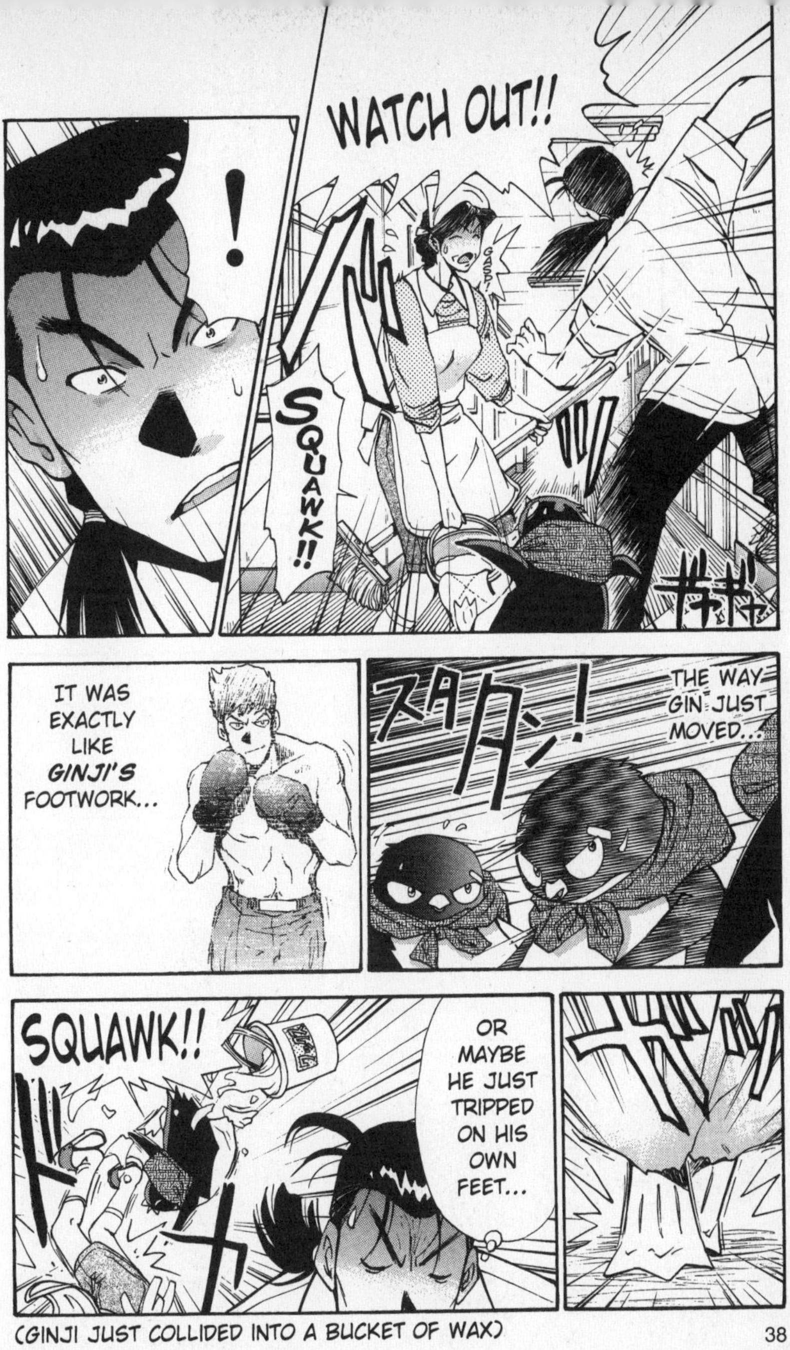
WATCH OUT!!
GASP!
SQUAWK!!
!
スタタン!
THE WAY GIN JUST MOVED...
IT WAS EXACTLY LIKE GINJI'S FOOTWORK...
OR MAYBE HE JUST TRIPPED ON HIS OWN FEET...
SQUAWK!!

(GINJI JUST COLLIDED INTO A BUCKET OF WAX)

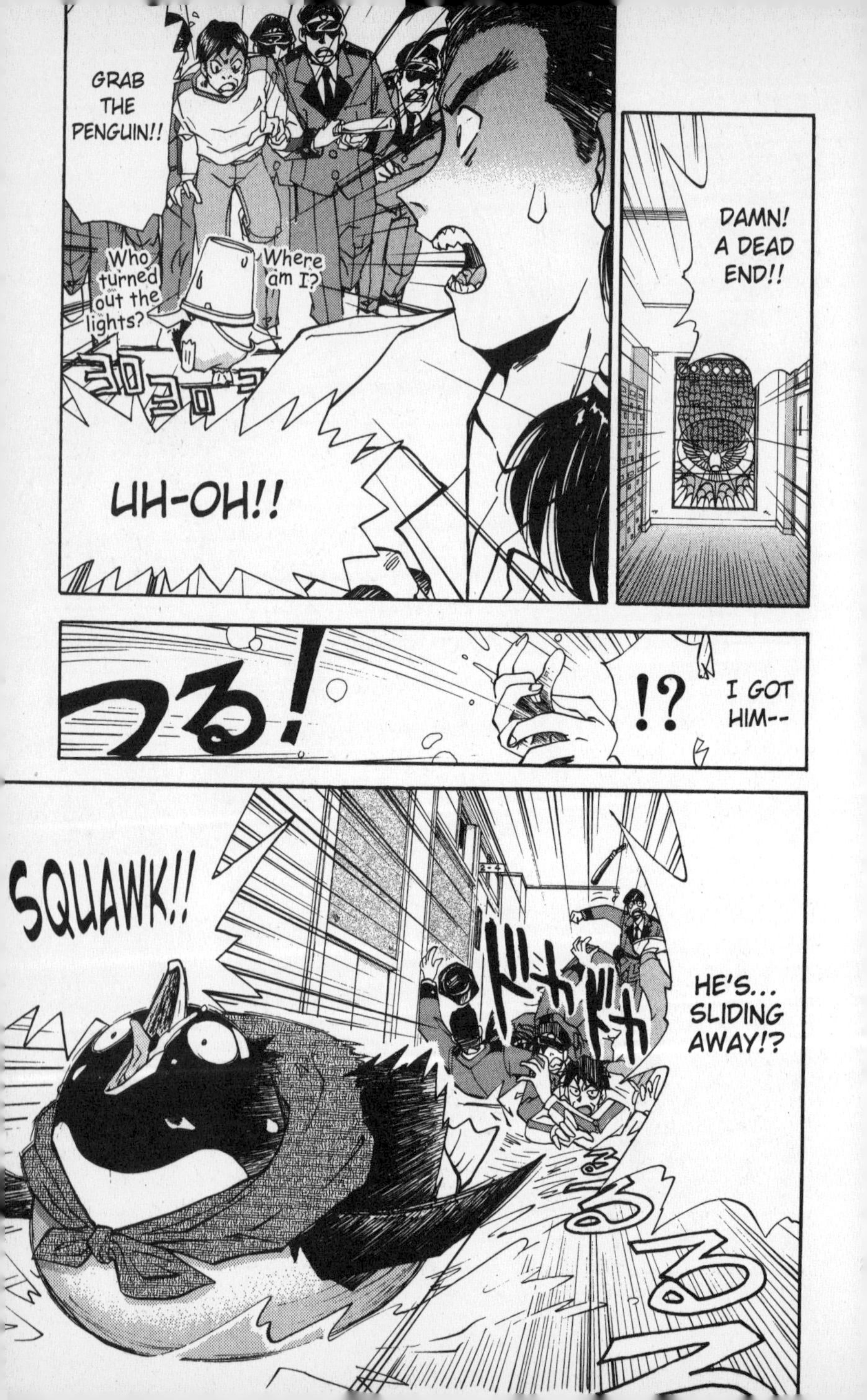
DAMN! A DEAD END!!
GRAB THE PENGUIN!!
Where am I?
Who turned out the lights?
UH-OH!!
I GOT HIM--
!?
つる!
HE'S... SLIDING AWAY!?
SQUAWK!!

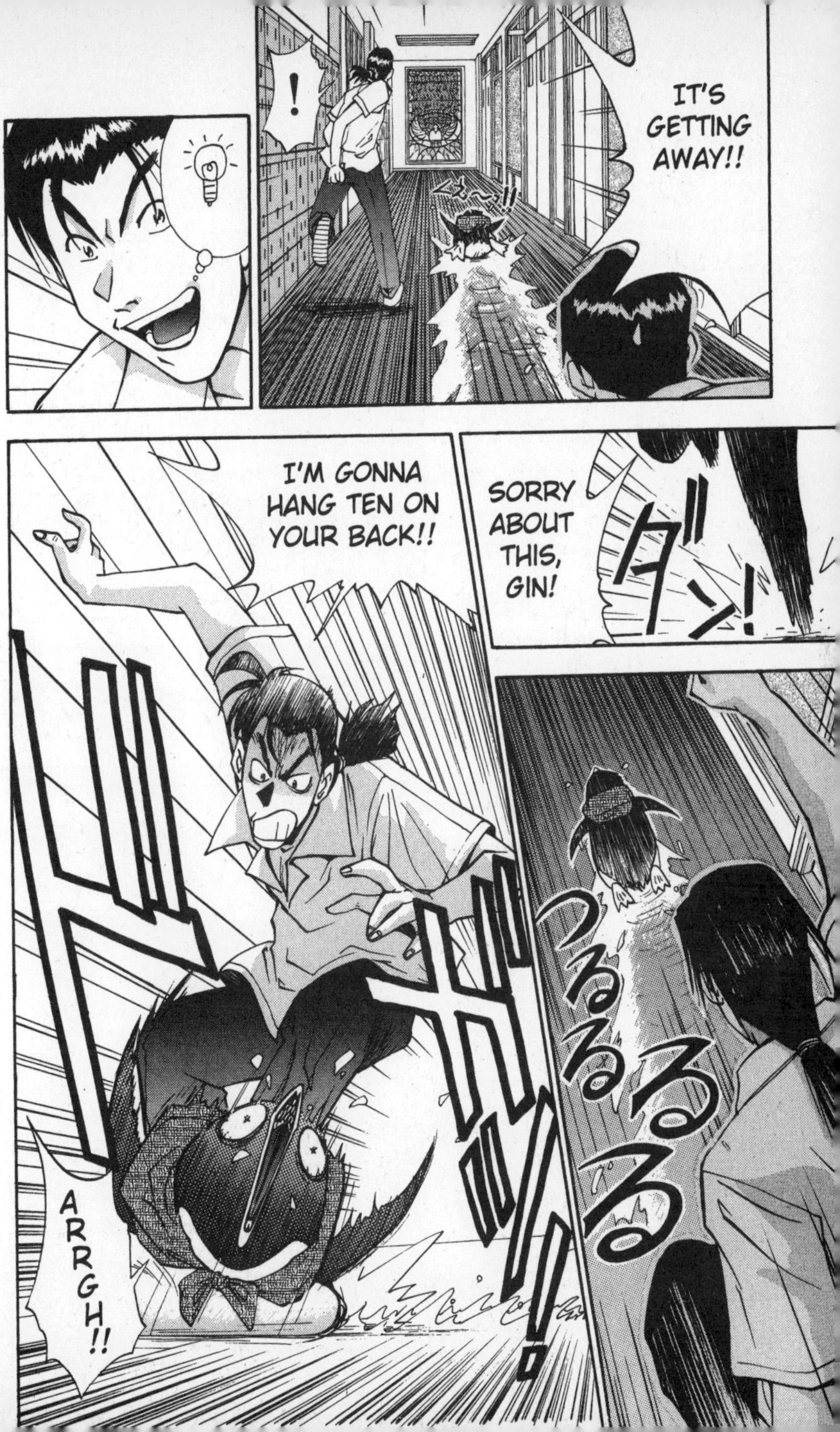
!
IT'S GETTING AWAY!!
SORRY ABOUT THIS, GIN!
ダン!
つるるるる
I'M GONNA HANG TEN ON YOUR BACK!!
ARRGH!!

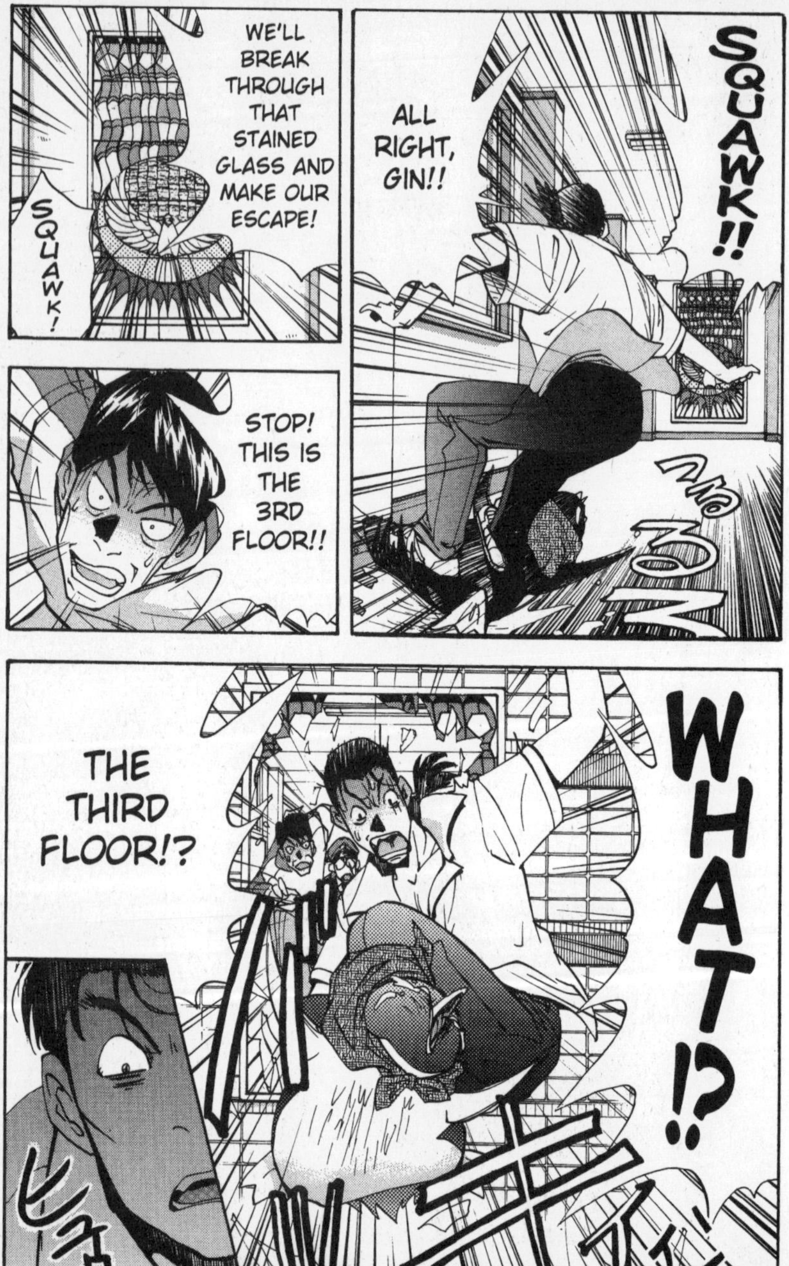
SQUAWK!!
ALL RIGHT, GIN!!
WE'LL BREAK THROUGH THAT STAINED GLASS AND MAKE OUR ESCAPE!
SQUAWK!
STOP! THIS IS THE 3RD FLOOR!!
WHAT!?!!
THE THIRD FLOOR!?

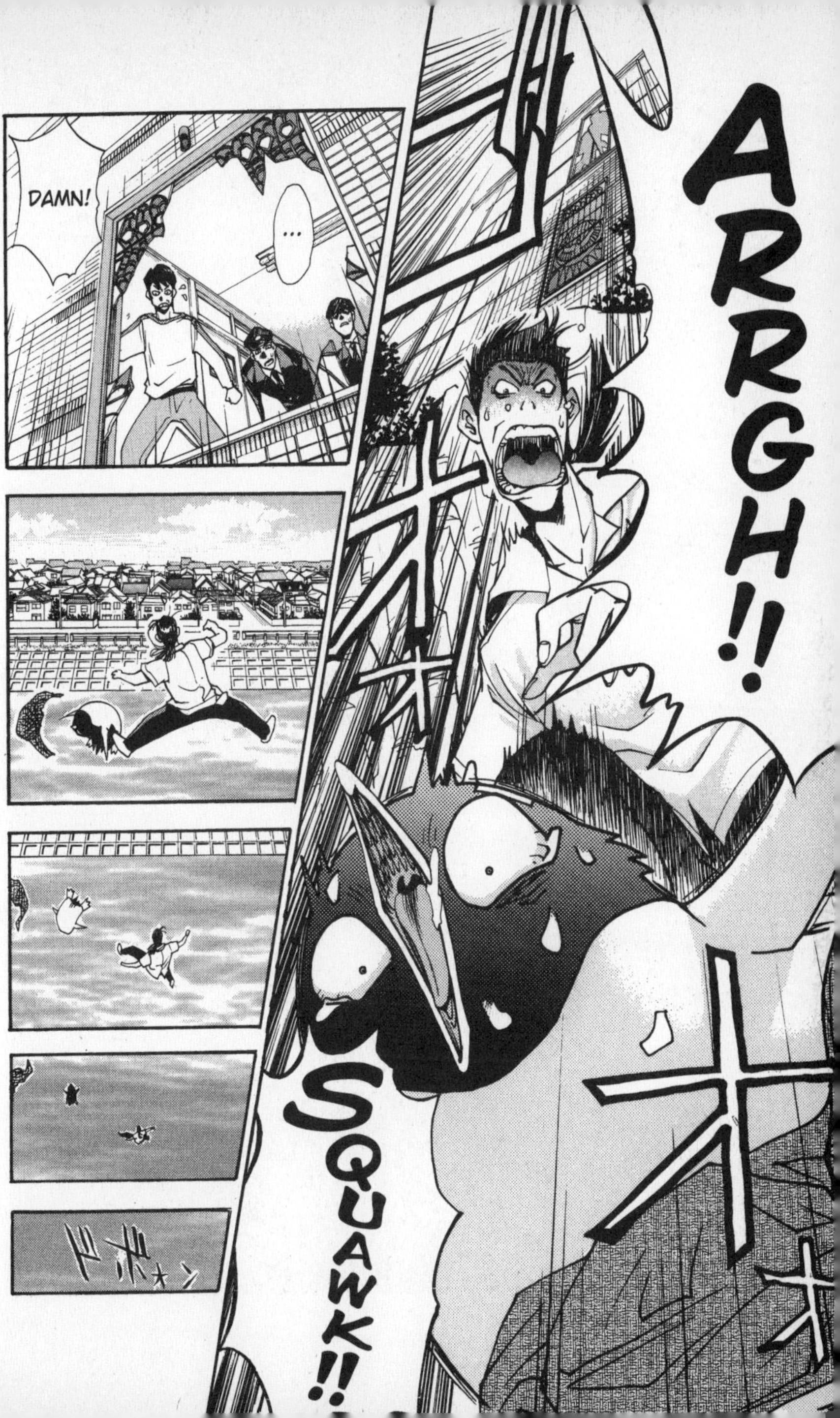
ARRGH!!
SQUAWK!!
DAMN!
...

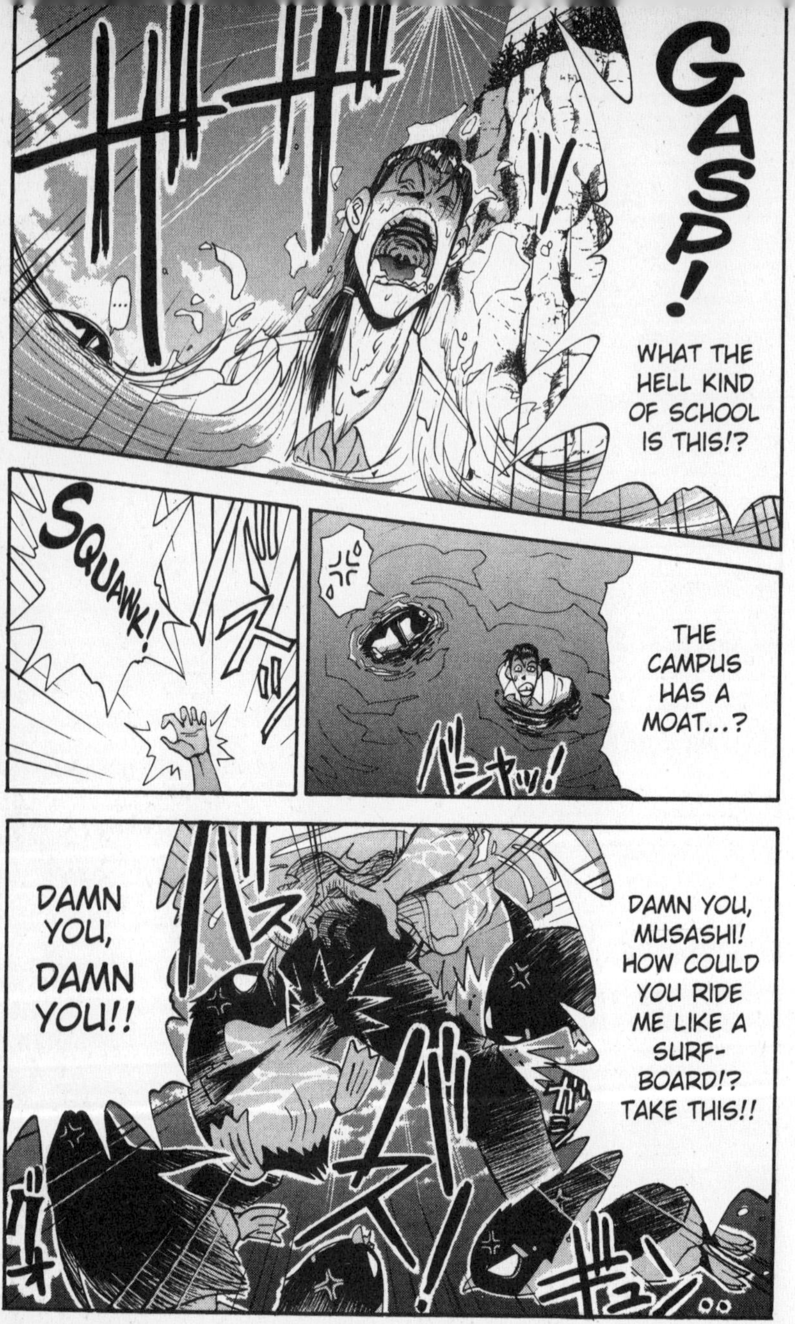
GASP!
WHAT THE HELL KIND OF SCHOOL IS THIS!?
THE CAMPUS HAS A MOAT...?
SQUAWK!
DAMN YOU, MUSASHI! HOW COULD YOU RIDE ME LIKE A SURF-BOARD!? TAKE THIS!!
DAMN YOU, DAMN YOU!!

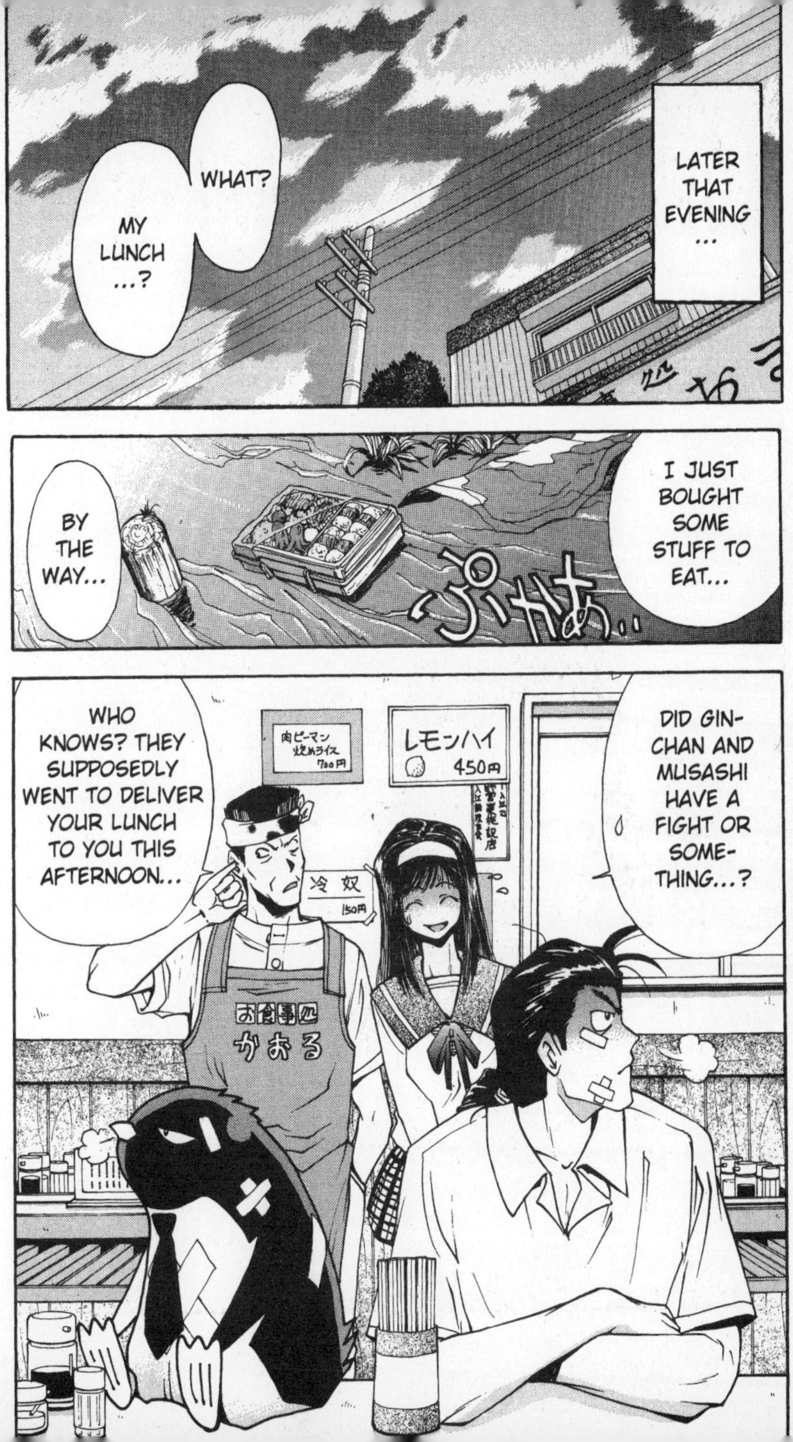
LATER THAT EVENING...
WHAT?
MY LUNCH...?
I JUST BOUGHT SOME STUFF TO EAT...
ぷかあ..
BY THE WAY...
DID GIN-CHAN AND MUSASHI HAVE A FIGHT OR SOMETHING...?
レモンハイ 450円
肉ピーマン 炒めライス 700円
冷奴 150円
お食事処 かおる
WHO KNOWS? THEY SUPPOSEDLY WENT TO DELIVER YOUR LUNCH TO YOU THIS AFTERNOON...

CHAPTER 2
LOVE COMMUNICATION

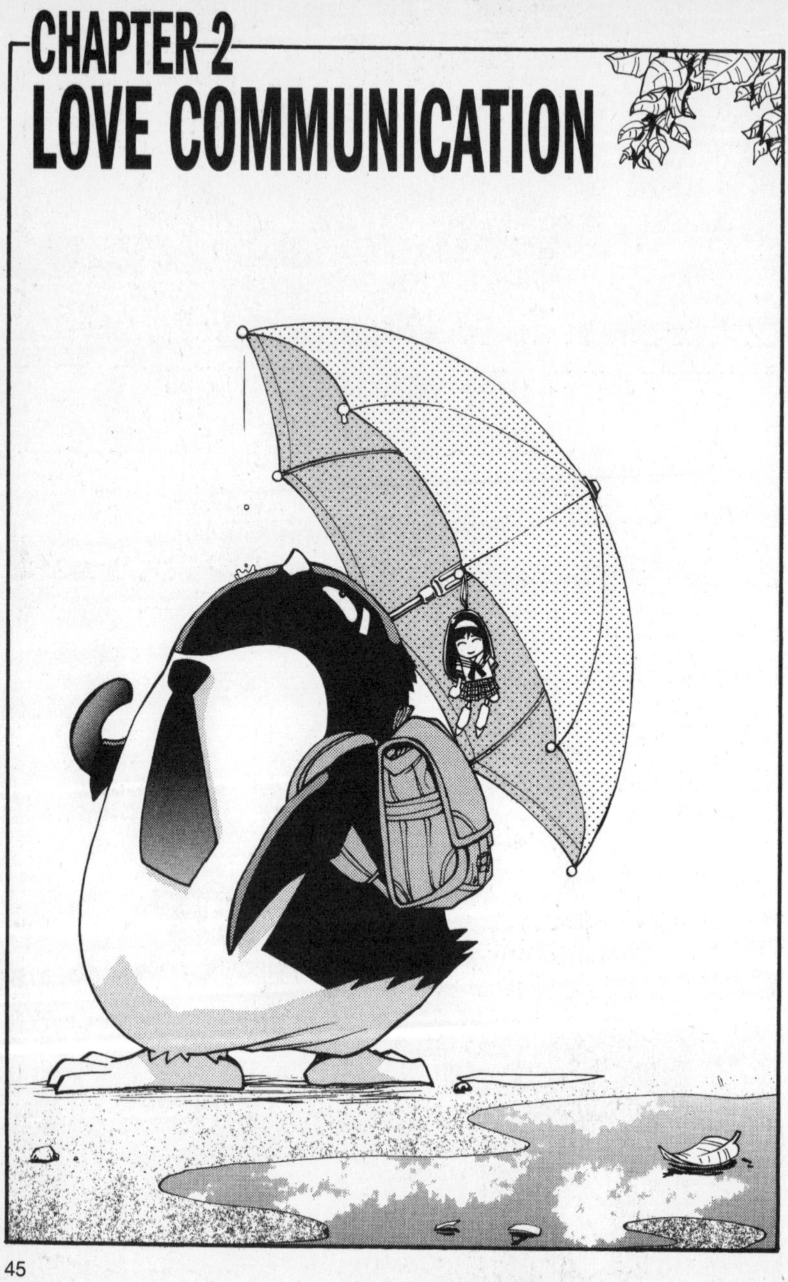

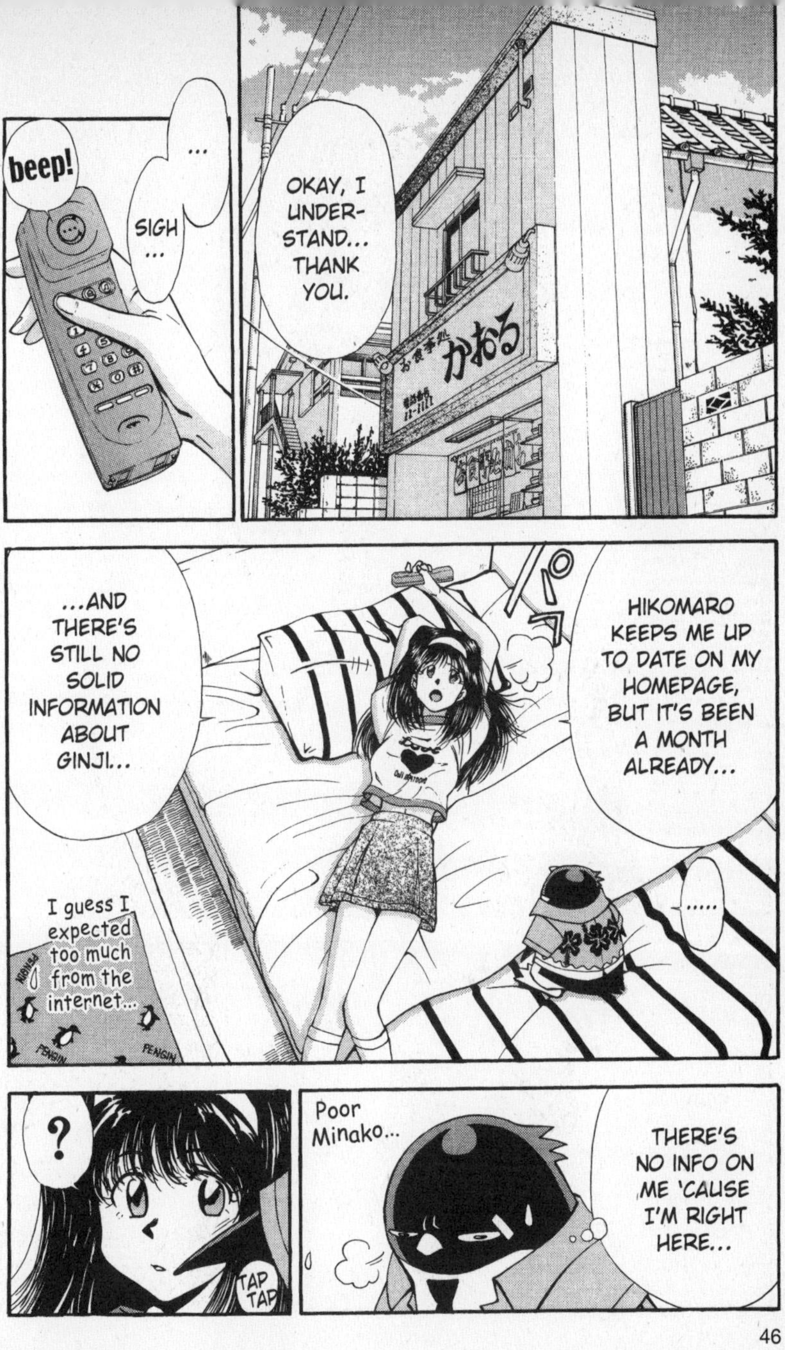

OKAY, I UNDER-STAND... THANK YOU.
お食事処 かおる
...
SIGH ...
beep!
HIKOMARO KEEPS ME UP TO DATE ON MY HOMEPAGE, BUT IT'S BEEN A MONTH ALREADY...
...AND THERE'S STILL NO SOLID INFORMATION ABOUT GINJI...
.....
I guess I expected too much from the internet...
PENGIN
Poor Minako...
THERE'S NO INFO ON ME 'CAUSE I'M RIGHT HERE...
?
TAP TAP

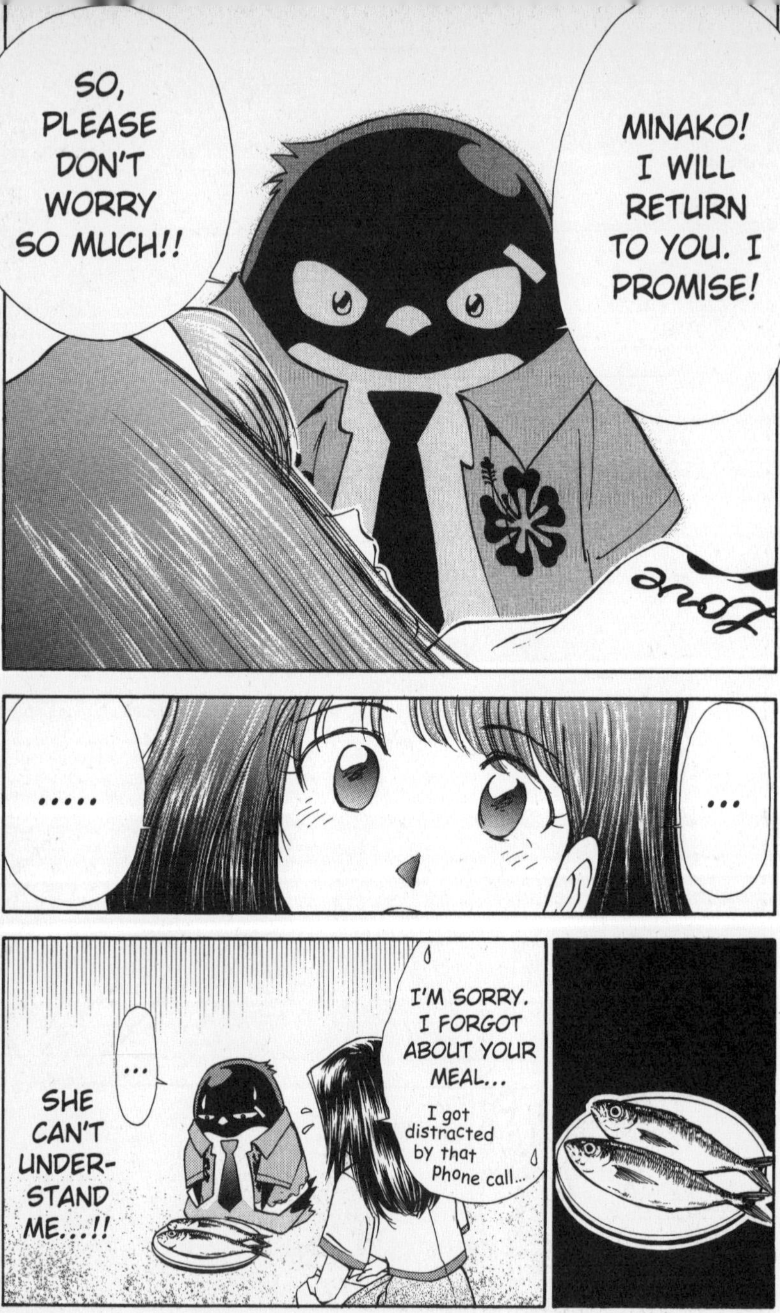
MINAKO! I WILL RETURN TO YOU. I PROMISE!
SO, PLEASE DON'T WORRY SO MUCH!!
Love
...
.....
I'M SORRY. I FORGOT ABOUT YOUR MEAL...
I got distracted by that phone call...
...
SHE CAN'T UNDER-STAND ME...!!

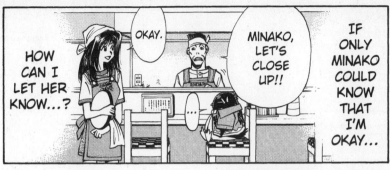

IF ONLY MINAKO COULD KNOW THAT I'M OKAY...
MINAKO, LET'S CLOSE UP!!
OKAY.
...
HOW CAN I LET HER KNOW...?
THERE MUST BE SOME WAY TO COM-MUNICATE WITH HER...
...?
THIS...
THIS IS IT!!
4月
特集
手旗信号は男の言葉!!
IF I CAN'T TALK TO HER...
THEN, MAYBE THIS'LL WORK!
左
原姿

(NAVAL MANIA! SPECIAL FEATURE ON SEMAPHORE!)

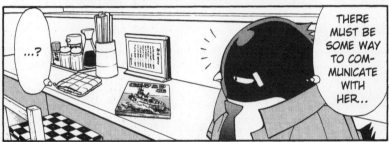

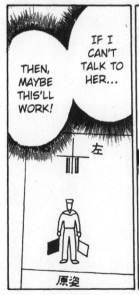

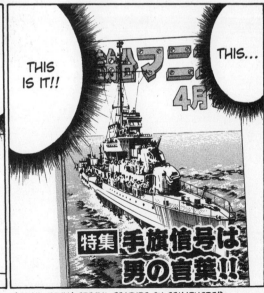

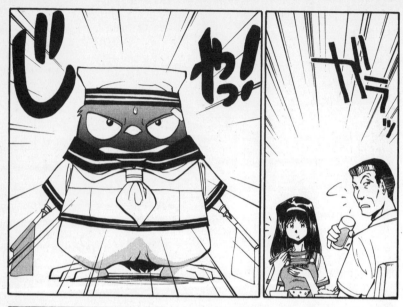

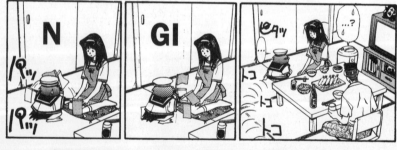

N

GI

...?

GI-N-JI
IS OK
– end message

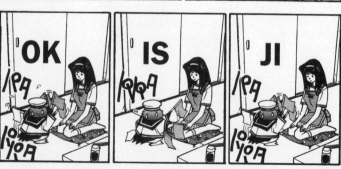

OK

IS

JI

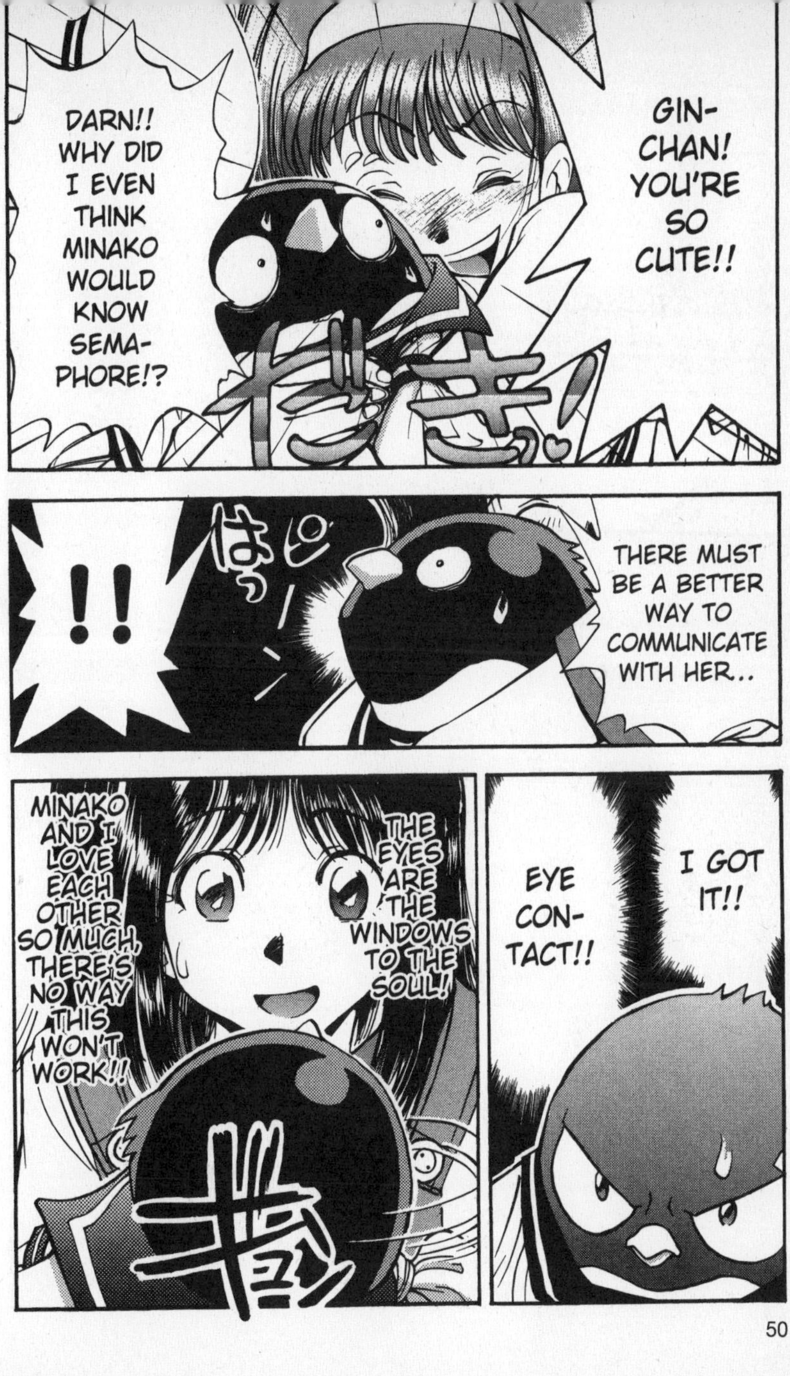
GIN-CHAN! YOU'RE SO CUTE!!
DARN!! WHY DID I EVEN THINK MINAKO WOULD KNOW SEMA-PHORE!?
THERE MUST BE A BETTER WAY TO COMMUNICATE WITH HER...
はっ
!!
I GOT IT!!
EYE CON-TACT!!
THE EYES ARE THE WINDOWS TO THE SOUL!
MINAKO AND I LOVE EACH OTHER SO MUCH, THERE'S NO WAY THIS WON'T WORK!!

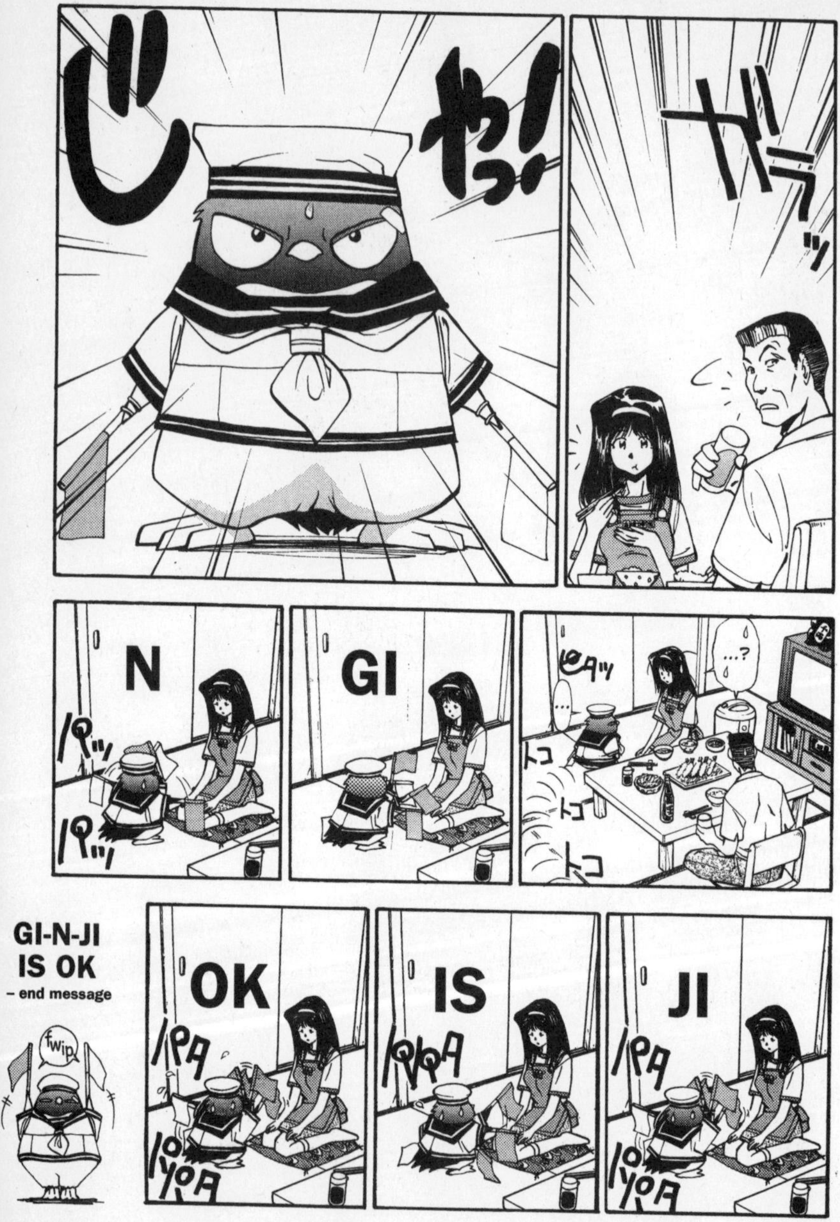
ガラッ
じゃっ!
ピタッ
…
…?
トコ
トコ
トコ
GI
N
パッ
パッ
JI
パタ
パタ
IS
パタパタ
パタ
OK
パタ
パタ
GI-N-JI
IS OK
– end message
fwip

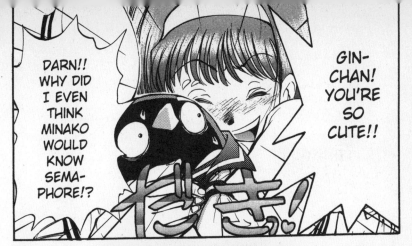

DARN!! WHY DID I EVEN THINK MINAKO WOULD KNOW SEMAPHORE!?

GIN-CHAN! YOU'RE SO CUTE!!

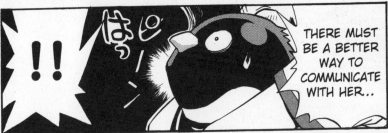

!!

THERE MUST BE A BETTER WAY TO COMMUNICATE WITH HER..

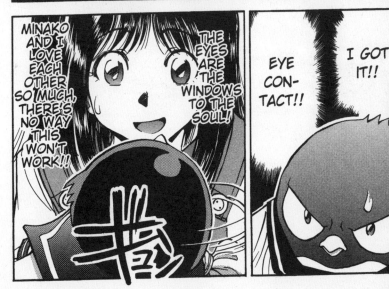

MINAKO AND I LOVE EACH OTHER SO MUCH, THERE'S NO WAY THIS WON'T WORK!!

THE EYES ARE THE WINDOWS TO THE SOUL!

EYE CON-TACT!!

I GOT IT!!

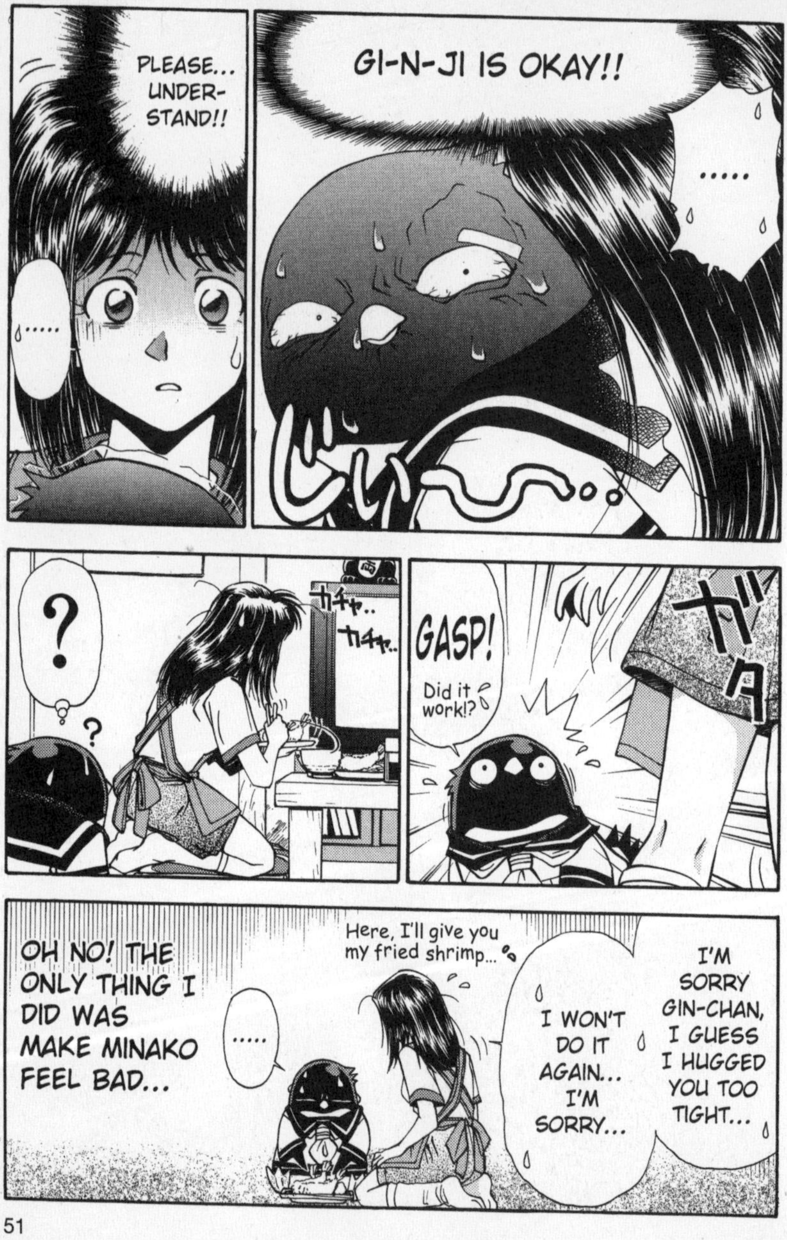
GI-N-JI IS OKAY!!
.....
じぃ～～
PLEASE... UNDER-STAND!!
.....
GASP!
Did it work!?
ガバ
?
?
カチャ..
カチャ..
I'M SORRY GIN-CHAN, I GUESS I HUGGED YOU TOO TIGHT...
I WON'T DO IT AGAIN... I'M SORRY...
Here, I'll give you my fried shrimp...
.....
OH NO! THE ONLY THING I DID WAS MAKE MINAKO FEEL BAD...

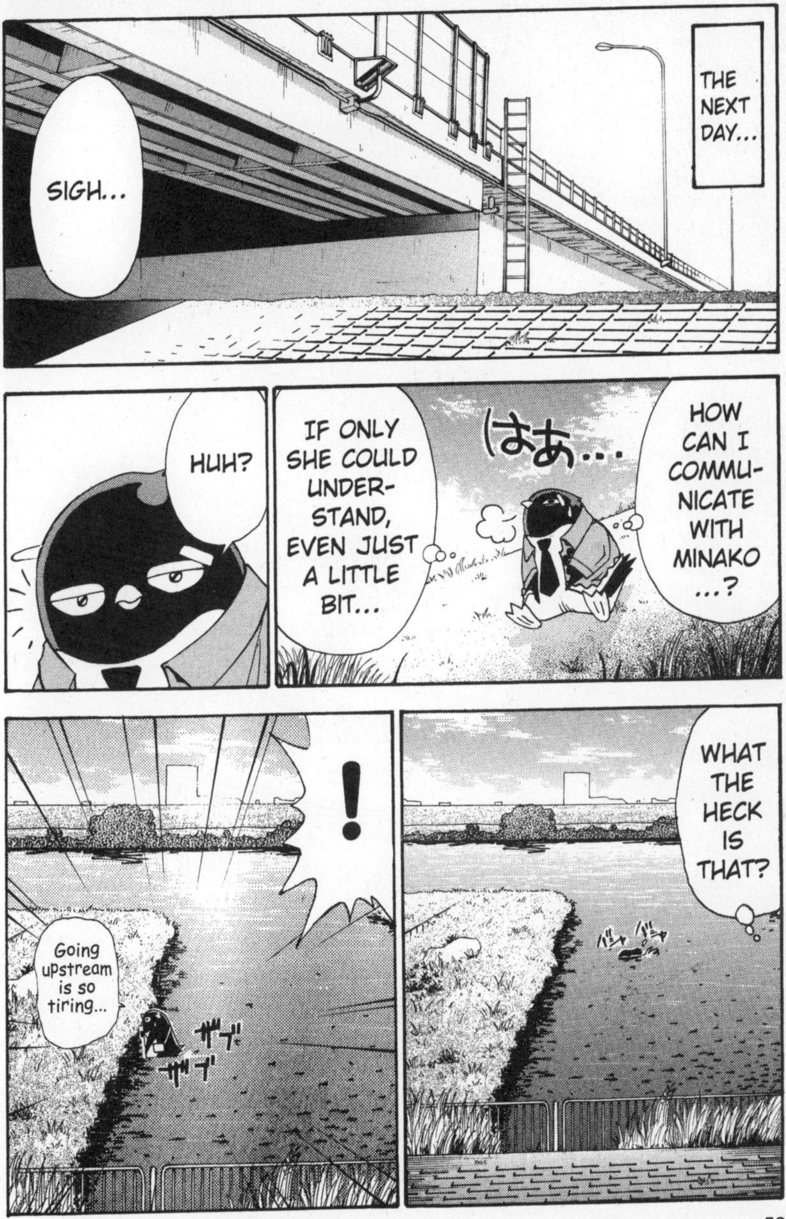
THE NEXT DAY...
SIGH...
HOW CAN I COMMUNICATE WITH MINAKO ...?
はあ...
IF ONLY SHE COULD UNDERSTAND, EVEN JUST A LITTLE BIT...
HUH?
WHAT THE HECK IS THAT?
バシャ バシャ
!
Going upstream is so tiring...
ザブ ザブ

MIKE!!
WAH!! DON'T STARTLE ME.
BOSS!! FANCY MEETING YOU HERE!
MIKE WHAT'RE YOU DOING HERE? I THOUGHT YOU WENT BACK TO THE AQUARIUM!
THEY HAVEN'T REPAIRED THAT SEWER GRATE, YET! I CAN COME AND GO AS I PLEASE!!
I FORGOT THE ZOO HAD SUCH CRUMMY MAINTE-NANCE...
BUT, I HAVE TO GO BACK IN TWO DAYS!
WHY?
I HAVE A TV COM-MERCIAL TO SHOOT!!
I'M SUCH A GENIUS, I WRITE NOTES TO MYSELF, LIKE THIS!!
あさって
HEY...

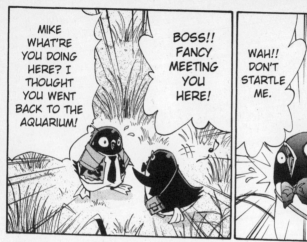

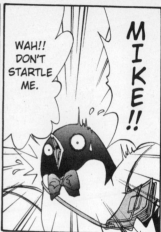

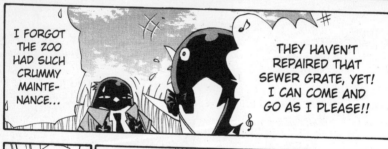

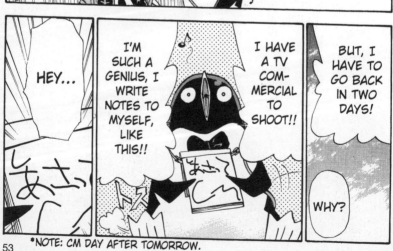

*NOTE: CM DAY AFTER TOMORROW.

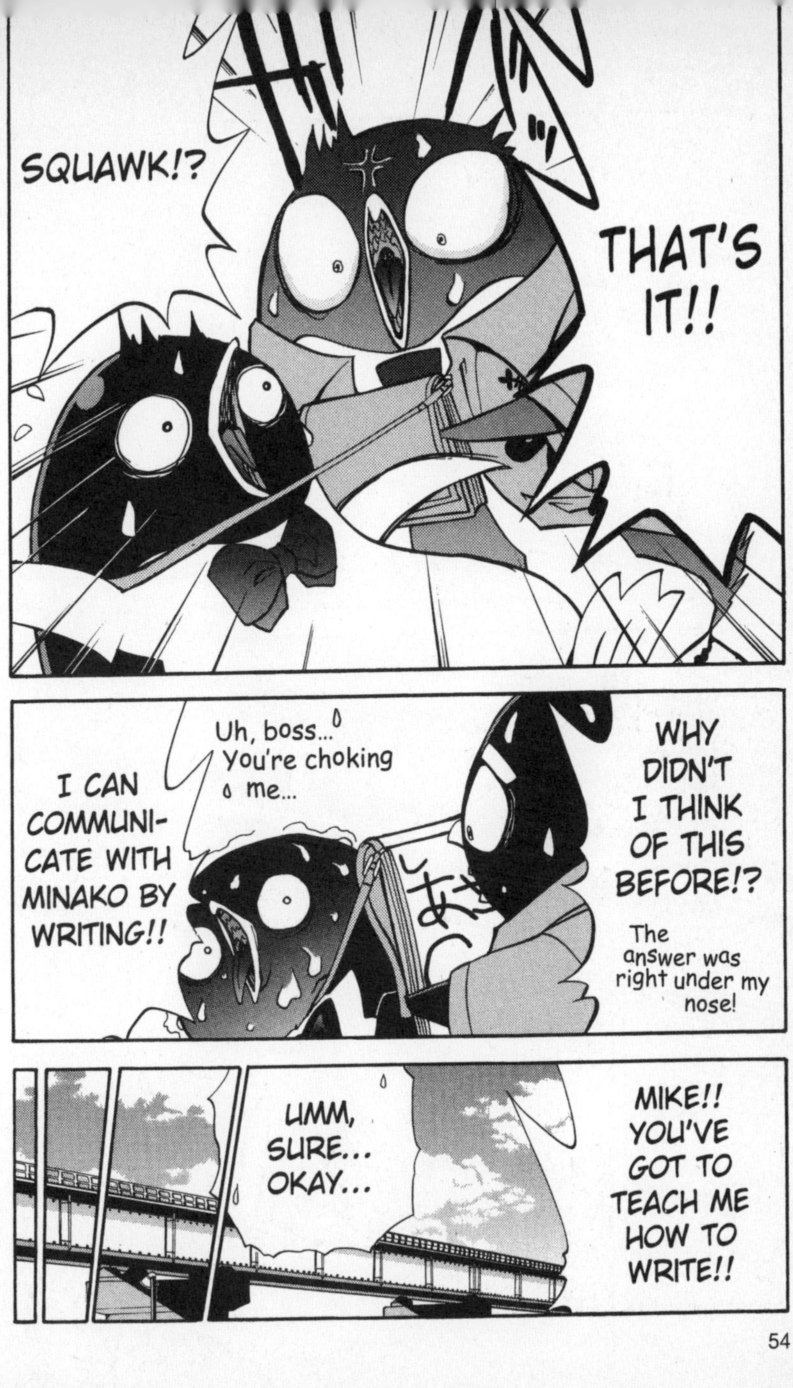
THAT'S IT!!
SQUAWK!?
WHY DIDN'T I THINK OF THIS BEFORE!?
The answer was right under my nose!
Uh, boss... You're choking me...
I CAN COMMUNICATE WITH MINAKO BY WRITING!!
MIKE!! YOU'VE GOT TO TEACH ME HOW TO WRITE!!
UMM, SURE... OKAY...

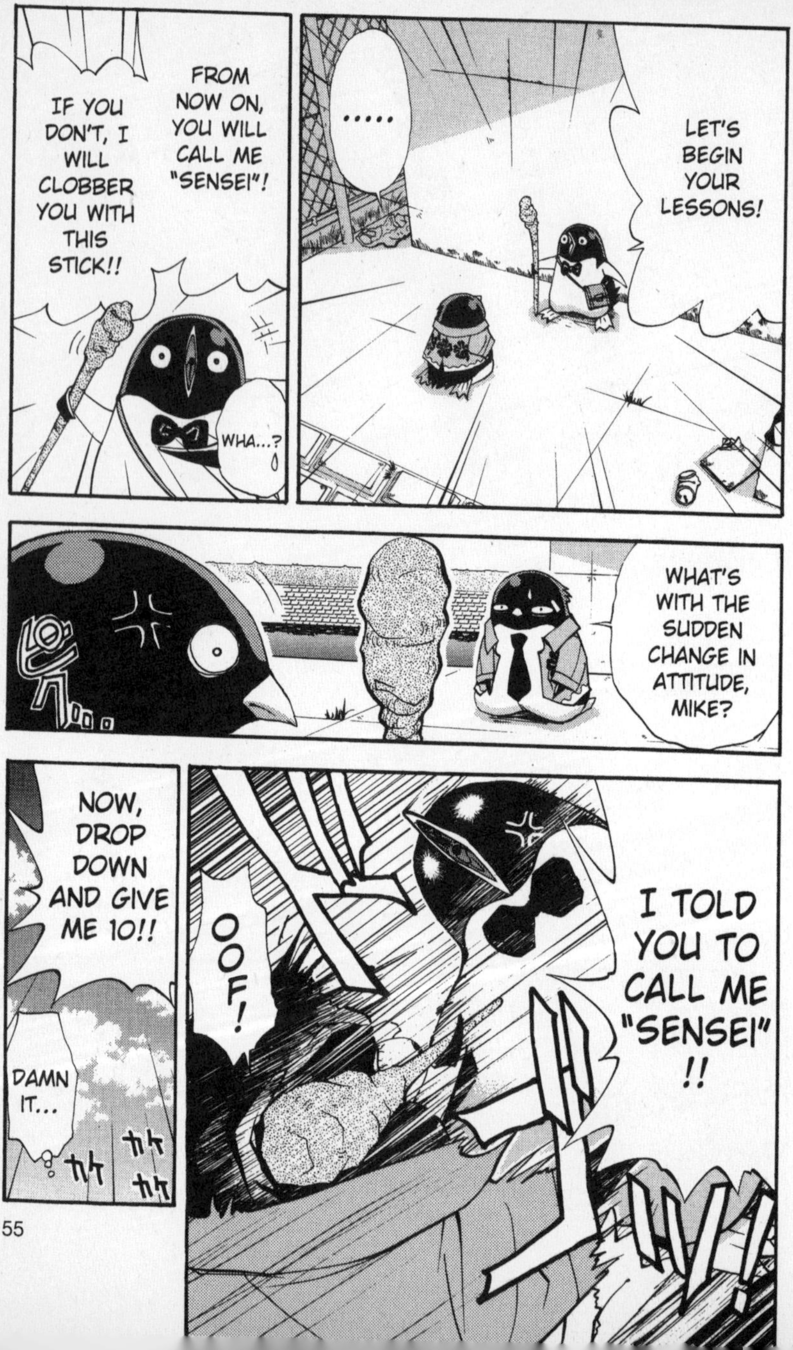
LET'S BEGIN YOUR LESSONS!
.....
FROM NOW ON, YOU WILL CALL ME "SENSEI"!
IF YOU DON'T, I WILL CLOBBER YOU WITH THIS STICK!!
WHA...?
WHAT'S WITH THE SUDDEN CHANGE IN ATTITUDE, MIKE?
I TOLD YOU TO CALL ME "SENSEI" !!
OOF!
NOW, DROP DOWN AND GIVE ME 10!!
DAMN IT...

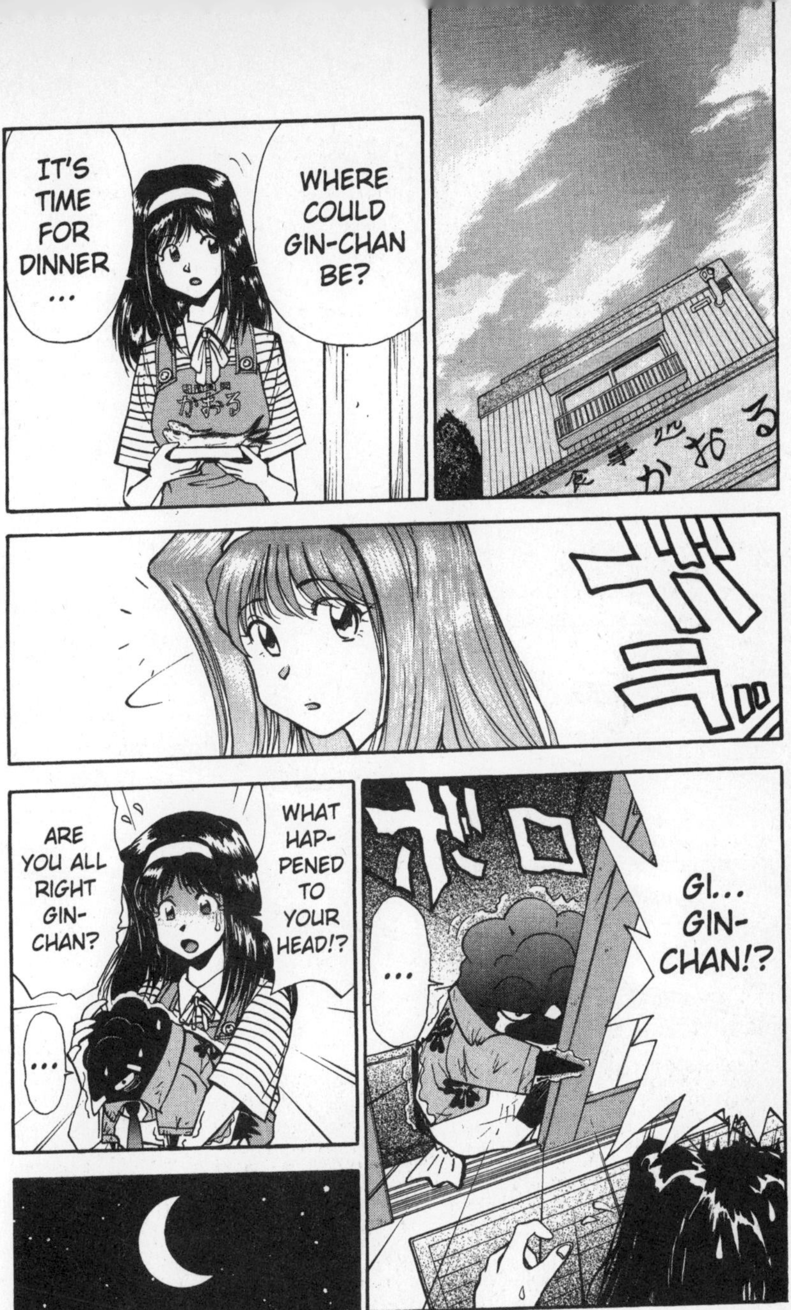

食事処 かおる
WHERE COULD GIN-CHAN BE?
IT'S TIME FOR DINNER ...
かおる
ガラッ
GI... GIN-CHAN!?
ボロ
...
WHAT HAP-PENED TO YOUR HEAD!?
ARE YOU ALL RIGHT GIN-CHAN?
...

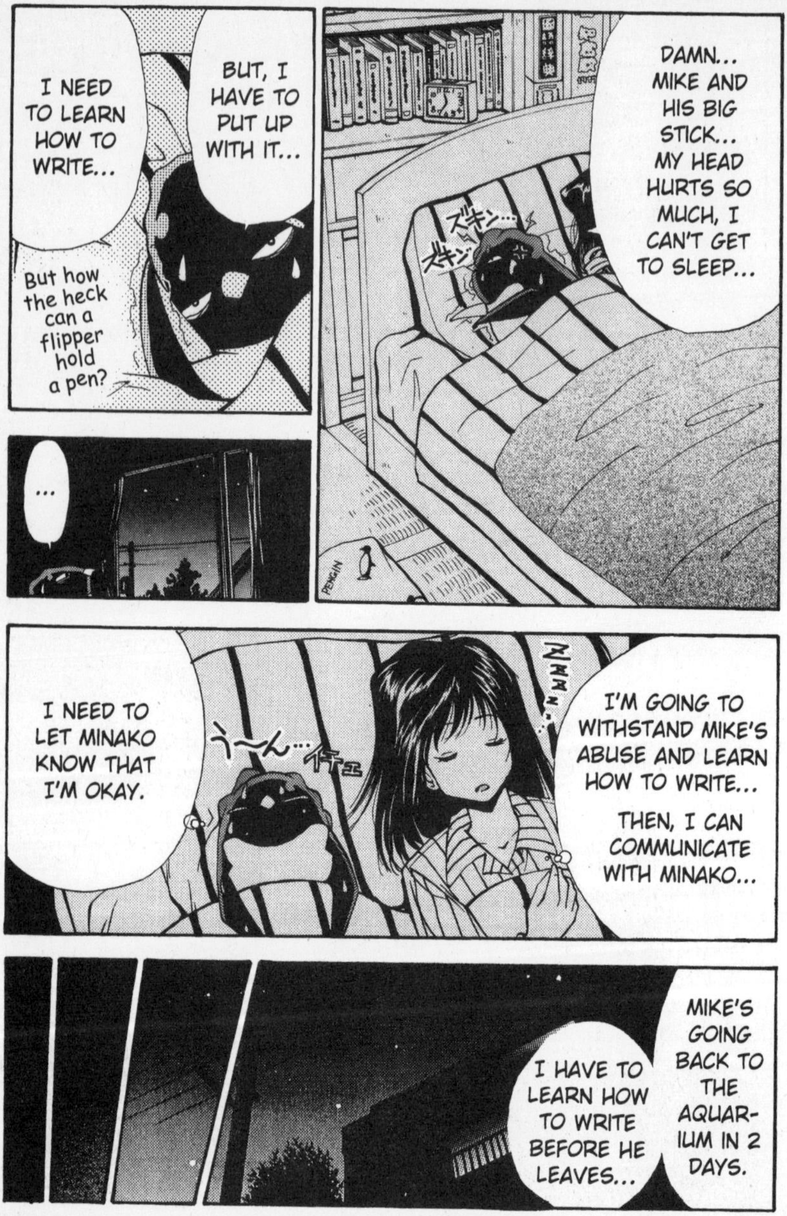
DAMN... MIKE AND HIS BIG STICK... MY HEAD HURTS SO MUCH, I CAN'T GET TO SLEEP...
ズキン…
ズキン
PENGIN
BUT, I HAVE TO PUT UP WITH IT...
I NEED TO LEARN HOW TO WRITE...
But how the heck can a flipper hold a pen?
...
I'M GOING TO WITHSTAND MIKE'S ABUSE AND LEARN HOW TO WRITE...
THEN, I CAN COMMUNICATE WITH MINAKO...
I NEED TO LET MINAKO KNOW THAT I'M OKAY.
MIKE'S GOING BACK TO THE AQUARIUM IN 2 DAYS.
I HAVE TO LEARN HOW TO WRITE BEFORE HE LEAVES...

THE NEXT DAY...
SQUAWK!
THAT'S ALL WRONG!!
YIKES!
WHAT'S THE MATTER WITH YOU!?
I TOLD YOU TO WRITE "MU"!!
This is "mu"!
I CAN'T EVEN TELL WHAT IT IS THAT YOU WROTE!
BUT IT SURE IS IRRITATING ME!!
I GUESS I HAVE NO CHOICE!!
I'M GONNA BEAT THIS LESSON INTO YOU!!
DAMN YOU, MIKE...
HUH?
WHAT'S WITH THE ATTITUDE!? I'M YOUR SENSEI!!
...

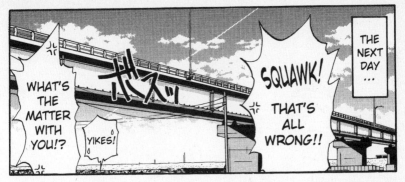

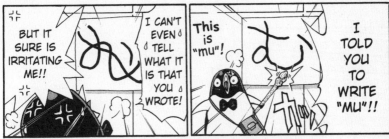

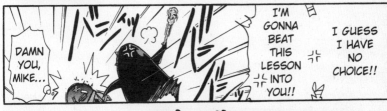

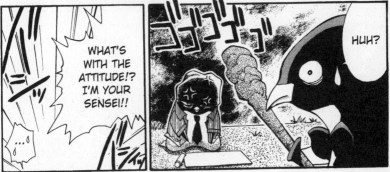

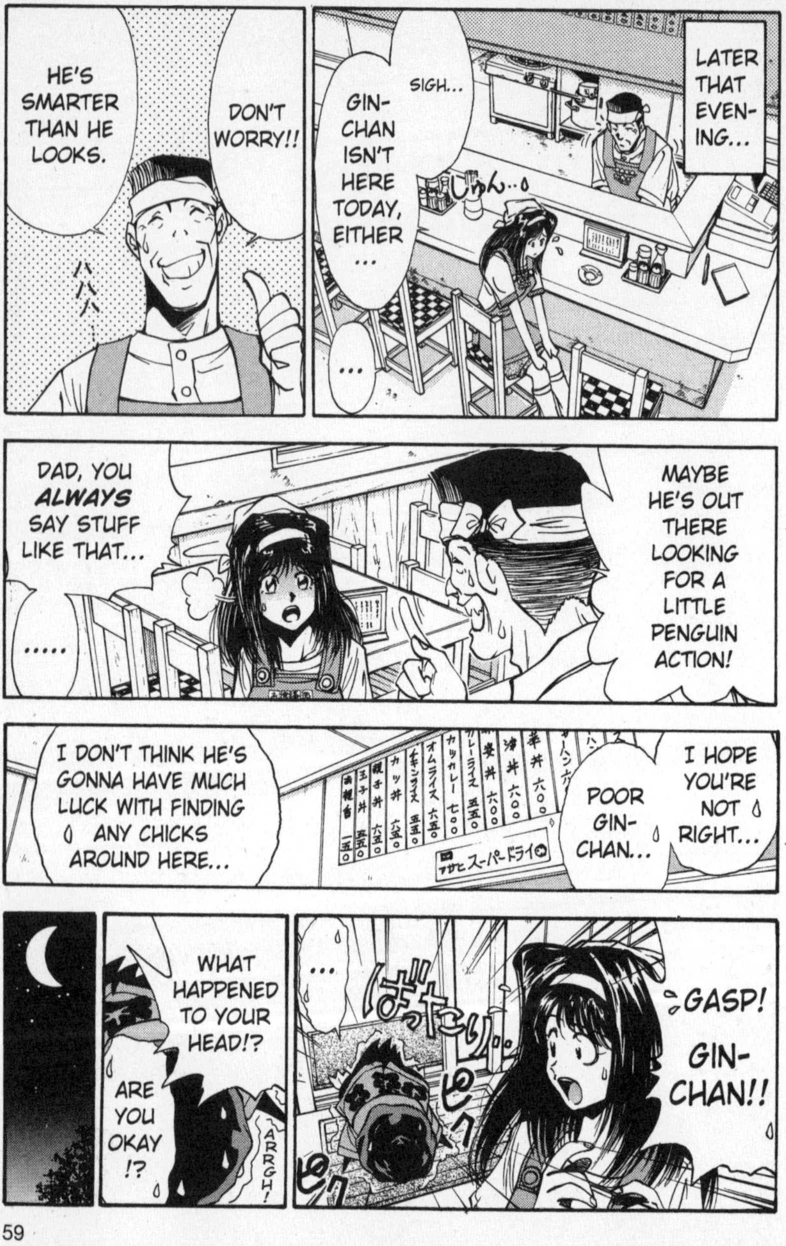
LATER THAT EVEN-ING...
SIGH...
GIN-CHAN ISN'T HERE TODAY, EITHER...
じゅん..
...
DON'T WORRY!!
HE'S SMARTER THAN HE LOOKS.
ハハハ
MAYBE HE'S OUT THERE LOOKING FOR A LITTLE PENGUIN ACTION!
DAD, YOU ALWAYS SAY STUFF LIKE THAT...
.....
I HOPE YOU'RE NOT RIGHT...
POOR GIN-CHAN...
I DON'T THINK HE'S GONNA HAVE MUCH LUCK WITH FINDING ANY CHICKS AROUND HERE...
GASP!
GIN-CHAN!!
ばったり。
ピク
...
WHAT HAPPENED TO YOUR HEAD!?
ARE YOU OKAY!?
ARRGH!

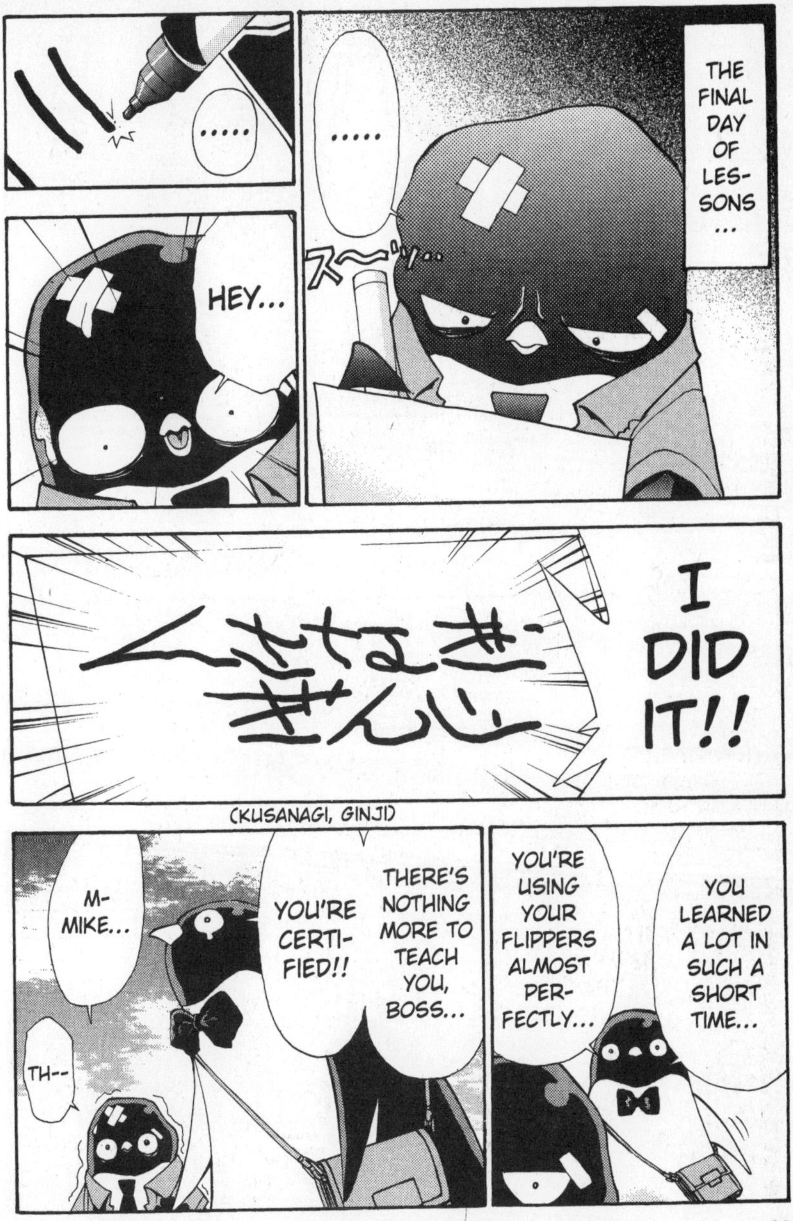
THE FINAL DAY OF LES- SONS...
.....
.....
HEY...
I DID IT!!
くさなぎ ぎんじ
(KUSANAGI, GINJI)
YOU LEARNED A LOT IN SUCH A SHORT TIME...
YOU'RE USING YOUR FLIPPERS ALMOST PER- FECTLY...
THERE'S NOTHING MORE TO TEACH YOU, BOSS...
YOU'RE CERTI- FIED!!
M- MIKE...
TH--

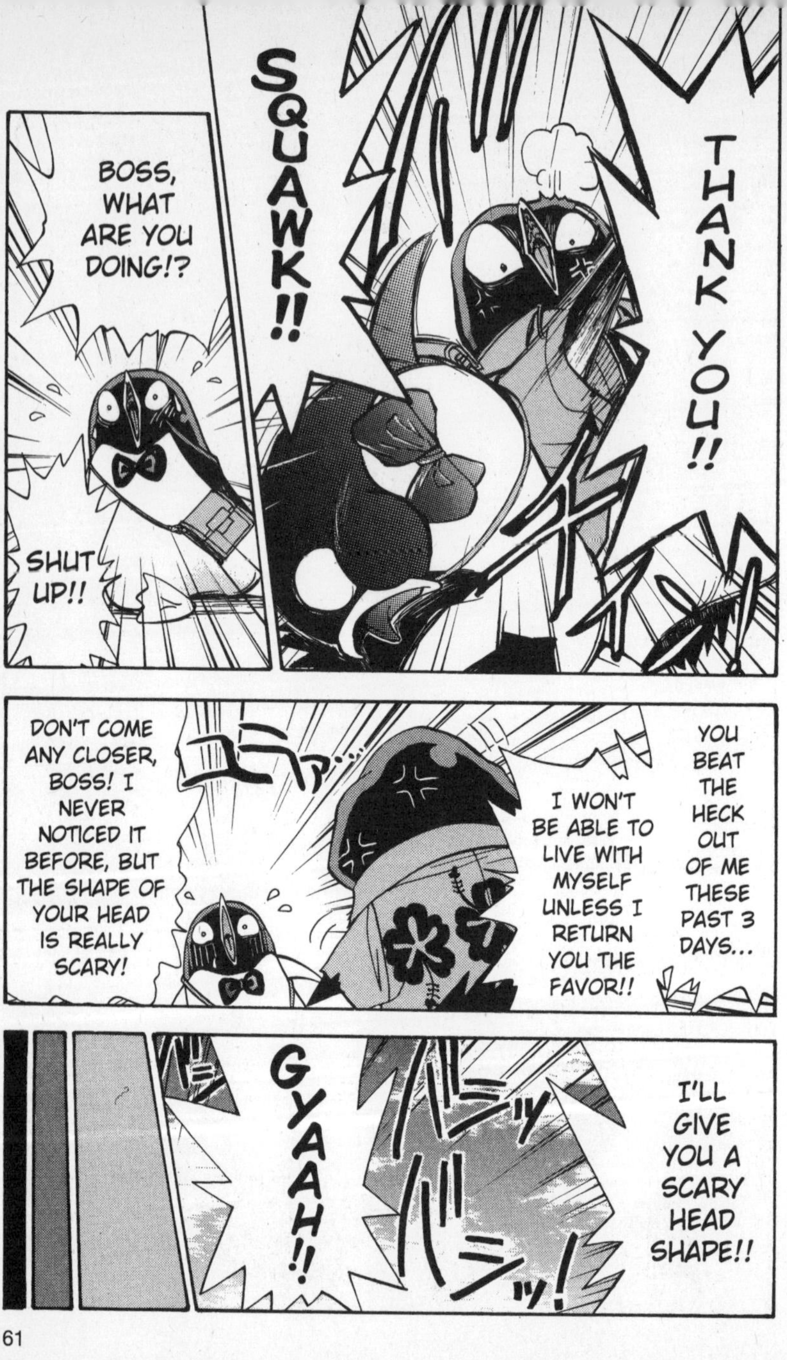
THANK YOU!!
SQUAWK!!
BOSS, WHAT ARE YOU DOING!?
SHUT UP!!
YOU BEAT THE HECK OUT OF ME THESE PAST 3 DAYS...
I WON'T BE ABLE TO LIVE WITH MYSELF UNLESS I RETURN YOU THE FAVOR!!
DON'T COME ANY CLOSER, BOSS! I NEVER NOTICED IT BEFORE, BUT THE SHAPE OF YOUR HEAD IS REALLY SCARY!
I'LL GIVE YOU A SCARY HEAD SHAPE!!
GYAAH!!

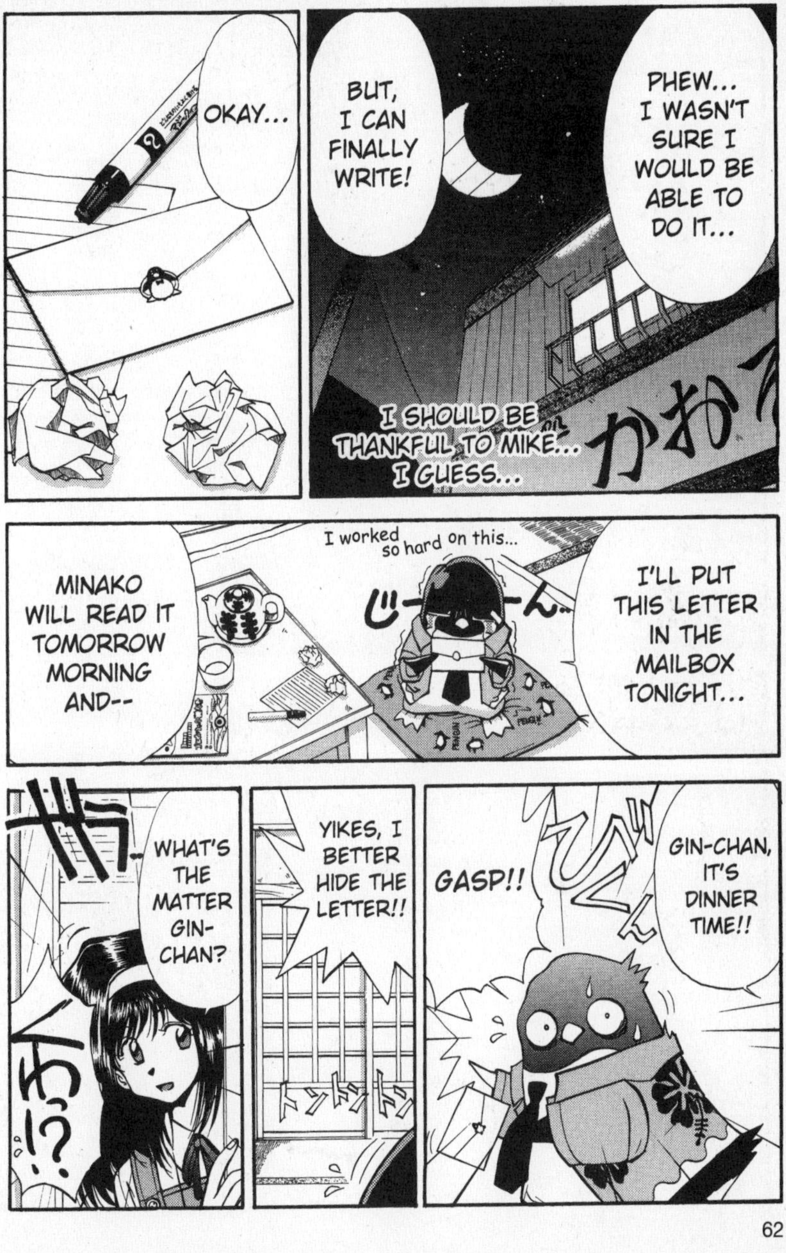
PHEW... I WASN'T SURE I WOULD BE ABLE TO DO IT...
BUT, I CAN FINALLY WRITE!
I SHOULD BE THANKFUL TO MIKE... I GUESS...
OKAY...
I'LL PUT THIS LETTER IN THE MAILBOX TONIGHT...
I worked so hard on this...
MINAKO WILL READ IT TOMORROW MORNING AND--
GIN-CHAN, IT'S DINNER TIME!!
GASP!!
YIKES, I BETTER HIDE THE LETTER!!
WHAT'S THE MATTER GIN-CHAN?

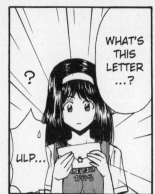

HM?
GASP!
OH NO! THE LETTER!!
WHAT'S THIS LETTER ...?
?
ULP...
MAYBE, AS LONG AS SHE CAN READ IT, IT DOESN'T MATTER HOW SHE GETS THE LETTER!
MY MESSAGE FROM THE HEART, TO TELL HER THAT...
"I'M OKAY! --GIN"
.....

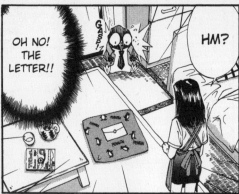

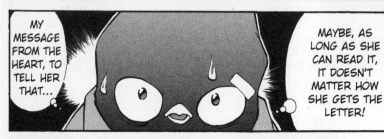

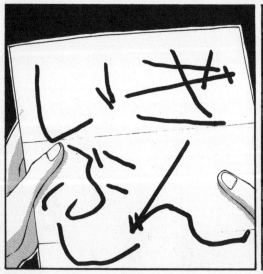

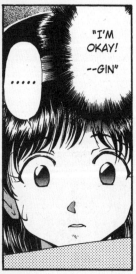

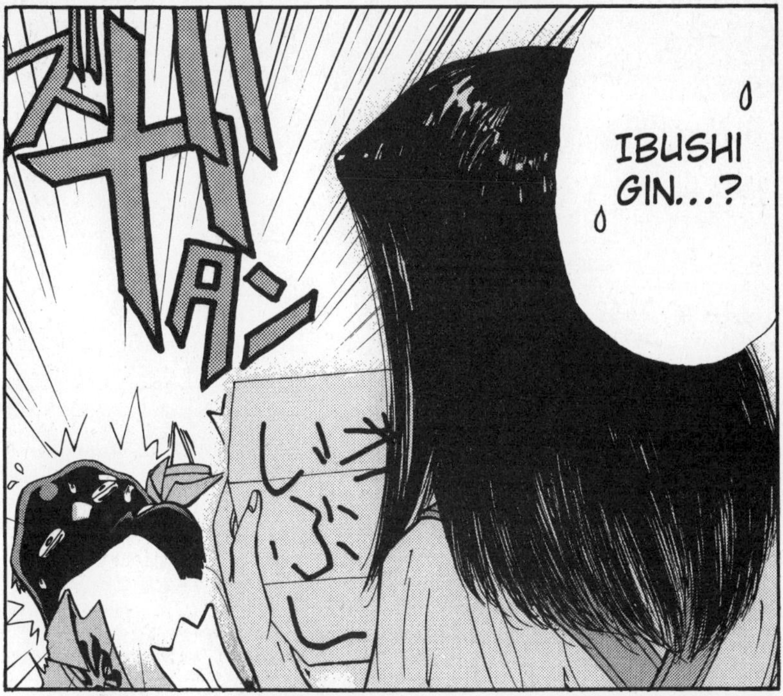
IBUSHI GIN...?

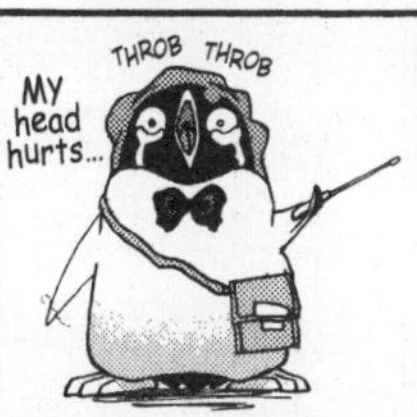
THROB THROB
My head hurts...

A Word From Mike the Genius Penguin

You probably already know this, but here's the definition of "Ibushi Gin"

i·bu·shi gin 1. *n.* oxidized silver created from a process utilizing the smoke of sulfur; a somber silver color. 2. *adj.* refined.

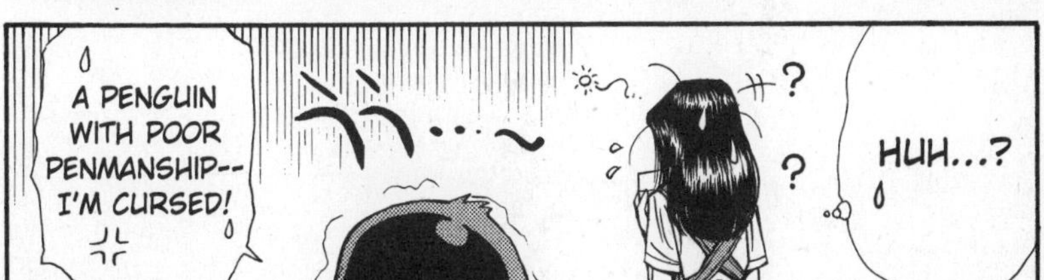
HUH...?
A PENGUIN WITH POOR PENMANSHIP-- I'M CURSED!
ちゃんちゃん♪

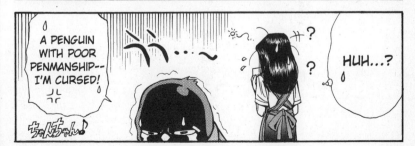

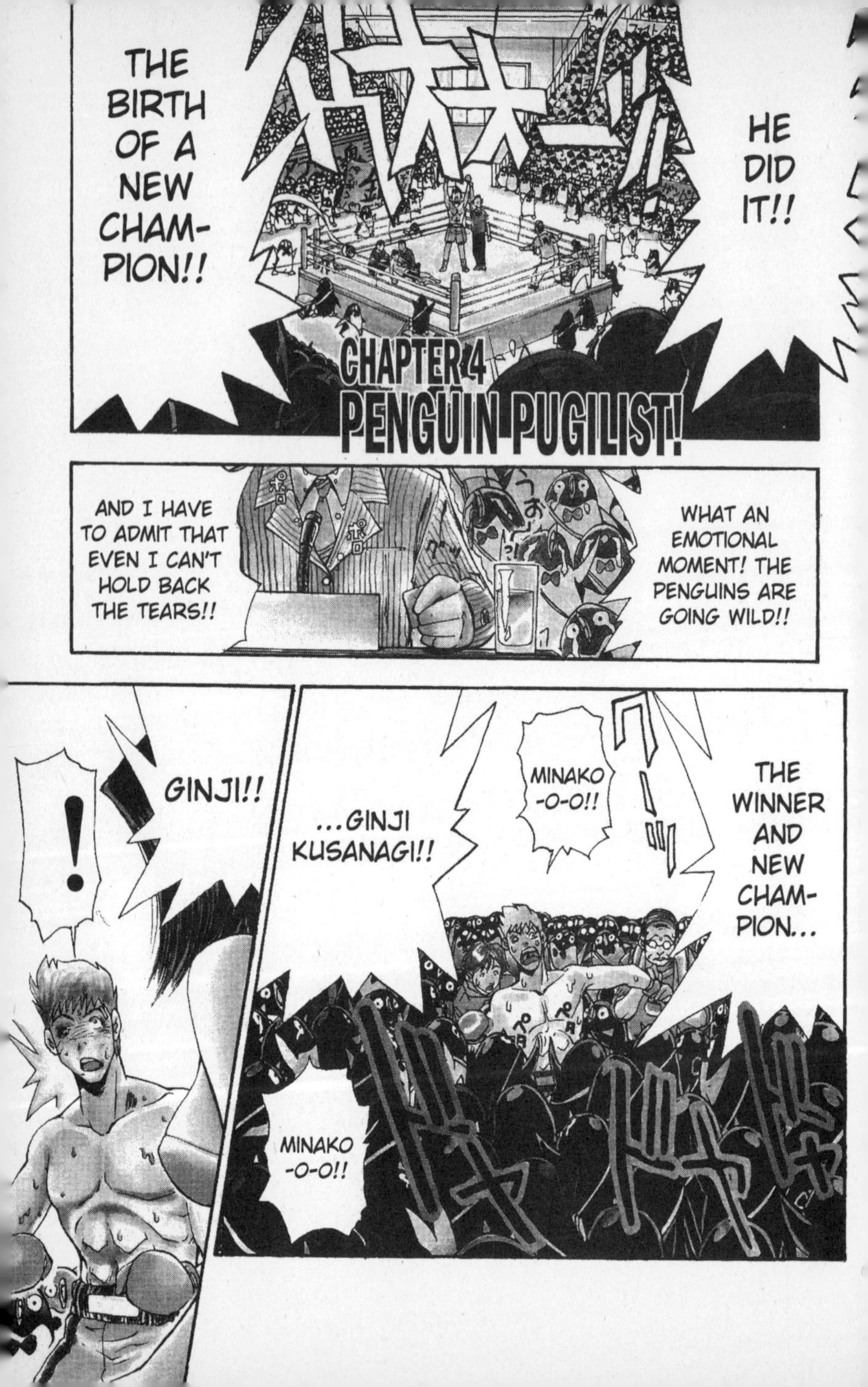
HE DID IT!!
THE BIRTH OF A NEW CHAMPION!!
CHAPTER 4
PENGUIN PUGILIST!
WHAT AN EMOTIONAL MOMENT! THE PENGUINS ARE GOING WILD!!
AND I HAVE TO ADMIT THAT EVEN I CAN'T HOLD BACK THE TEARS!!
THE WINNER AND NEW CHAMPION...
MINAKO-O-O!!
...GINJI KUSANAGI!!
MINAKO-O-O!!
GINJI!!
!

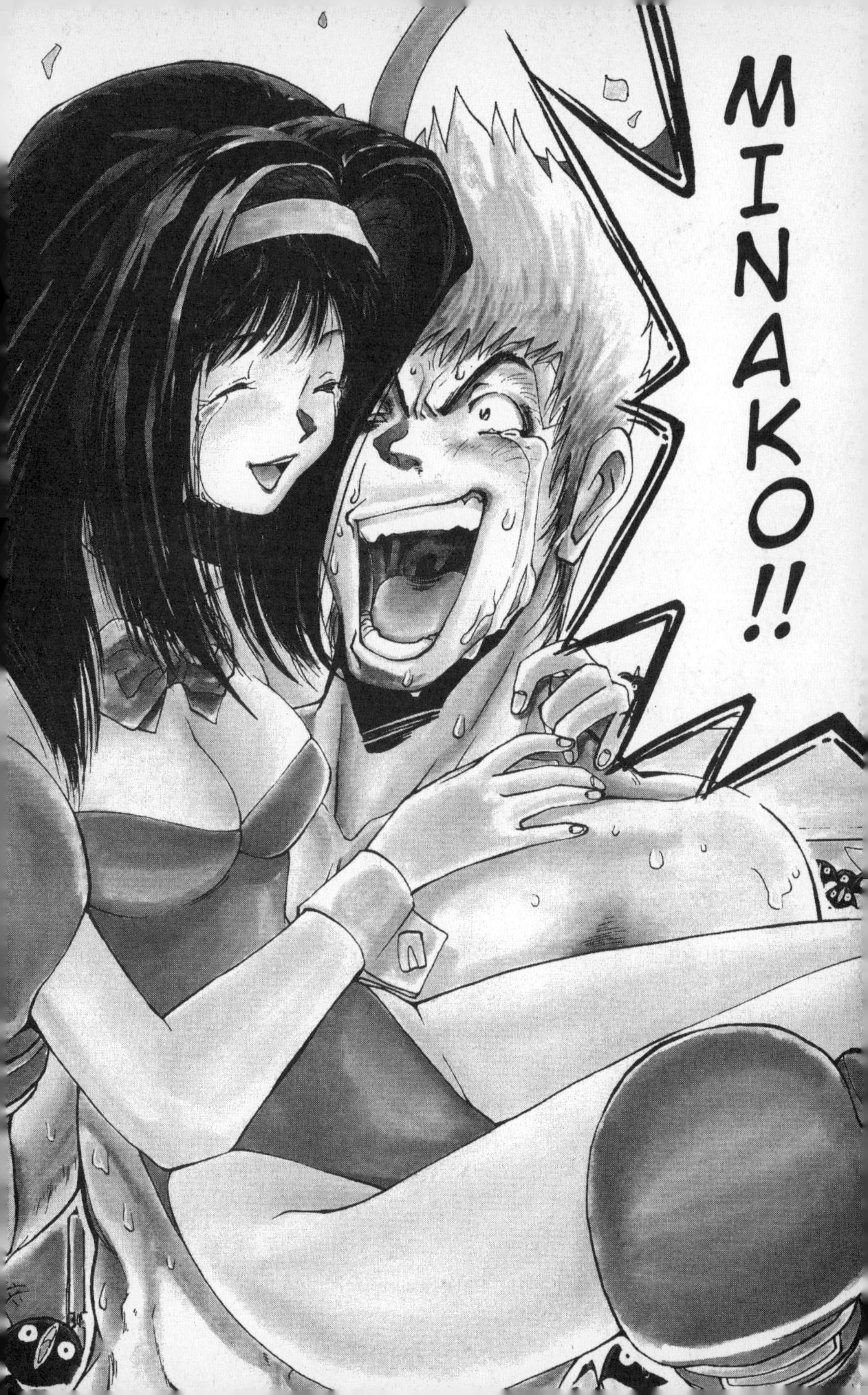
MINAKO!!

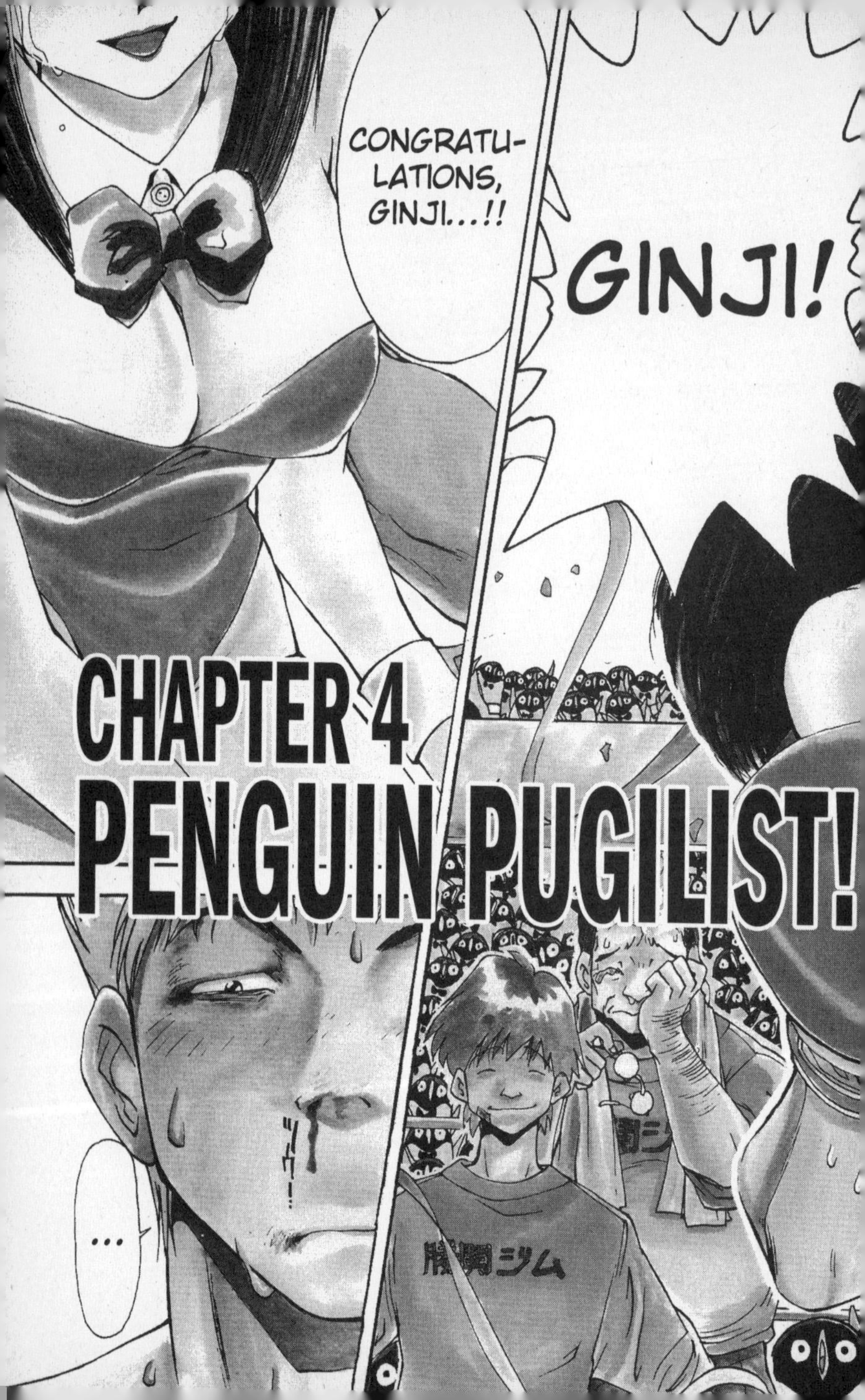
GINJI!
CONGRATULATIONS, GINJI...!!
CHAPTER 4
PENGUIN PUGILIST!
...

TUXEDO GIN

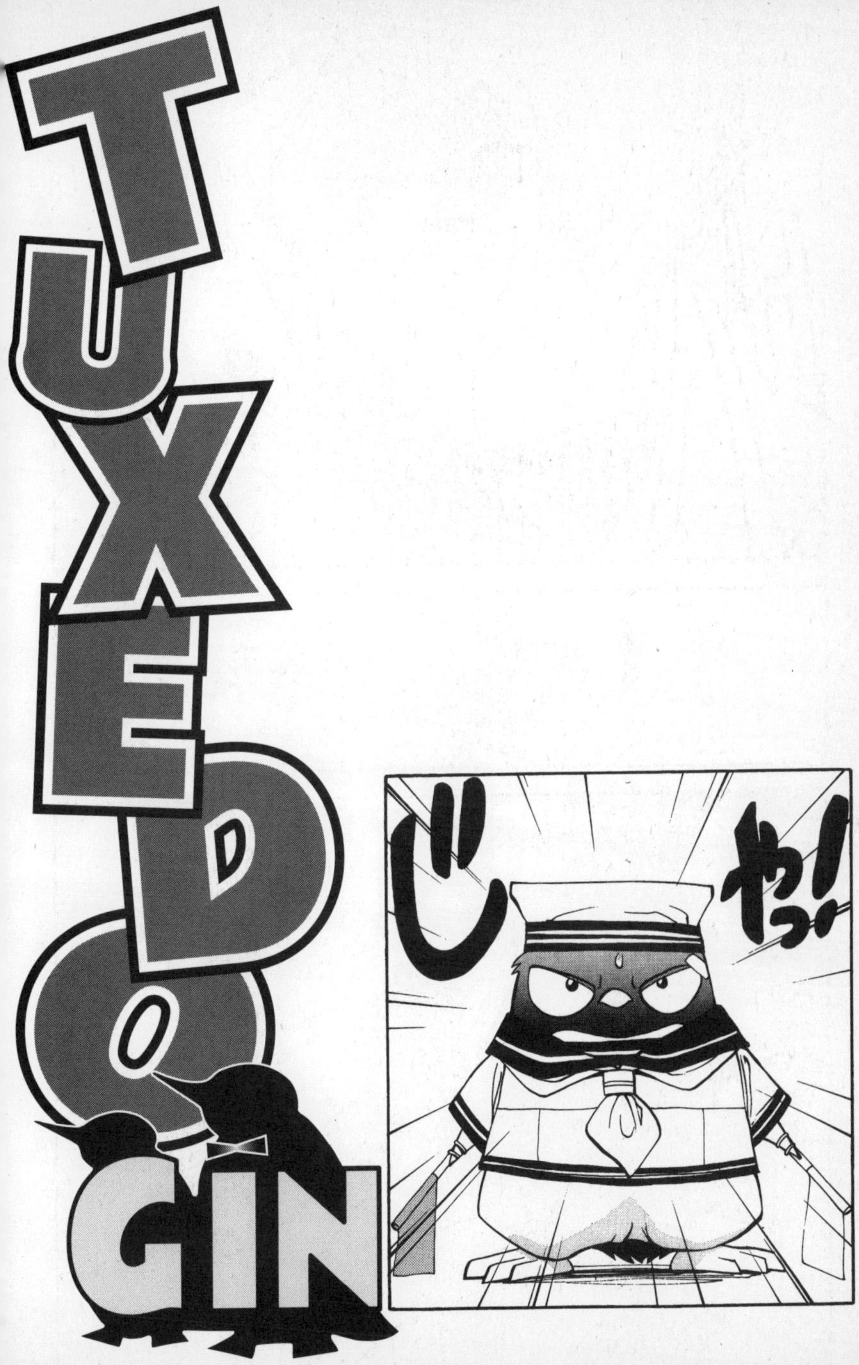
じやっ!

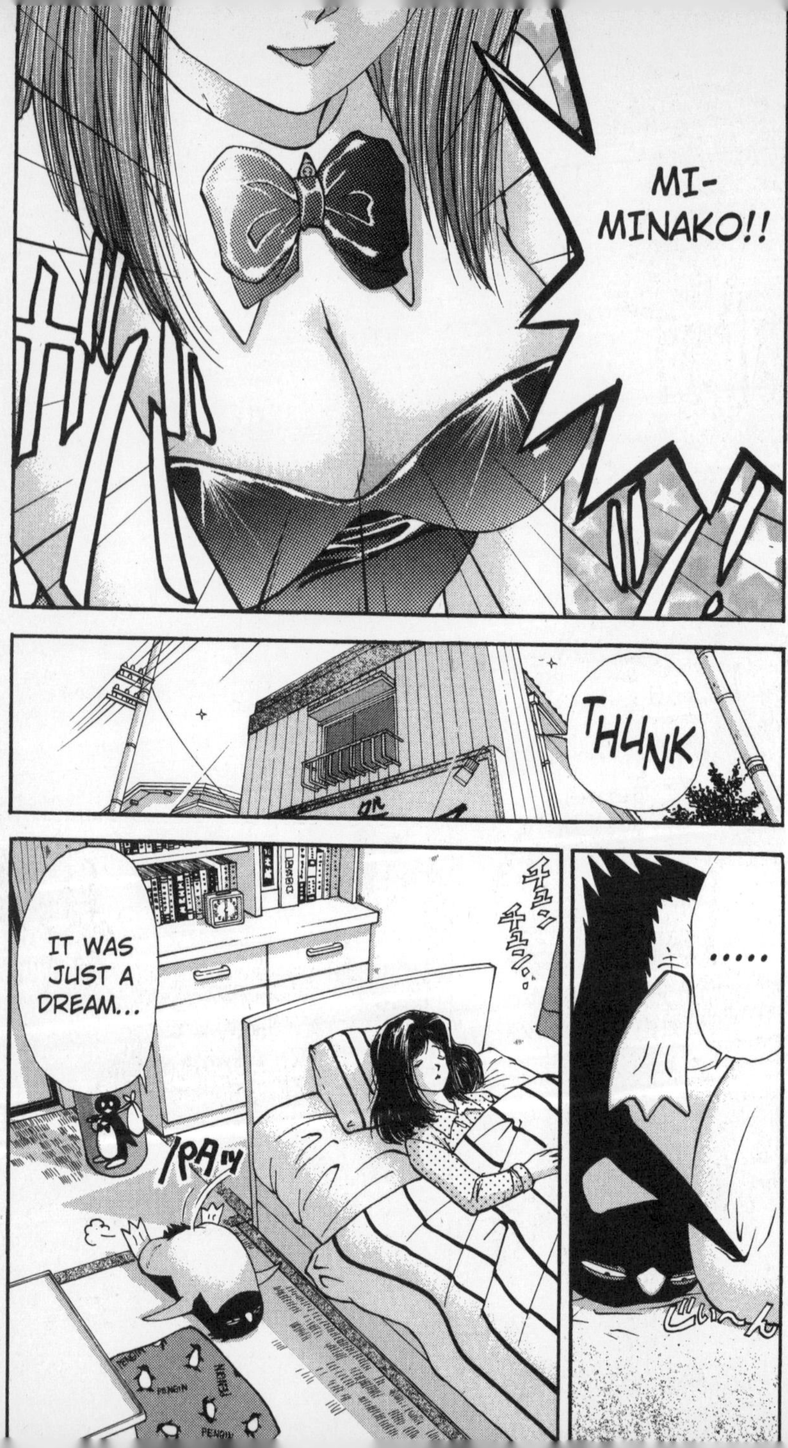
MI-
MINAKO!!
THUNK
.....
IT WAS JUST A DREAM...
PA

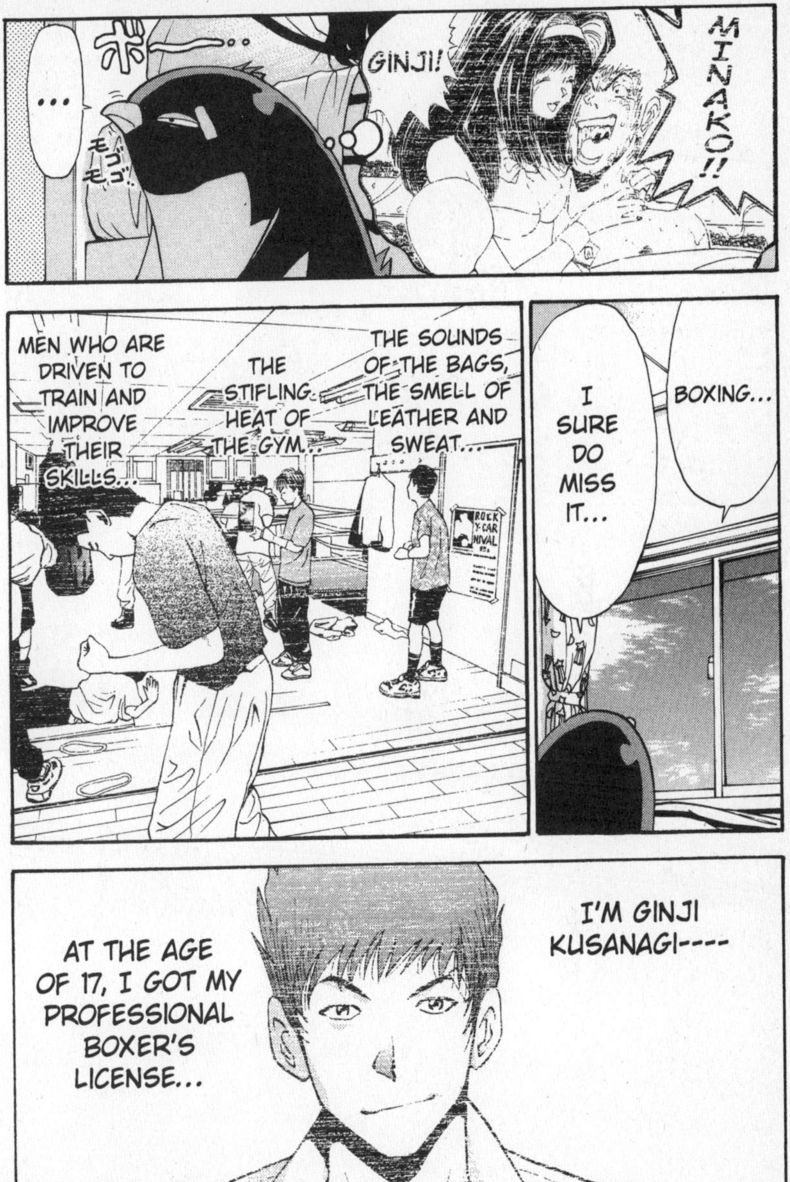
MINAKO!!
GINJI!
...
ボー
モゴモゴ
BOXING...
I SURE DO MISS IT...
THE SOUNDS OF THE BAGS, THE SMELL OF LEATHER AND SWEAT...
THE STIFLING HEAT OF THE GYM...
MEN WHO ARE DRIVEN TO TRAIN AND IMPROVE THEIR SKILLS...
ROCKY CARNIVAL
I'M GINJI KUSANAGI----
AT THE AGE OF 17, I GOT MY PROFESSIONAL BOXER'S LICENSE...

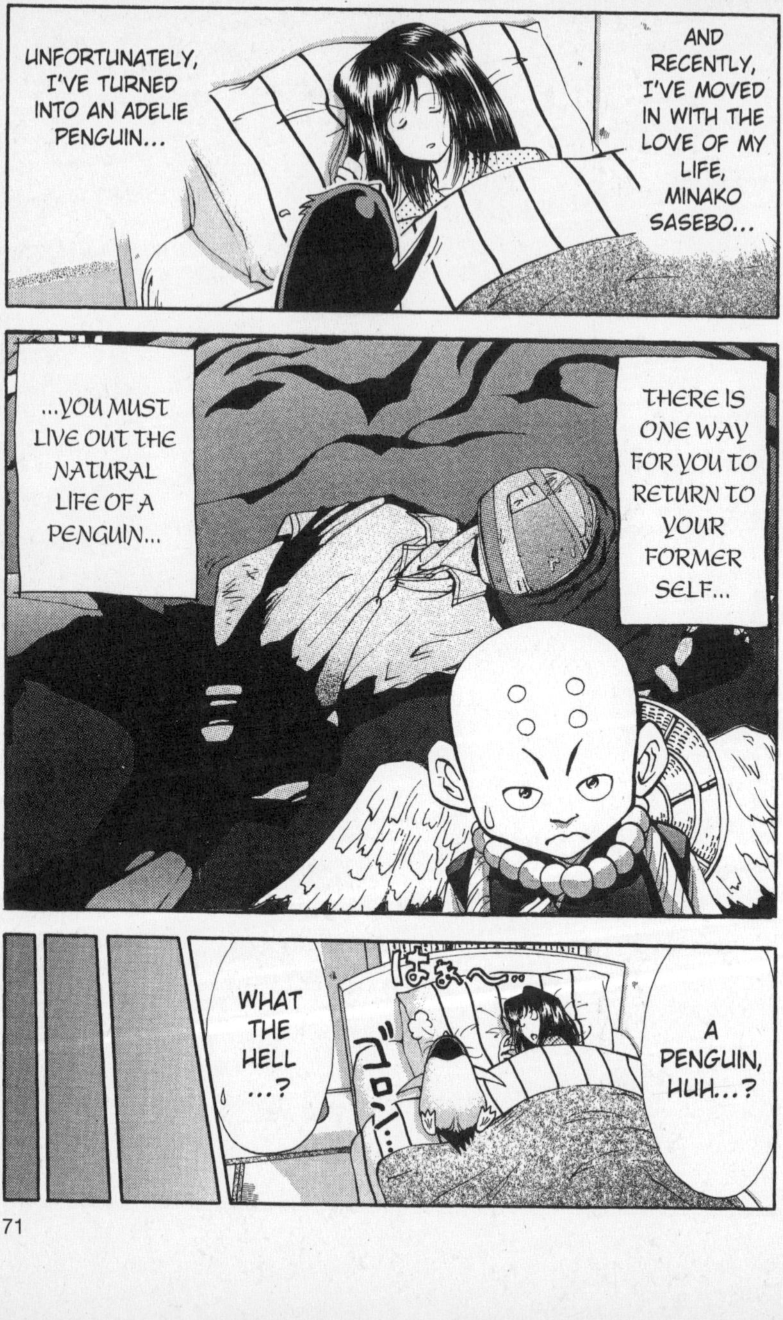
AND RECENTLY, I'VE MOVED IN WITH THE LOVE OF MY LIFE, MINAKO SASEBO...
UNFORTUNATELY, I'VE TURNED INTO AN ADELIE PENGUIN...
THERE IS ONE WAY FOR YOU TO RETURN TO YOUR FORMER SELF...
...YOU MUST LIVE OUT THE NATURAL LIFE OF A PENGUIN...
A PENGUIN, HUH...?
はぁ〜..
ゴロン…
WHAT THE HELL ...?

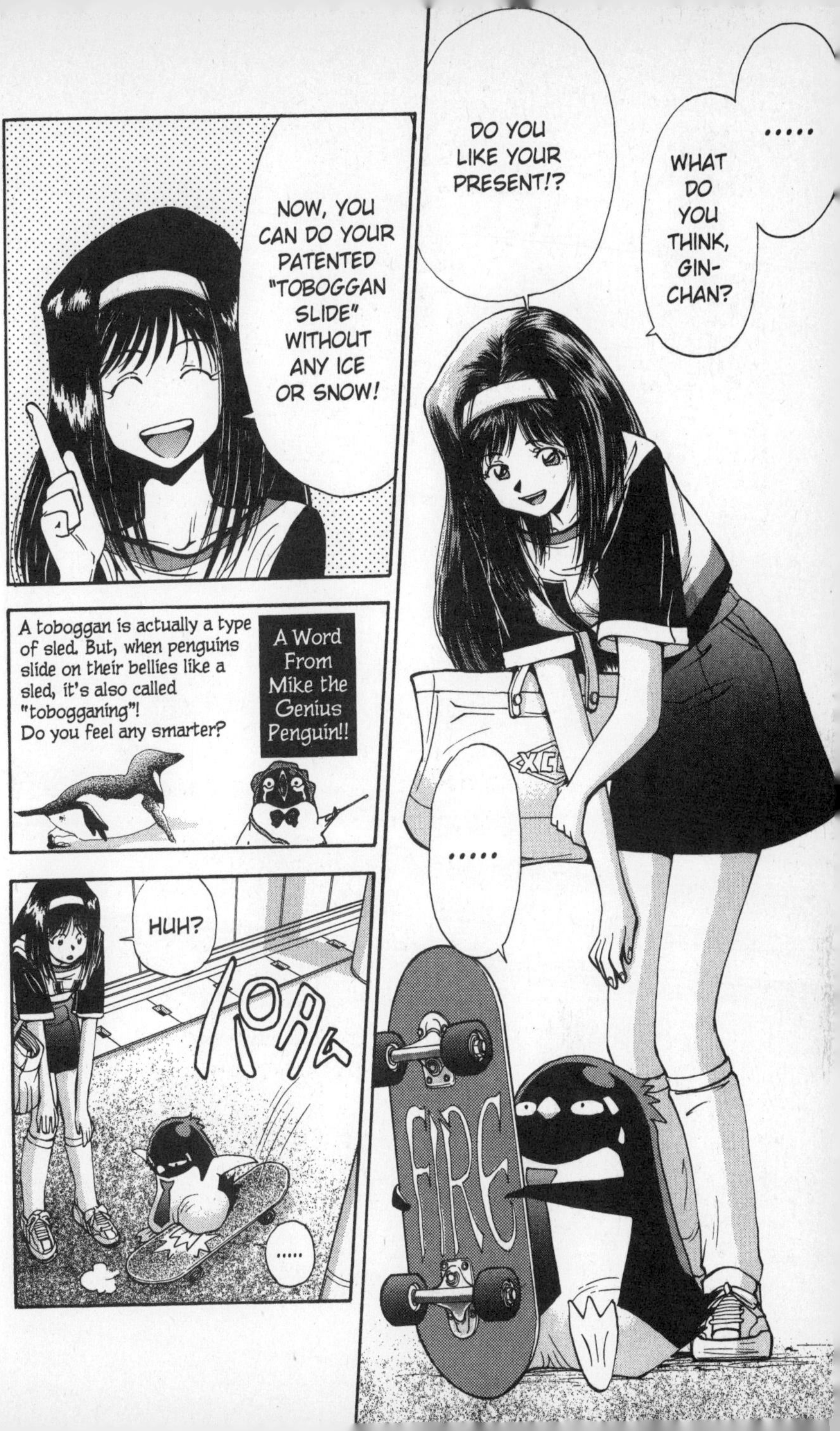
.....
WHAT DO YOU THINK, GIN-CHAN?
DO YOU LIKE YOUR PRESENT!?
.....
NOW, YOU CAN DO YOUR PATENTED "TOBOGGAN SLIDE" WITHOUT ANY ICE OR SNOW!
A Word From Mike the Genius Penguin!!
A toboggan is actually a type of sled. But, when penguins slide on their bellies like a sled, it's also called "tobogganing"! Do you feel any smarter?
HUH?
.....

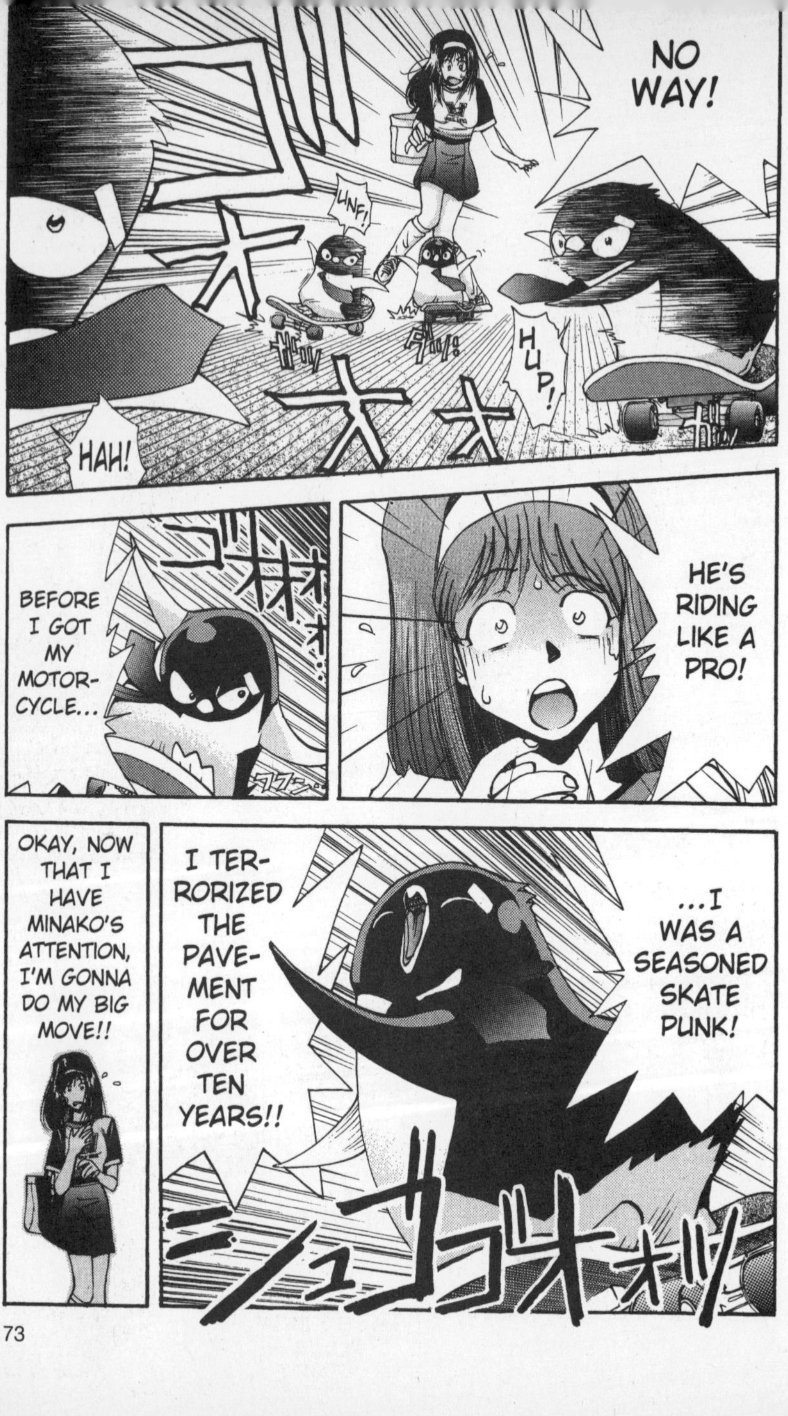
NO WAY!
HUP!
UNF!
HAH!
HE'S RIDING LIKE A PRO!
BEFORE I GOT MY MOTORCYCLE...
...I WAS A SEASONED SKATE PUNK!
I TERRORIZED THE PAVEMENT FOR OVER TEN YEARS!!
OKAY, NOW THAT I HAVE MINAKO'S ATTENTION, I'M GONNA DO MY BIG MOVE!!

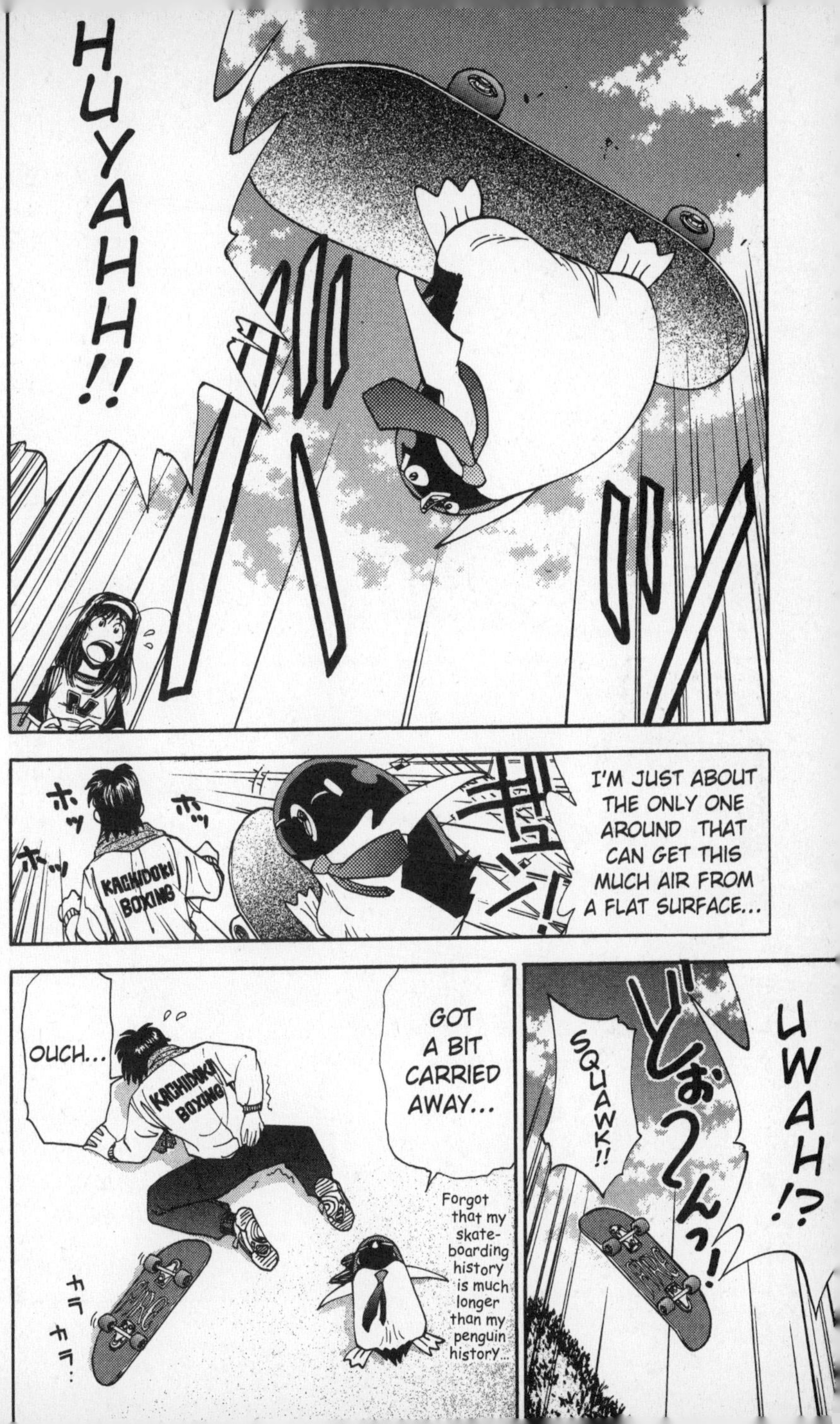
HUYAHH!!
I'M JUST ABOUT THE ONLY ONE AROUND THAT CAN GET THIS MUCH AIR FROM A FLAT SURFACE...
ホッ
ホッ
ホッ
UWAH!?
どぉ〜んっ!
SQUAWK!!
GOT A BIT CARRIED AWAY...
OUCH...
Forgot that my skate-boarding history is much longer than my penguin history...
カラ
カラ

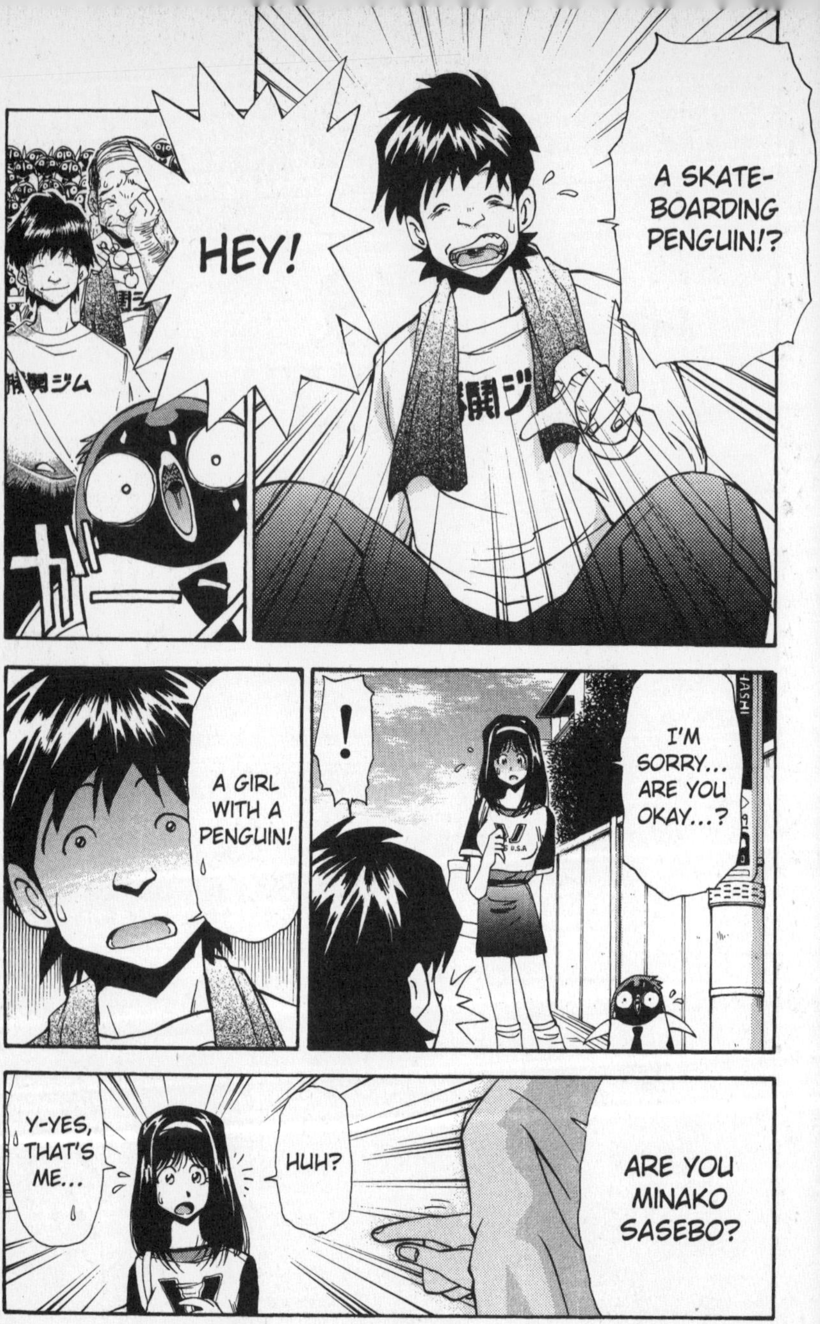
A SKATE-BOARDING PENGUIN!?
HEY!
I'M SORRY... ARE YOU OKAY...?
!
A GIRL WITH A PENGUIN!
ARE YOU MINAKO SASEBO?
HUH?
Y-YES, THAT'S ME...

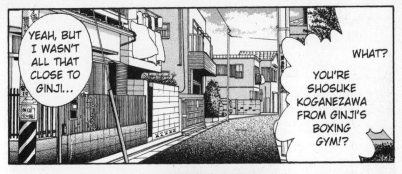

WHAT?
YOU'RE SHOSUKE KOGANEZAWA FROM GINJI'S BOXING GYM!?
YEAH, BUT I WASN'T ALL THAT CLOSE TO GINJI...
I DIDN'T THINK YOU WERE GOING TO BE THIS CUTE. AND THE RUMORS ARE TRUE--
YOU'RE WALKING AROUND WITH A PENGUIN!
Uh.. Well, thanks..
RUMORS? MUSASHI MUST BE SPREADING THE WORD...
HEY! WHY DON'T YOU COME VISIT THE GYM!?
REALLY?
Yippee!!
MAYBE IT'LL CHEER COACH UP TO MEET A FRIEND OF GINJI'S!
HUH?
WHY WOULD THAT MANIAC OF A COACH NEED CHEERING UP...?
HA HA HA

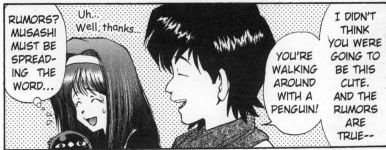

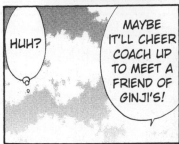

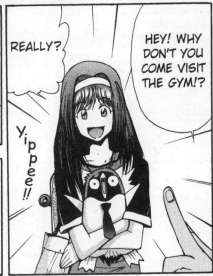

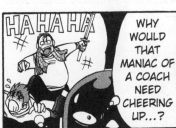

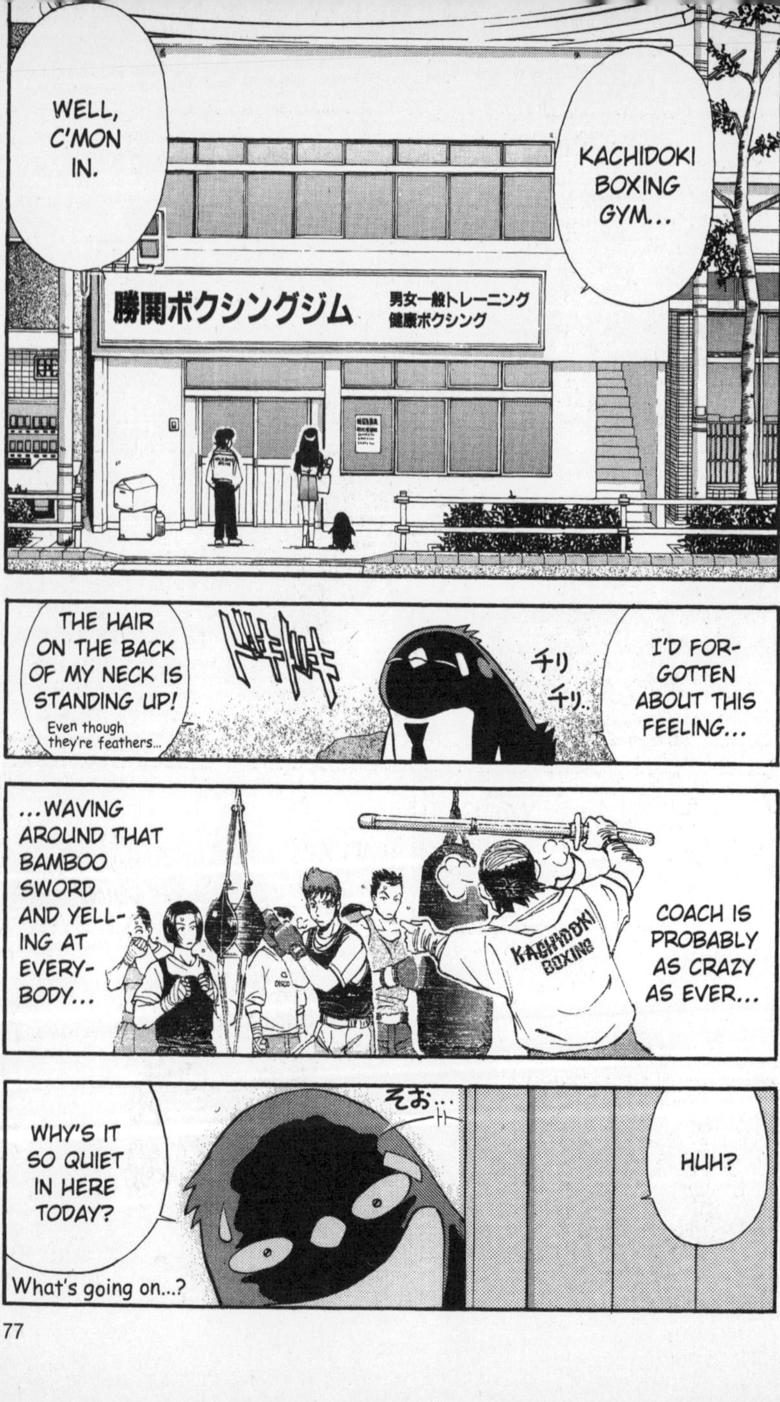
KACHIDOKI BOXING GYM...
WELL, C'MON IN.
勝鬨ボクシングジム
男女一般トレーニング
健康ボクシング
I'D FOR-GOTTEN ABOUT THIS FEELING...
チリ チリ..
ドキドキ
THE HAIR ON THE BACK OF MY NECK IS STANDING UP!
Even though they're feathers...
COACH IS PROBABLY AS CRAZY AS EVER...
KACHIDOKI BOXING
...WAVING AROUND THAT BAMBOO SWORD AND YELL-ING AT EVERY-BODY...
HUH?
そお…
WHY'S IT SO QUIET IN HERE TODAY?
What's going on...?

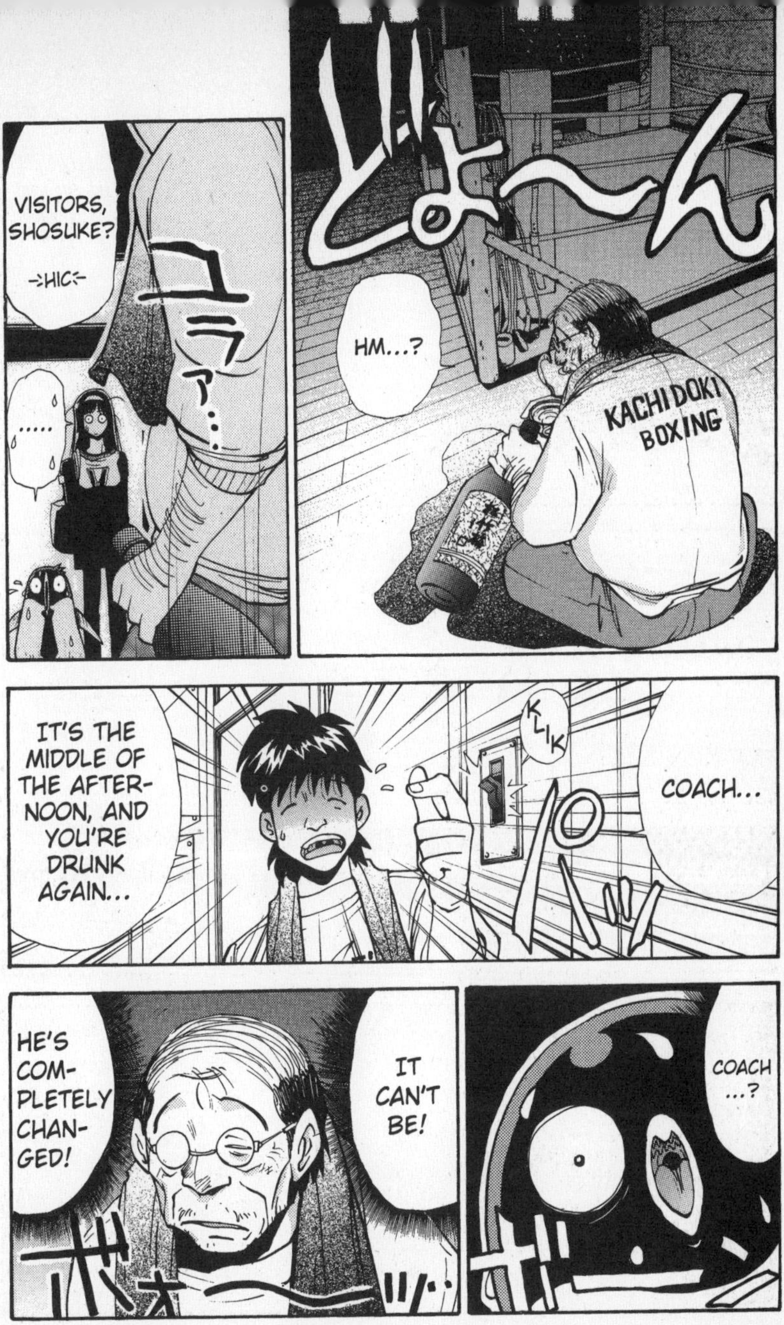
どよ～ん
HM...?
KACHIDOKI BOXING
VISITORS, SHOSUKE?
-HIC-
ユラァ…
.....
COACH...
KLIK
IT'S THE MIDDLE OF THE AFTER-NOON, AND YOU'RE DRUNK AGAIN...
COACH ...?
IT CAN'T BE!
HE'S COM-PLETELY CHAN-GED!

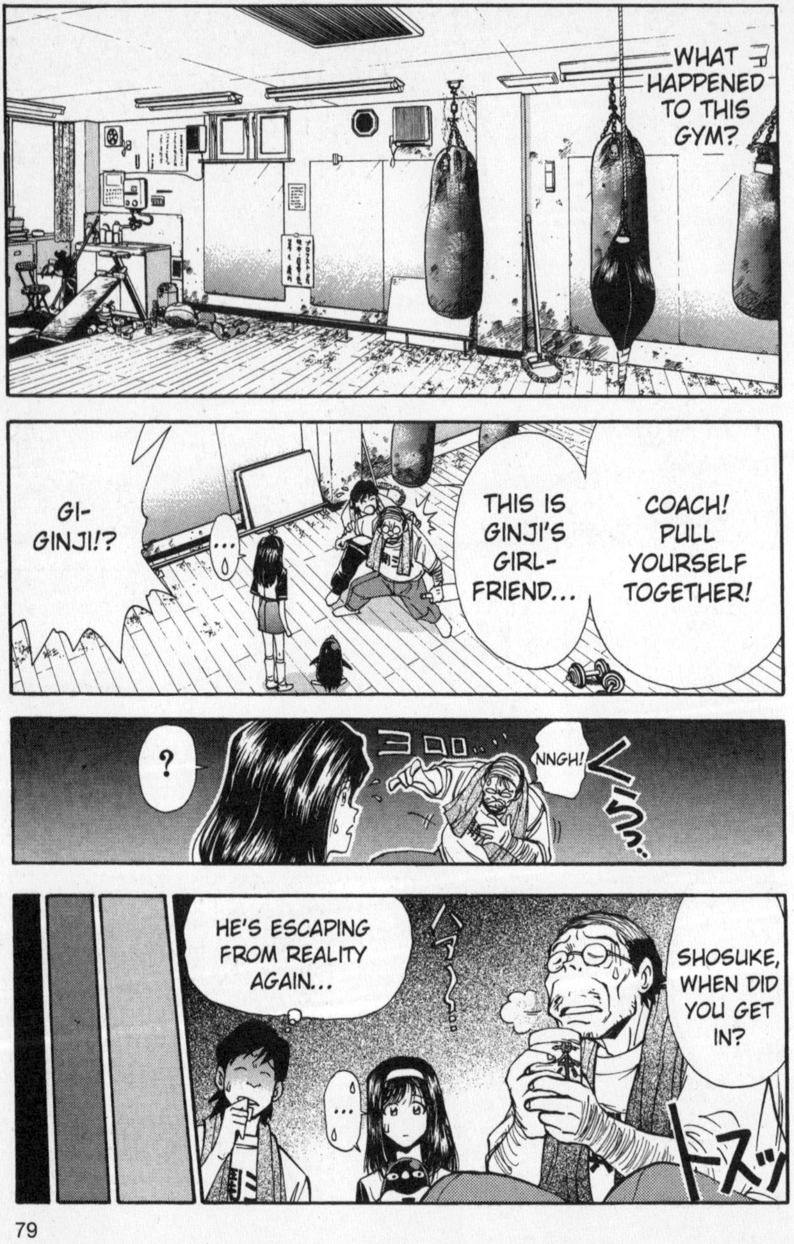
WHAT HAPPENED TO THIS GYM?
COACH! PULL YOURSELF TOGETHER!
THIS IS GINJI'S GIRL-FRIEND...
...
GI-GINJI!?
くらっ
NNGH!
ヨロ
?
SHOSUKE, WHEN DID YOU GET IN?
トスッ
ハァ〜
HE'S ESCAPING FROM REALITY AGAIN...
...

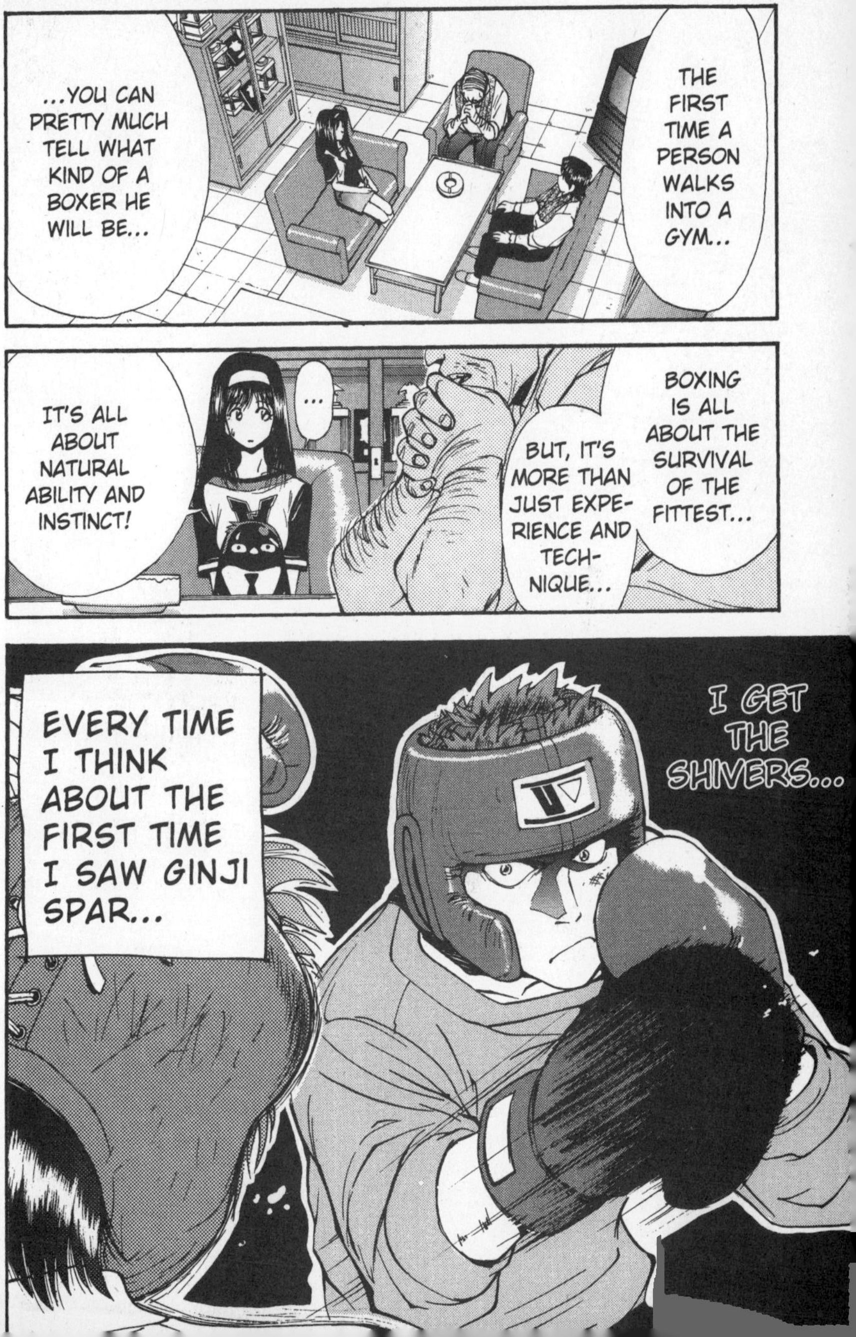
THE FIRST TIME A PERSON WALKS INTO A GYM...
...YOU CAN PRETTY MUCH TELL WHAT KIND OF A BOXER HE WILL BE...
BOXING IS ALL ABOUT THE SURVIVAL OF THE FITTEST...
BUT, IT'S MORE THAN JUST EXPERIENCE AND TECHNIQUE...
...
IT'S ALL ABOUT NATURAL ABILITY AND INSTINCT!
I GET THE SHIVERS...
EVERY TIME I THINK ABOUT THE FIRST TIME I SAW GINJI SPAR...

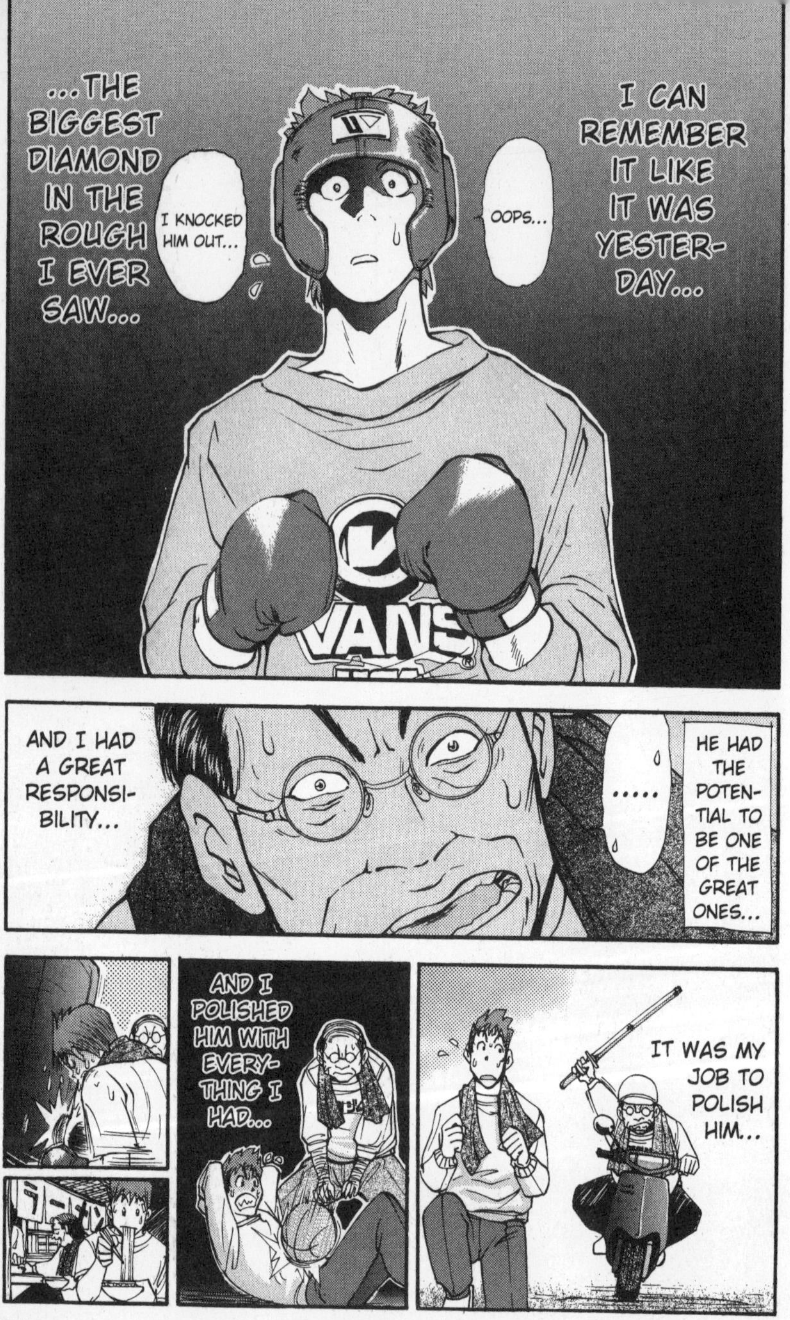
I CAN REMEMBER IT LIKE IT WAS YESTER-DAY...
OOPS...
I KNOCKED HIM OUT...
...THE BIGGEST DIAMOND IN THE ROUGH I EVER SAW...
HE HAD THE POTEN-TIAL TO BE ONE OF THE GREAT ONES...
.....
AND I HAD A GREAT RESPONSI-BILITY...
IT WAS MY JOB TO POLISH HIM...
AND I POLISHED HIM WITH EVERY-THING I HAD...

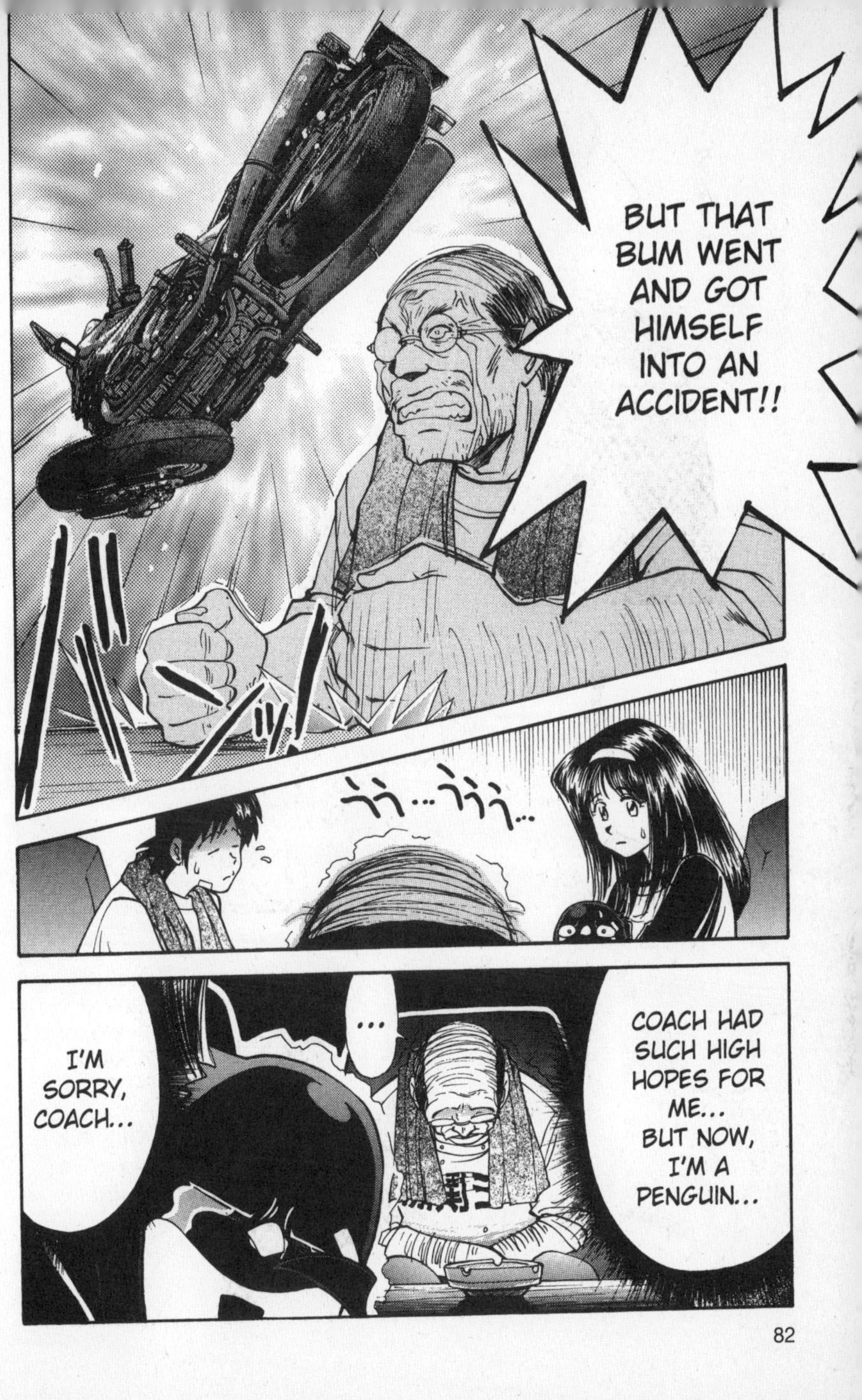
BUT THAT BUM WENT AND GOT HIMSELF INTO AN ACCIDENT!!
うう…ううう…
COACH HAD SUCH HIGH HOPES FOR ME... BUT NOW, I'M A PENGUIN...
...
I'M SORRY, COACH...

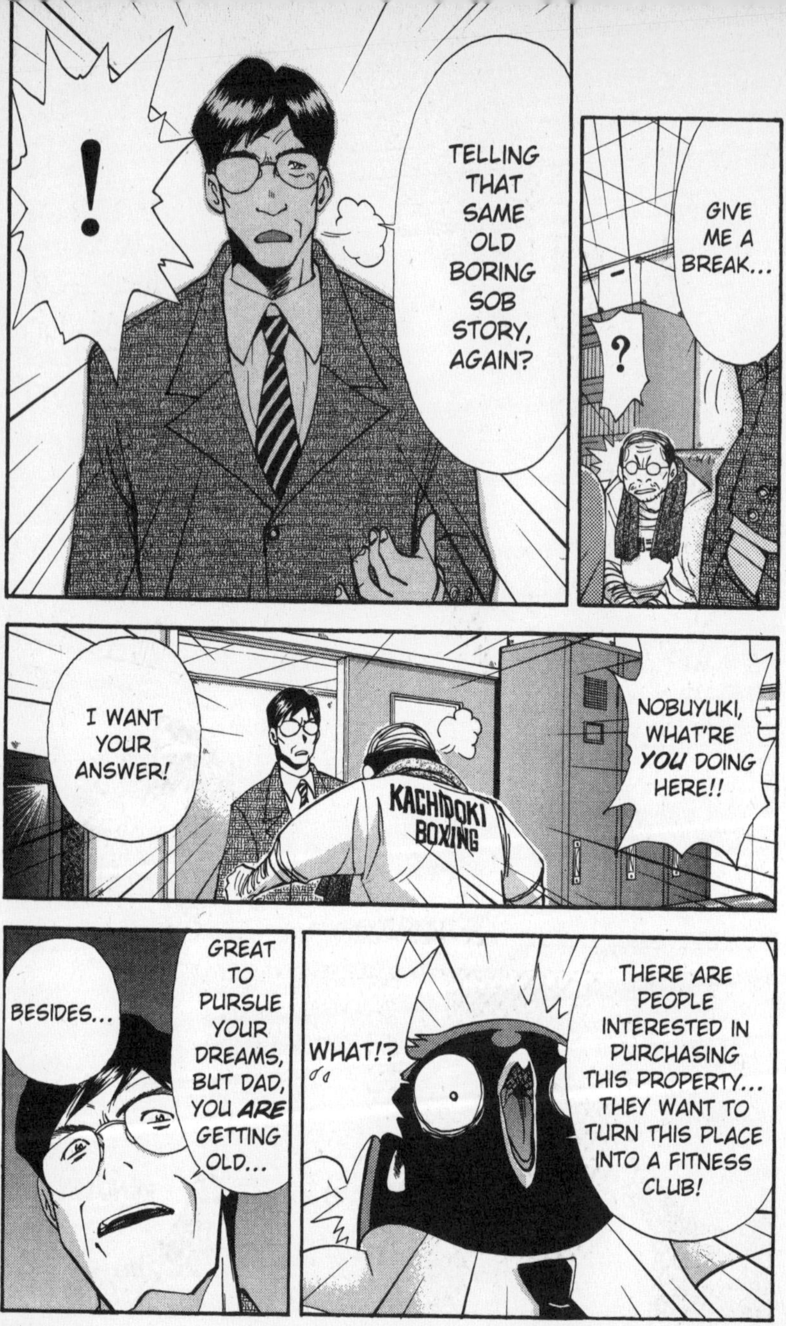
GIVE ME A BREAK...
?
TELLING THAT SAME OLD BORING SOB STORY, AGAIN?
!
NOBUYUKI, WHAT'RE *YOU* DOING HERE!!
I WANT YOUR ANSWER!
KACHIDOKI BOXING
THERE ARE PEOPLE INTERESTED IN PURCHASING THIS PROPERTY... THEY WANT TO TURN THIS PLACE INTO A FITNESS CLUB!
WHAT!?
GREAT TO PURSUE YOUR DREAMS, BUT DAD, YOU *ARE* GETTING OLD...
BESIDES...

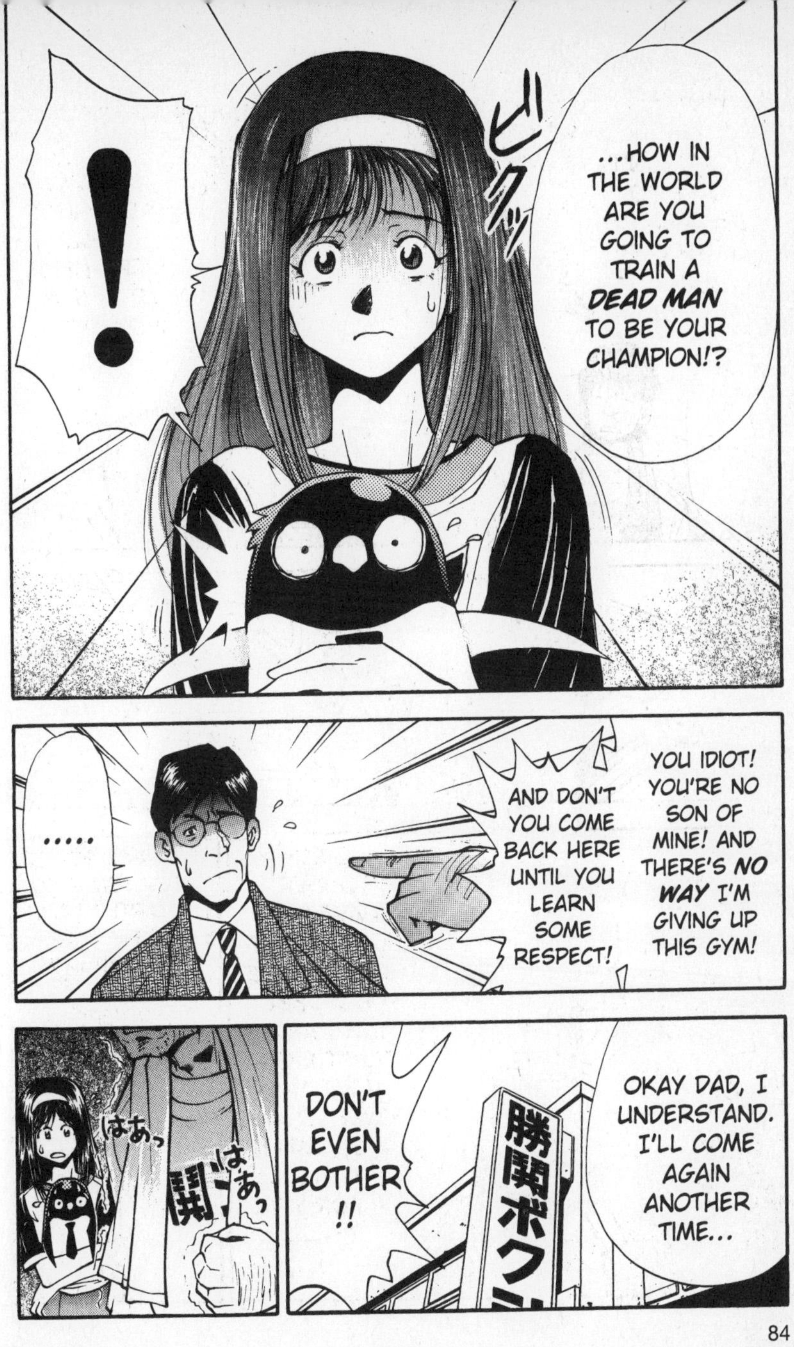

...HOW IN THE WORLD ARE YOU GOING TO TRAIN A DEAD MAN TO BE YOUR CHAMPION!?
ビクッ
!
YOU IDIOT! YOU'RE NO SON OF MINE! AND THERE'S NO WAY I'M GIVING UP THIS GYM!
AND DON'T YOU COME BACK HERE UNTIL YOU LEARN SOME RESPECT!
.....
OKAY DAD, I UNDERSTAND. I'LL COME AGAIN ANOTHER TIME...
DON'T EVEN BOTHER!!
はあっ
はあっ

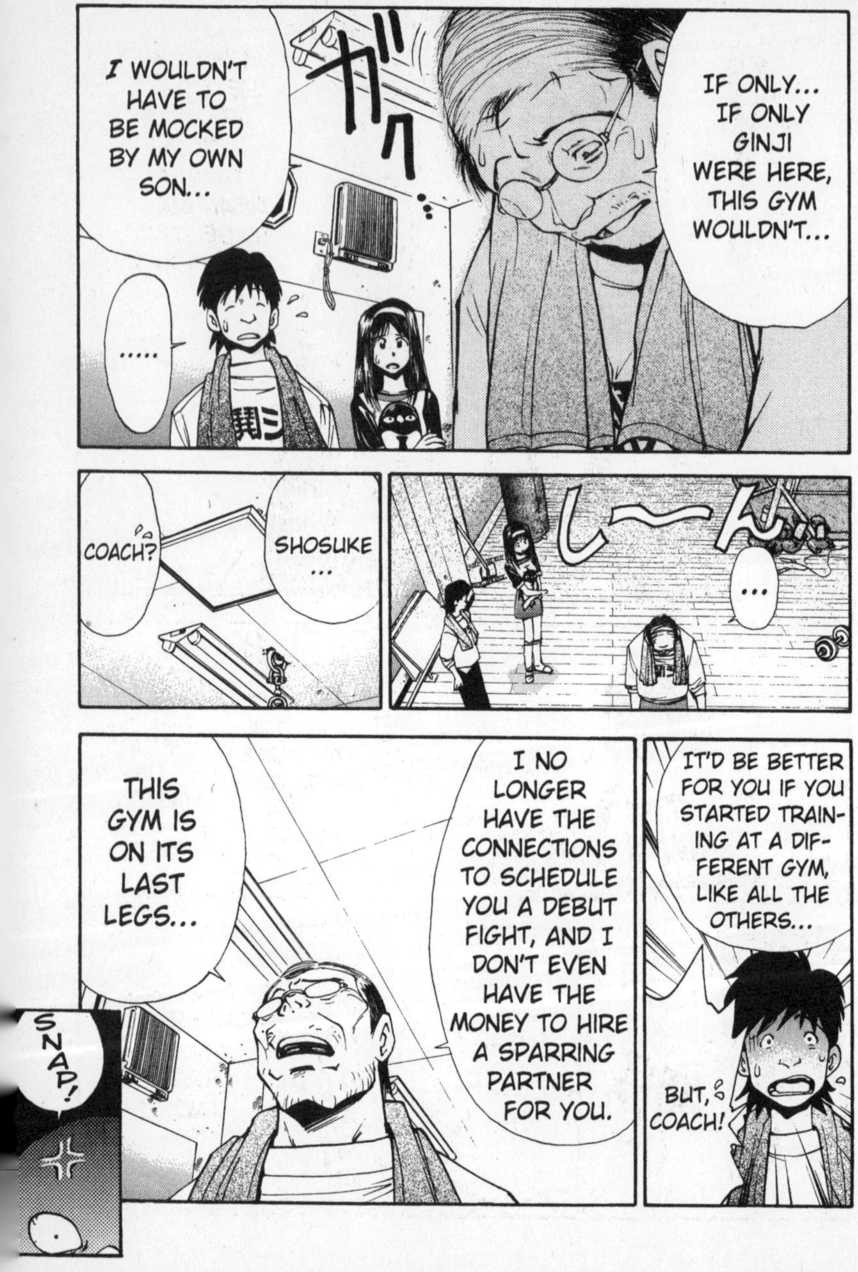
IF ONLY... IF ONLY GINJI WERE HERE, THIS GYM WOULDN'T...
ガク
I WOULDN'T HAVE TO BE MOCKED BY MY OWN SON...
.....
しーん
...
SHOSUKE ...
COACH?
IT'D BE BETTER FOR YOU IF YOU STARTED TRAIN-ING AT A DIF-FERENT GYM, LIKE ALL THE OTHERS...
BUT, COACH!
I NO LONGER HAVE THE CONNECTIONS TO SCHEDULE YOU A DEBUT FIGHT, AND I DON'T EVEN HAVE THE MONEY TO HIRE A SPARRING PARTNER FOR YOU.
THIS GYM IS ON ITS LAST LEGS...
SNAP!

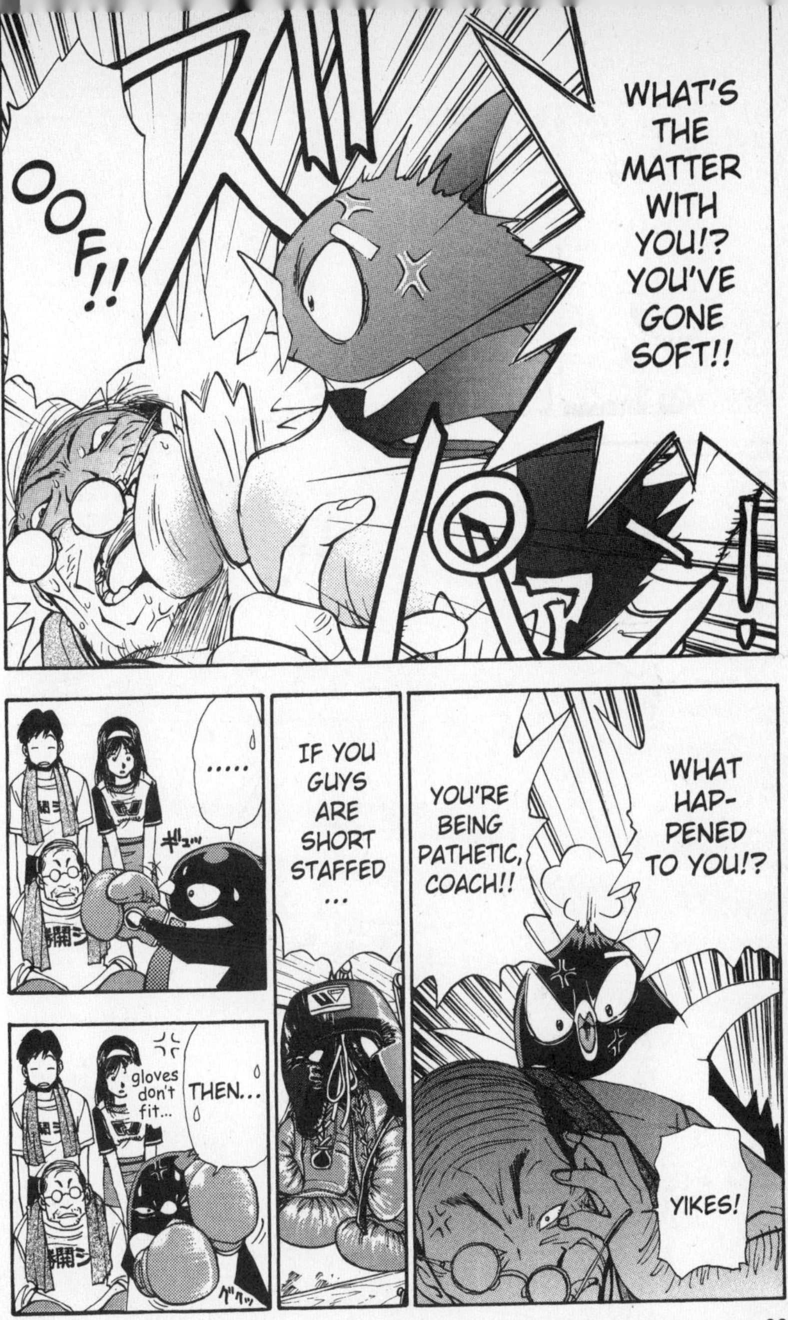
WHAT'S THE MATTER WITH YOU!? YOU'VE GONE SOFT!!
OOF!!
WHAT HAP-PENED TO YOU!?
YOU'RE BEING PATHETIC, COACH!!
YIKES!
IF YOU GUYS ARE SHORT STAFFED ...
.....
ギュッ
THEN...
gloves don't fit...

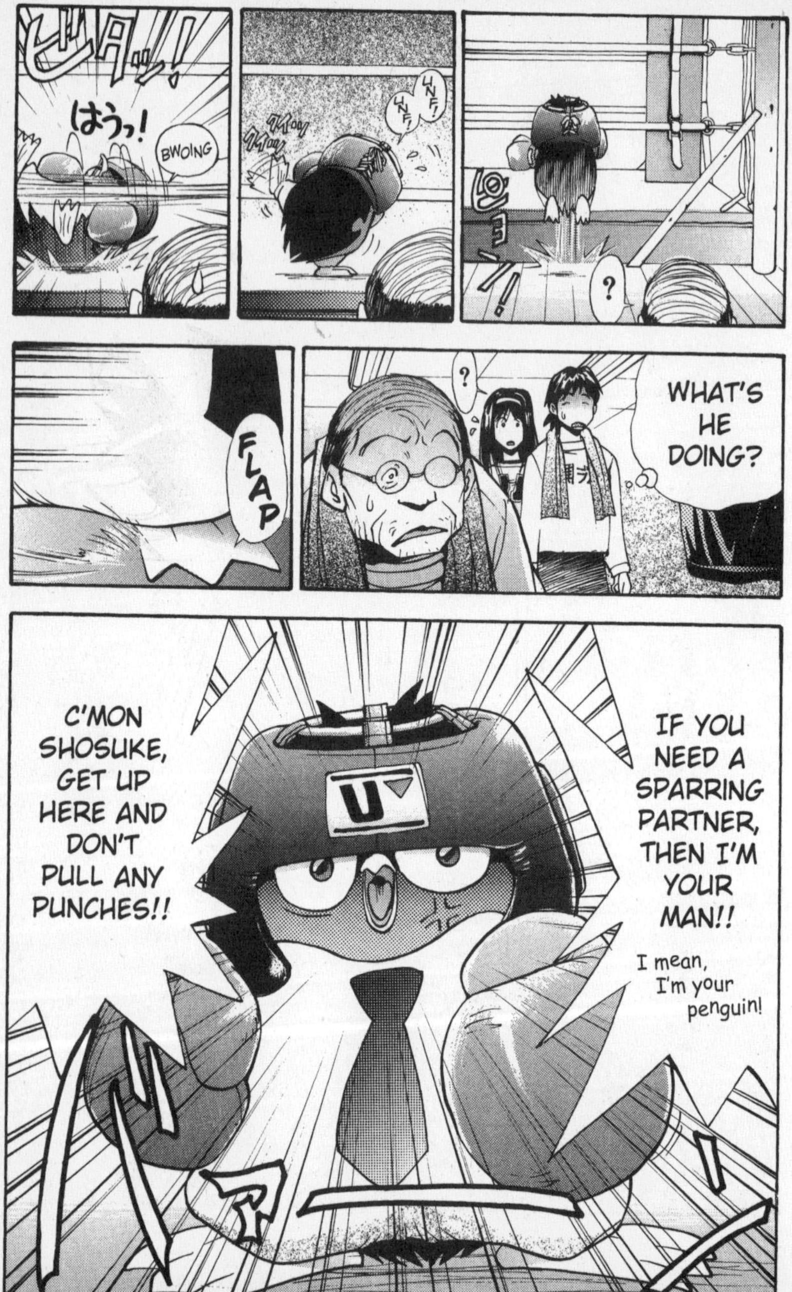
?
UNF! UNF!
ビタッ!!
はうっ!
BWOING
?
WHAT'S HE DOING?
FLAP
IF YOU NEED A SPARRING PARTNER, THEN I'M YOUR MAN!!
I mean, I'm your penguin!
C'MON SHOSUKE, GET UP HERE AND DON'T PULL ANY PUNCHES!!

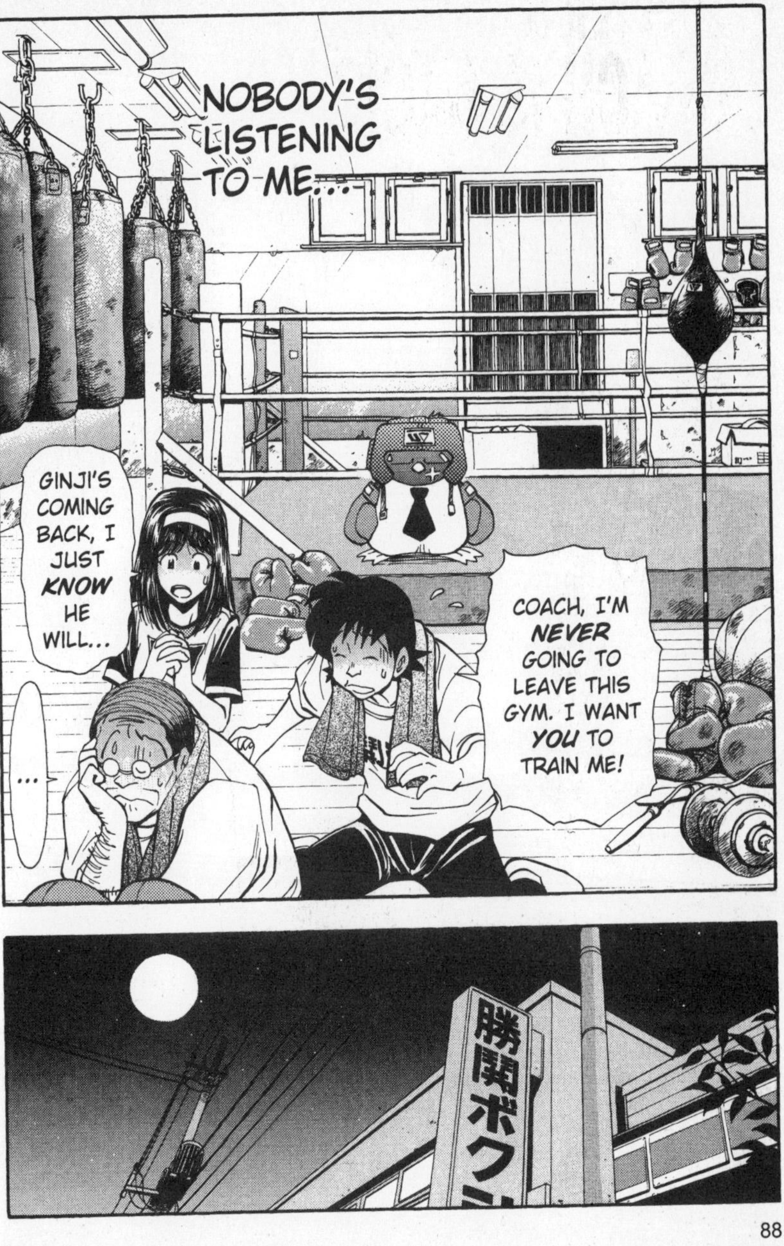
NOBODY'S LISTENING TO ME...
COACH, I'M *NEVER* GOING TO LEAVE THIS GYM. I WANT *YOU* TO TRAIN ME!
GINJI'S COMING BACK, I JUST *KNOW* HE WILL...
...
勝関ボク

CHAPTER 5
COACH IS BACK!

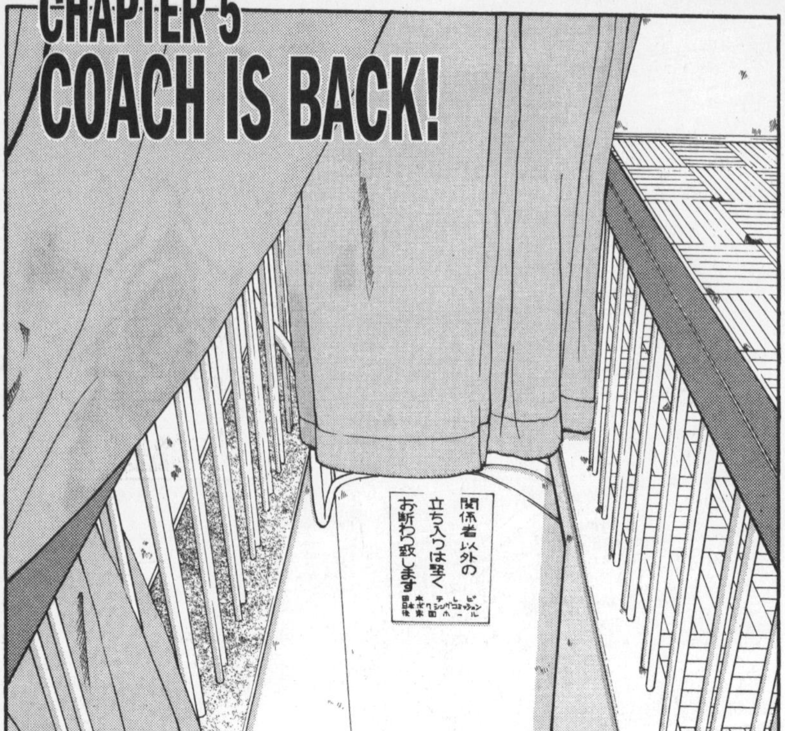
関係者以外の
立ち入りは堅く
お断わり致します
日本テレビ
日本ボクシングコミッション
後楽園ホール

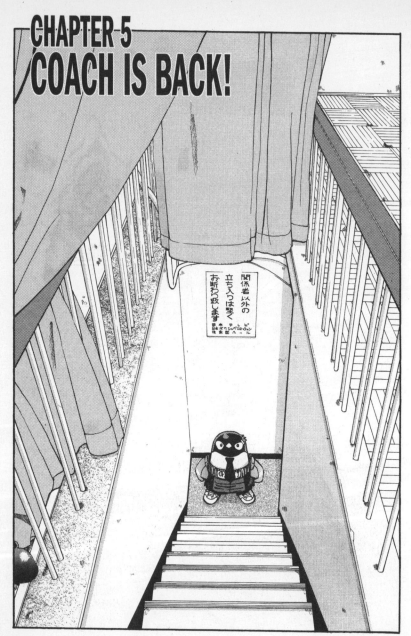

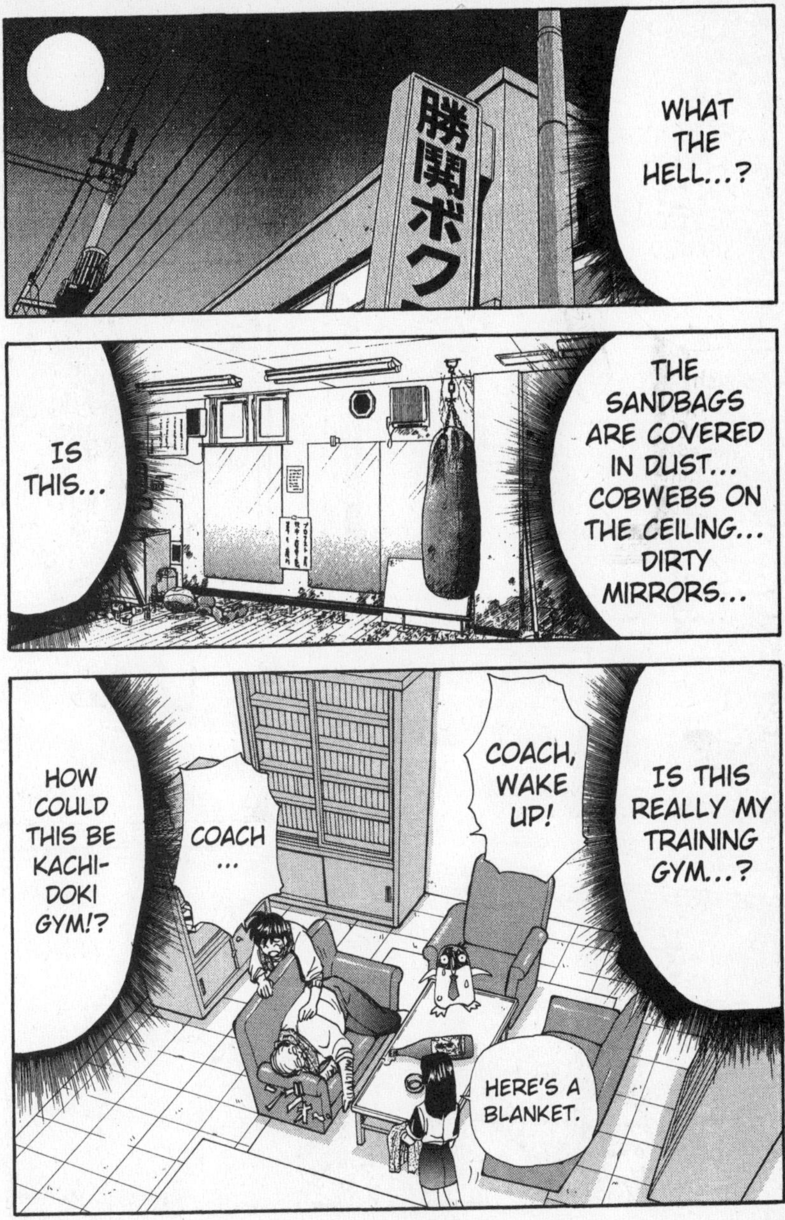
勝関ボク
WHAT THE HELL...?
THE SANDBAGS ARE COVERED IN DUST... COBWEBS ON THE CEILING... DIRTY MIRRORS...
IS THIS...
IS THIS REALLY MY TRAINING GYM...?
COACH, WAKE UP!
COACH ...
HOW COULD THIS BE KACHI-DOKI GYM!?
HERE'S A BLANKET.

IF HE FALLS ASLEEP HERE, HE MIGHT CATCH A COLD...
IT'S GINJI!!
YEAH... THAT'S A PHOTO OF GINJI'S DEBUT FIGHT...
GINJI
Coach really had high hopes for him...
I WISH I COULD HAVE IT...
.....
GO AHEAD AND TAKE IT.
REALLY!?
ARE YOU SURE!?
ちょっと幸福..
I'LL TREASURE IT FOR THE REST OF MY LIFE!!
BLUSH
She's going to treasure it?

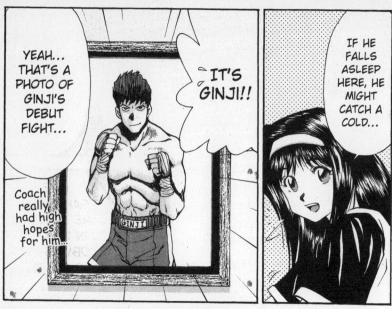

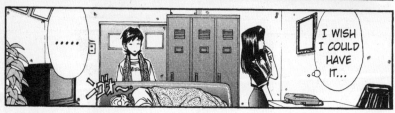

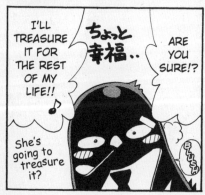

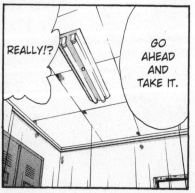

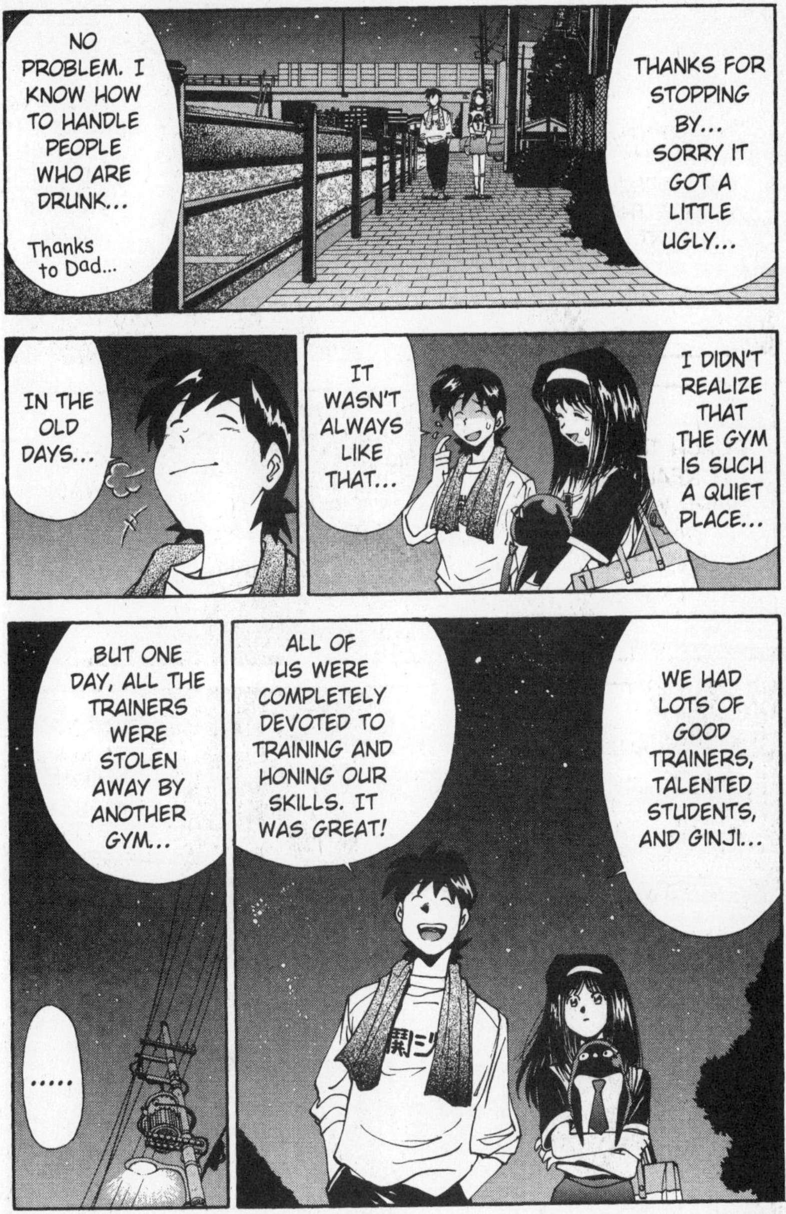
THANKS FOR STOPPING BY... SORRY IT GOT A LITTLE UGLY...
NO PROBLEM. I KNOW HOW TO HANDLE PEOPLE WHO ARE DRUNK...
Thanks to Dad...
I DIDN'T REALIZE THAT THE GYM IS SUCH A QUIET PLACE...
IT WASN'T ALWAYS LIKE THAT...
IN THE OLD DAYS...
WE HAD LOTS OF GOOD TRAINERS, TALENTED STUDENTS, AND GINJI...
ALL OF US WERE COMPLETELY DEVOTED TO TRAINING AND HONING OUR SKILLS. IT WAS GREAT!
BUT ONE DAY, ALL THE TRAINERS WERE STOLEN AWAY BY ANOTHER GYM...
.....

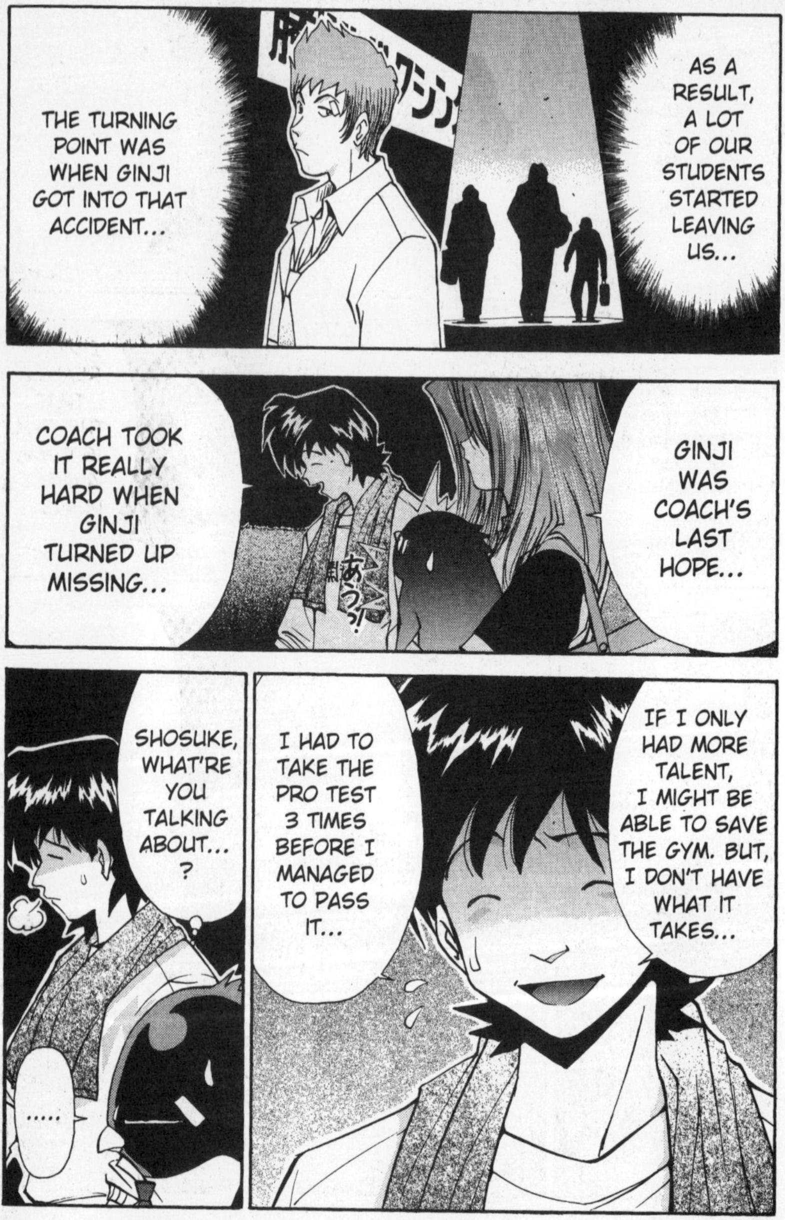
AS A RESULT, A LOT OF OUR STUDENTS STARTED LEAVING US...
THE TURNING POINT WAS WHEN GINJI GOT INTO THAT ACCIDENT...
GINJI WAS COACH'S LAST HOPE...
COACH TOOK IT REALLY HARD WHEN GINJI TURNED UP MISSING...
あうっ!
IF I ONLY HAD MORE TALENT, I MIGHT BE ABLE TO SAVE THE GYM. BUT, I DON'T HAVE WHAT IT TAKES...
I HAD TO TAKE THE PRO TEST 3 TIMES BEFORE I MANAGED TO PASS IT...
SHOSUKE, WHAT'RE YOU TALKING ABOUT...?
.....

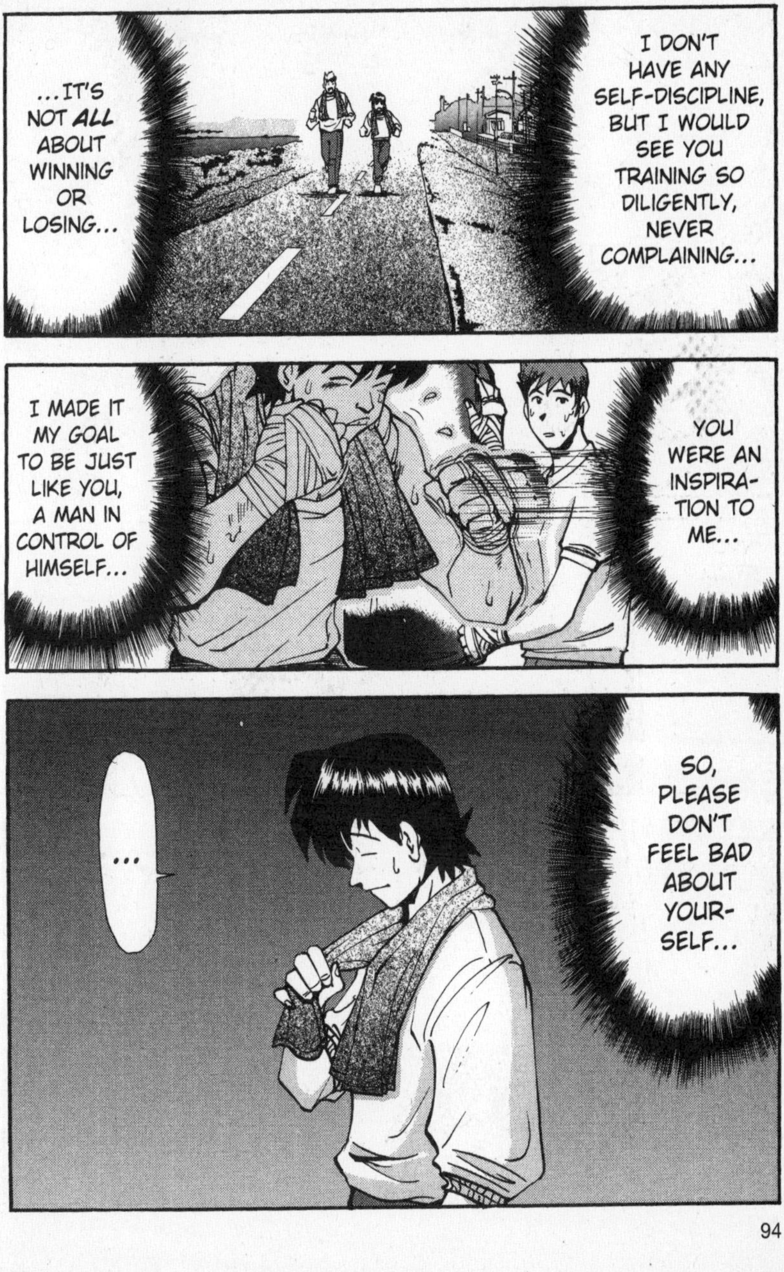
I DON'T HAVE ANY SELF-DISCIPLINE, BUT I WOULD SEE YOU TRAINING SO DILIGENTLY, NEVER COMPLAINING...
...IT'S NOT ALL ABOUT WINNING OR LOSING...
YOU WERE AN INSPIRA-TION TO ME...
I MADE IT MY GOAL TO BE JUST LIKE YOU, A MAN IN CONTROL OF HIMSELF...
SO, PLEASE DON'T FEEL BAD ABOUT YOUR-SELF...
...

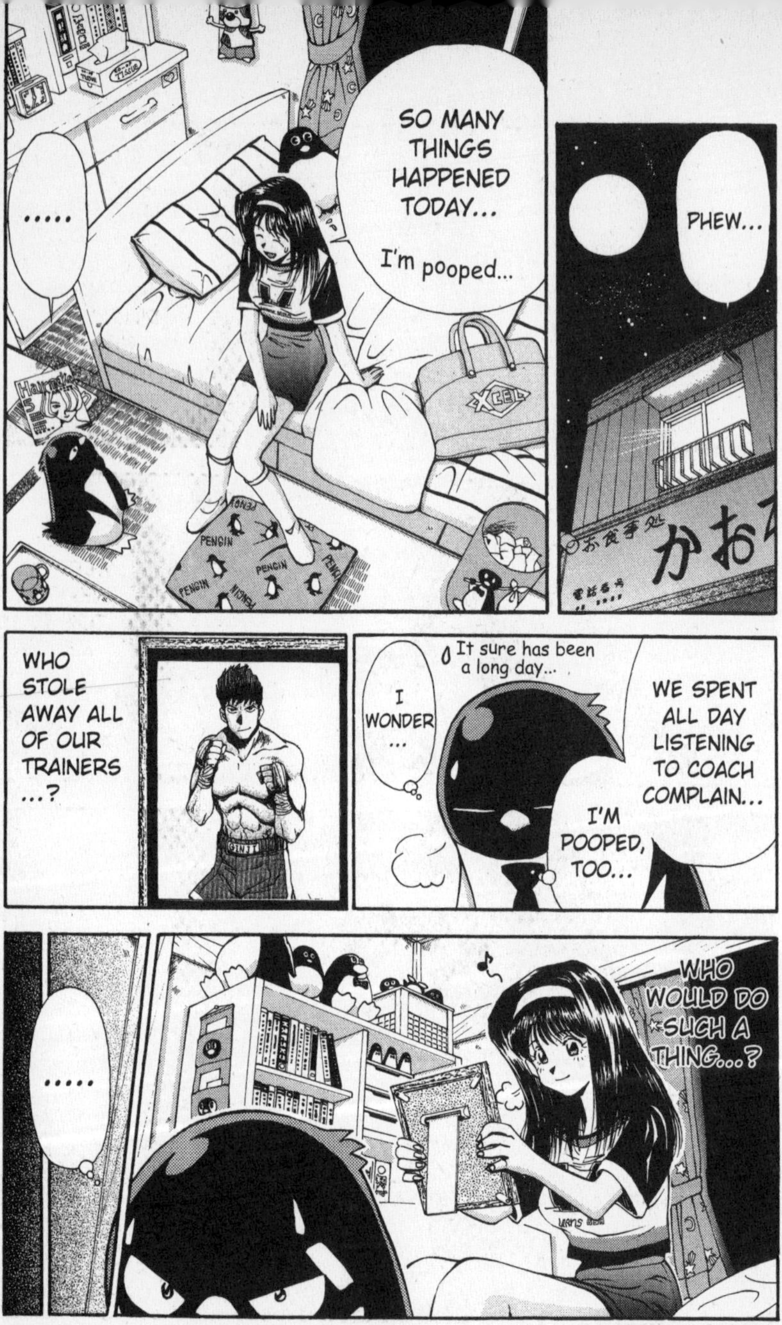
PHEW...
お食事処
SO MANY THINGS HAPPENED TODAY...
I'm pooped...
.....
WE SPENT ALL DAY LISTENING TO COACH COMPLAIN...
I'M POOPED, TOO...
It sure has been a long day...
I WONDER...
WHO STOLE AWAY ALL OF OUR TRAINERS...?
WHO WOULD DO SUCH A THING...?
.....

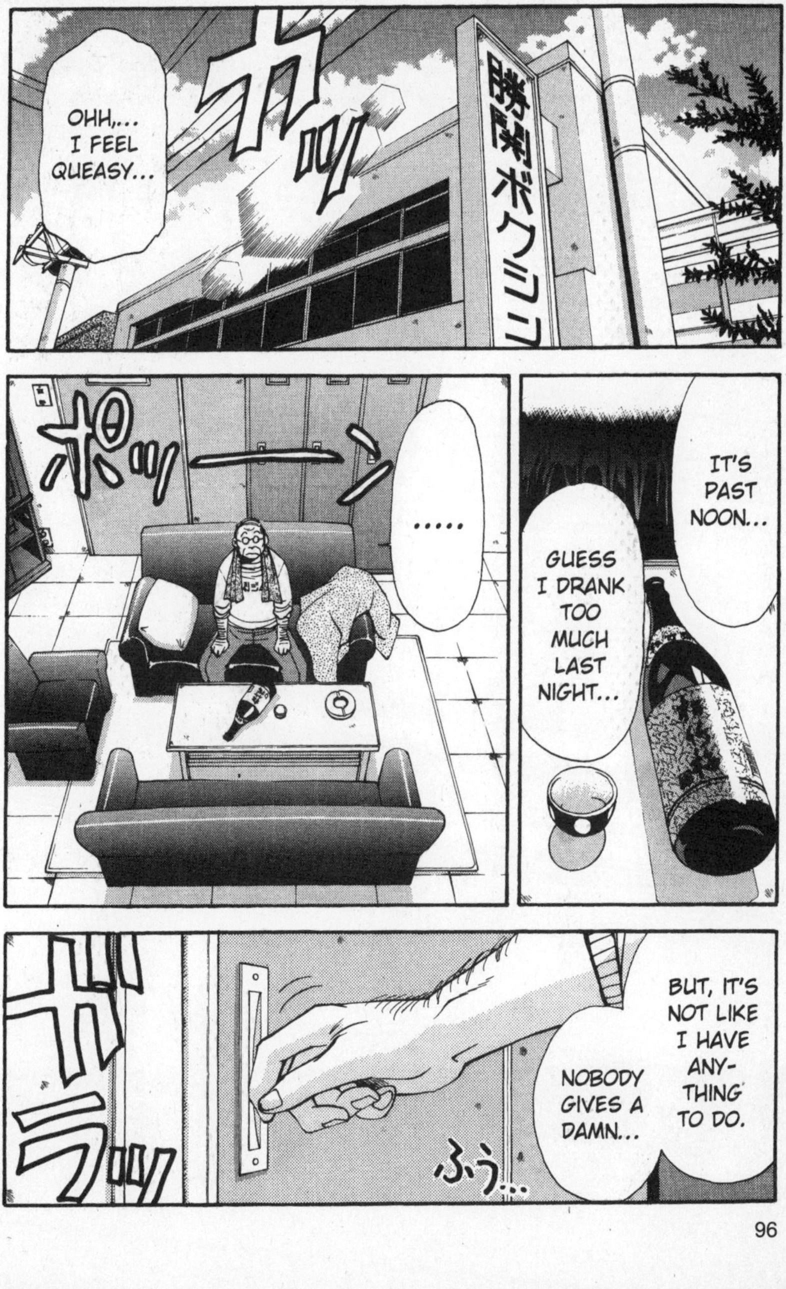
ガッ
勝関ボクシン
OHH,... I FEEL QUEASY...
IT'S PAST NOON...
GUESS I DRANK TOO MUCH LAST NIGHT...
ポツーン
.....
BUT, IT'S NOT LIKE I HAVE ANYTHING TO DO.
NOBODY GIVES A DAMN...
ふう...
ガラッ

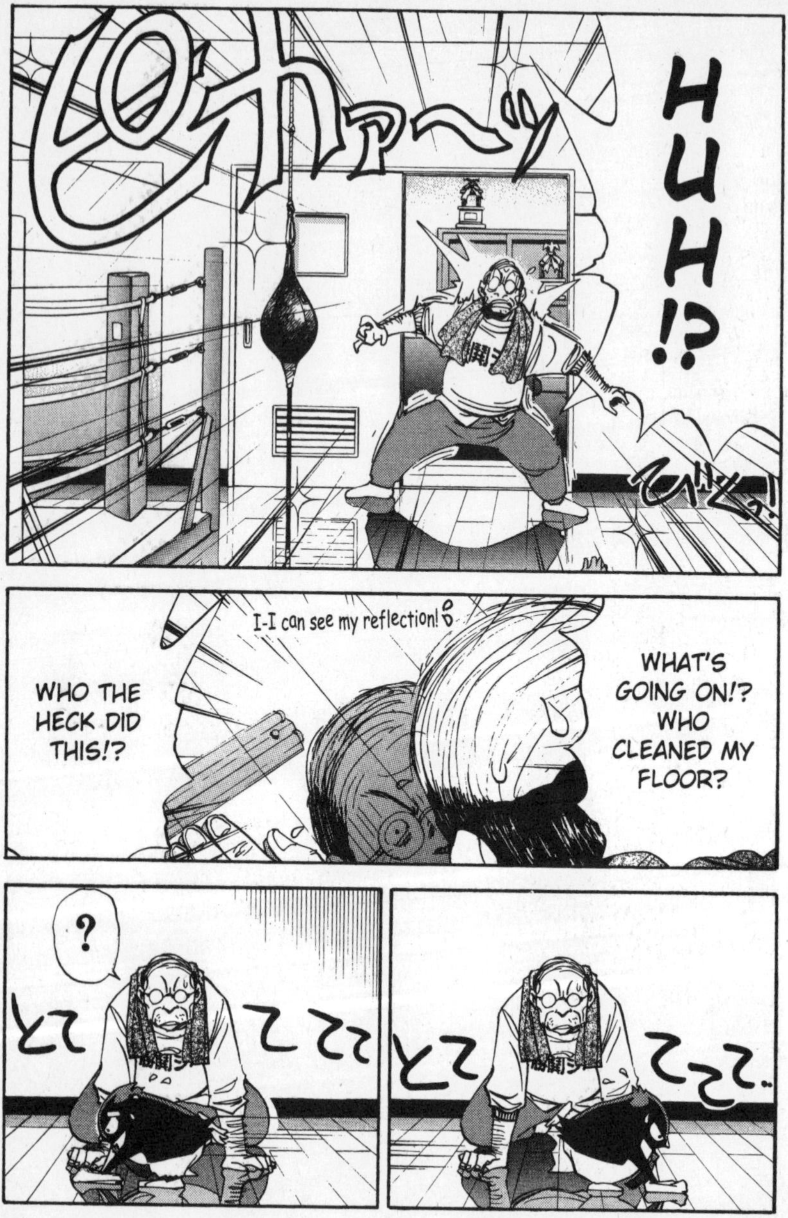
HUH!?
WHAT'S GOING ON!? WHO CLEANED MY FLOOR?
I-I can see my reflection!
WHO THE HECK DID THIS!?
?

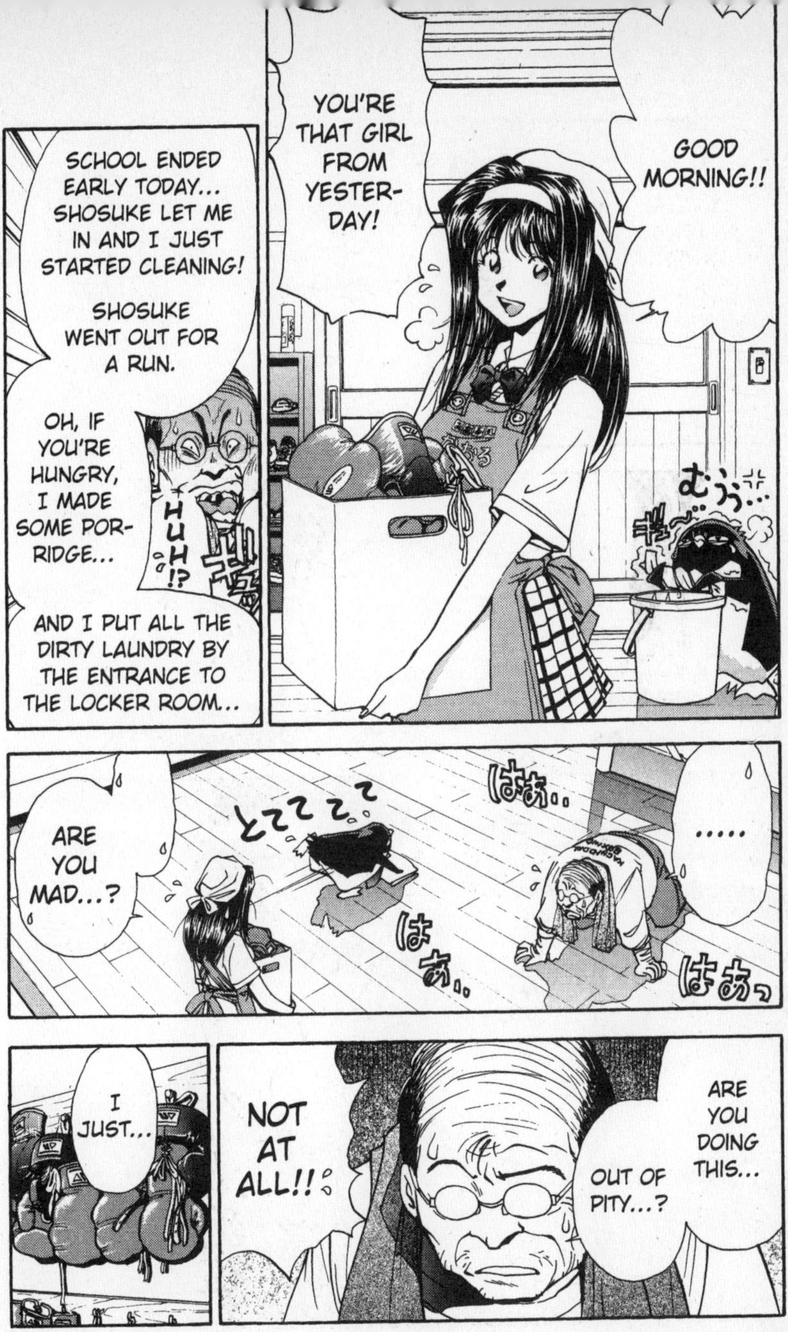
GOOD MORNING!!
YOU'RE THAT GIRL FROM YESTER-DAY!
むぅ…
SCHOOL ENDED EARLY TODAY... SHOSUKE LET ME IN AND I JUST STARTED CLEANING!
SHOSUKE WENT OUT FOR A RUN.
OH, IF YOU'RE HUNGRY, I MADE SOME POR-RIDGE...
HUH!?
AND I PUT ALL THE DIRTY LAUNDRY BY THE ENTRANCE TO THE LOCKER ROOM...
.....
はあ。。
はあっ
はあ。。
とててててて
ARE YOU MAD...?
ARE YOU DOING THIS...
OUT OF PITY...?
NOT AT ALL!!
I JUST...

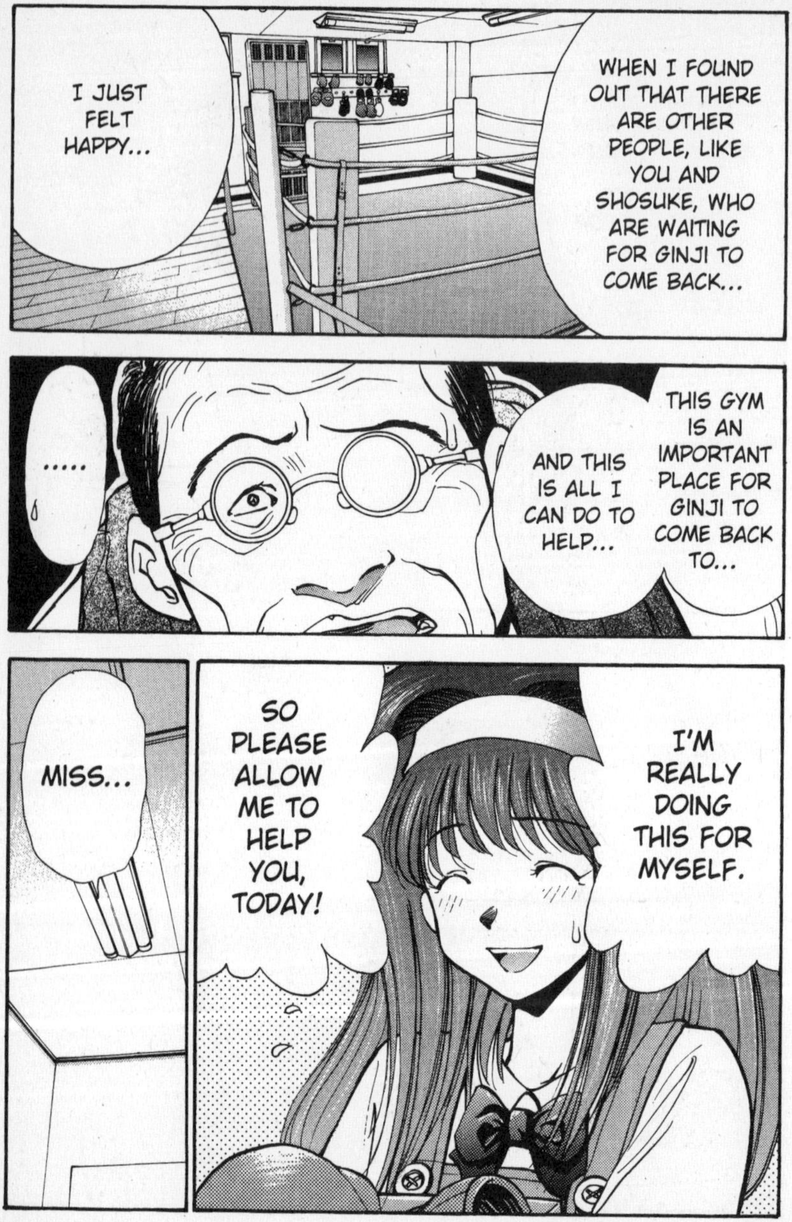
WHEN I FOUND OUT THAT THERE ARE OTHER PEOPLE, LIKE YOU AND SHOSUKE, WHO ARE WAITING FOR GINJI TO COME BACK...
I JUST FELT HAPPY...
THIS GYM IS AN IMPORTANT PLACE FOR GINJI TO COME BACK TO...
AND THIS IS ALL I CAN DO TO HELP...
.....
I'M REALLY DOING THIS FOR MYSELF.
SO PLEASE ALLOW ME TO HELP YOU, TODAY!
MISS...

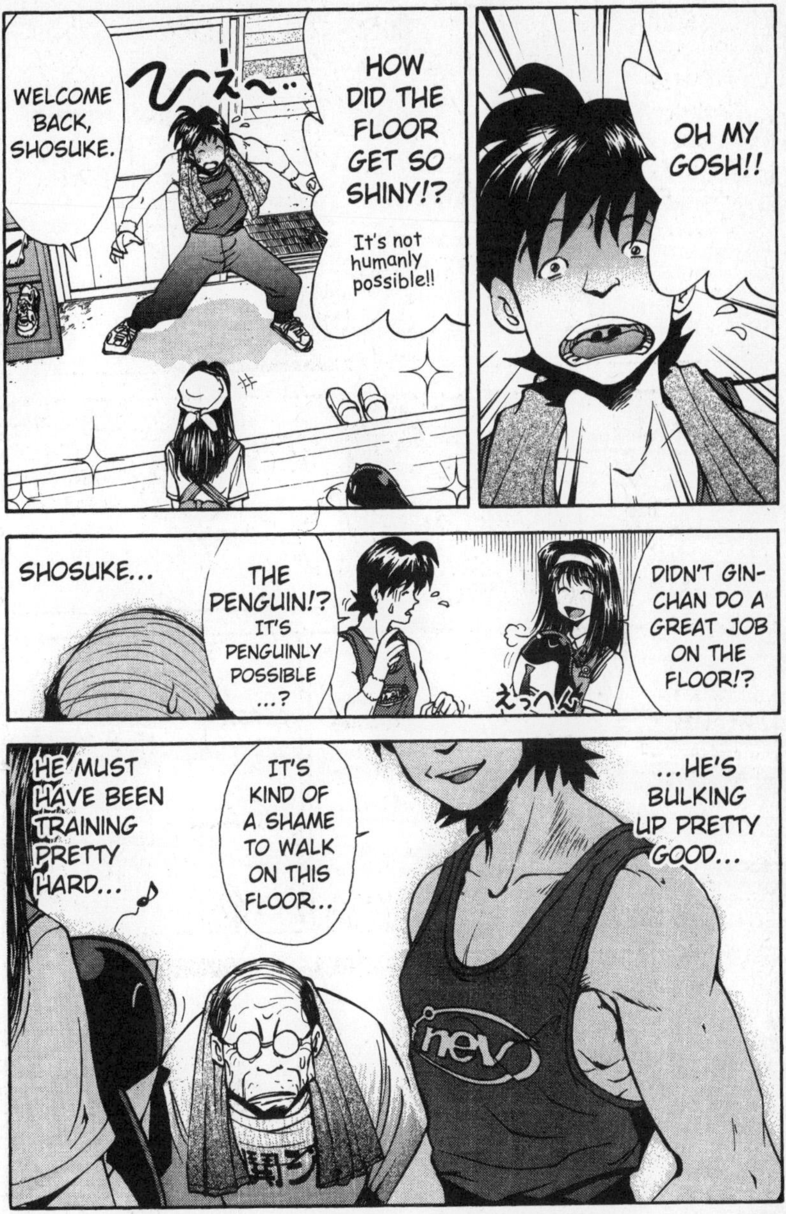
OH MY GOSH!!
HOW DID THE FLOOR GET SO SHINY!?
It's not humanly possible!!
ひぇ~..
WELCOME BACK, SHOSUKE.
DIDN'T GIN-CHAN DO A GREAT JOB ON THE FLOOR!?
えっへん
THE PENGUIN!? IT'S PENGUINLY POSSIBLE ...?
SHOSUKE...
...HE'S BULKING UP PRETTY GOOD...
IT'S KIND OF A SHAME TO WALK ON THIS FLOOR...
HE MUST HAVE BEEN TRAINING PRETTY HARD...

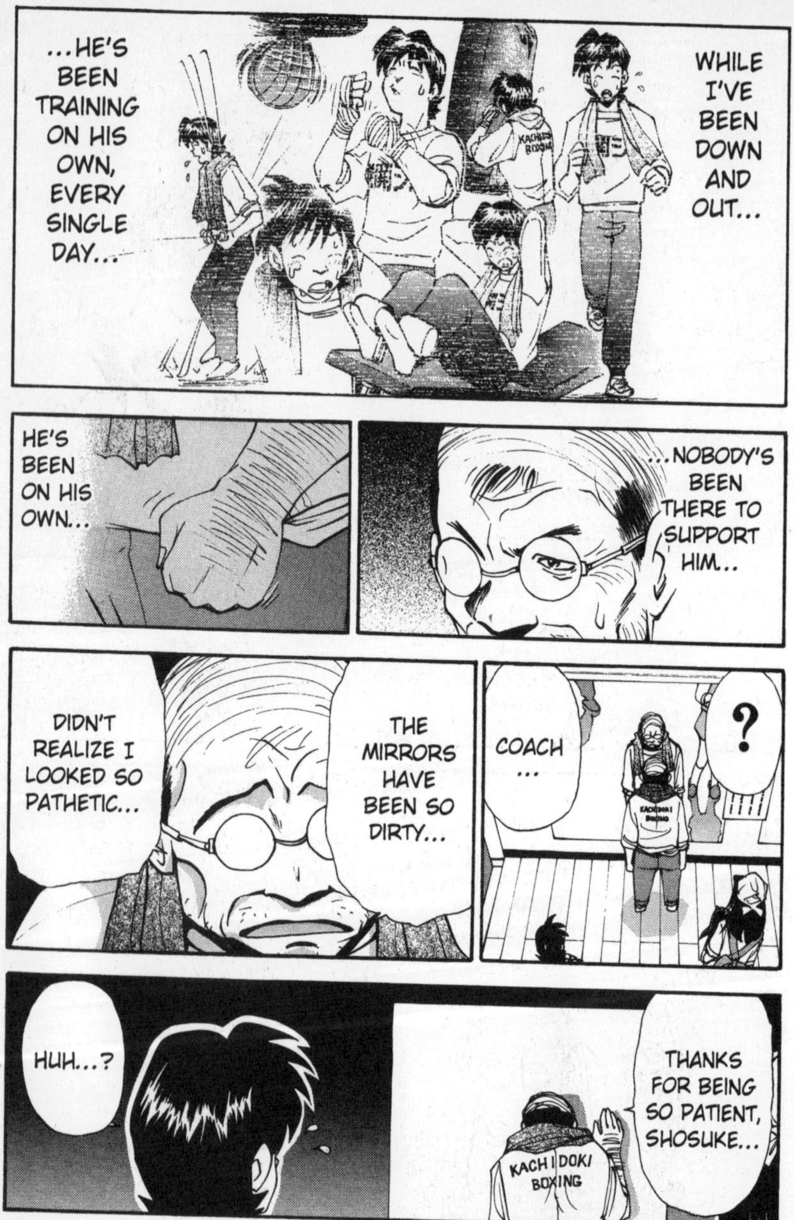
WHILE I'VE BEEN DOWN AND OUT...
...HE'S BEEN TRAINING ON HIS OWN, EVERY SINGLE DAY...
...NOBODY'S BEEN THERE TO SUPPORT HIM...
HE'S BEEN ON HIS OWN...
?
COACH ...
THE MIRRORS HAVE BEEN SO DIRTY...
DIDN'T REALIZE I LOOKED SO PATHETIC...
THANKS FOR BEING SO PATIENT, SHOSUKE...
KACHIDOKI BOXING
HUH...?

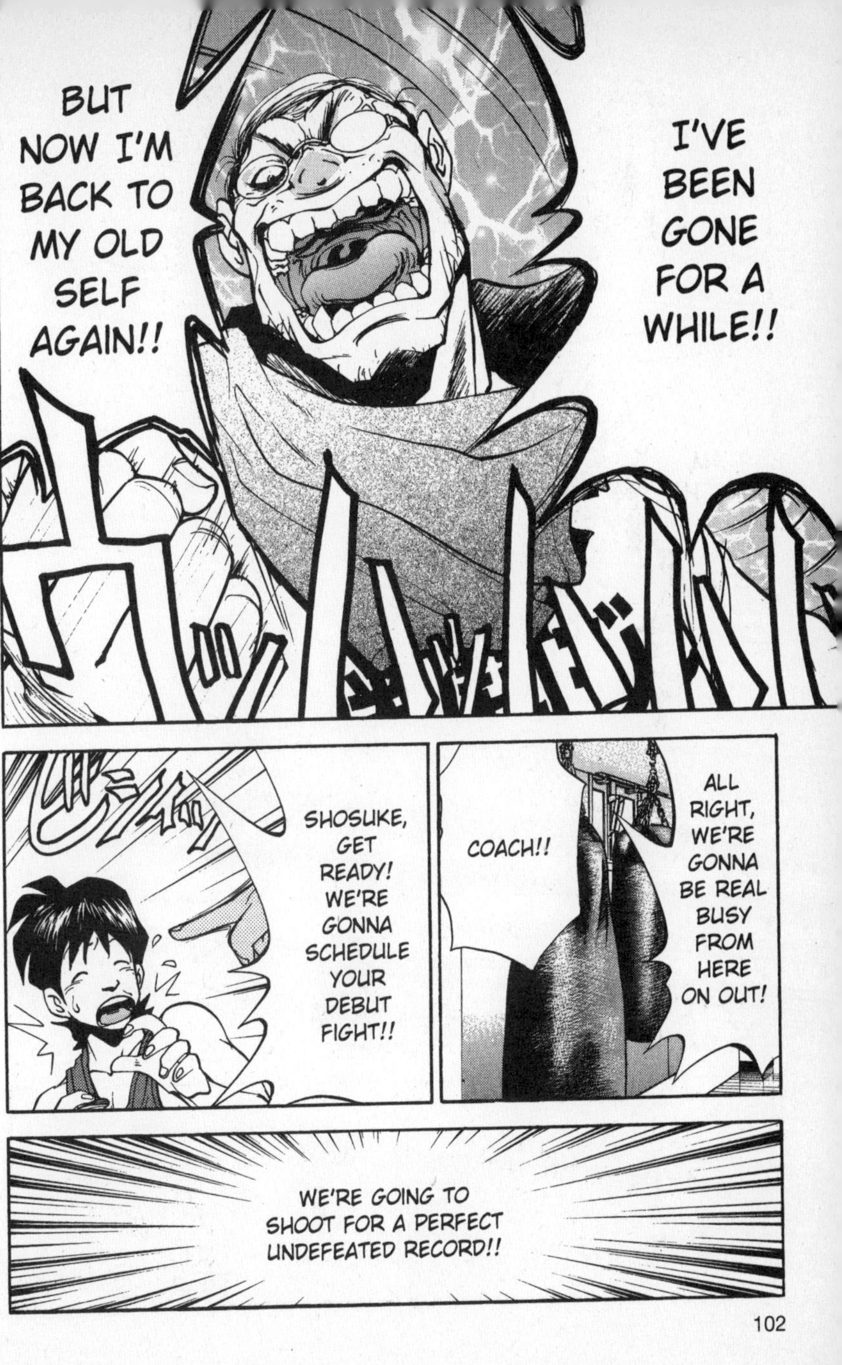
I'VE BEEN GONE FOR A WHILE!!
BUT NOW I'M BACK TO MY OLD SELF AGAIN!!
ALL RIGHT, WE'RE GONNA BE REAL BUSY FROM HERE ON OUT!
COACH!!
SHOSUKE, GET READY! WE'RE GONNA SCHEDULE YOUR DEBUT FIGHT!!
WE'RE GOING TO SHOOT FOR A PERFECT UNDEFEATED RECORD!!

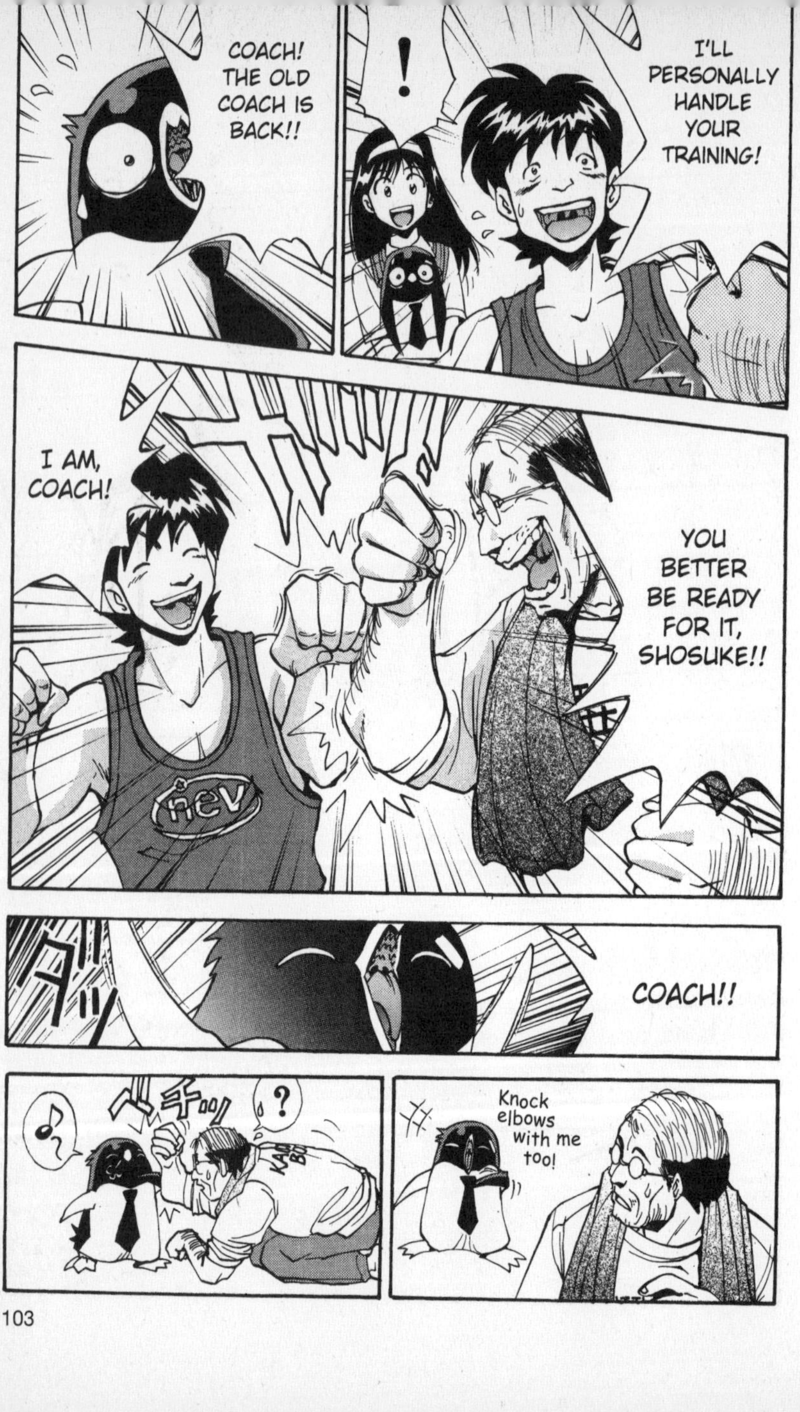
I'LL PERSONALLY HANDLE YOUR TRAINING!
!
COACH! THE OLD COACH IS BACK!!
YOU BETTER BE READY FOR IT, SHOSUKE!!
I AM, COACH!
COACH!!
Knock elbows with me too!
?

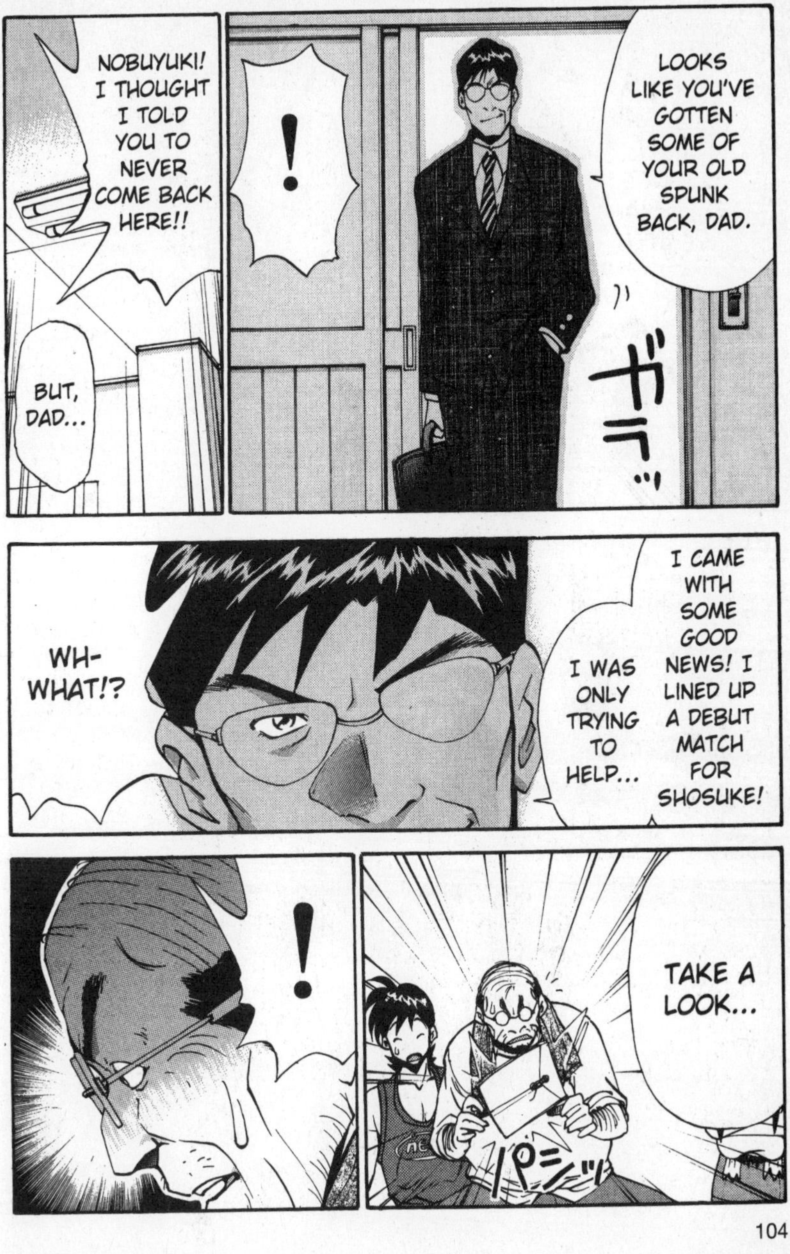
LOOKS LIKE YOU'VE GOTTEN SOME OF YOUR OLD SPUNK BACK, DAD.
ガラッ
!
NOBUYUKI! I THOUGHT I TOLD YOU TO NEVER COME BACK HERE!!
BUT, DAD...
I CAME WITH SOME GOOD NEWS! I LINED UP A DEBUT MATCH FOR SHOSUKE!
I WAS ONLY TRYING TO HELP...
WH-WHAT!?
TAKE A LOOK...
!

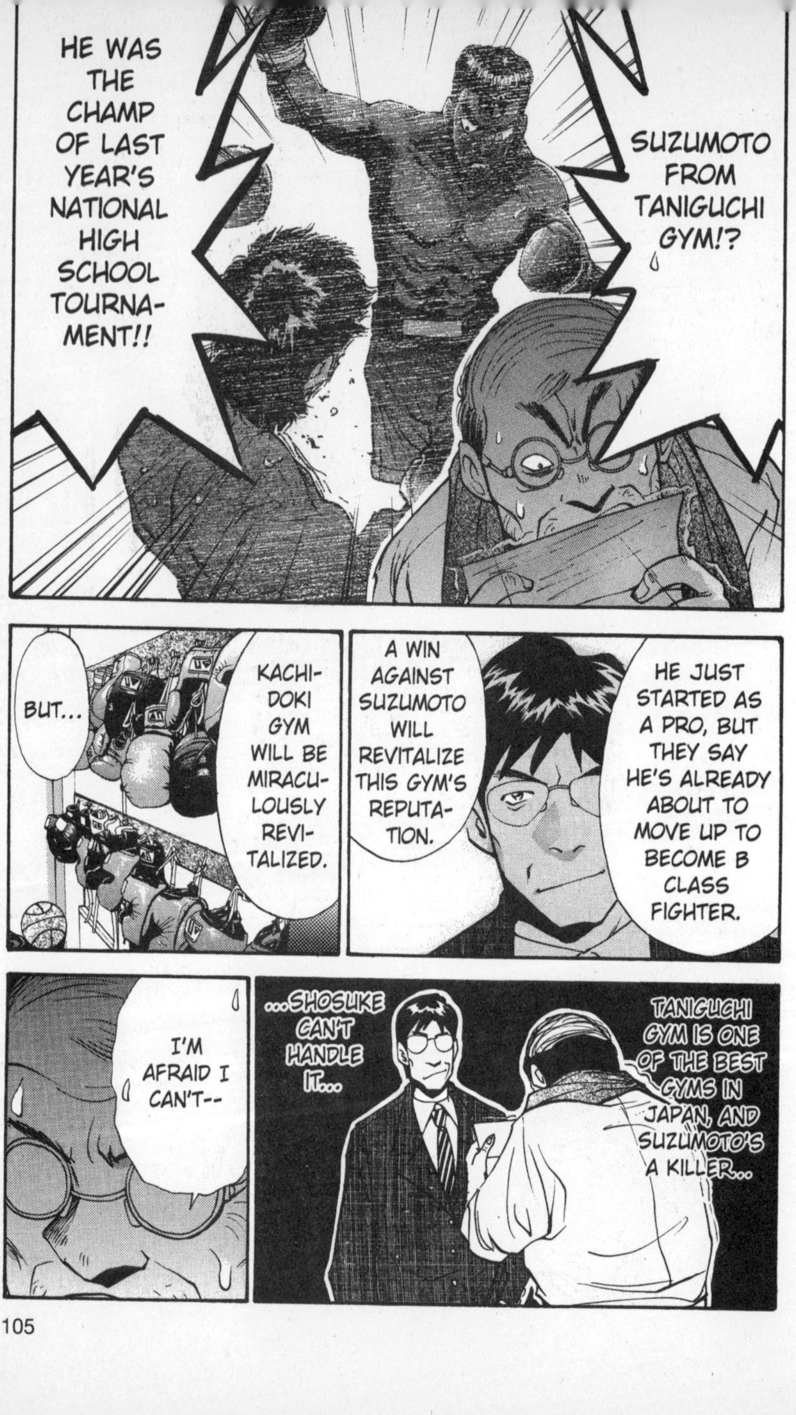
SUZUMOTO FROM TANIGUCHI GYM!?
HE WAS THE CHAMP OF LAST YEAR'S NATIONAL HIGH SCHOOL TOURNAMENT!!
HE JUST STARTED AS A PRO, BUT THEY SAY HE'S ALREADY ABOUT TO MOVE UP TO BECOME B CLASS FIGHTER.
A WIN AGAINST SUZUMOTO WILL REVITALIZE THIS GYM'S REPUTATION.
KACHIDOKI GYM WILL BE MIRACULOUSLY REVITALIZED.
BUT...
TANIGUCHI GYM IS ONE OF THE BEST GYMS IN JAPAN, AND SUZUMOTO'S A KILLER...
...SHOSUKE CAN'T HANDLE IT...
I'M AFRAID I CAN'T--

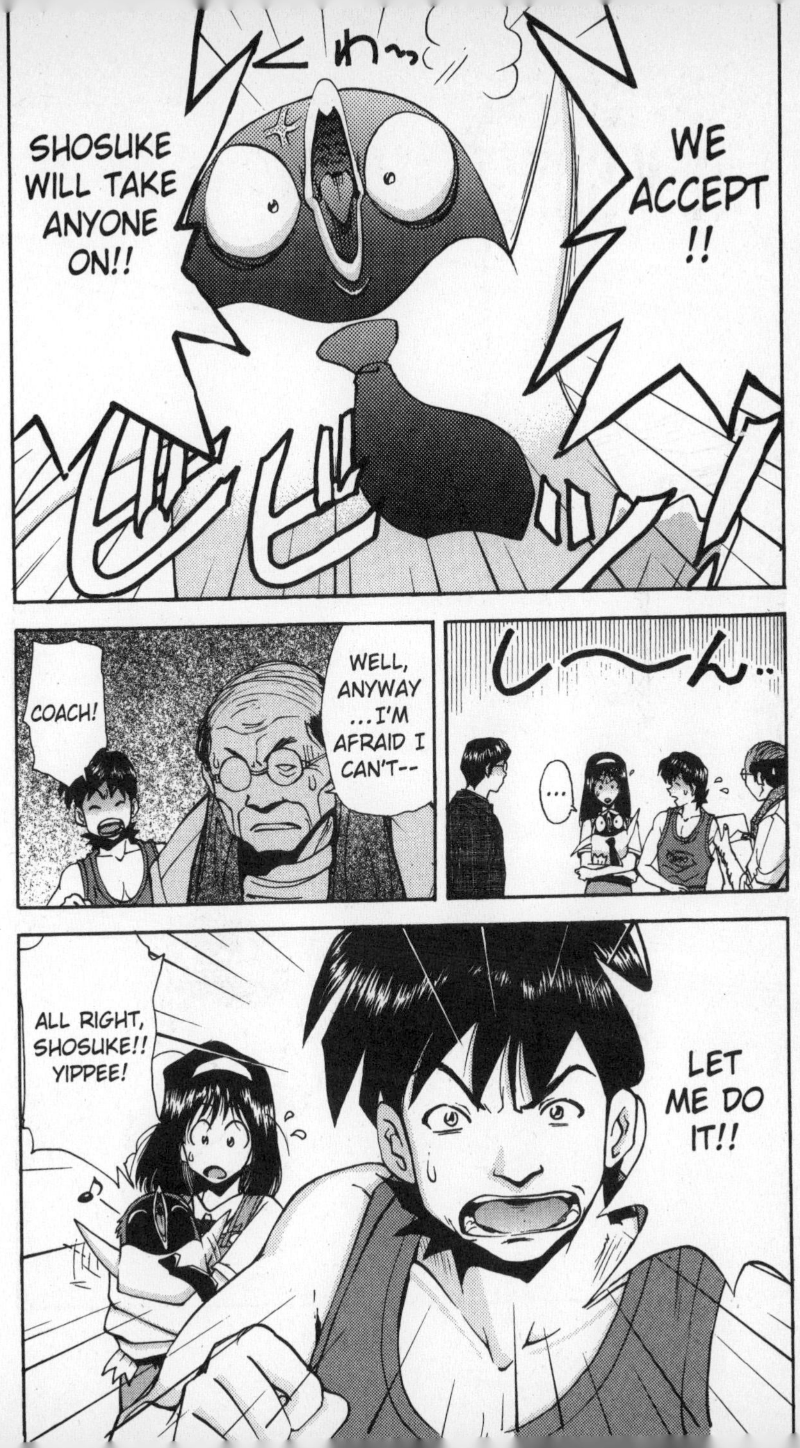
WE ACCEPT!!
くわ～っ
SHOSUKE WILL TAKE ANYONE ON!!
し～ん..
...
WELL, ANYWAY ...I'M AFRAID I CAN'T--
COACH!
LET ME DO IT!!
ALL RIGHT, SHOSUKE!! YIPPEE!

CHAPTER-6
NEW SUPER-MOVE!?

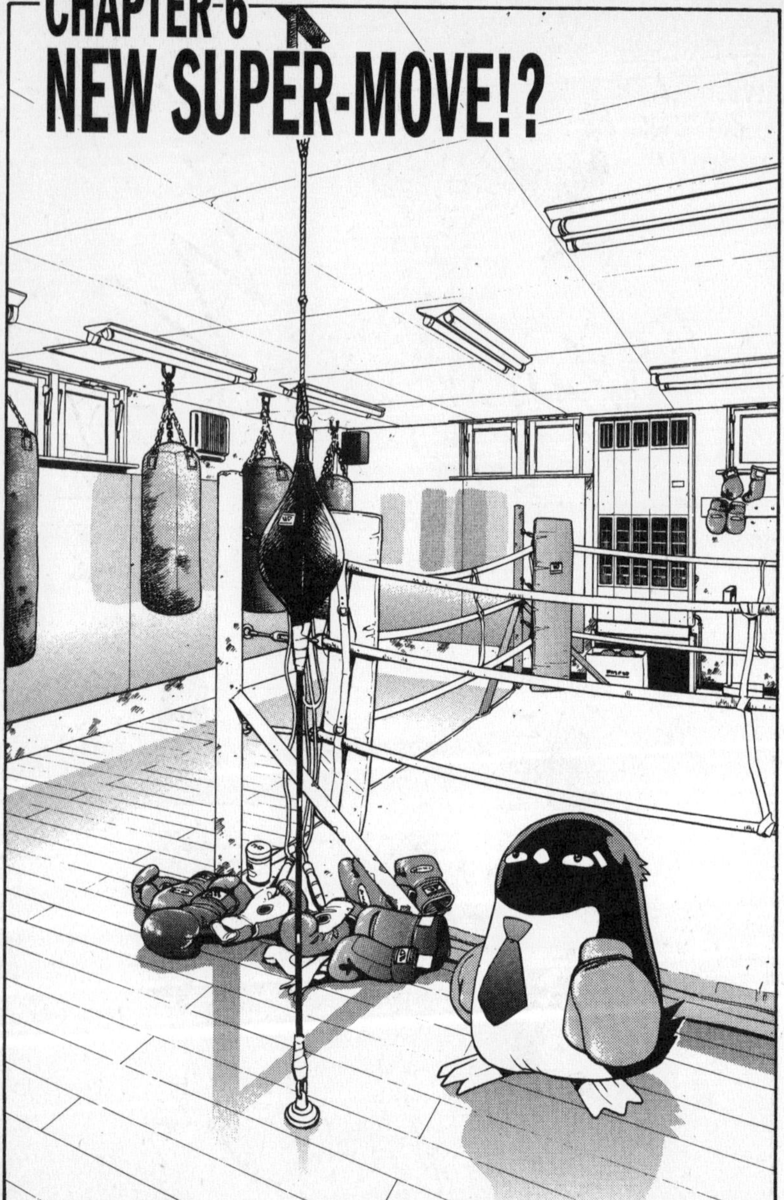

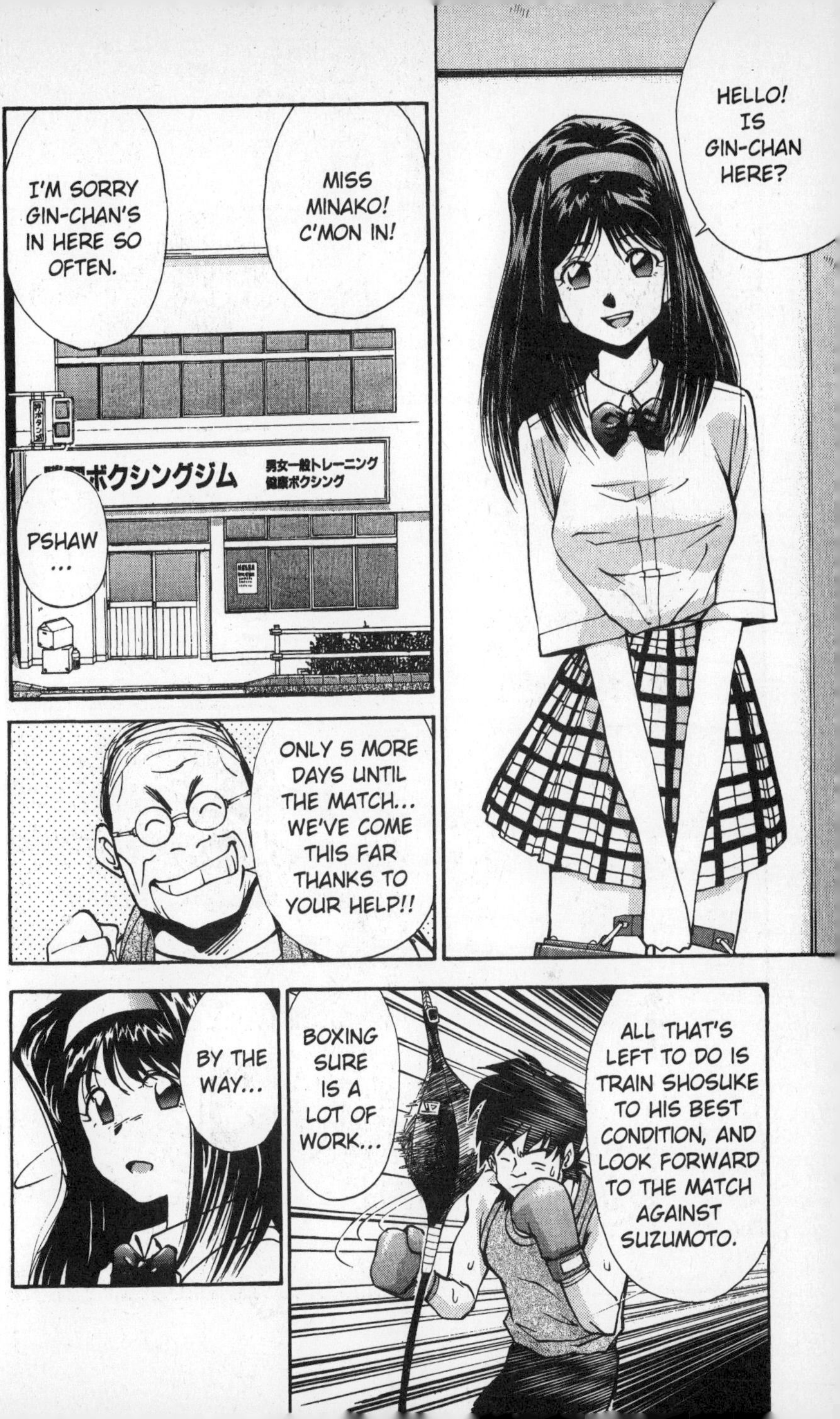
HELLO! IS GIN-CHAN HERE?
MISS MINAKO! C'MON IN!
I'M SORRY GIN-CHAN'S IN HERE SO OFTEN.
ボクシングジム
男女一般トレーニング
健康ボクシング
PSHAW...
ONLY 5 MORE DAYS UNTIL THE MATCH... WE'VE COME THIS FAR THANKS TO YOUR HELP!!
ALL THAT'S LEFT TO DO IS TRAIN SHOSUKE TO HIS BEST CONDITION, AND LOOK FORWARD TO THE MATCH AGAINST SUZUMOTO.
BOXING SURE IS A LOT OF WORK...
BY THE WAY...

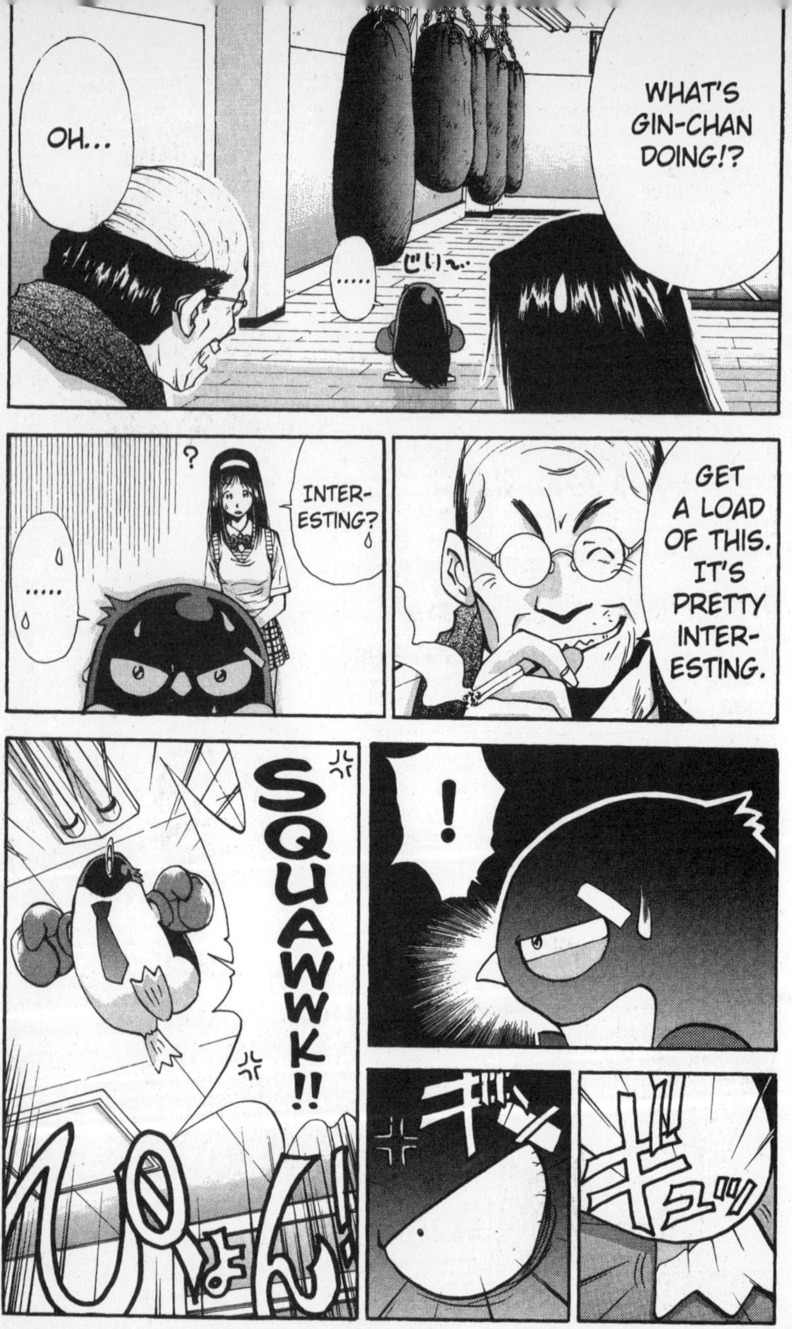
WHAT'S GIN-CHAN DOING!?
OH...
.....
GET A LOAD OF THIS. IT'S PRETTY INTER-ESTING.
INTER-ESTING?
?
.....
!
SQUAWWK!!

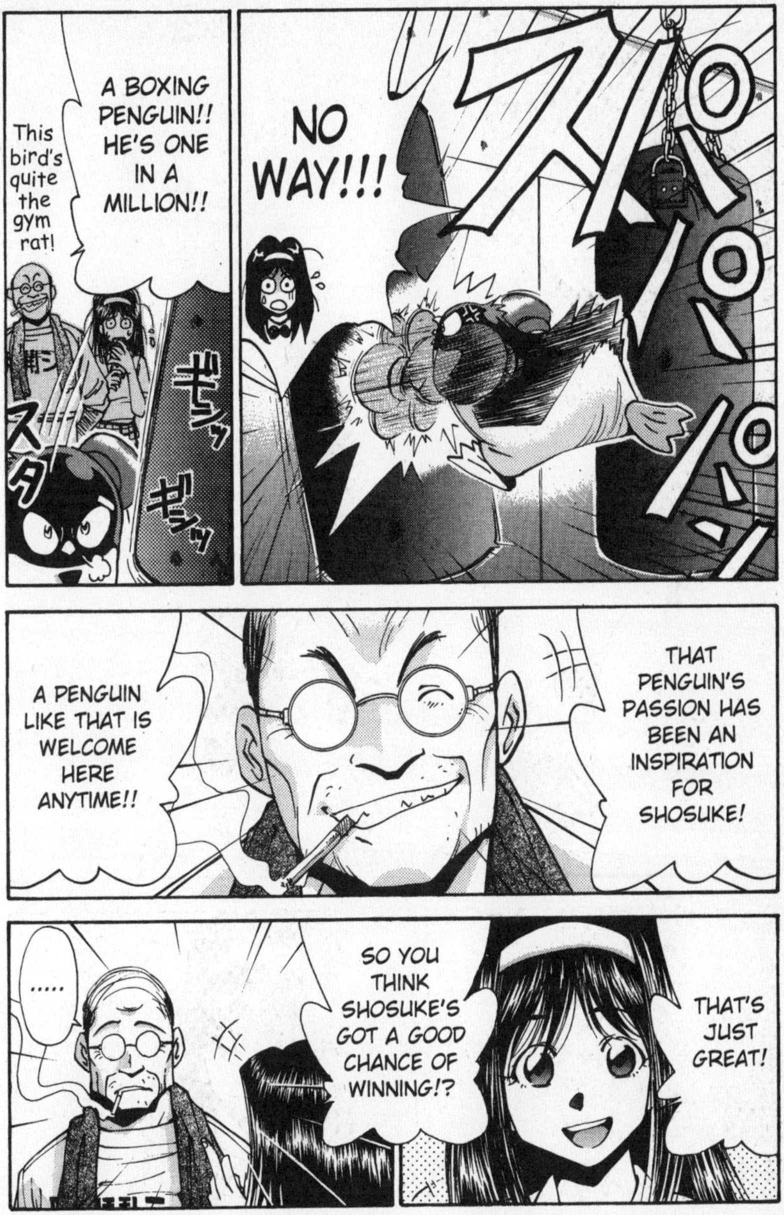
NO WAY!!!
A BOXING PENGUIN!! HE'S ONE IN A MILLION!!
This bird's quite the gym rat!
THAT PENGUIN'S PASSION HAS BEEN AN INSPIRATION FOR SHOSUKE!
A PENGUIN LIKE THAT IS WELCOME HERE ANYTIME!!
THAT'S JUST GREAT!
SO YOU THINK SHOSUKE'S GOT A GOOD CHANCE OF WINNING!?
.....

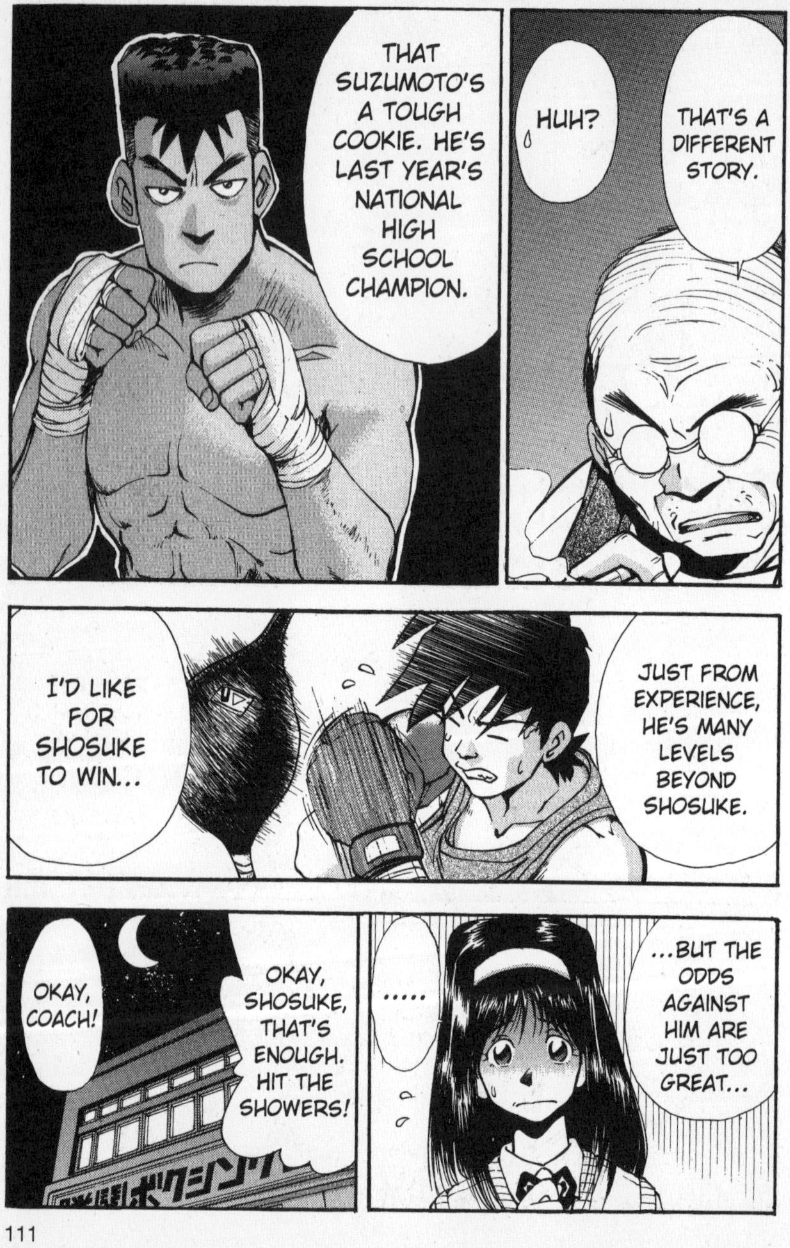
THAT'S A DIFFERENT STORY.
HUH?
THAT SUZUMOTO'S A TOUGH COOKIE. HE'S LAST YEAR'S NATIONAL HIGH SCHOOL CHAMPION.
JUST FROM EXPERIENCE, HE'S MANY LEVELS BEYOND SHOSUKE.
I'D LIKE FOR SHOSUKE TO WIN...
...BUT THE ODDS AGAINST HIM ARE JUST TOO GREAT...
.....
OKAY, SHOSUKE, THAT'S ENOUGH. HIT THE SHOWERS!
OKAY, COACH!

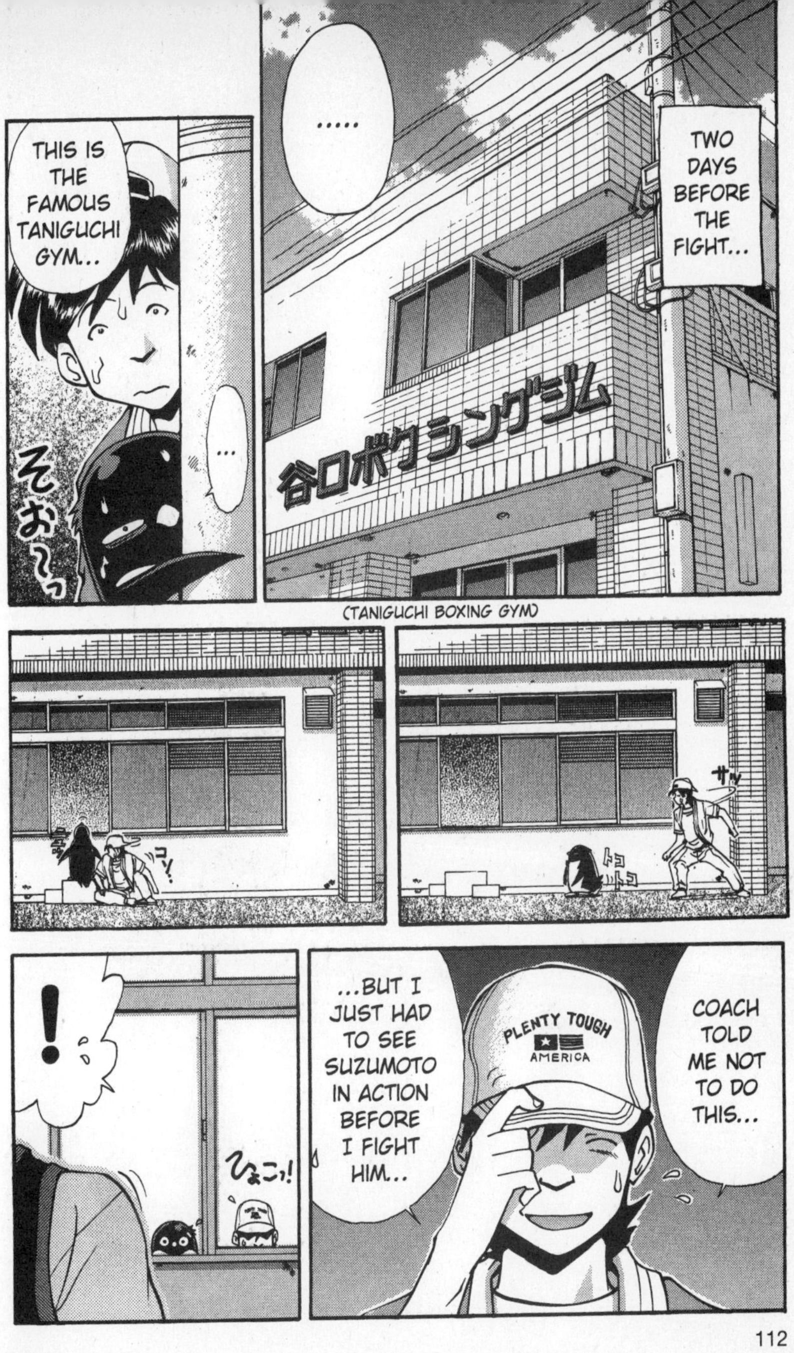
TWO DAYS BEFORE THE FIGHT...
......
谷口ボクシングジム
(TANIGUCHI BOXING GYM)
THIS IS THE FAMOUS TANIGUCHI GYM...
...
そぉ～っ
サッ
トコトコ
COACH TOLD ME NOT TO DO THIS...
...BUT I JUST HAD TO SEE SUZUMOTO IN ACTION BEFORE I FIGHT HIM...
PLENTY TOUGH
AMERICA
!
ひょこっ!

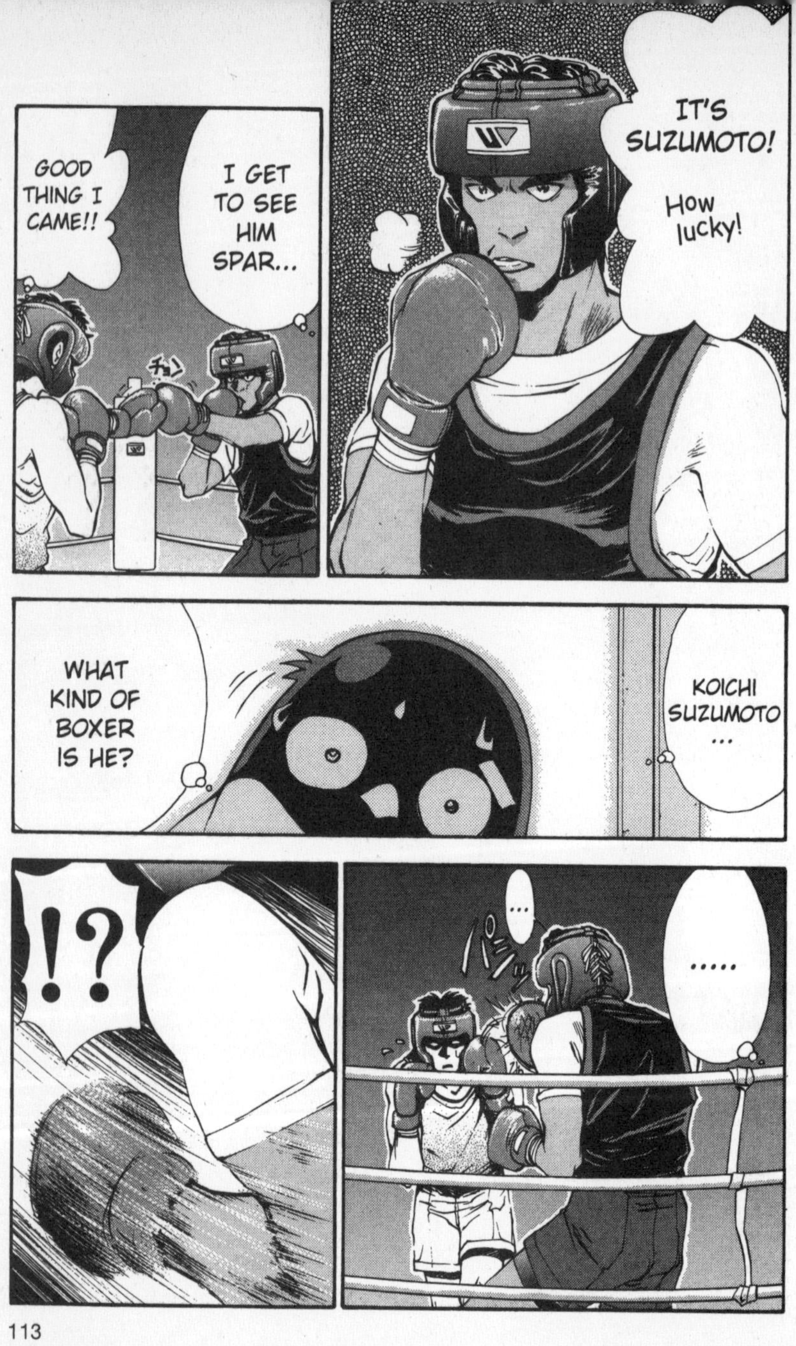
IT'S SUZUMOTO!
How lucky!
I GET TO SEE HIM SPAR...
チョン
GOOD THING I CAME!!
KOICHI SUZUMOTO ...
WHAT KIND OF BOXER IS HE?
.....
...
!?

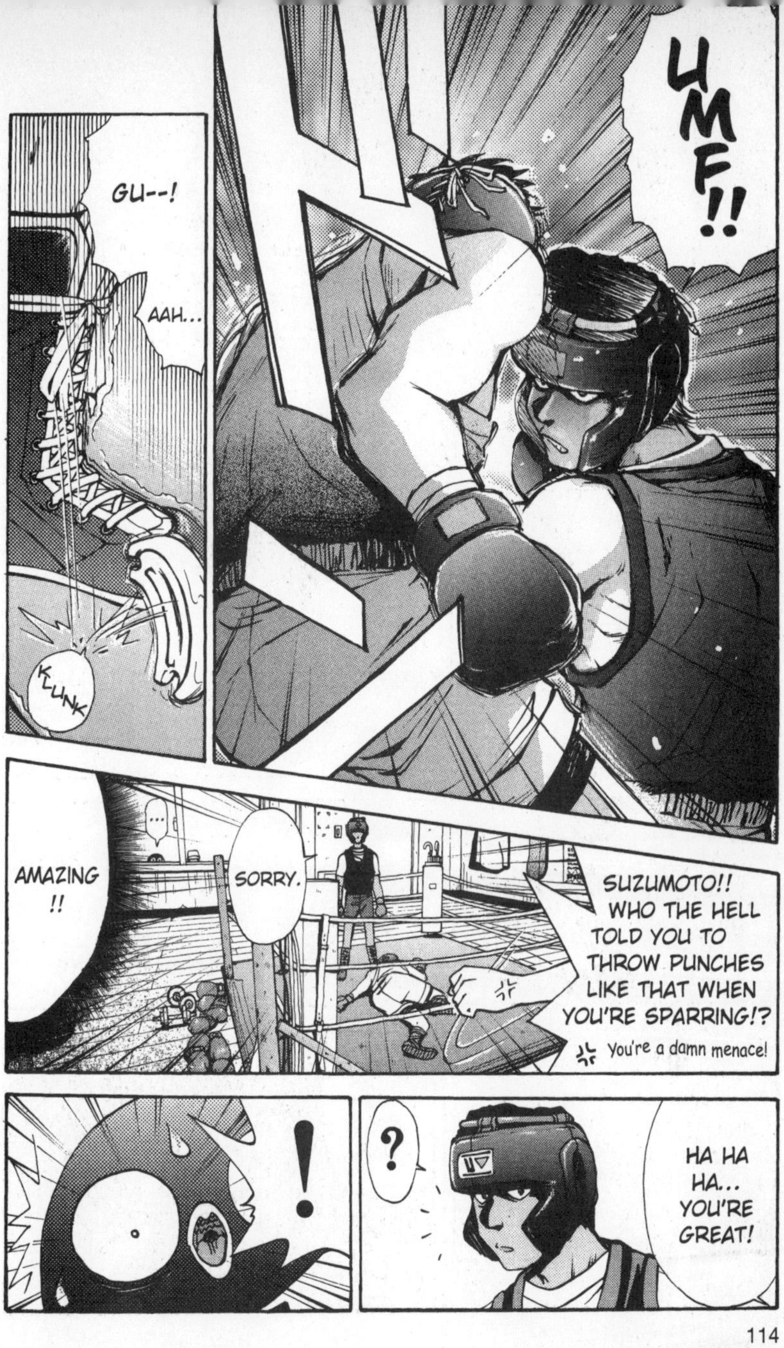
UMF!!
GU--!
AAH...
KLUNK
SUZUMOTO!! WHO THE HELL TOLD YOU TO THROW PUNCHES LIKE THAT WHEN YOU'RE SPARRING!?
You're a damn menace!
SORRY.
...
AMAZING!!
HA HA HA... YOU'RE GREAT!
?
!

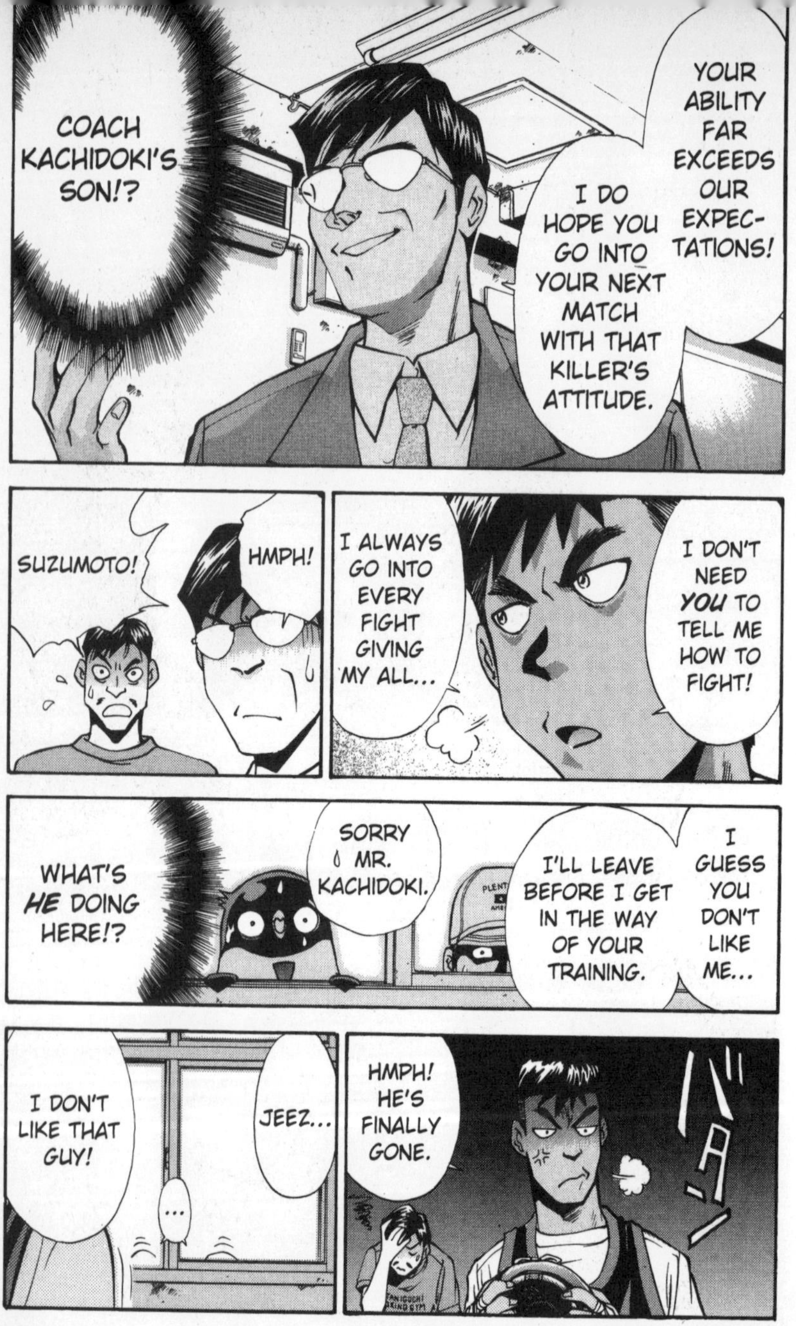
YOUR ABILITY FAR EXCEEDS OUR EXPECTATIONS!
I DO HOPE YOU GO INTO YOUR NEXT MATCH WITH THAT KILLER'S ATTITUDE.
COACH KACHIDOKI'S SON!?
I DON'T NEED *YOU* TO TELL ME HOW TO FIGHT!
I ALWAYS GO INTO EVERY FIGHT GIVING MY ALL...
HMPH!
SUZUMOTO!
I GUESS YOU DON'T LIKE ME...
I'LL LEAVE BEFORE I GET IN THE WAY OF YOUR TRAINING.
SORRY MR. KACHIDOKI.
WHAT'S *HE* DOING HERE!?
バタン！
HMPH! HE'S FINALLY GONE.
JEEZ...
I DON'T LIKE THAT GUY!
...

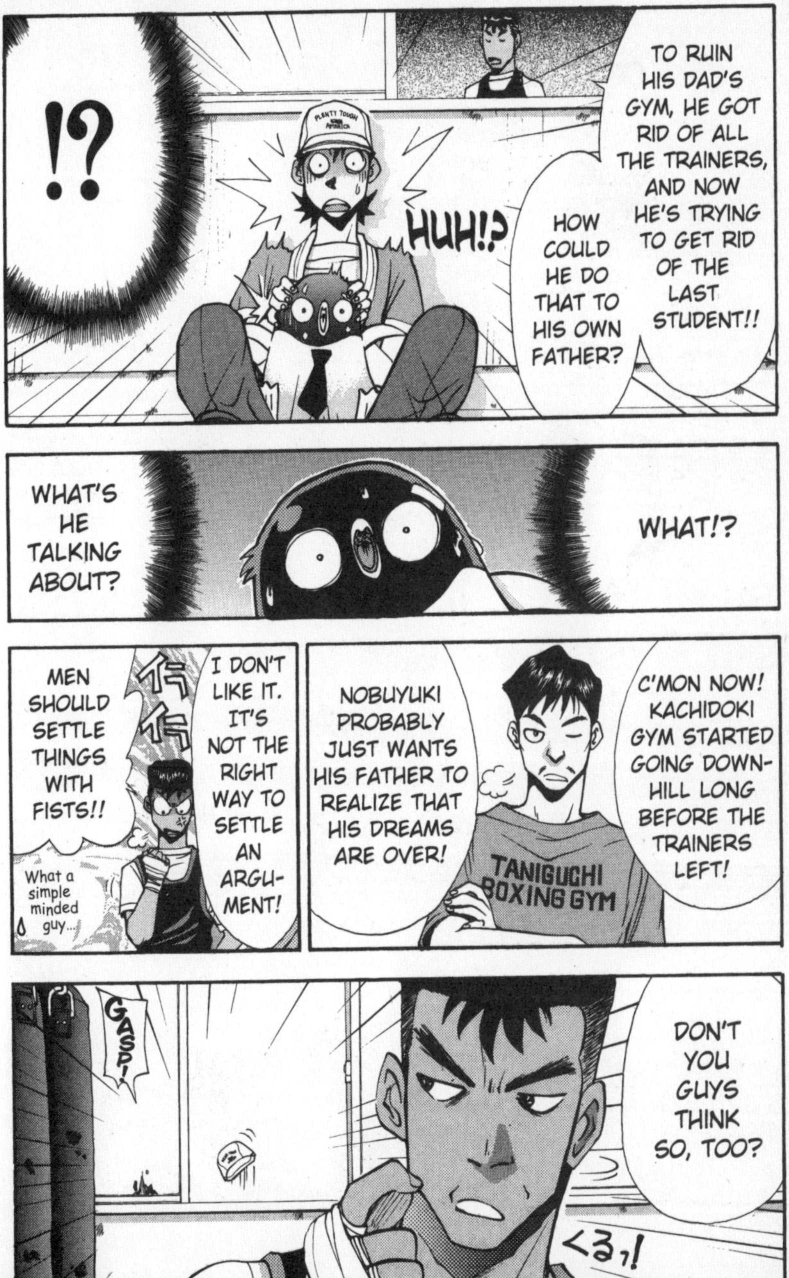
TO RUIN HIS DAD'S GYM, HE GOT RID OF ALL THE TRAINERS, AND NOW HE'S TRYING TO GET RID OF THE LAST STUDENT!!
HOW COULD HE DO THAT TO HIS OWN FATHER?
HUH!?
!?
WHAT!?
WHAT'S HE TALKING ABOUT?
C'MON NOW! KACHIDOKI GYM STARTED GOING DOWN-HILL LONG BEFORE THE TRAINERS LEFT!
NOBUYUKI PROBABLY JUST WANTS HIS FATHER TO REALIZE THAT HIS DREAMS ARE OVER!
TANIGUCHI BOXING GYM
I DON'T LIKE IT. IT'S NOT THE RIGHT WAY TO SETTLE AN ARGU-MENT!
イラ イラ
MEN SHOULD SETTLE THINGS WITH FISTS!!
What a simple minded guy...
DON'T YOU GUYS THINK SO, TOO?
くるっ!
GASP!

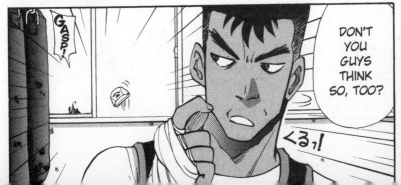

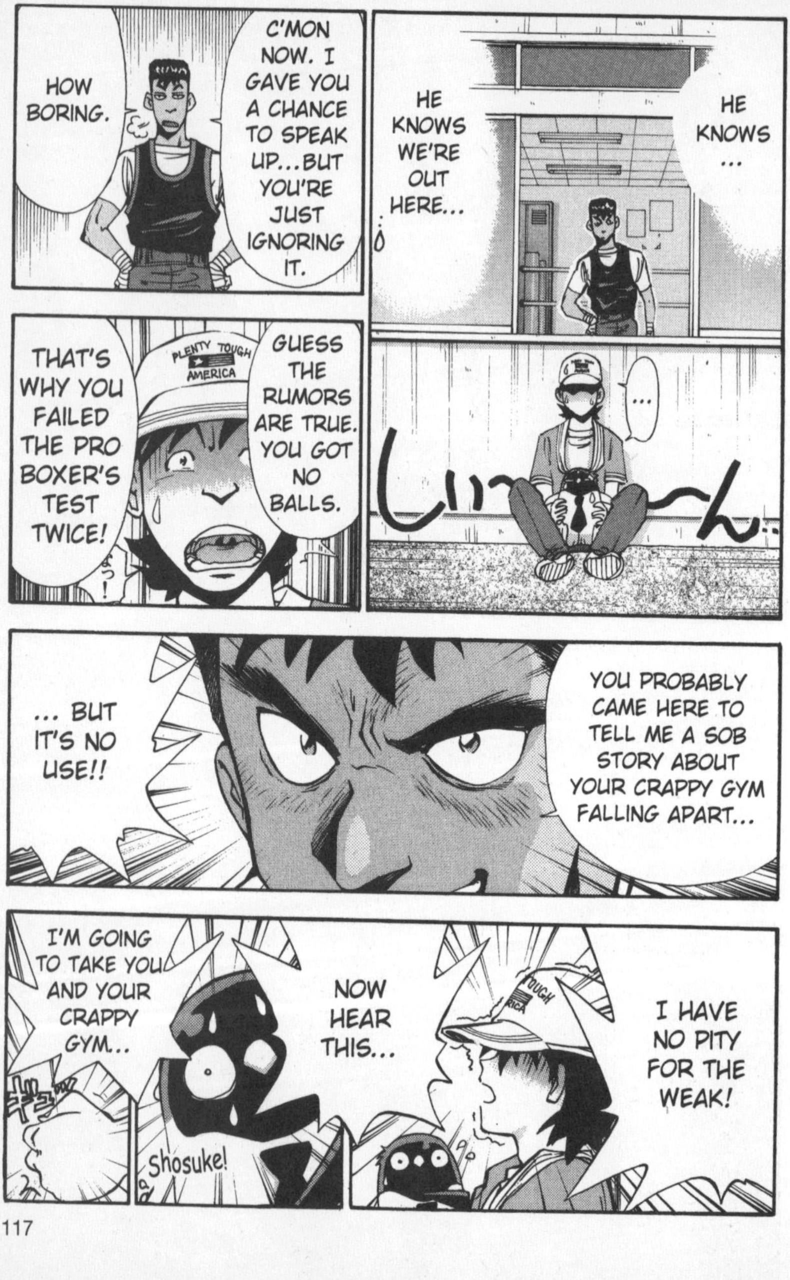
HE KNOWS ...
HE KNOWS WE'RE OUT HERE...
C'MON NOW. I GAVE YOU A CHANCE TO SPEAK UP...BUT YOU'RE JUST IGNORING IT.
HOW BORING.
...
GUESS THE RUMORS ARE TRUE. YOU GOT NO BALLS.
THAT'S WHY YOU FAILED THE PRO BOXER'S TEST TWICE!
PLENTY TOUGH AMERICA
YOU PROBABLY CAME HERE TO TELL ME A SOB STORY ABOUT YOUR CRAPPY GYM FALLING APART...
... BUT IT'S NO USE!!
I HAVE NO PITY FOR THE WEAK!
NOW HEAR THIS...
I'M GOING TO TAKE YOU AND YOUR CRAPPY GYM...
Shosuke!

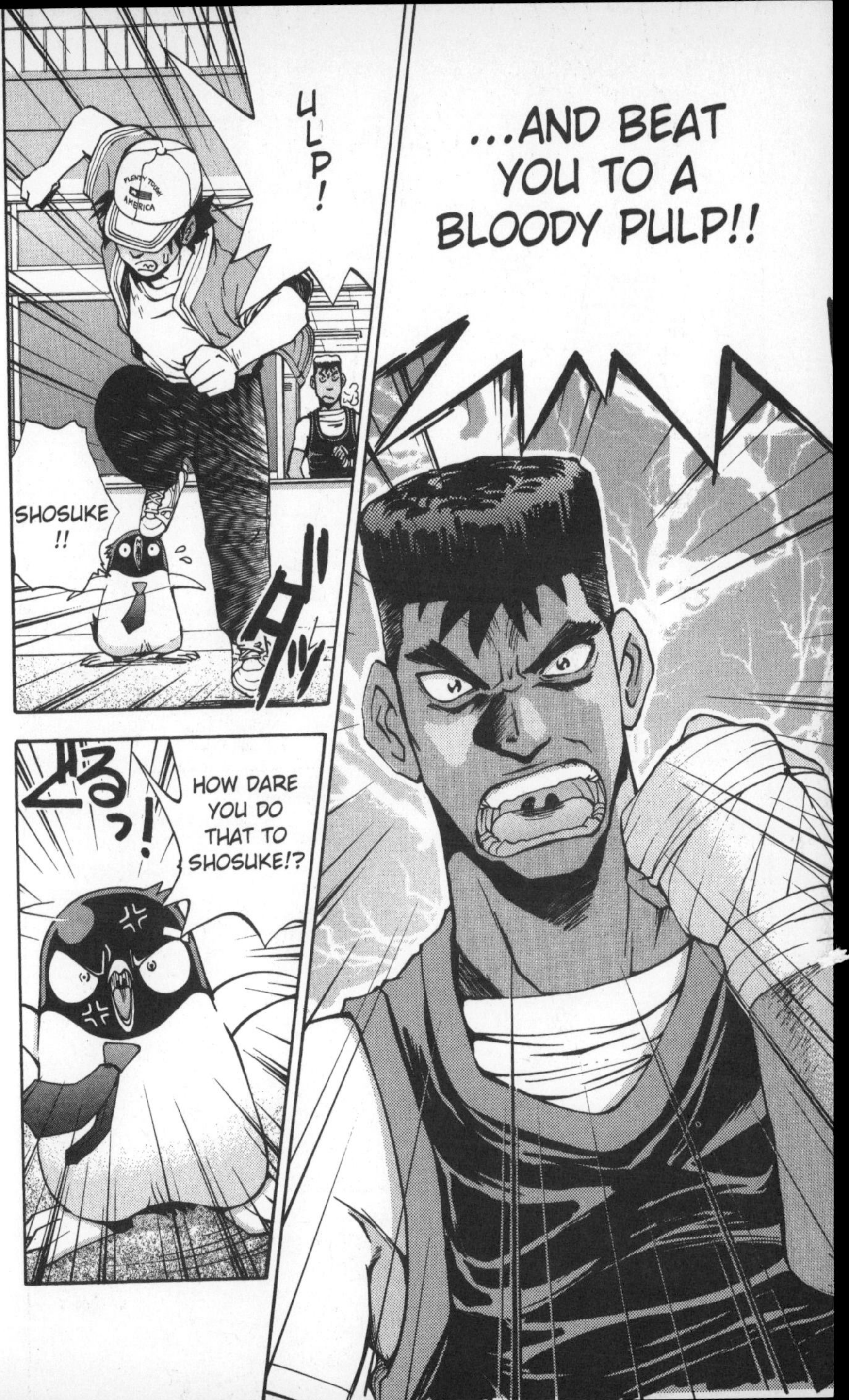
...AND BEAT YOU TO A BLOODY PULP!!
ULP!
SHOSUKE !!
HOW DARE YOU DO THAT TO SHOSUKE!?

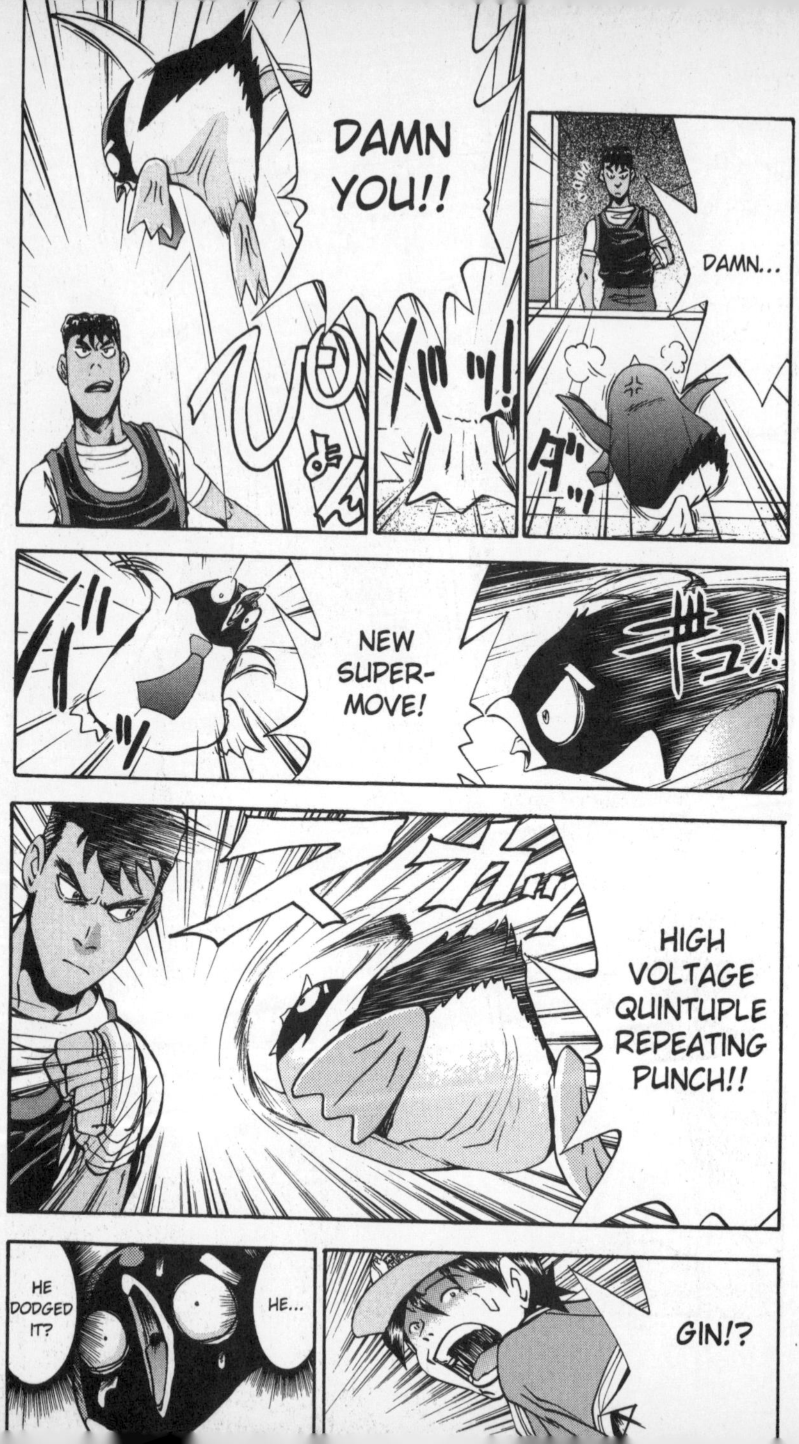
DAMN...
DAMN YOU!!
NEW SUPER-MOVE!
HIGH VOLTAGE QUINTUPLE REPEATING PUNCH!!
GIN!?
HE...
HE DODGED IT?

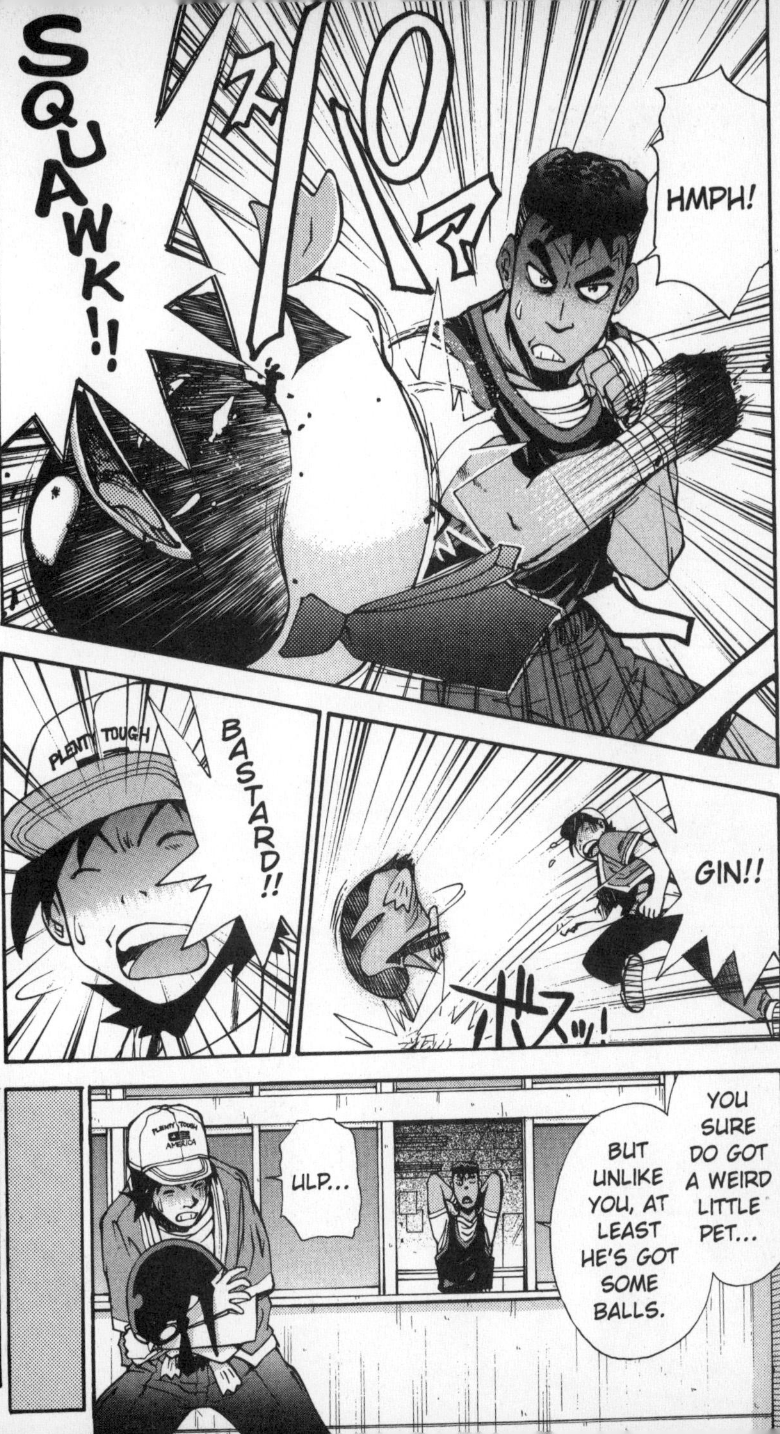
HMPH!
SQUAWK!!
GIN!!
ボスッ!
BASTARD!!
PLENTY TOUGH
YOU SURE DO GOT A WEIRD LITTLE PET...
BUT UNLIKE YOU, AT LEAST HE'S GOT SOME BALLS.
ULP...
PLENTY TOUGH AMERICA

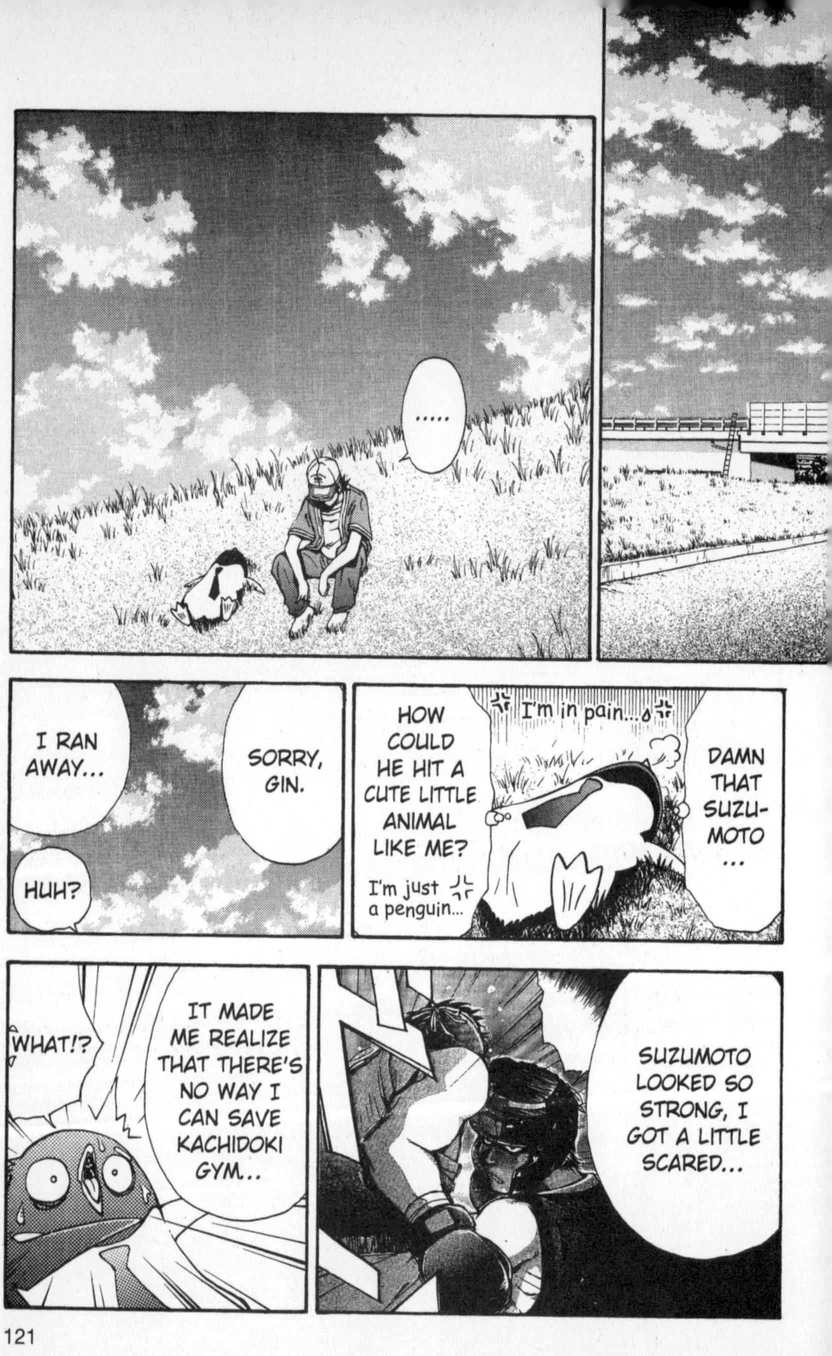
.....
I'm in pain...
DAMN THAT SUZU-MOTO...
HOW COULD HE HIT A CUTE LITTLE ANIMAL LIKE ME?
I'm just a penguin...
SORRY, GIN.
I RAN AWAY...
HUH?
SUZUMOTO LOOKED SO STRONG, I GOT A LITTLE SCARED...
IT MADE ME REALIZE THAT THERE'S NO WAY I CAN SAVE KACHIDOKI GYM...
WHAT!?

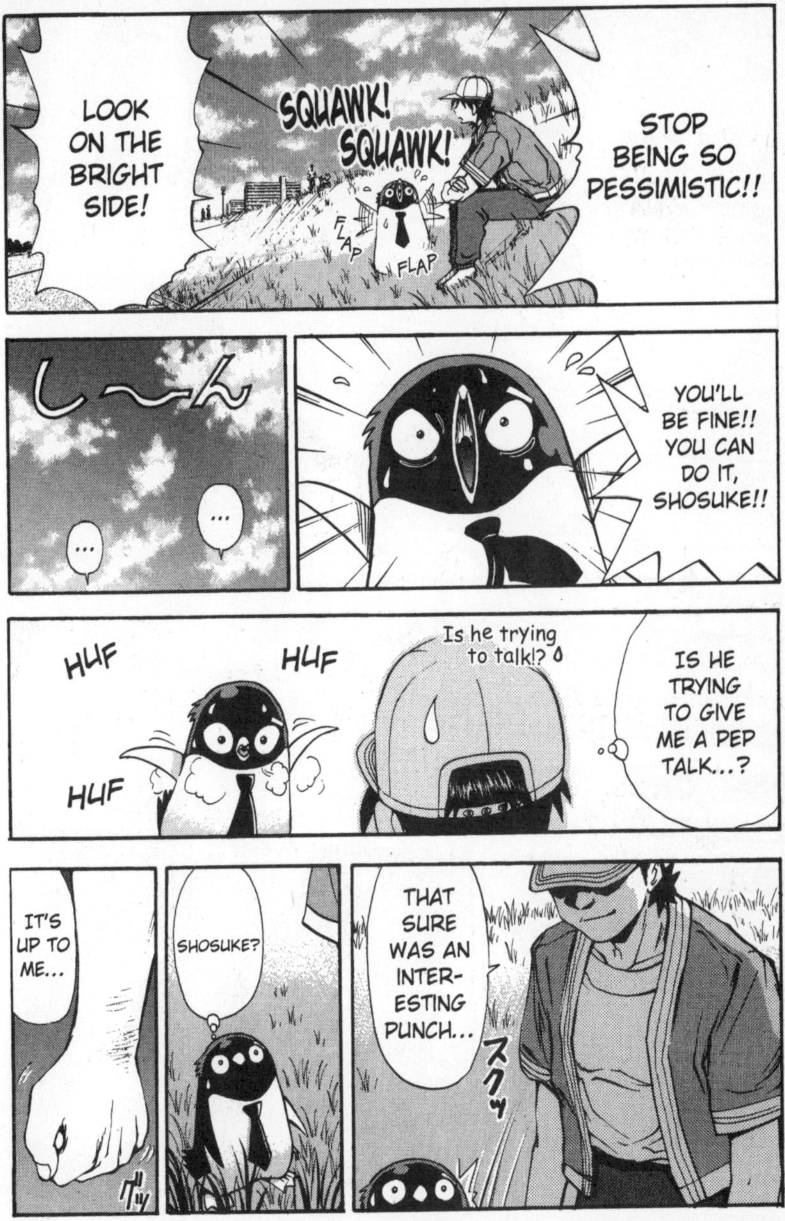
STOP BEING SO PESSIMISTIC!!
SQUAWK! SQUAWK!
LOOK ON THE BRIGHT SIDE!
FLAP FLAP
YOU'LL BE FINE!! YOU CAN DO IT, SHOSUKE!!
しーん
...
...
IS HE TRYING TO GIVE ME A PEP TALK...?
Is he trying to talk!?
HUF HUF
HUF
THAT SURE WAS AN INTER-ESTING PUNCH...
スクッ
SHOSUKE?
IT'S UP TO ME...
グッ

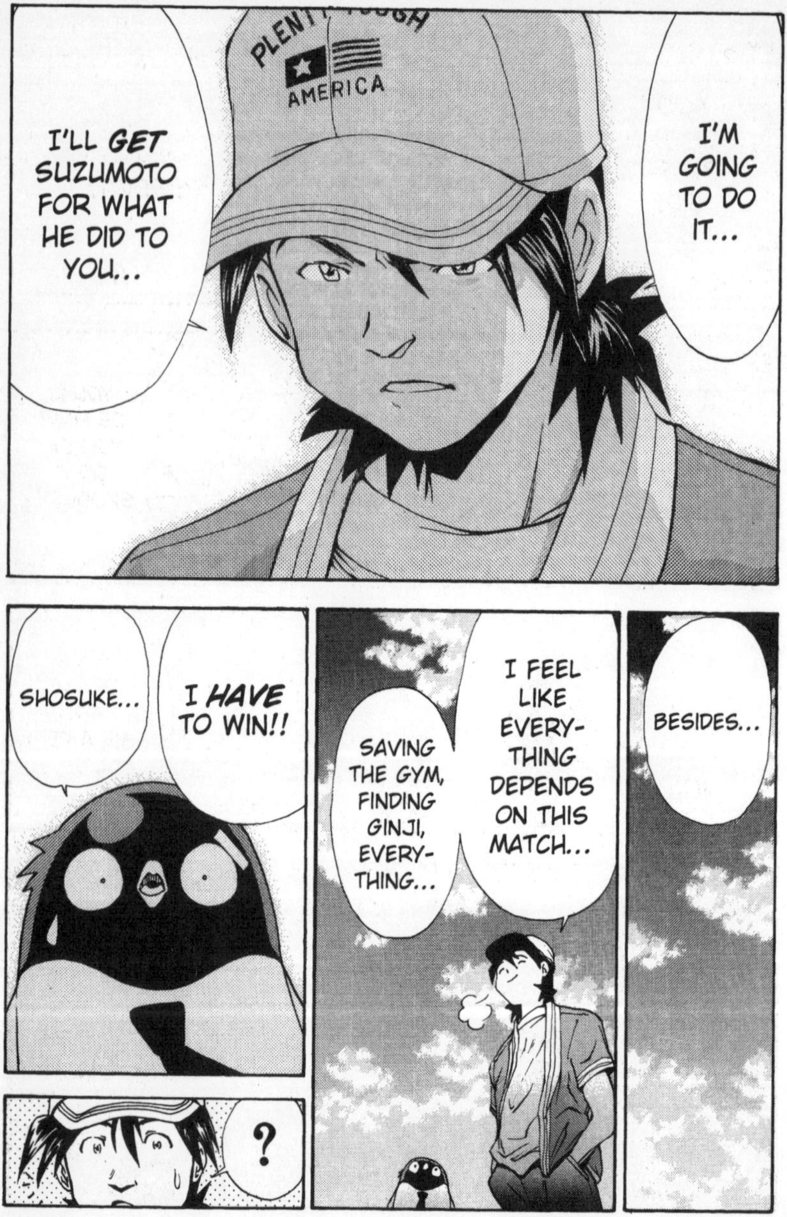
AMERICA
I'M GOING TO DO IT...
I'LL *GET* SUZUMOTO FOR WHAT HE DID TO YOU...
BESIDES...
I FEEL LIKE EVERY-THING DEPENDS ON THIS MATCH...
SAVING THE GYM, FINDING GINJI, EVERY-THING...
I *HAVE* TO WIN!!
SHOSUKE...
?

fwip
.....
fwip
LET'S GO FOR IT!!
BUMP

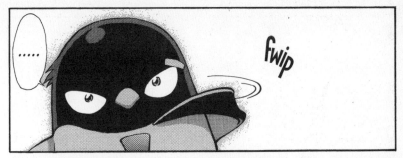

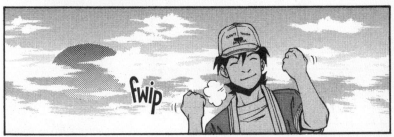

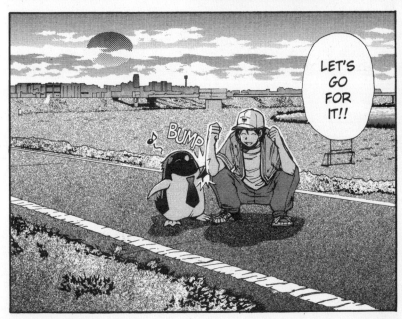

CHAPTER 7
FIGHT NIGHT!!

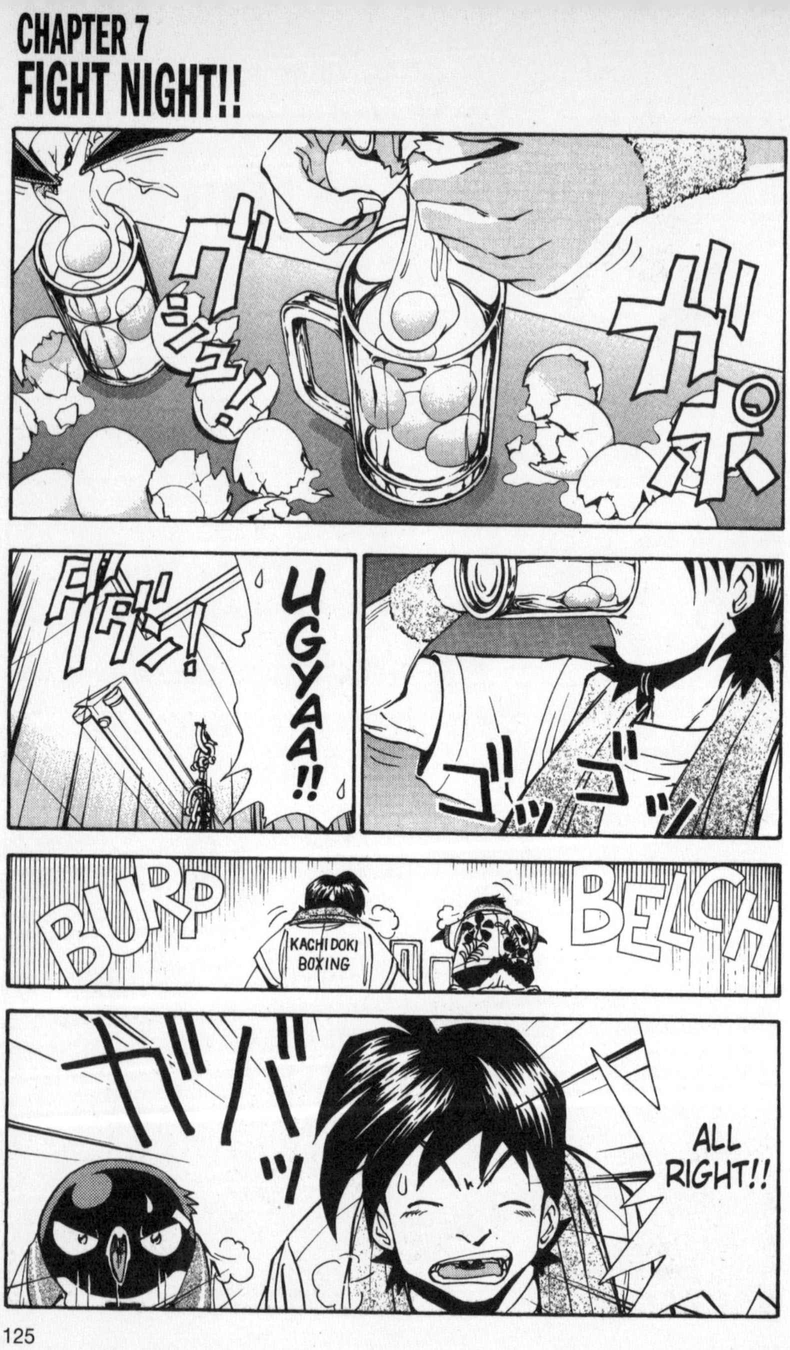
ガポ.
ゴッゴッ
UGYAA!!
BELCH
KACHIDOKI BOXING
BURP
ALL RIGHT!!
ガバッ

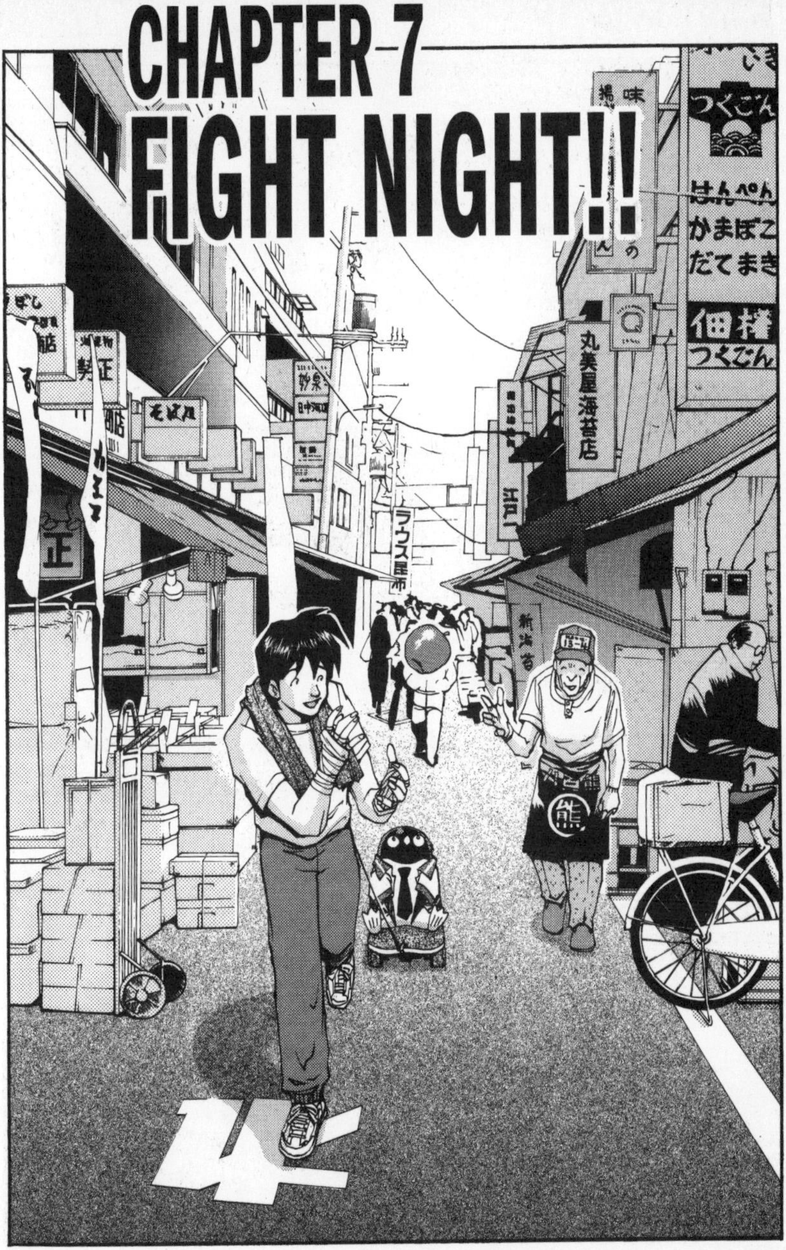
CHAPTER 7
FIGHT NIGHT!!

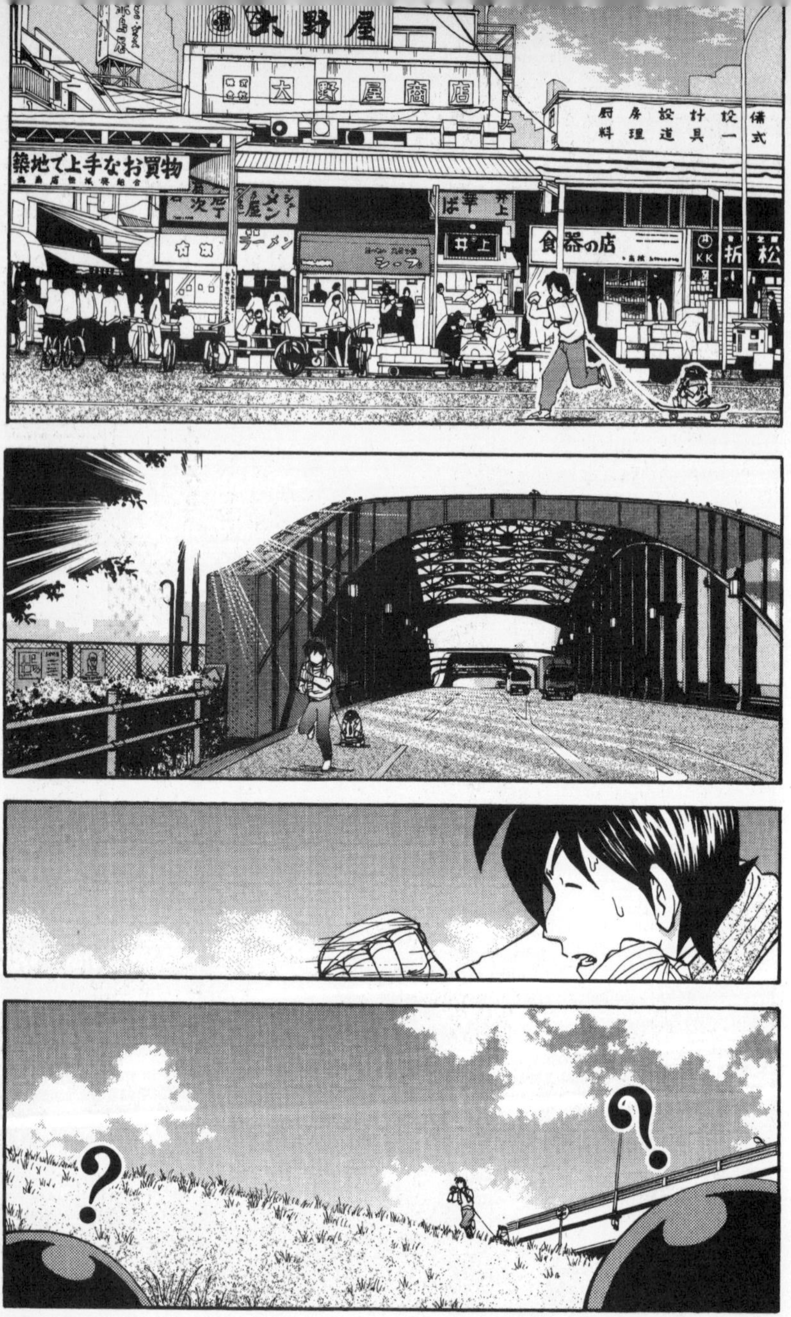
大野屋
大野屋商店
厨房設計設備
料理道具一式
築地で上手なお買物
ラーメン
井上
食器の店
?
?

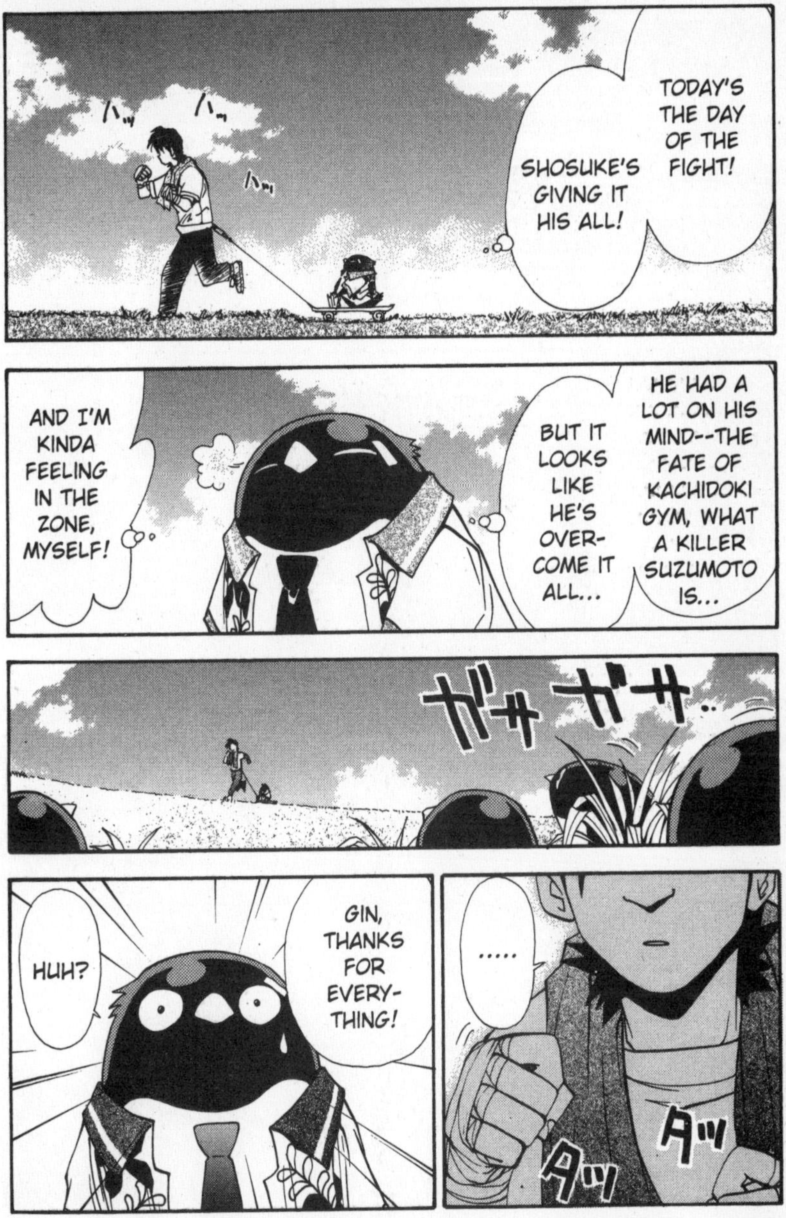
TODAY'S THE DAY OF THE FIGHT!
SHOSUKE'S GIVING IT HIS ALL!
ハッ ハッ ハッ
HE HAD A LOT ON HIS MIND--THE FATE OF KACHIDOKI GYM, WHAT A KILLER SUZUMOTO IS...
BUT IT LOOKS LIKE HE'S OVER-COME IT ALL...
AND I'M KINDA FEELING IN THE ZONE, MYSELF!
ガサ ガサ..
.....
ダッ ダッ
GIN, THANKS FOR EVERY-THING!
HUH?

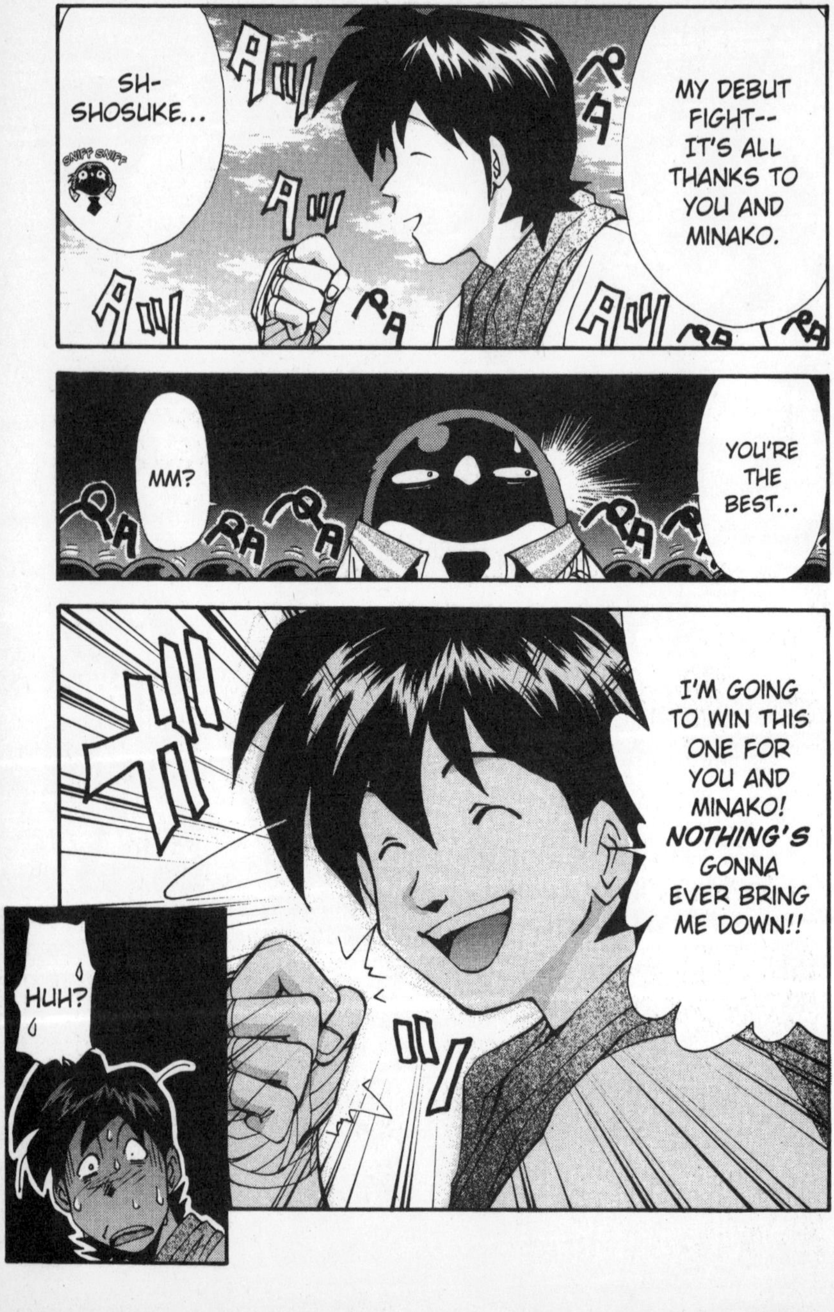
MY DEBUT FIGHT-- IT'S ALL THANKS TO YOU AND MINAKO.
SH- SHOSUKE...
SNIFF SNIFF
YOU'RE THE BEST...
MM?
I'M GOING TO WIN THIS ONE FOR YOU AND MINAKO! *NOTHING'S* GONNA EVER BRING ME DOWN!!
HUH?

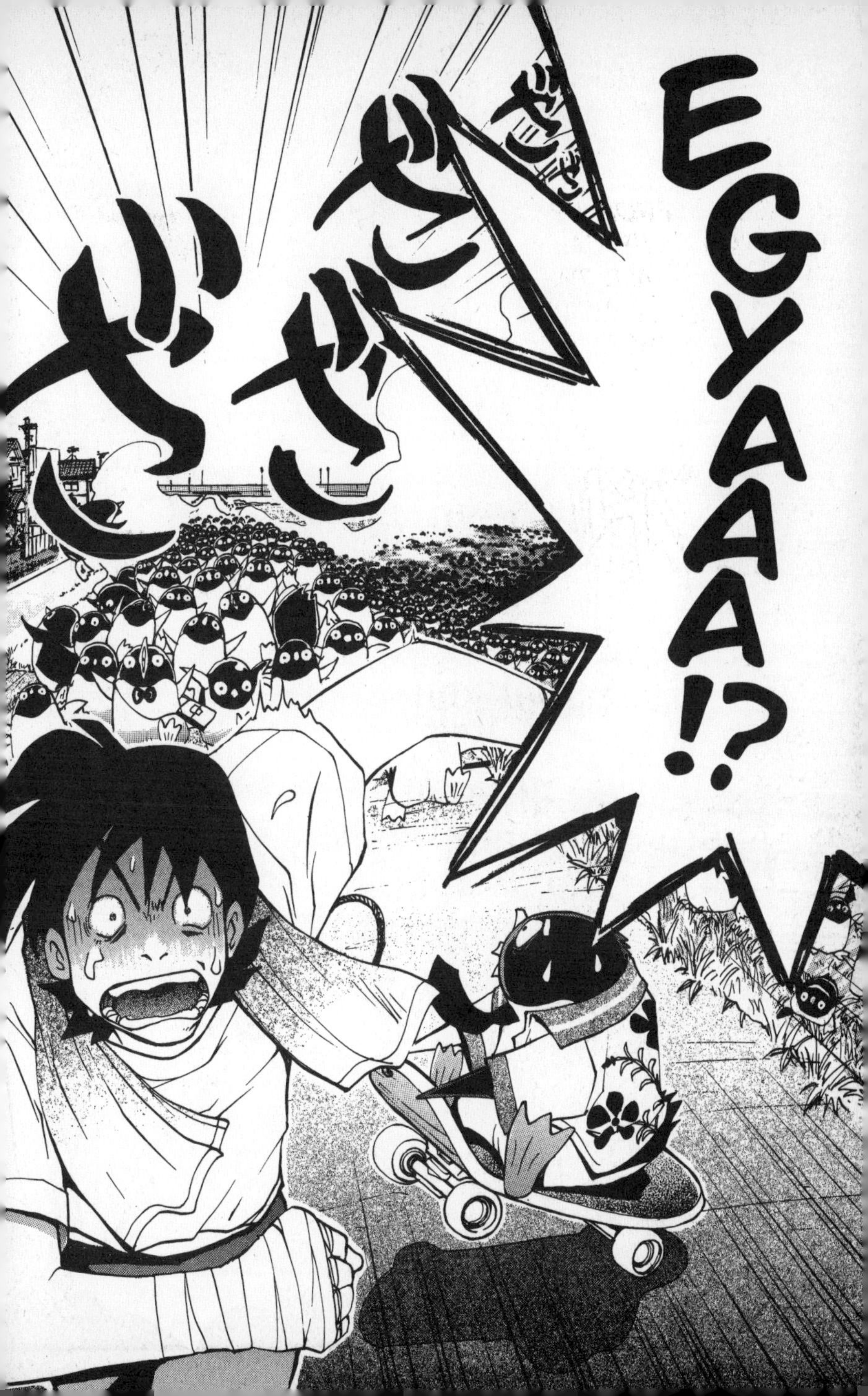
EGYAAA!?
ざざ
ざざざ

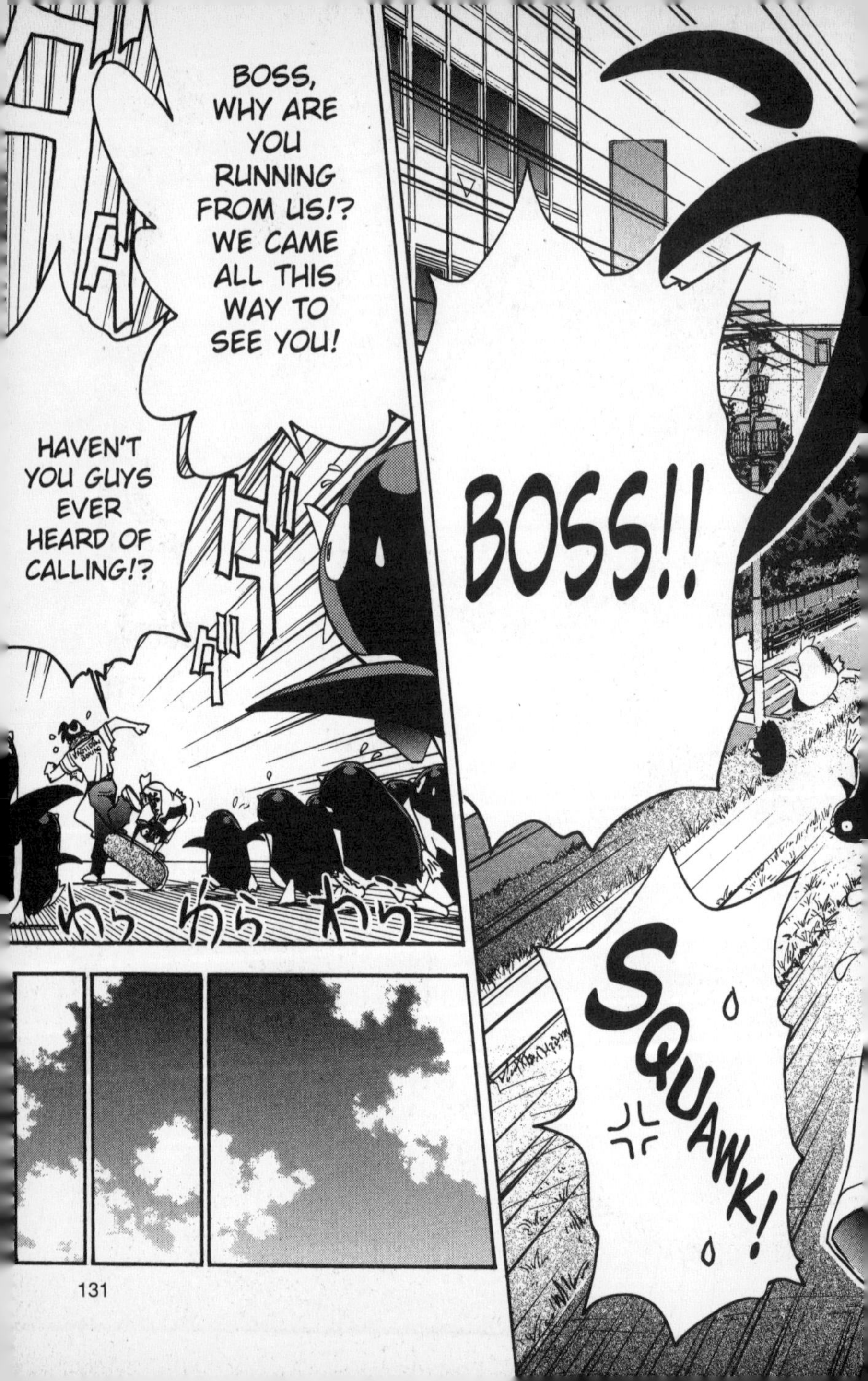
BOSS!!
SQUAWK!
BOSS, WHY ARE YOU RUNNING FROM US!? WE CAME ALL THIS WAY TO SEE YOU!
HAVEN'T YOU GUYS EVER HEARD OF CALLING!?

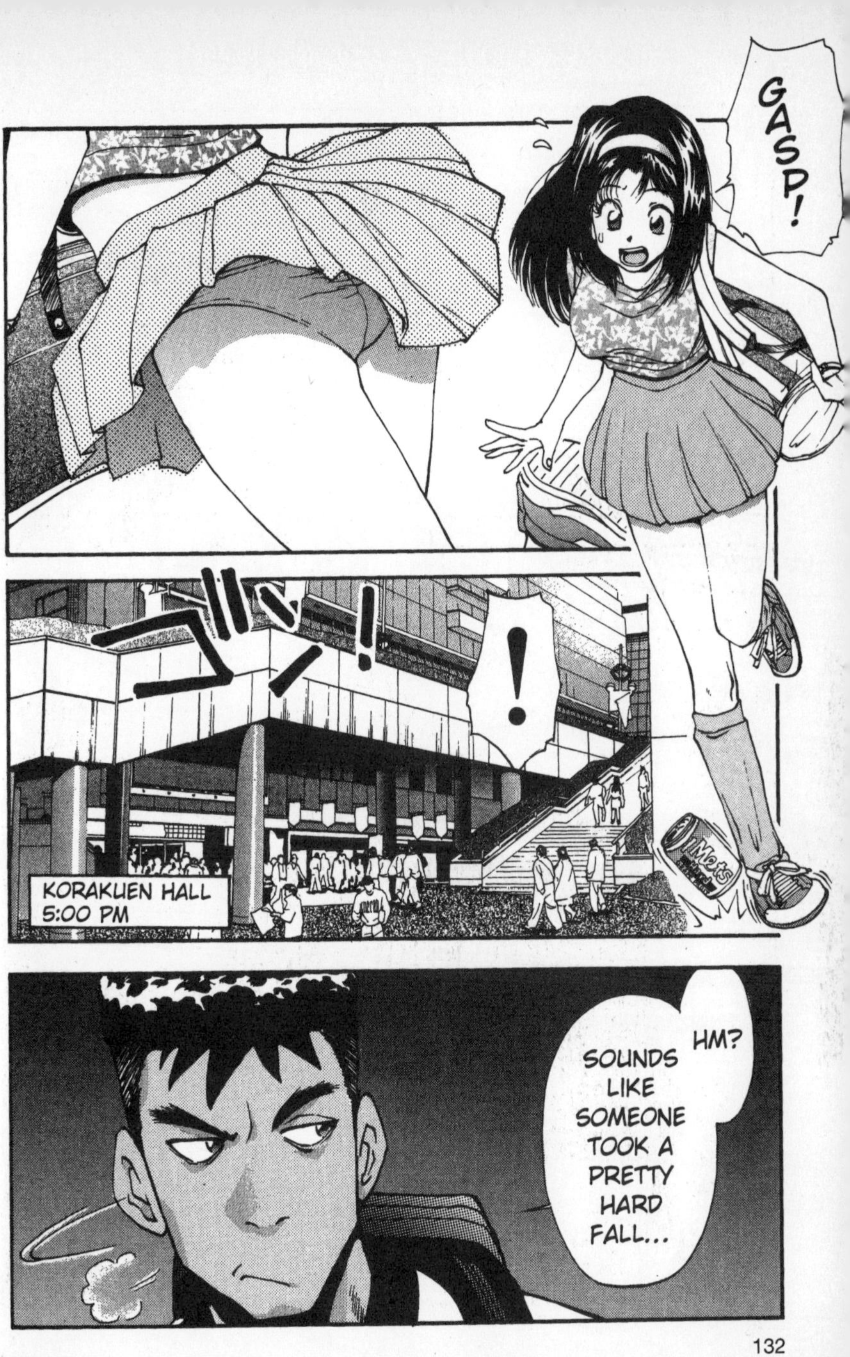
GASP!
!
KORAKUEN HALL
5:00 PM
HM?
SOUNDS LIKE SOMEONE TOOK A PRETTY HARD FALL...

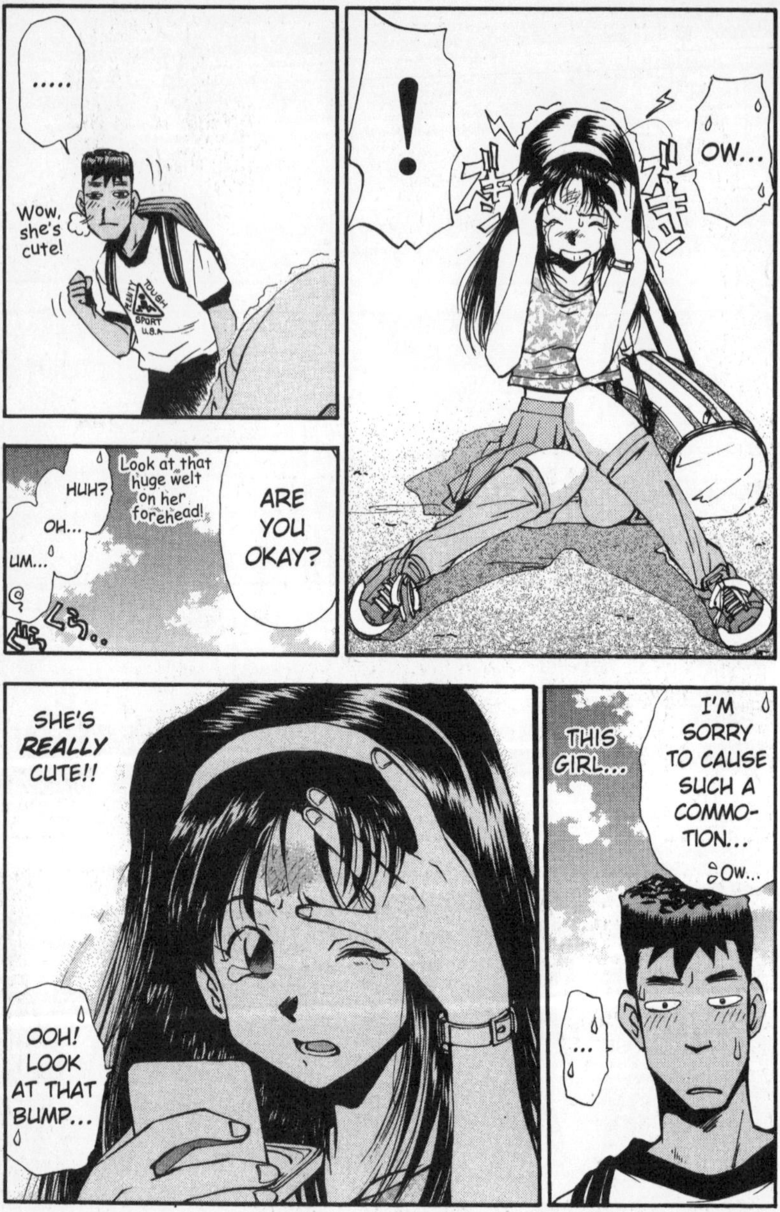
!
OW...
.....
Wow, she's cute!
ARE YOU OKAY?
Look at that huge welt on her forehead!
HUH?
OH...
UM...
I'M SORRY TO CAUSE SUCH A COMMOTION...
OW...
THIS GIRL...
...
SHE'S *REALLY* CUTE!!
OOH! LOOK AT THAT BUMP...

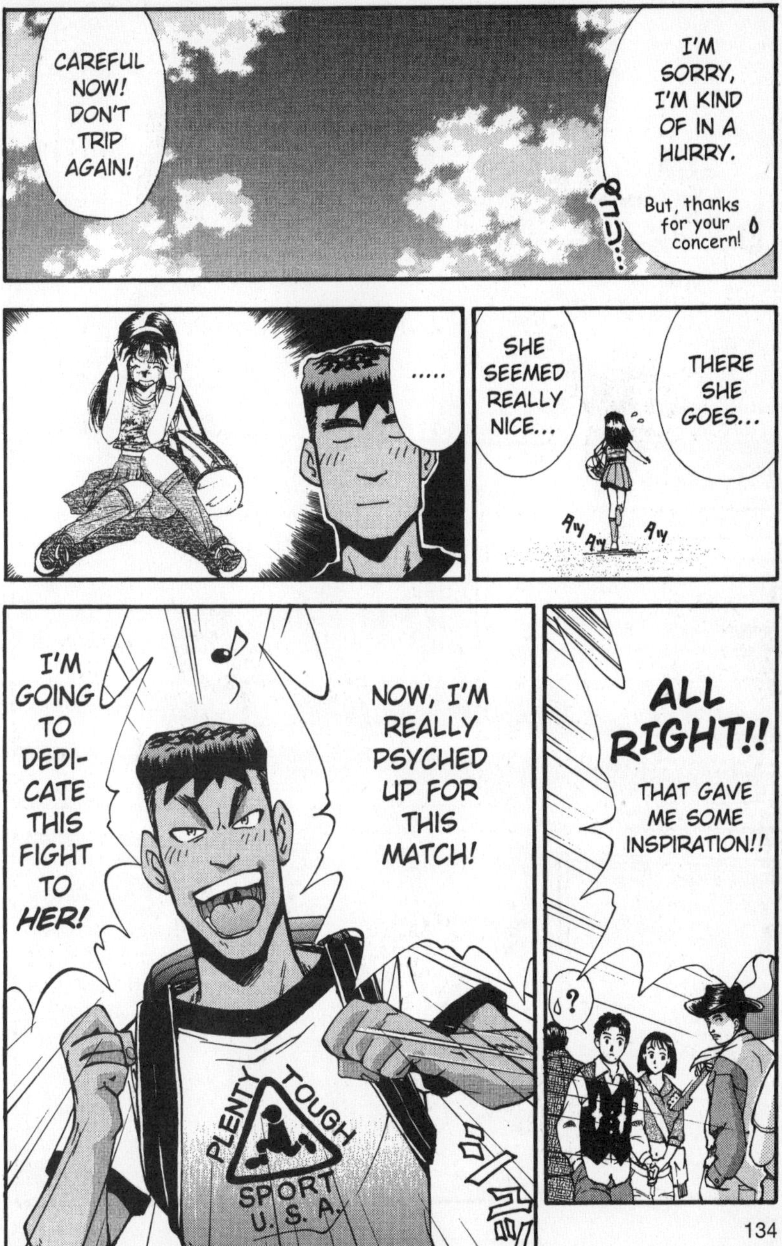
I'M SORRY, I'M KIND OF IN A HURRY.
But, thanks for your concern!
ペコリ…
CAREFUL NOW! DON'T TRIP AGAIN!
THERE SHE GOES...
SHE SEEMED REALLY NICE...
.....
ALL RIGHT!!
THAT GAVE ME SOME INSPIRATION!!
?
NOW, I'M REALLY PSYCHED UP FOR THIS MATCH!
I'M GOING TO DEDICATE THIS FIGHT TO HER!
PLENTY TOUGH
SPORT U. S. A.

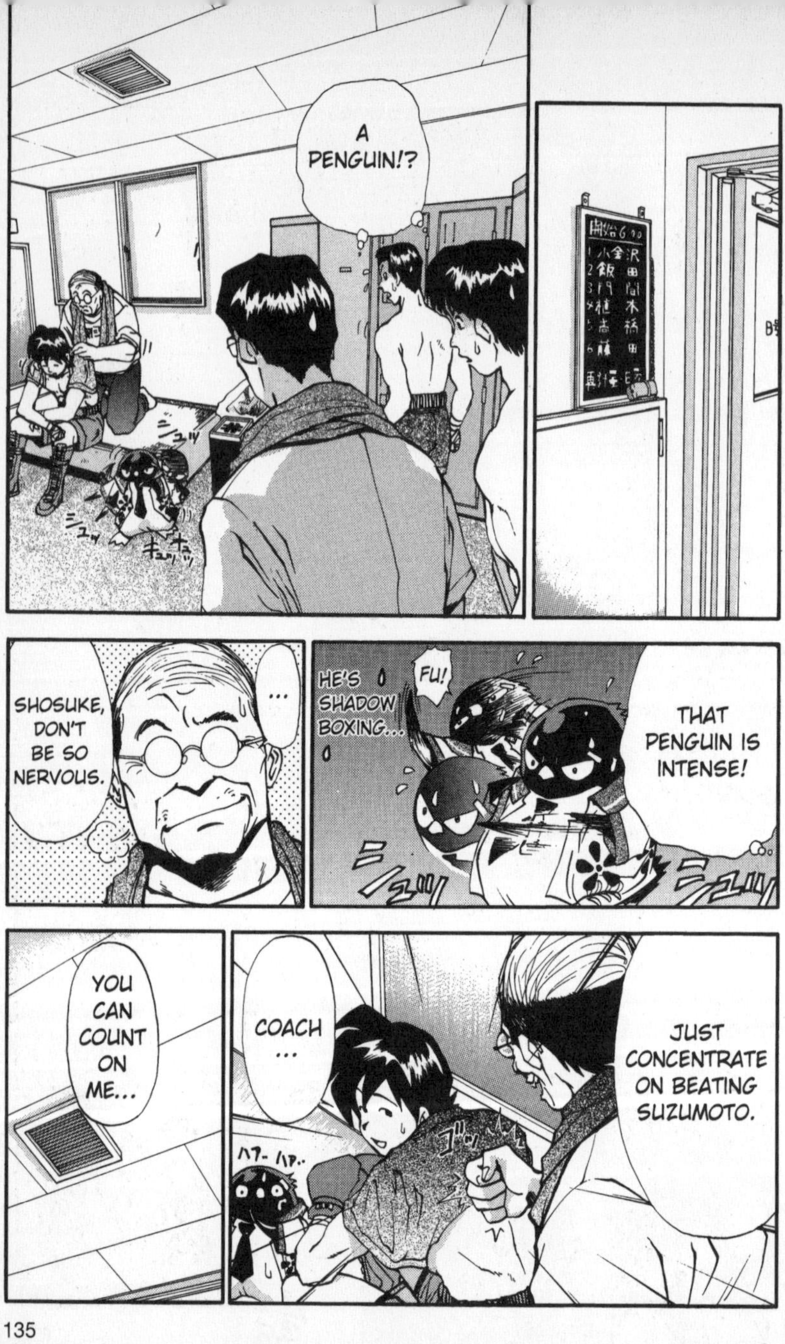
A PENGUIN!?
THAT PENGUIN IS INTENSE!
FU!
HE'S SHADOW BOXING...
...
SHOSUKE, DON'T BE SO NERVOUS.
JUST CONCENTRATE ON BEATING SUZUMOTO.
COACH ...
YOU CAN COUNT ON ME...

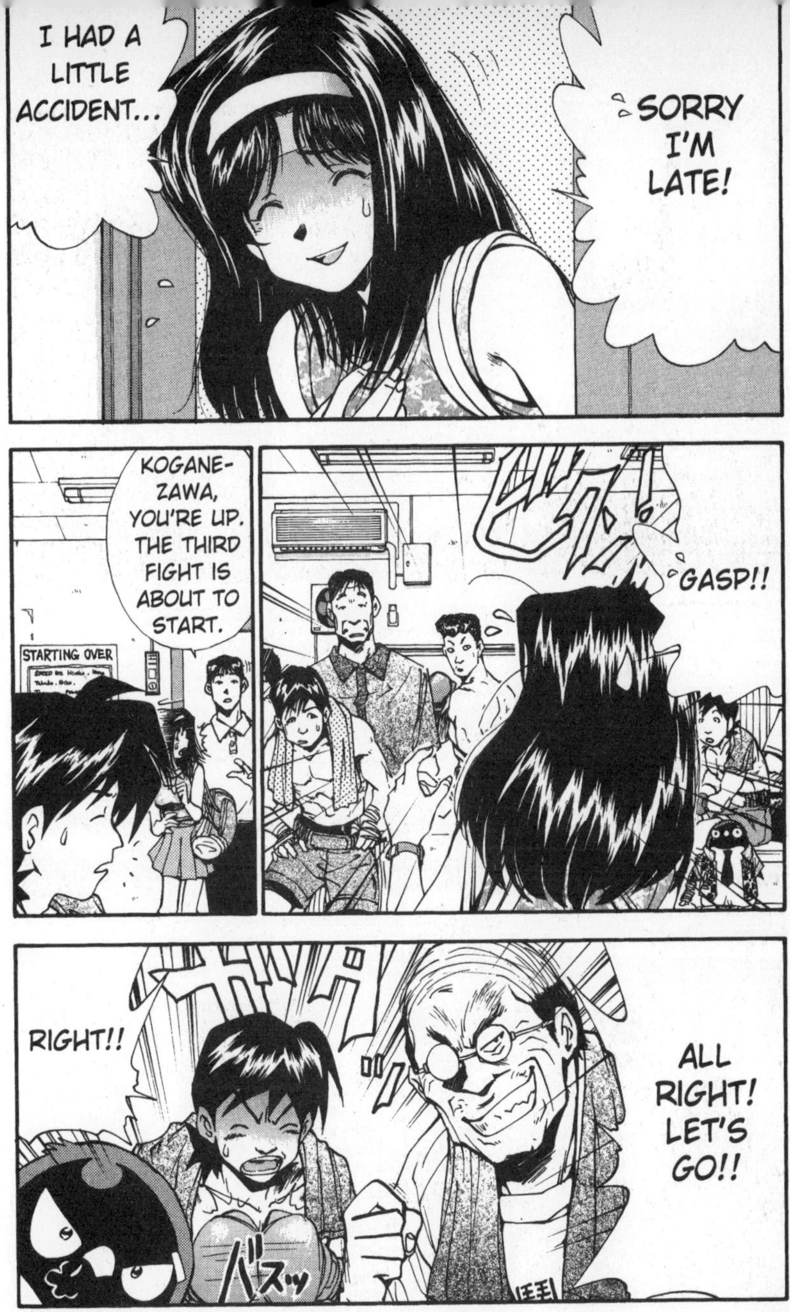
SORRY I'M LATE!
I HAD A LITTLE ACCIDENT...
GASP!!
KOGANE-ZAWA, YOU'RE UP. THE THIRD FIGHT IS ABOUT TO START.
STARTING OVER
ALL RIGHT! LET'S GO!!
RIGHT!!
バスッ

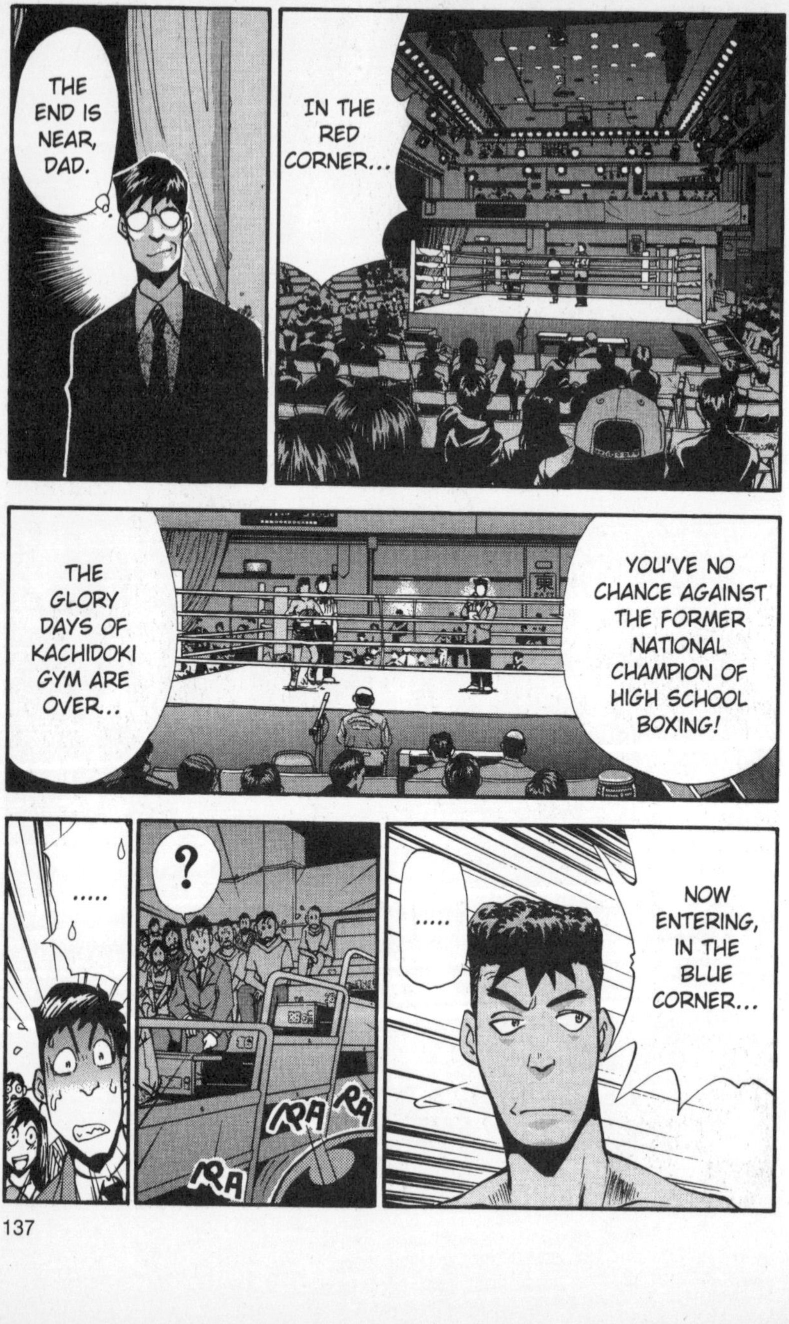
IN THE RED CORNER...
THE END IS NEAR, DAD.
YOU'VE NO CHANCE AGAINST THE FORMER NATIONAL CHAMPION OF HIGH SCHOOL BOXING!
THE GLORY DAYS OF KACHIDOKI GYM ARE OVER...
NOW ENTERING, IN THE BLUE CORNER...
.....
?
RA
RA
RA
.....

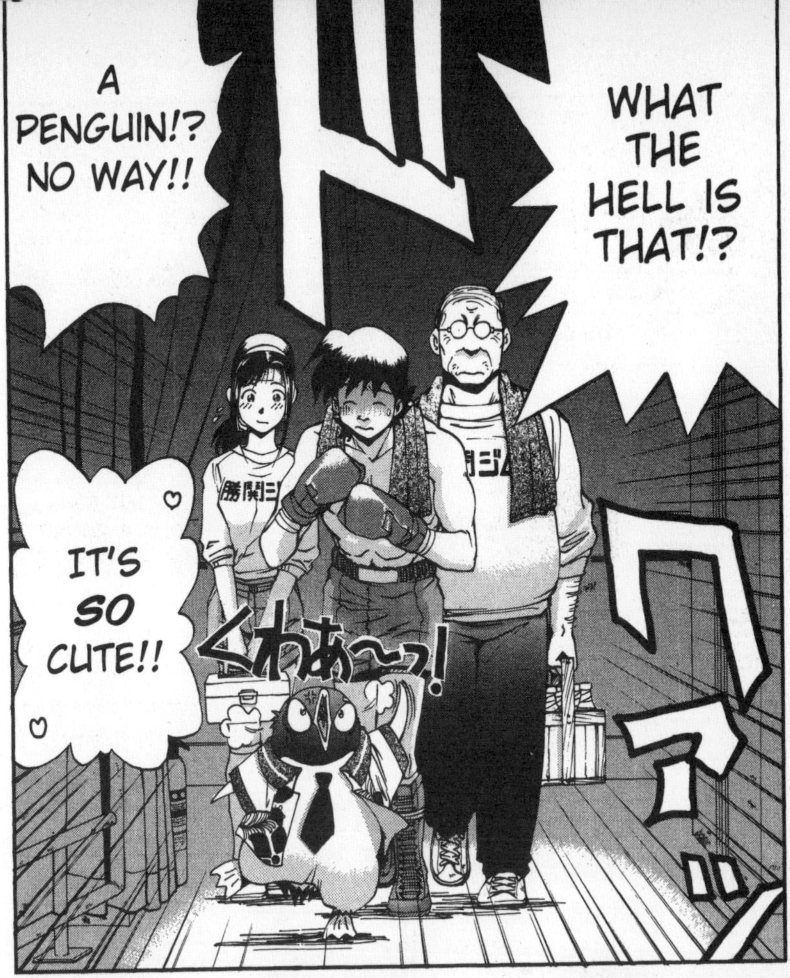
WHAT THE HELL IS THAT!?
A PENGUIN!? NO WAY!!
くわあ～っ!
IT'S *SO* CUTE!!

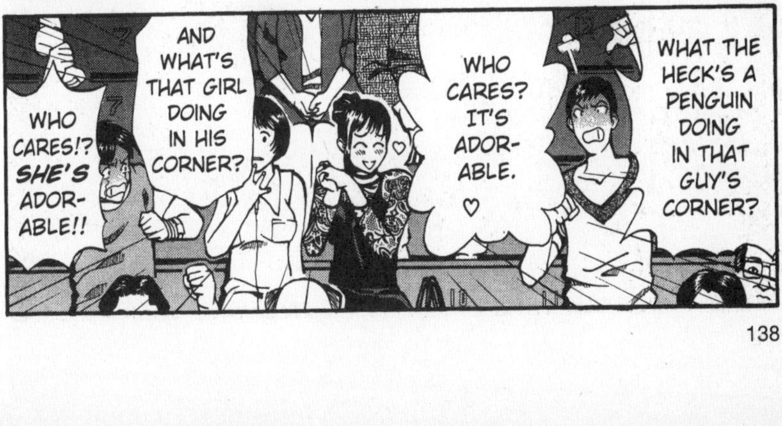
WHAT THE HECK'S A PENGUIN DOING IN THAT GUY'S CORNER?
WHO CARES? IT'S ADORABLE.
AND WHAT'S THAT GIRL DOING IN HIS CORNER?
WHO CARES!? *SHE'S* ADORABLE!!

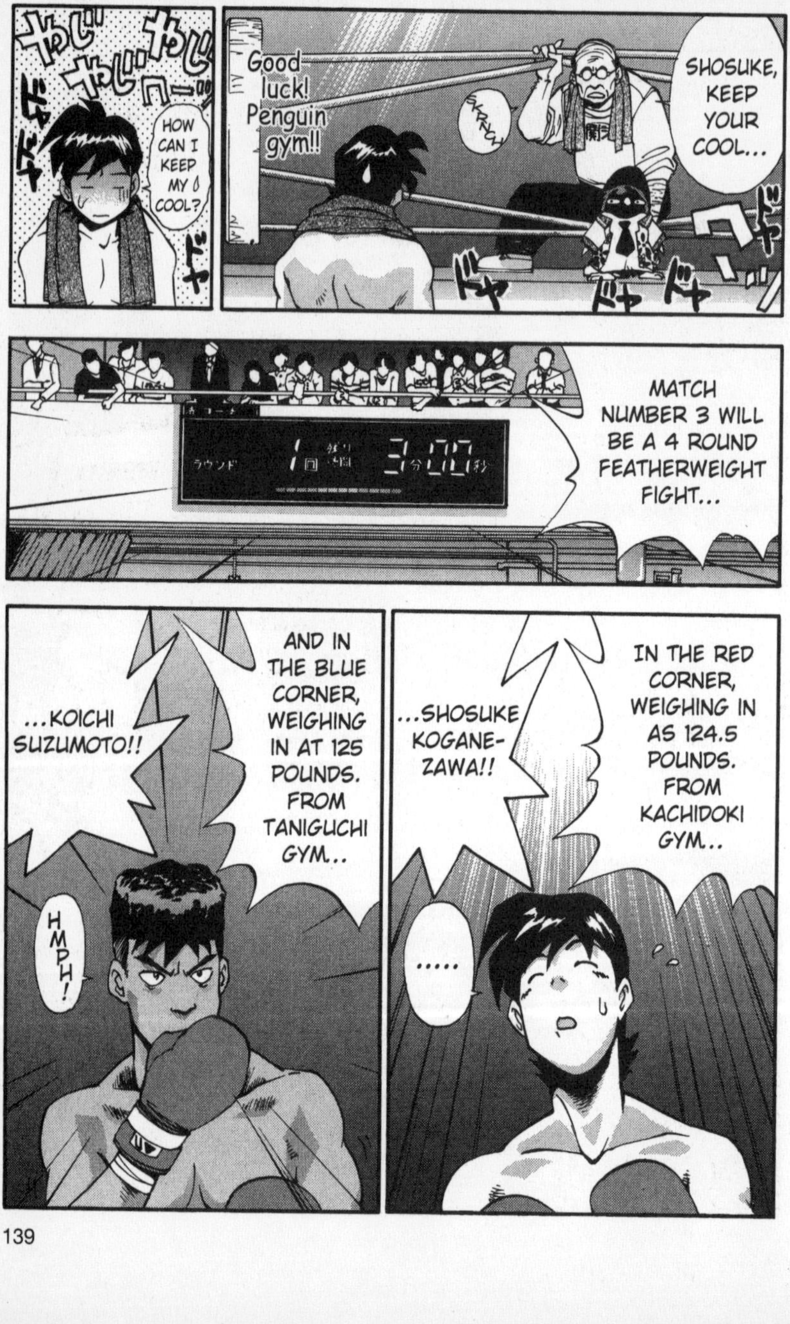
SHOSUKE, KEEP YOUR COOL...
SKRNCH
Good luck! Penguin gym!!
HOW CAN I KEEP MY COOL?
MATCH NUMBER 3 WILL BE A 4 ROUND FEATHERWEIGHT FIGHT...
IN THE RED CORNER, WEIGHING IN AS 124.5 POUNDS. FROM KACHIDOKI GYM...
...SHOSUKE KOGANE-ZAWA!!
.....
AND IN THE BLUE CORNER, WEIGHING IN AT 125 POUNDS. FROM TANIGUCHI GYM...
...KOICHI SUZUMOTO!!
HMPH!

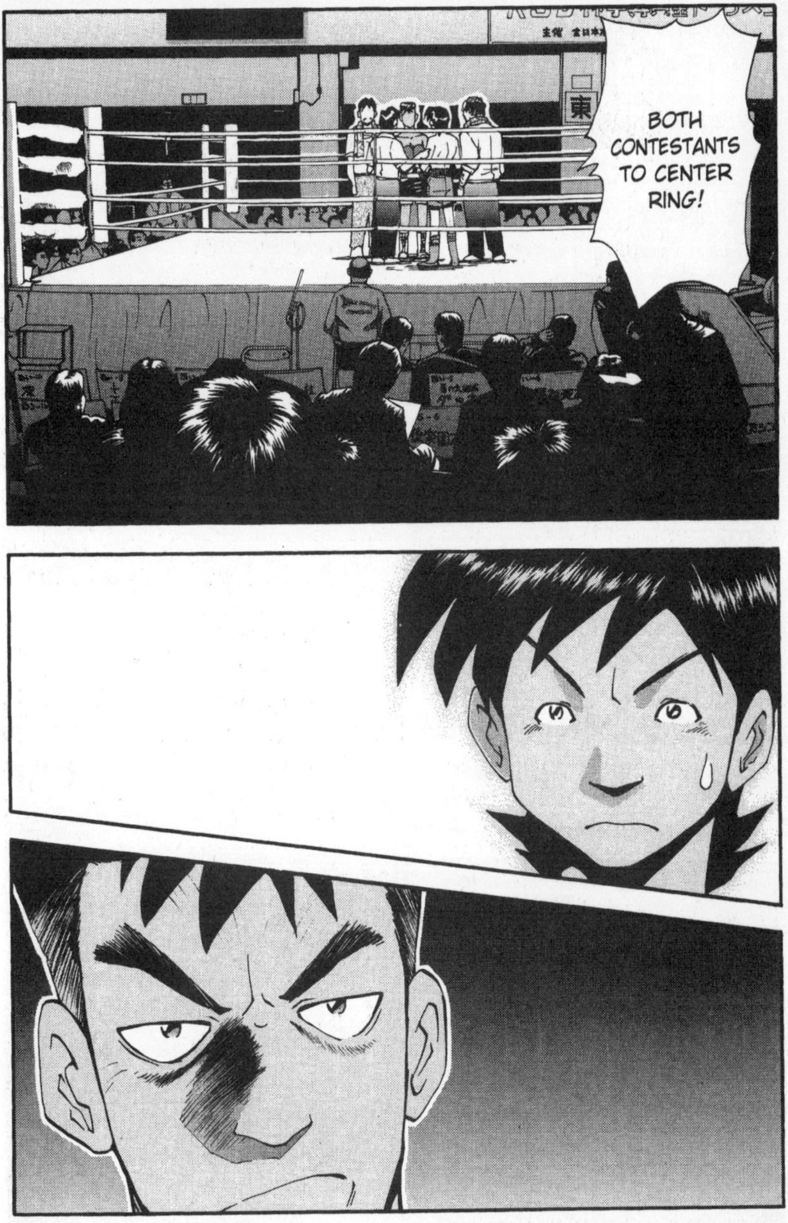
BOTH CONTESTANTS TO CENTER RING!

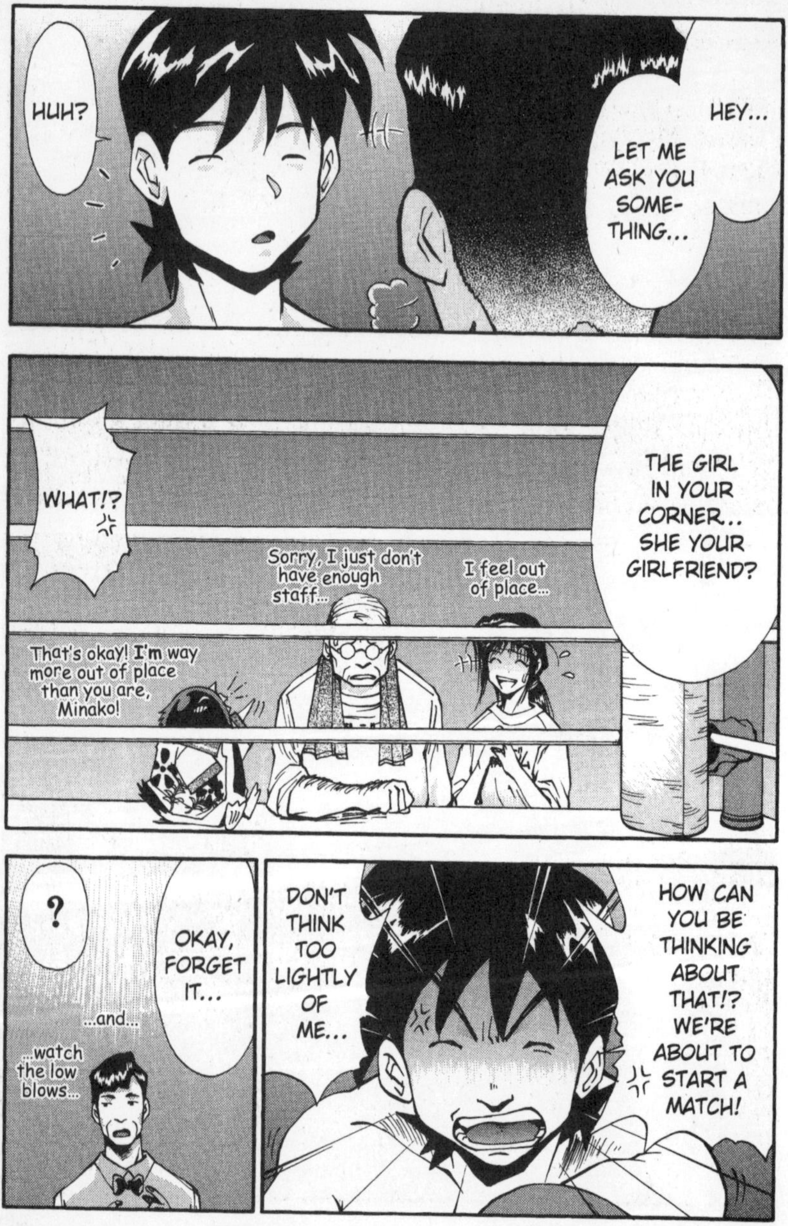
HEY... LET ME ASK YOU SOME-THING...
HUH?
THE GIRL IN YOUR CORNER.. SHE YOUR GIRLFRIEND?
WHAT!?
I feel out of place...
Sorry, I just don't have enough staff...
That's okay! I'm way more out of place than you are, Minako!
HOW CAN YOU BE THINKING ABOUT THAT!? WE'RE ABOUT TO START A MATCH!
DON'T THINK TOO LIGHTLY OF ME...
OKAY, FORGET IT...
?
...and...
...watch the low blows...

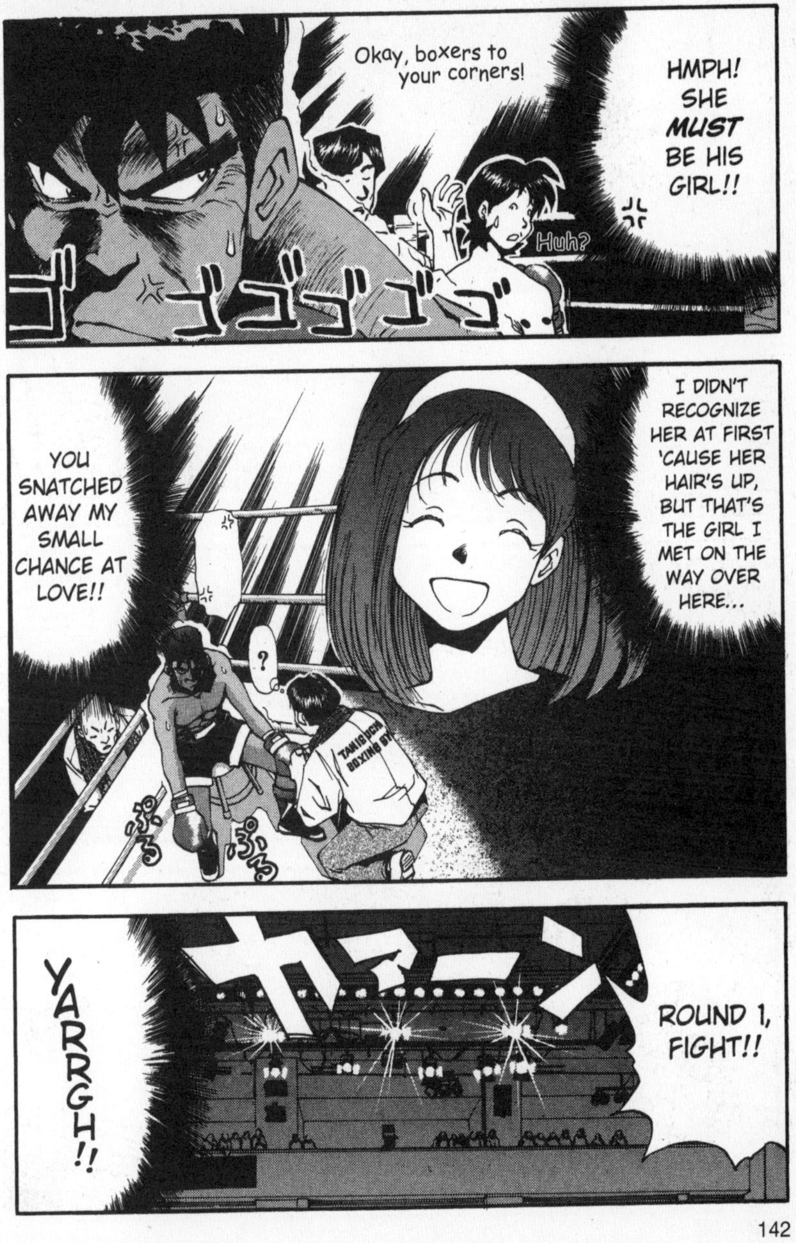
HMPH! SHE *MUST* BE HIS GIRL!!
Okay, boxers to your corners!
Huh?
I DIDN'T RECOGNIZE HER AT FIRST 'CAUSE HER HAIR'S UP, BUT THAT'S THE GIRL I MET ON THE WAY OVER HERE...
YOU SNATCHED AWAY MY SMALL CHANCE AT LOVE!!
?
ROUND 1, FIGHT!!
YARRGH!!

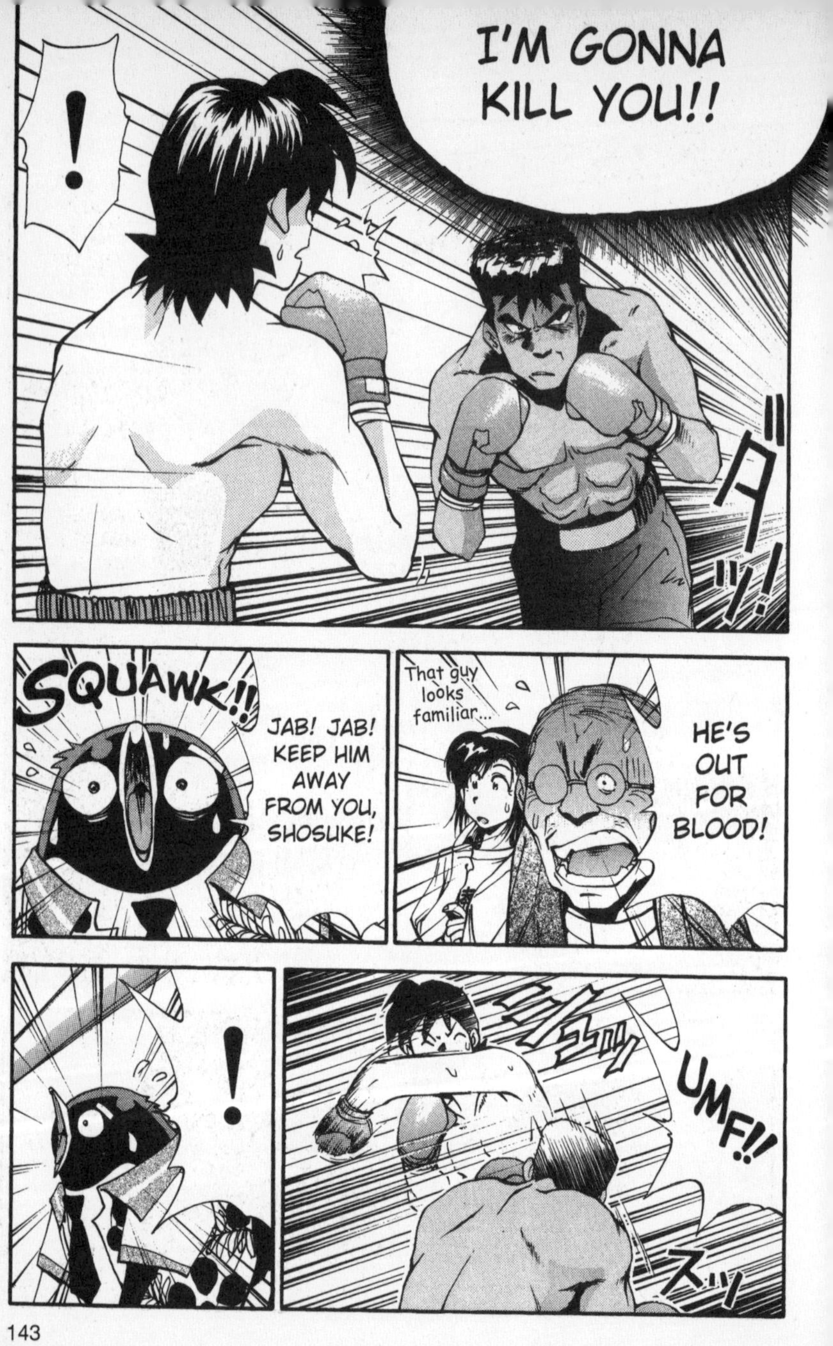
I'M GONNA KILL YOU!!
!
ダッ!!
HE'S OUT FOR BLOOD!
That guy looks familiar...
SQUAWK!!
JAB! JAB! KEEP HIM AWAY FROM YOU, SHOSUKE!
UMF!!
ズッ
!

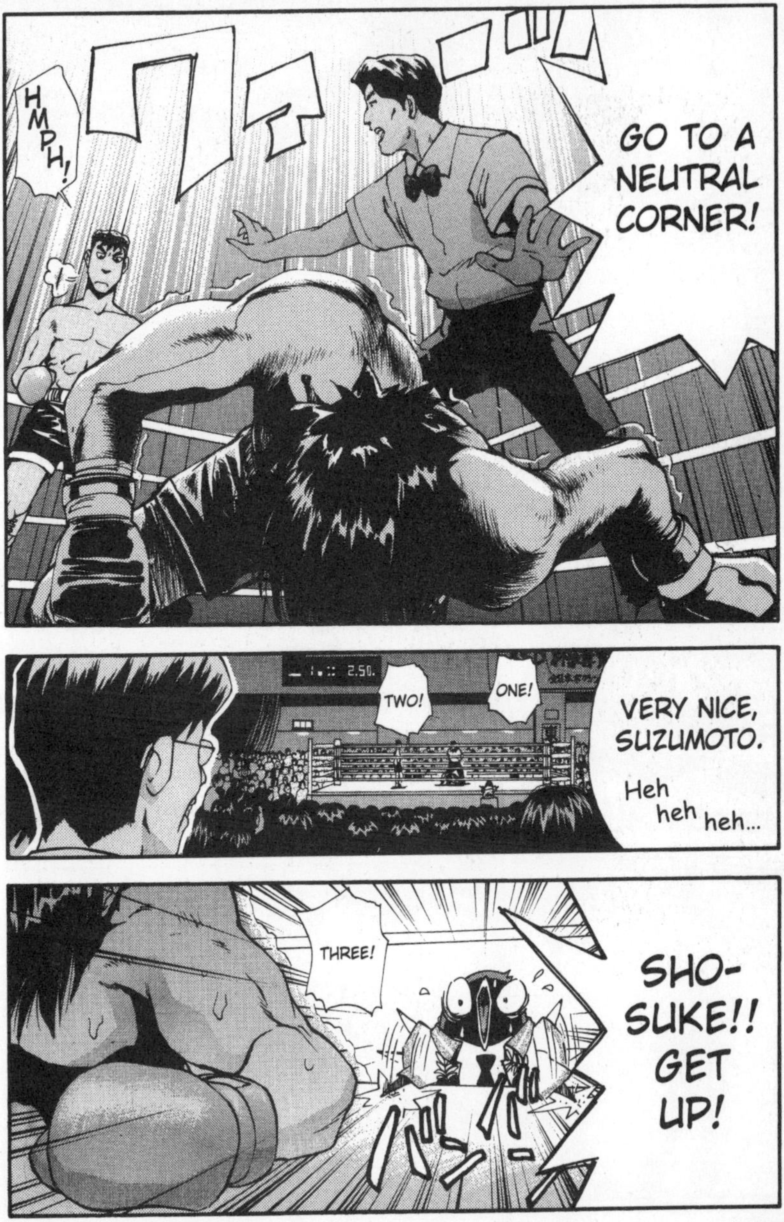
GO TO A NEUTRAL CORNER!
HMPH!
VERY NICE, SUZUMOTO.
Heh heh heh...
ONE!
TWO!
SHO-SUKE!! GET UP!
THREE!

CHAPTER 8
SPECIAL PUNCH!!

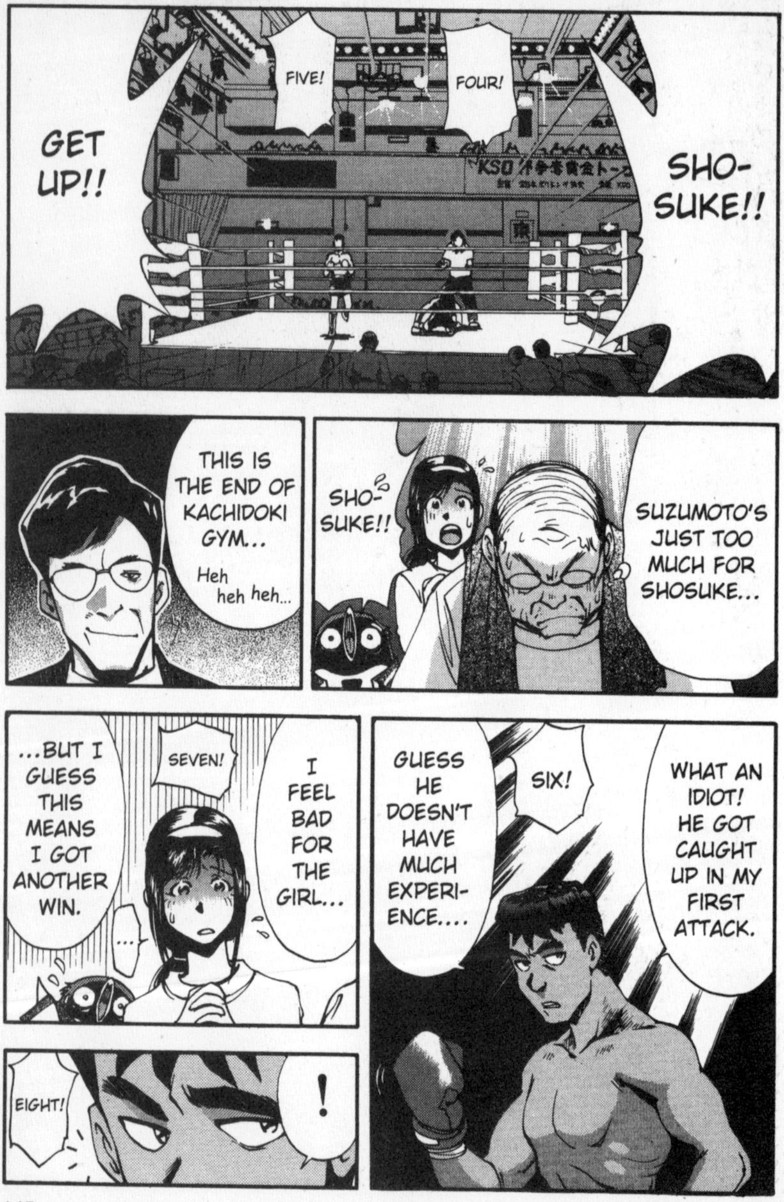

SHO-SUKE!!
FOUR!
FIVE!
GET UP!!
SUZUMOTO'S JUST TOO MUCH FOR SHOSUKE...
SHO-SUKE!!
THIS IS THE END OF KACHIDOKI GYM...
Heh heh heh...
WHAT AN IDIOT! HE GOT CAUGHT UP IN MY FIRST ATTACK.
SIX!
GUESS HE DOESN'T HAVE MUCH EXPERI-ENCE....
I FEEL BAD FOR THE GIRL...
SEVEN!
...BUT I GUESS THIS MEANS I GOT ANOTHER WIN.
...
!
EIGHT!

CHAPTER 8
SPECIAL PUNCH!

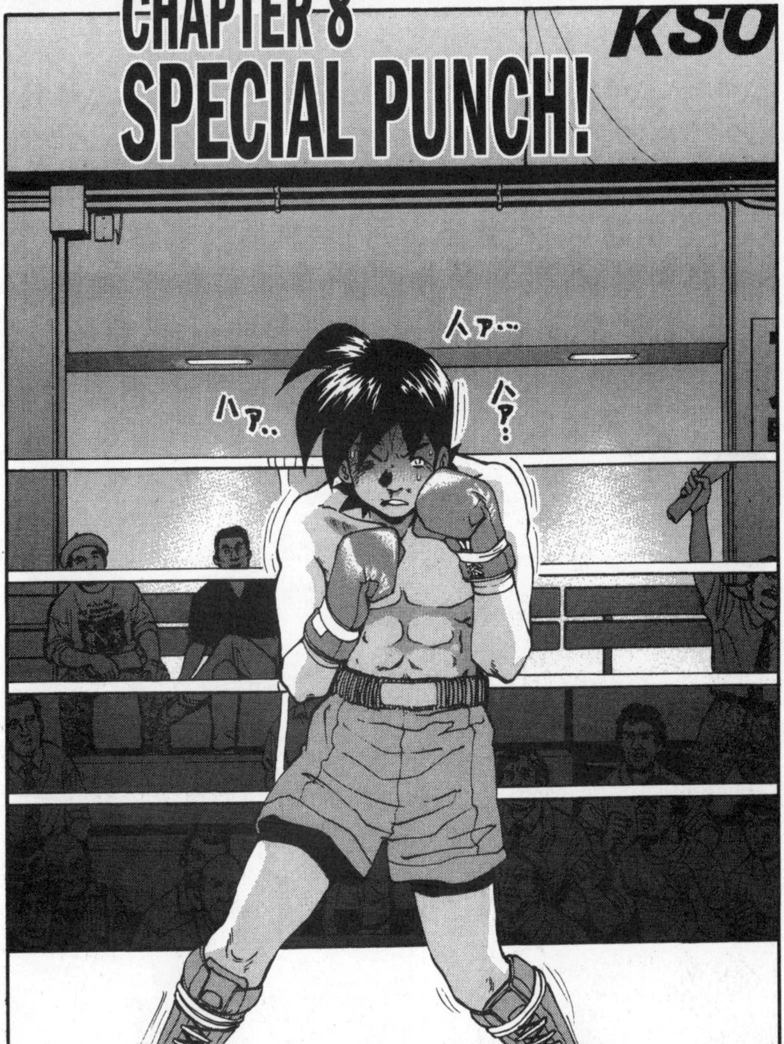

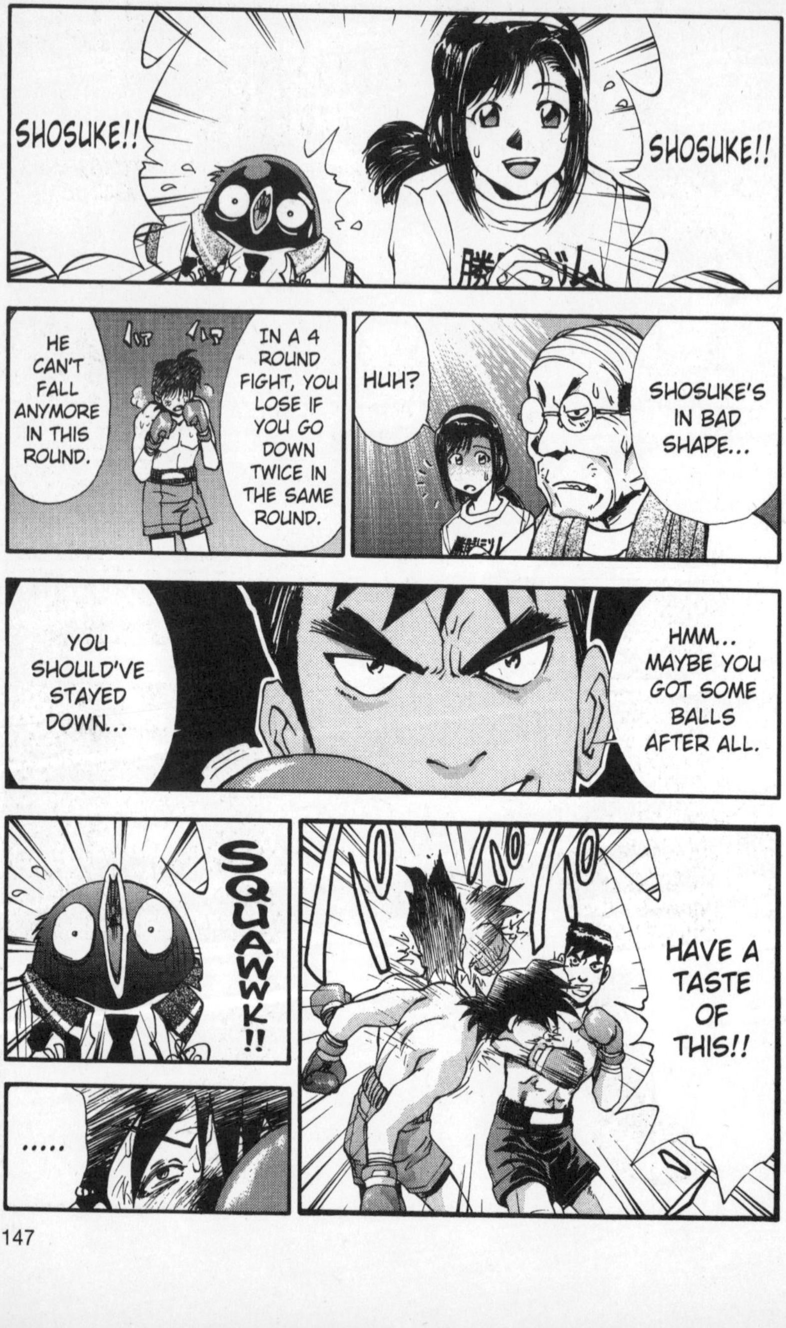
SHOSUKE!!
SHOSUKE!!
SHOSUKE'S IN BAD SHAPE...
HUH?
IN A 4 ROUND FIGHT, YOU LOSE IF YOU GO DOWN TWICE IN THE SAME ROUND.
HE CAN'T FALL ANYMORE IN THIS ROUND.
HMM... MAYBE YOU GOT SOME BALLS AFTER ALL.
YOU SHOULD'VE STAYED DOWN...
HAVE A TASTE OF THIS!!
SQUAWWK!!
.....

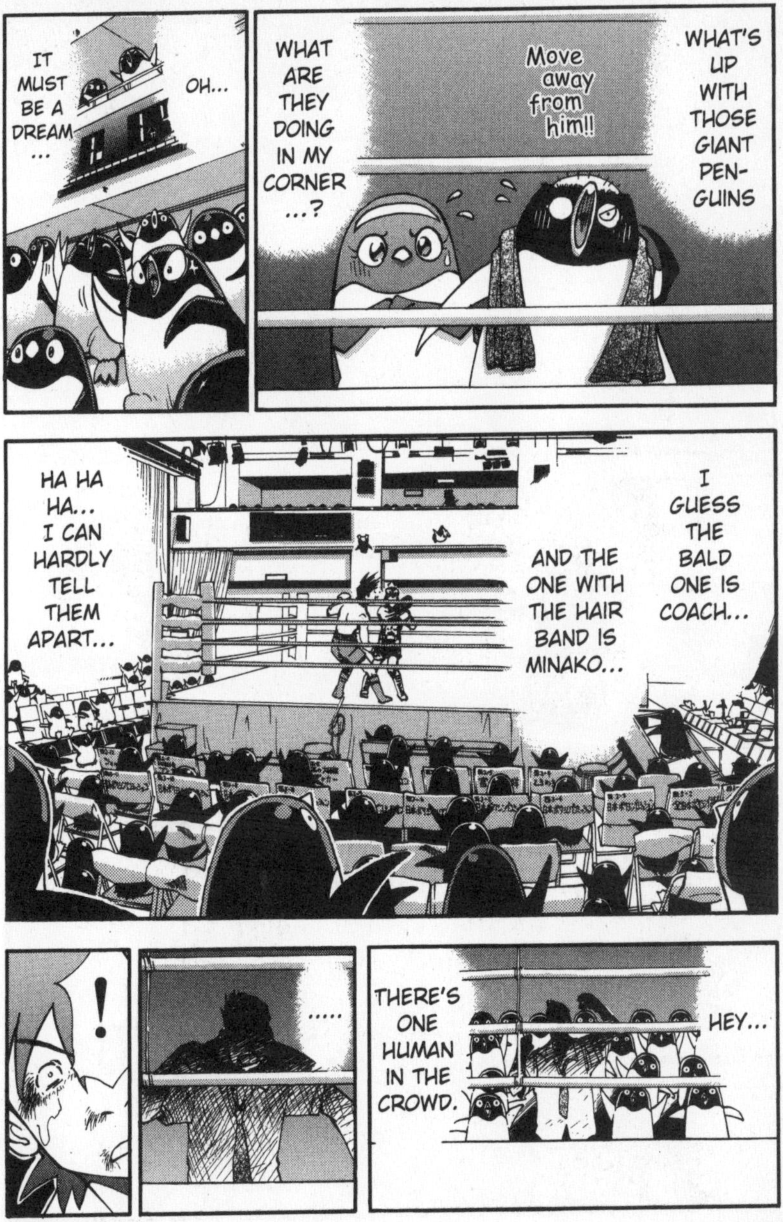
WHAT'S UP WITH THOSE GIANT PEN-GUINS
Move away from him!!
WHAT ARE THEY DOING IN MY CORNER ...?
OH...
IT MUST BE A DREAM ...
I GUESS THE BALD ONE IS COACH...
AND THE ONE WITH THE HAIR BAND IS MINAKO...
HA HA HA... I CAN HARDLY TELL THEM APART...
HEY...
THERE'S ONE HUMAN IN THE CROWD.
.....
!

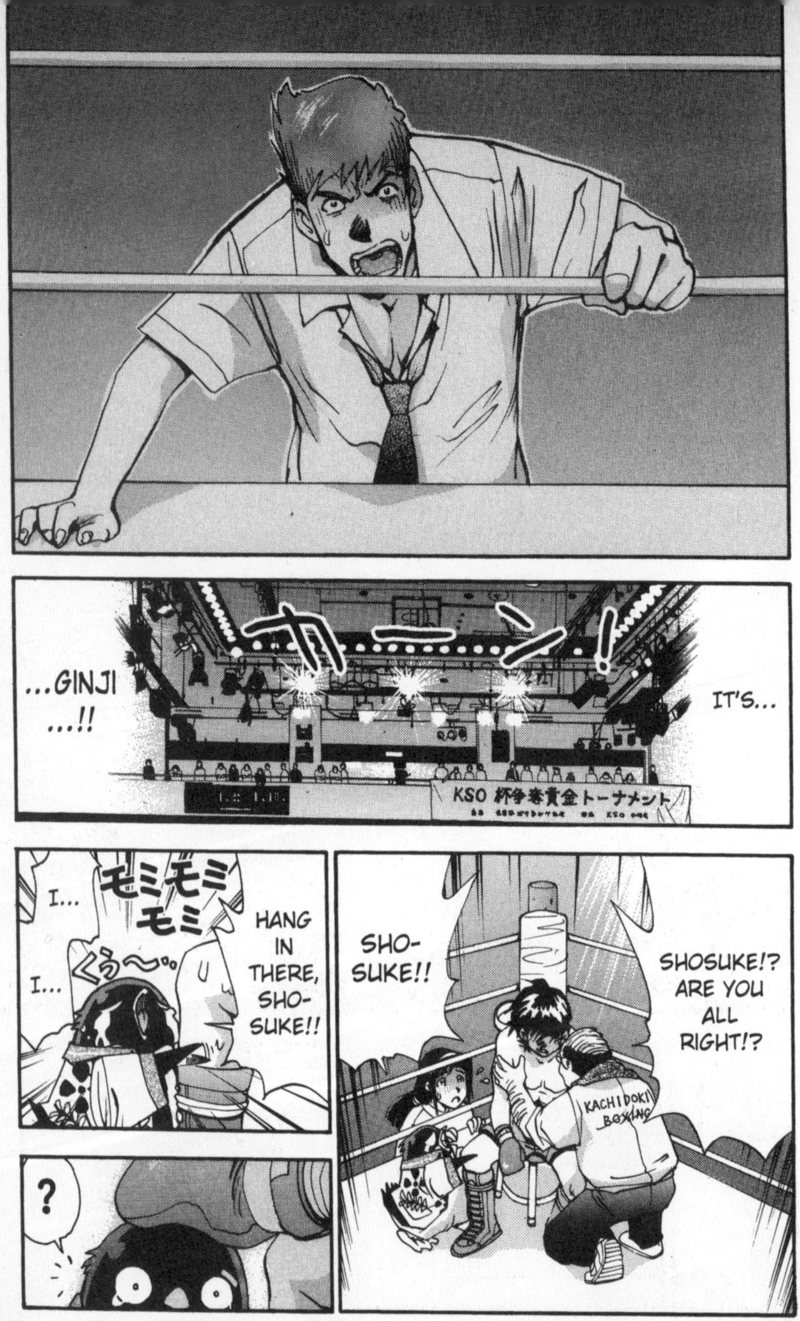
IT'S...
カーン!
...GINJI ...!!
KSO 杯争奪賞金トーナメント
SHOSUKE!? ARE YOU ALL RIGHT!?
SHO-SUKE!!
KACHIDOKI BOXING
HANG IN THERE, SHO-SUKE!!
モミモミモミ
I...
くぅ〜
I...
?

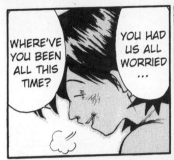

SHO-SUKE?
YOU HAD US ALL WORRIED ...
WHERE'VE YOU BEEN ALL THIS TIME?
GINJI...
HUH?
I'M SORRY, GINJI...
I'M NOT GOOD ENOUGH ...
I DON'T THINK I CAN SAVE THE GYM. YOU WON'T HAVE A PLACE TO COME BACK TO...
SHO-SUKE!
HE'S PUNCH DRUNK...
IT'S OKAY! YOU STILL HAVE A CHANCE!!
AND, YOU PROMISED ME YOU WOULD BEAT THIS GUY!!

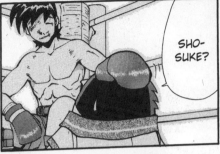

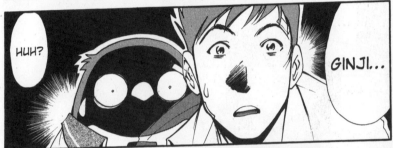

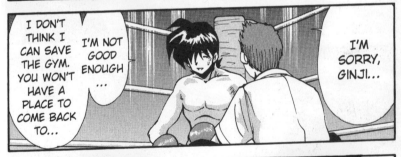

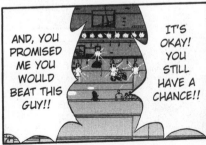

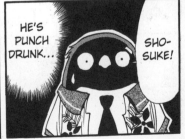

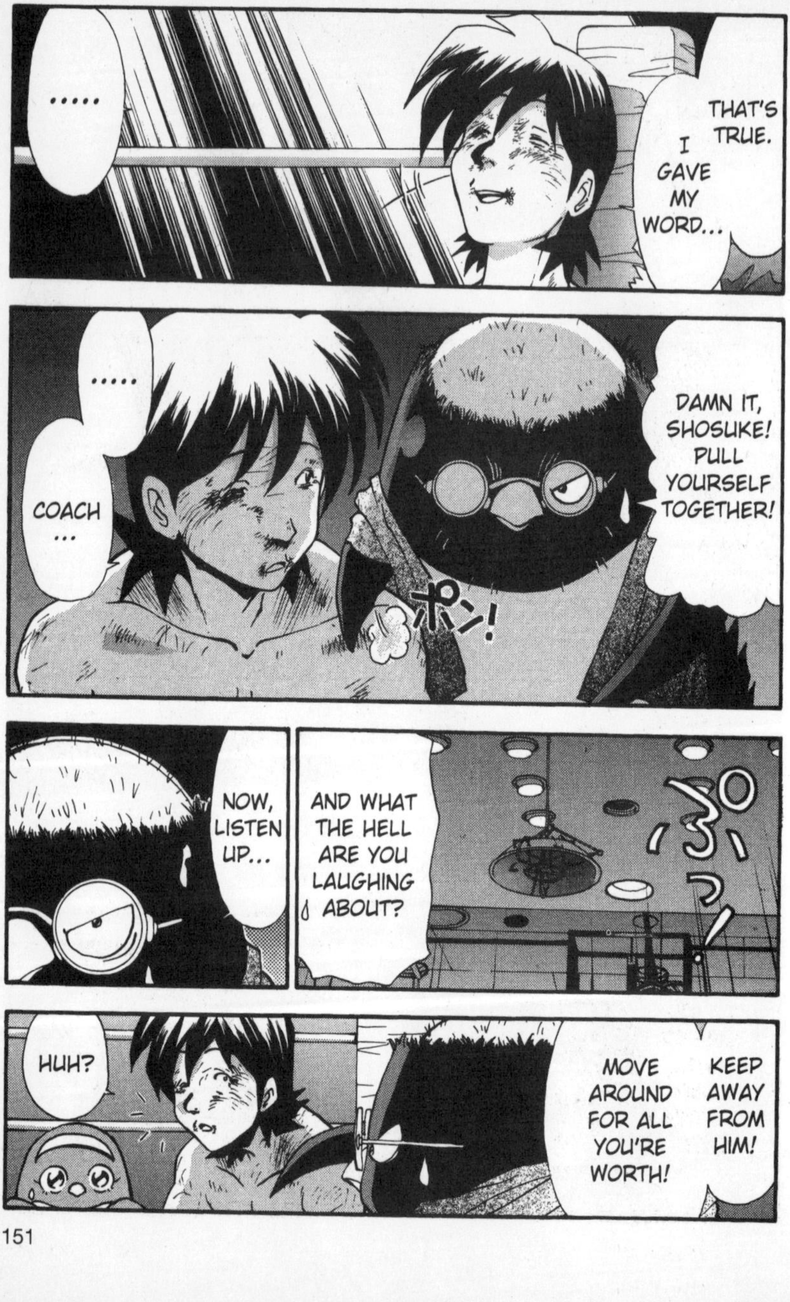
THAT'S TRUE. I GAVE MY WORD...
.....
DAMN IT, SHOSUKE! PULL YOURSELF TOGETHER!
ポン!
.....
COACH ...
ふっ!
AND WHAT THE HELL ARE YOU LAUGHING ABOUT?
NOW, LISTEN UP...
KEEP AWAY FROM HIM!
MOVE AROUND FOR ALL YOU'RE WORTH!
HUH?

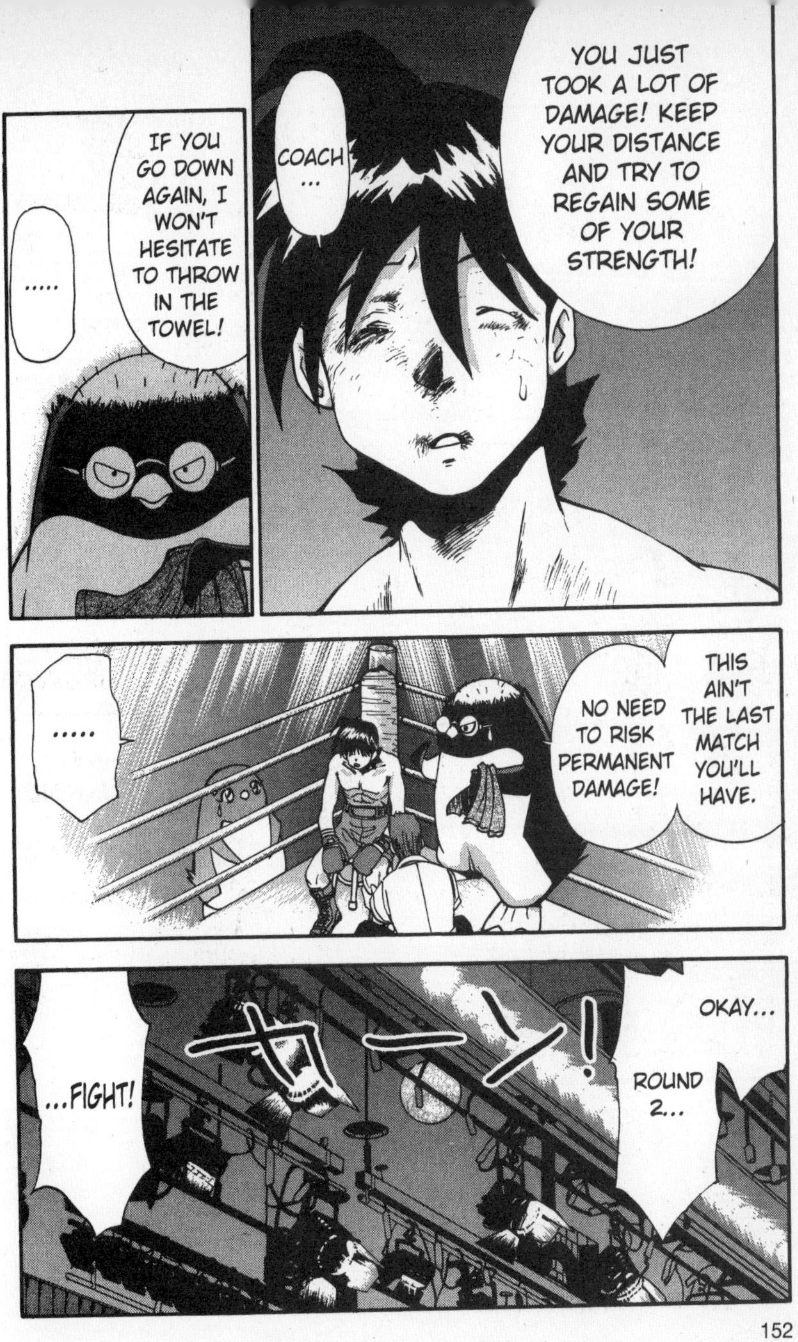
YOU JUST TOOK A LOT OF DAMAGE! KEEP YOUR DISTANCE AND TRY TO REGAIN SOME OF YOUR STRENGTH!
COACH ...
IF YOU GO DOWN AGAIN, I WON'T HESITATE TO THROW IN THE TOWEL!
.....
THIS AIN'T THE LAST MATCH YOU'LL HAVE.
NO NEED TO RISK PERMANENT DAMAGE!
.....
OKAY...
ROUND 2...
カーン!
...FIGHT!

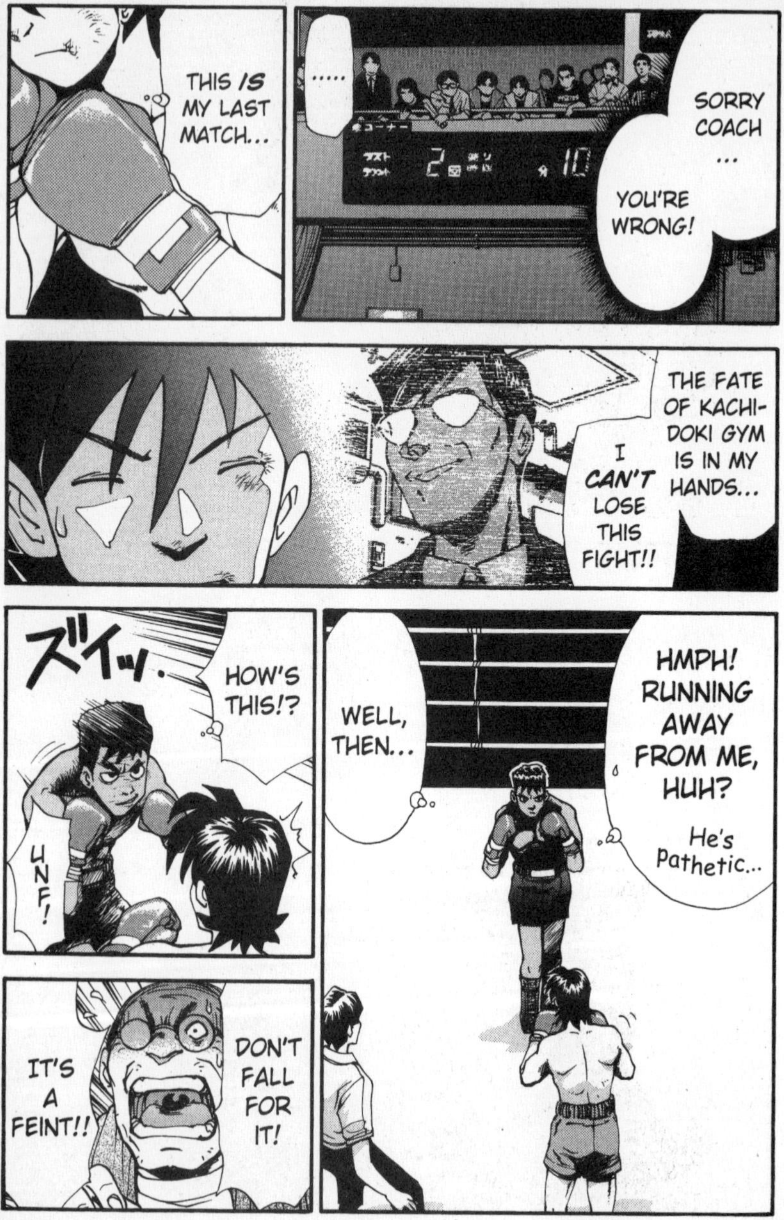

SORRY COACH ...
YOU'RE WRONG!
.....
THIS *IS* MY LAST MATCH...
THE FATE OF KACHI-DOKI GYM IS IN MY HANDS...
I *CAN'T* LOSE THIS FIGHT!!
HMPH! RUNNING AWAY FROM ME, HUH?
He's Pathetic...
WELL, THEN...
ズイッ
HOW'S THIS!?
UNF!
DON'T FALL FOR IT!
IT'S A FEINT!!

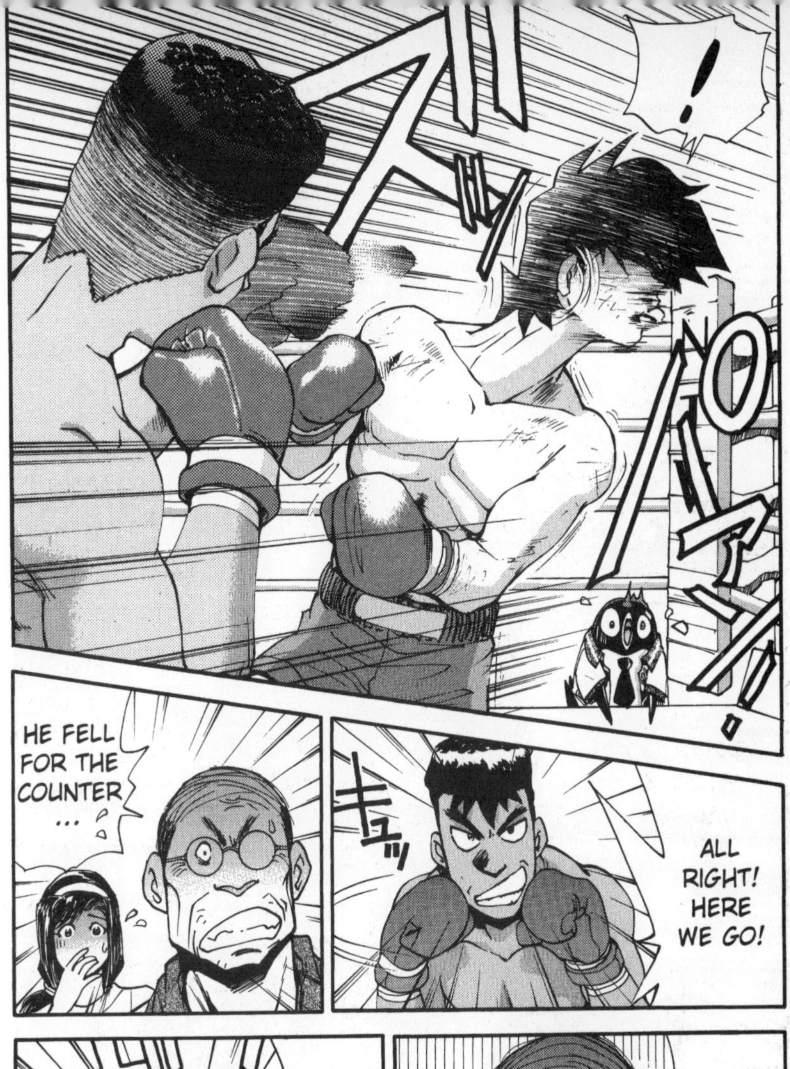
!
ALL RIGHT! HERE WE GO!
HE FELL FOR THE COUNTER ...
THAT'S IT...
!?

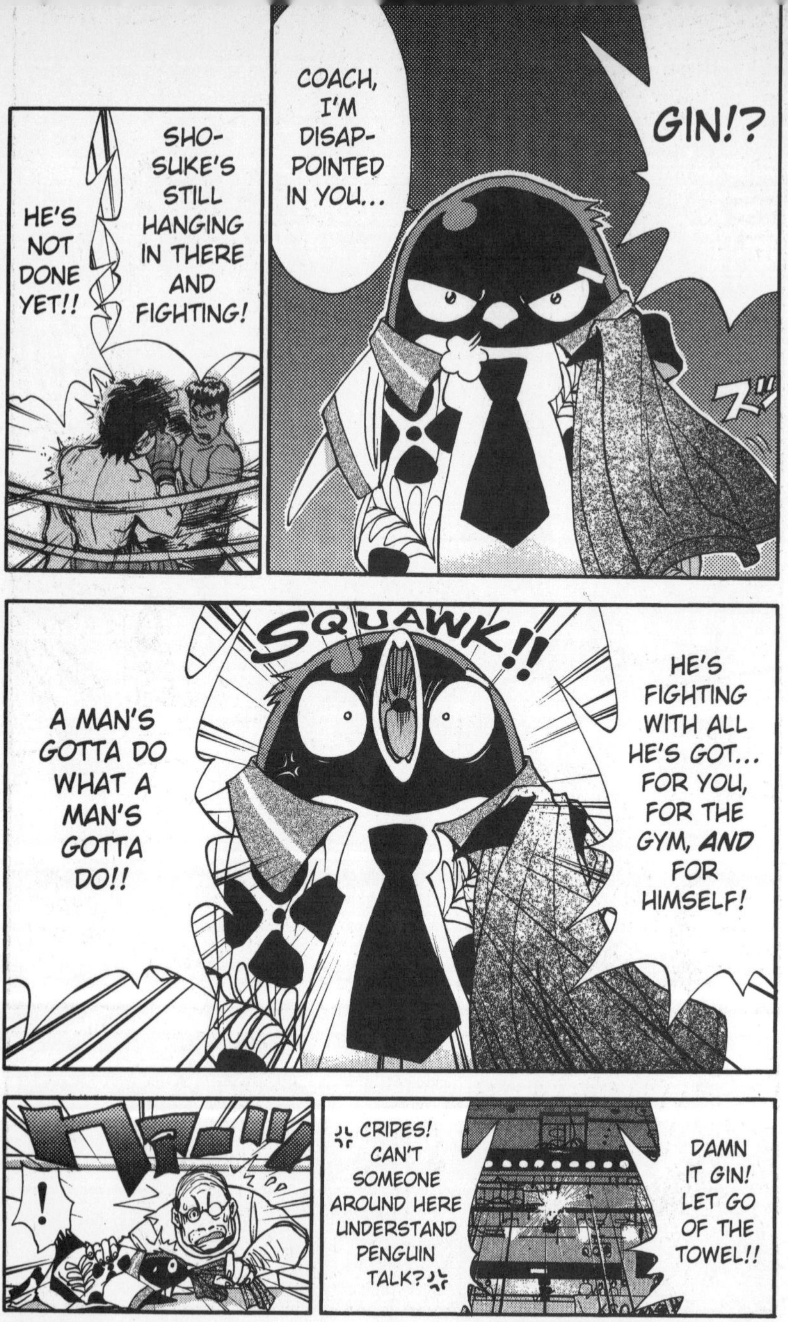
GIN!?
COACH, I'M DISAP-POINTED IN YOU...
SHO-SUKE'S STILL HANGING IN THERE AND FIGHTING!
HE'S NOT DONE YET!!
SQUAWK!!
HE'S FIGHTING WITH ALL HE'S GOT... FOR YOU, FOR THE GYM, AND FOR HIMSELF!
A MAN'S GOTTA DO WHAT A MAN'S GOTTA DO!!
DAMN IT GIN! LET GO OF THE TOWEL!!
CRIPES! CAN'T SOMEONE AROUND HERE UNDERSTAND PENGUIN TALK?
!

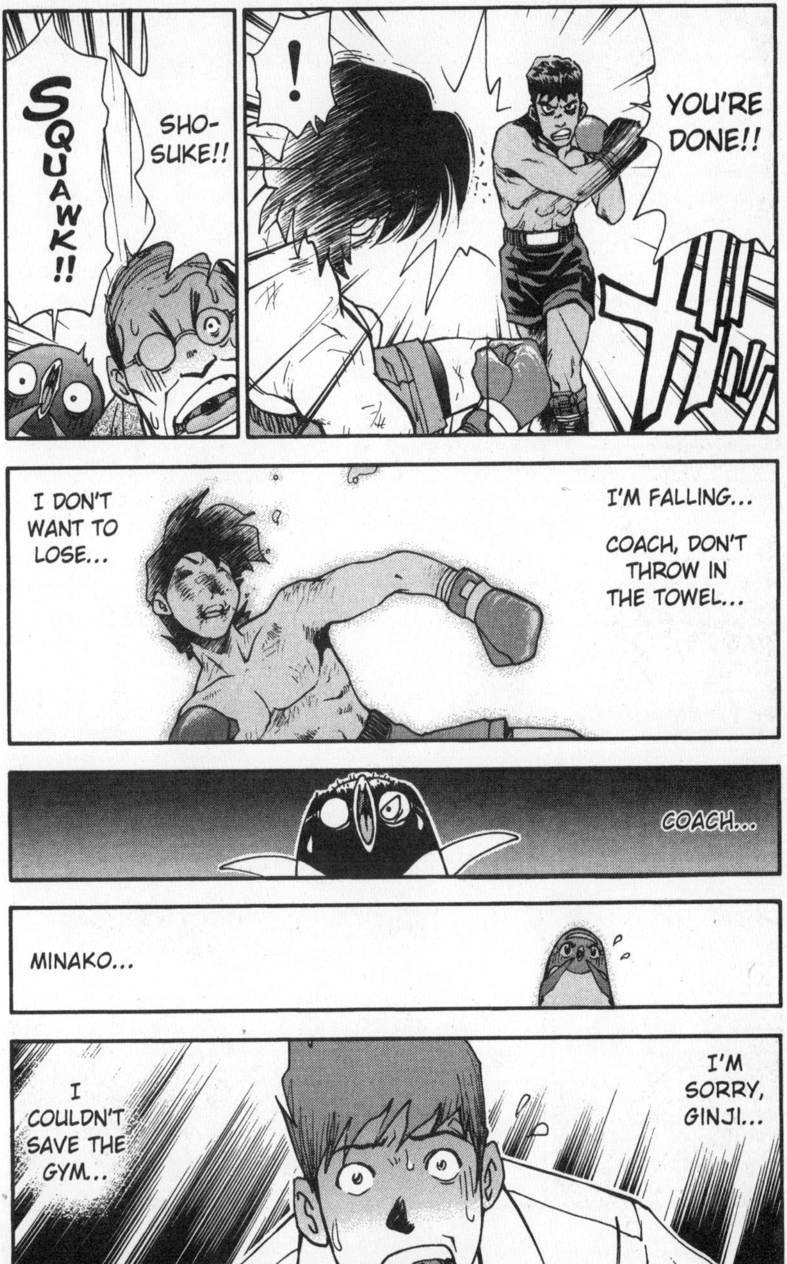
!
YOU'RE DONE!!
SHO-SUKE!!
SQUAWK!!
I'M FALLING...
COACH, DON'T THROW IN THE TOWEL...
I DON'T WANT TO LOSE...
COACH...
MINAKO...
I'M SORRY, GINJI...
I COULDN'T SAVE THE GYM...

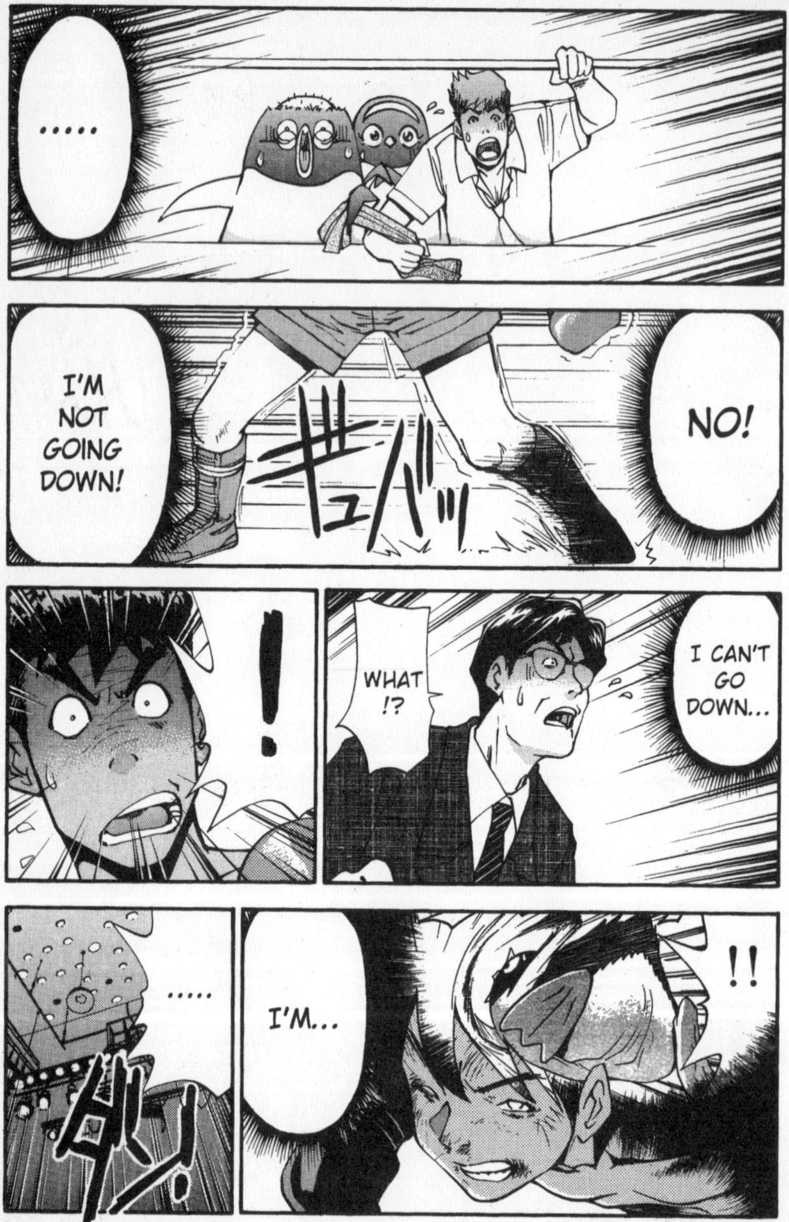
.....
NO!
ギュバッ
I'M NOT GOING DOWN!
I CAN'T GO DOWN...
WHAT !?
!
!!
I'M...
.....
ダッ

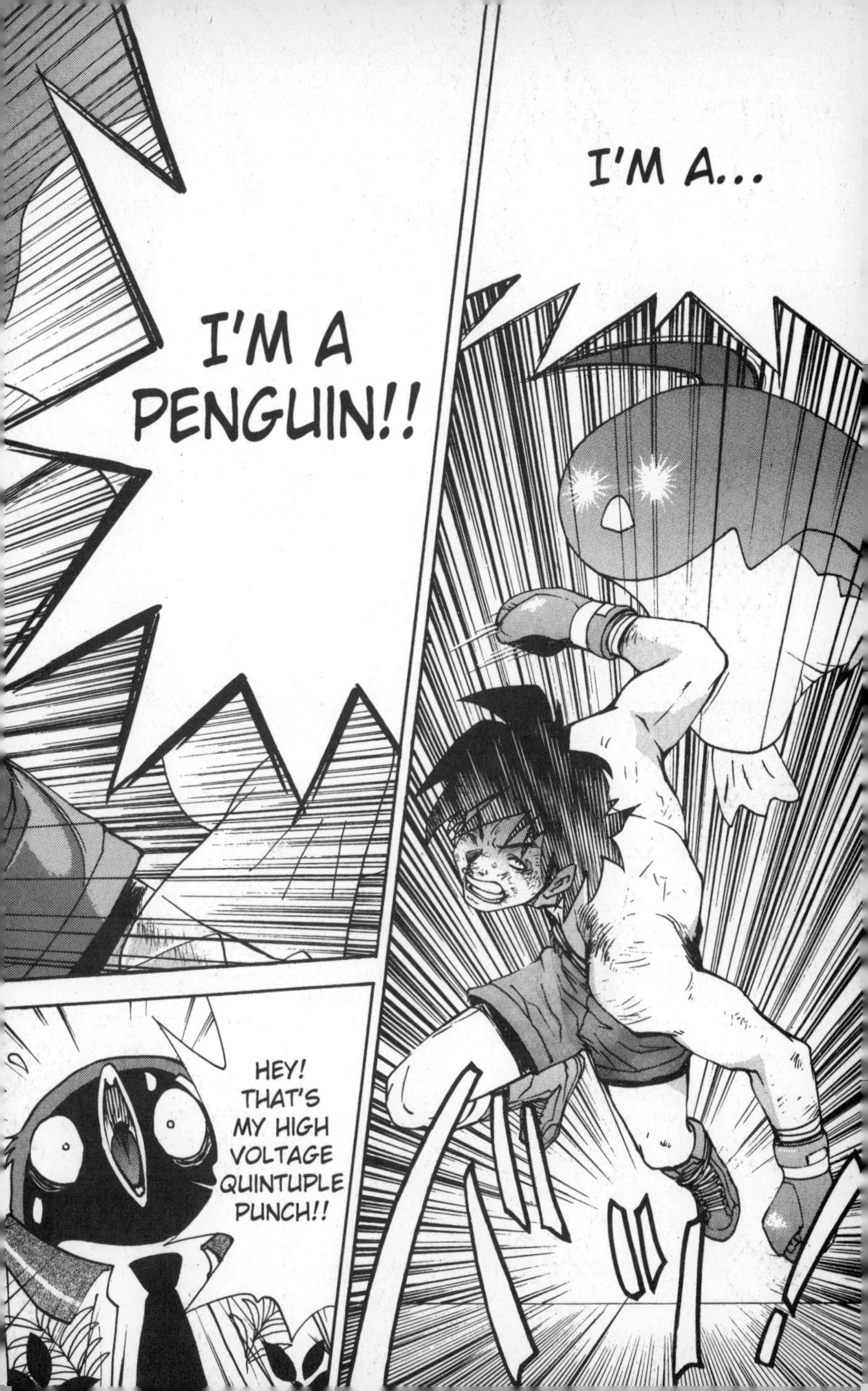
I'M A...
I'M A PENGUIN!!
HEY! THAT'S MY HIGH VOLTAGE QUINTUPLE PUNCH!!

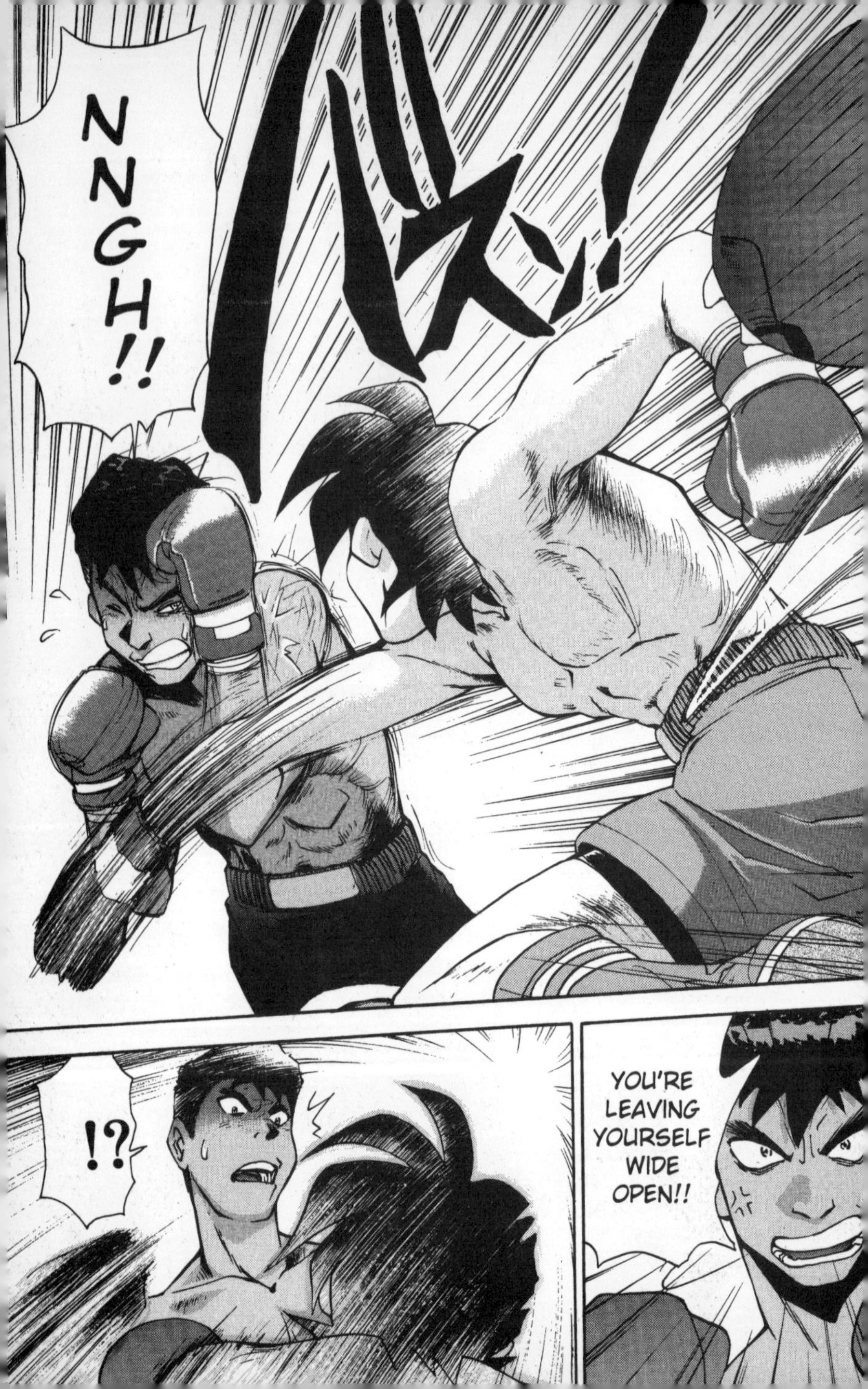
NNGH!!
YOU'RE LEAVING YOURSELF WIDE OPEN!!
!?

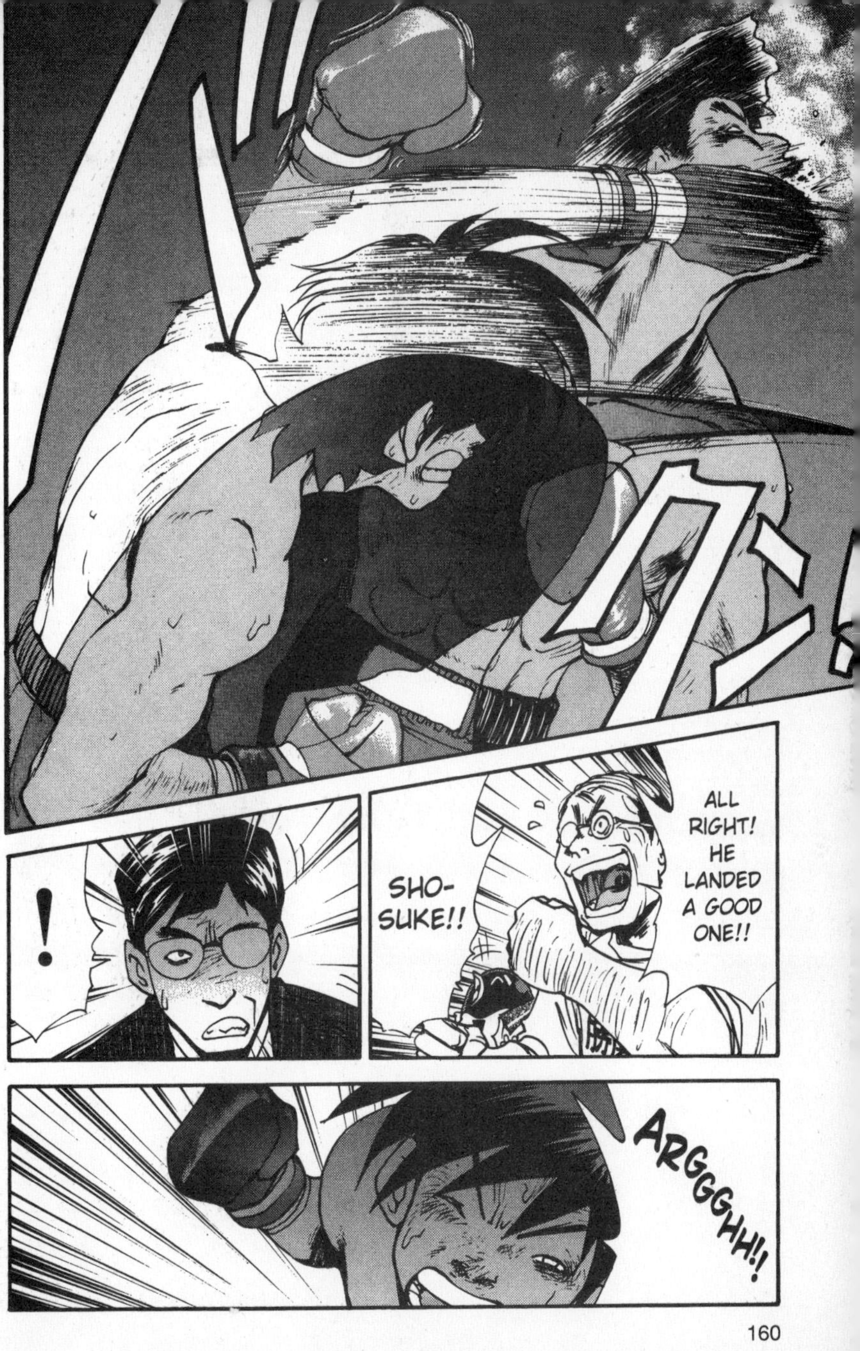
ALL RIGHT! HE LANDED A GOOD ONE!!
SHO-SUKE!!
!
ARGGGHH!!

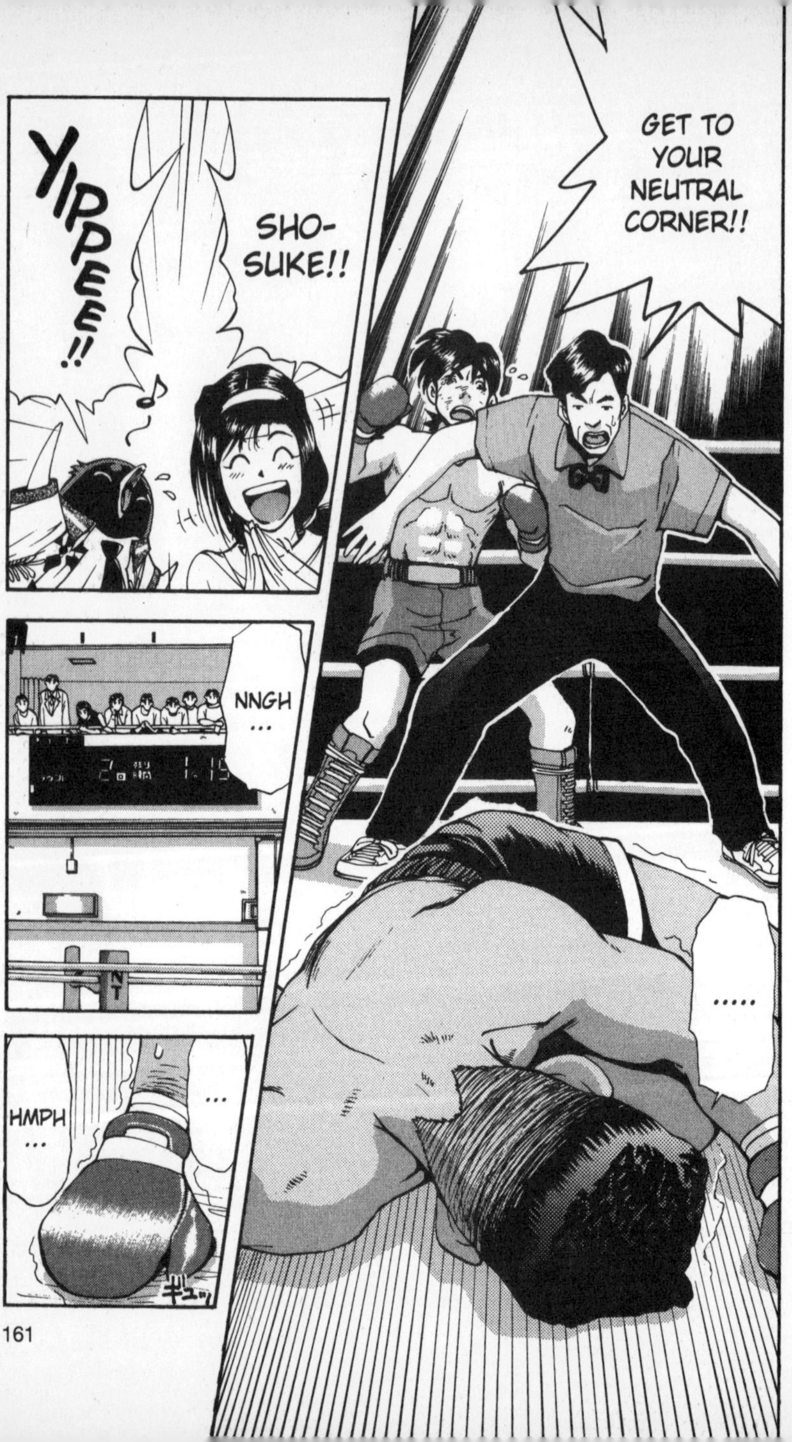
GET TO YOUR NEUTRAL CORNER!!
.....
SHO-SUKE!!
YIPPEE!!
NNGH ...
...
HMPH ...
ギュッ

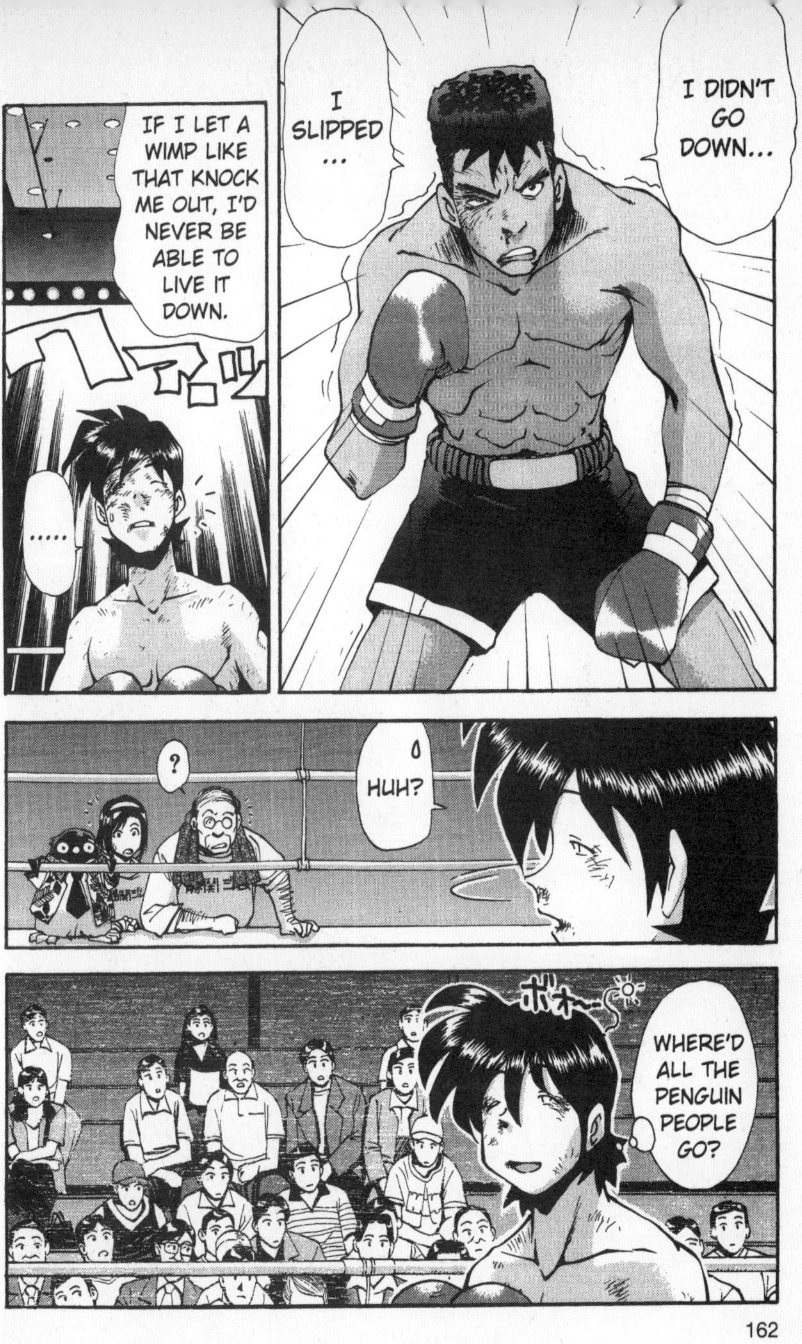
I DIDN'T GO DOWN...
I SLIPPED ...
IF I LET A WIMP LIKE THAT KNOCK ME OUT, I'D NEVER BE ABLE TO LIVE IT DOWN.
.....
HUH?
?
WHERE'D ALL THE PENGUIN PEOPLE GO?

CHAPTER 9
THE KACHIDOKI GYM COMEBACK!

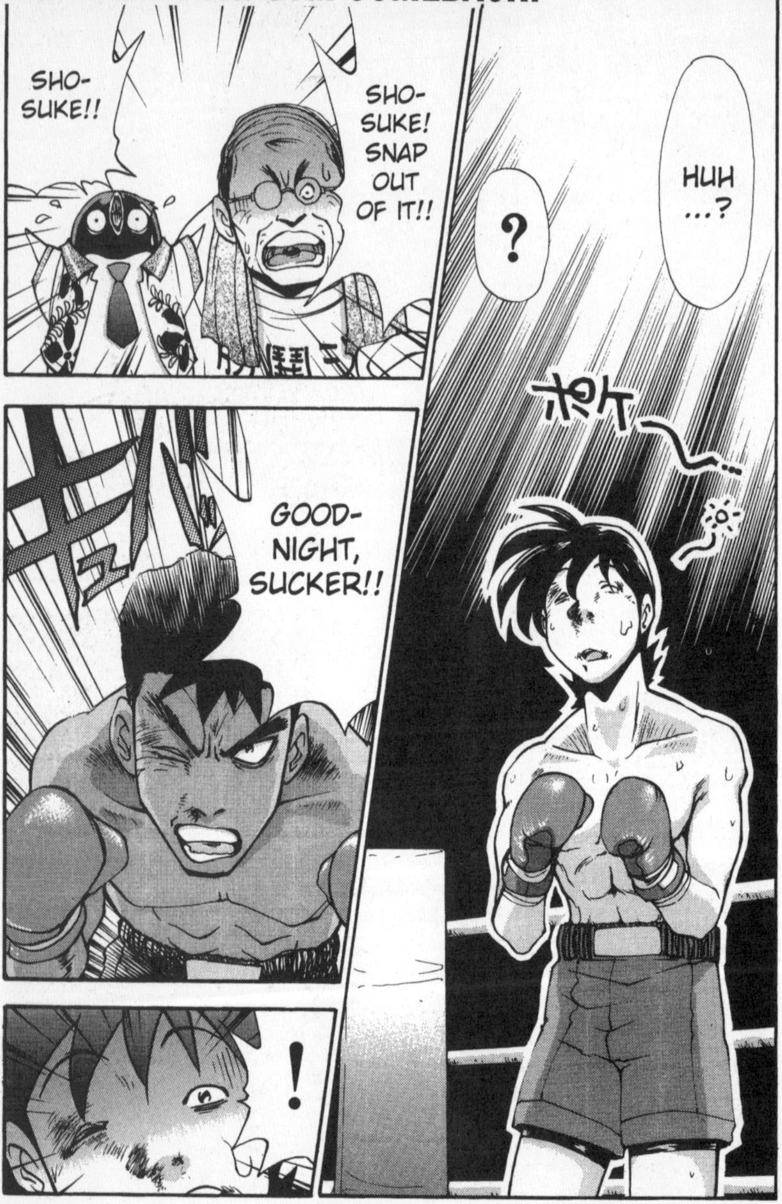
HUH ...?
?
SHO-SUKE! SNAP OUT OF IT!!
SHO-SUKE!!
GOOD-NIGHT, SUCKER!!
!

CHAPTER 9
THE KACHIDOKI GYM COMEBACK!

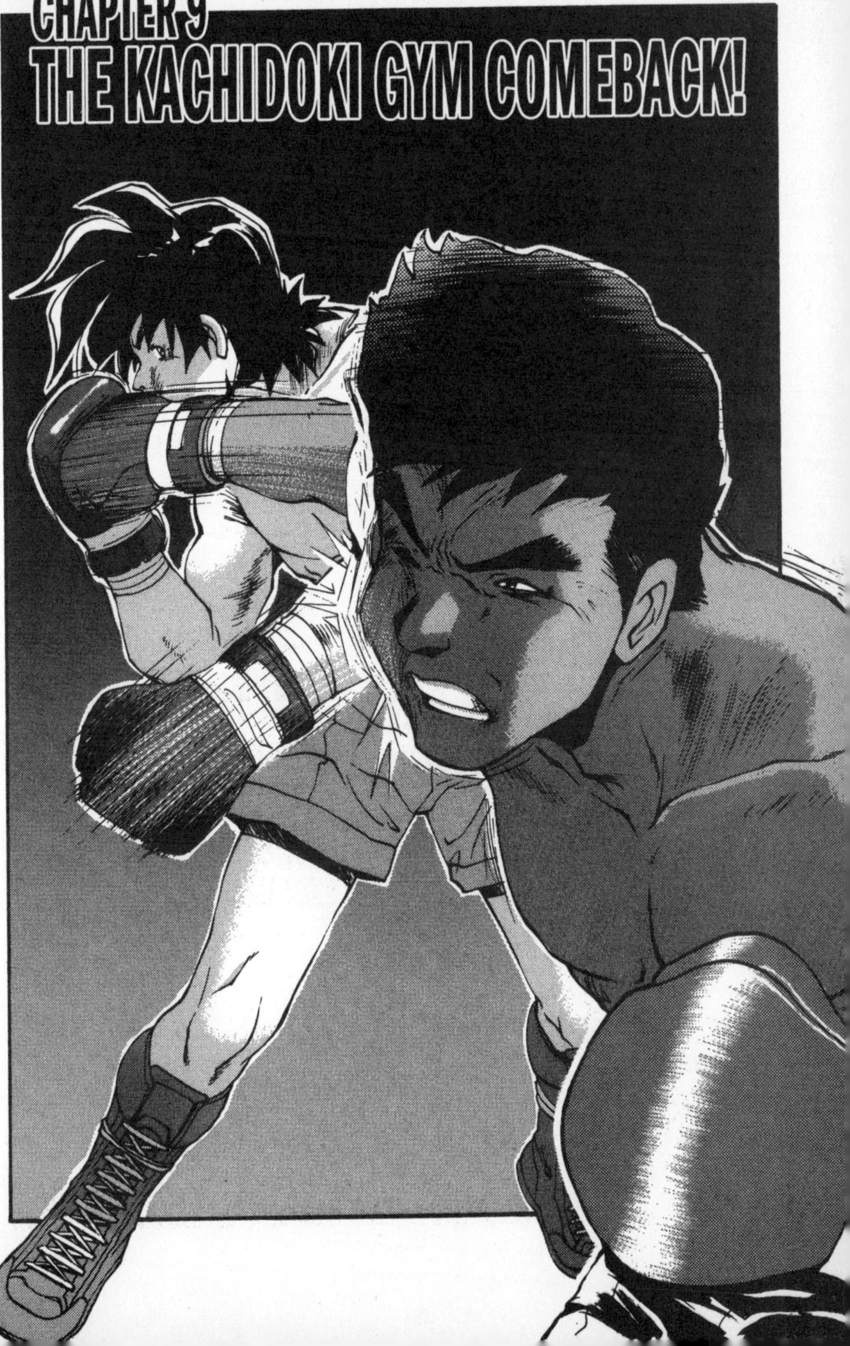

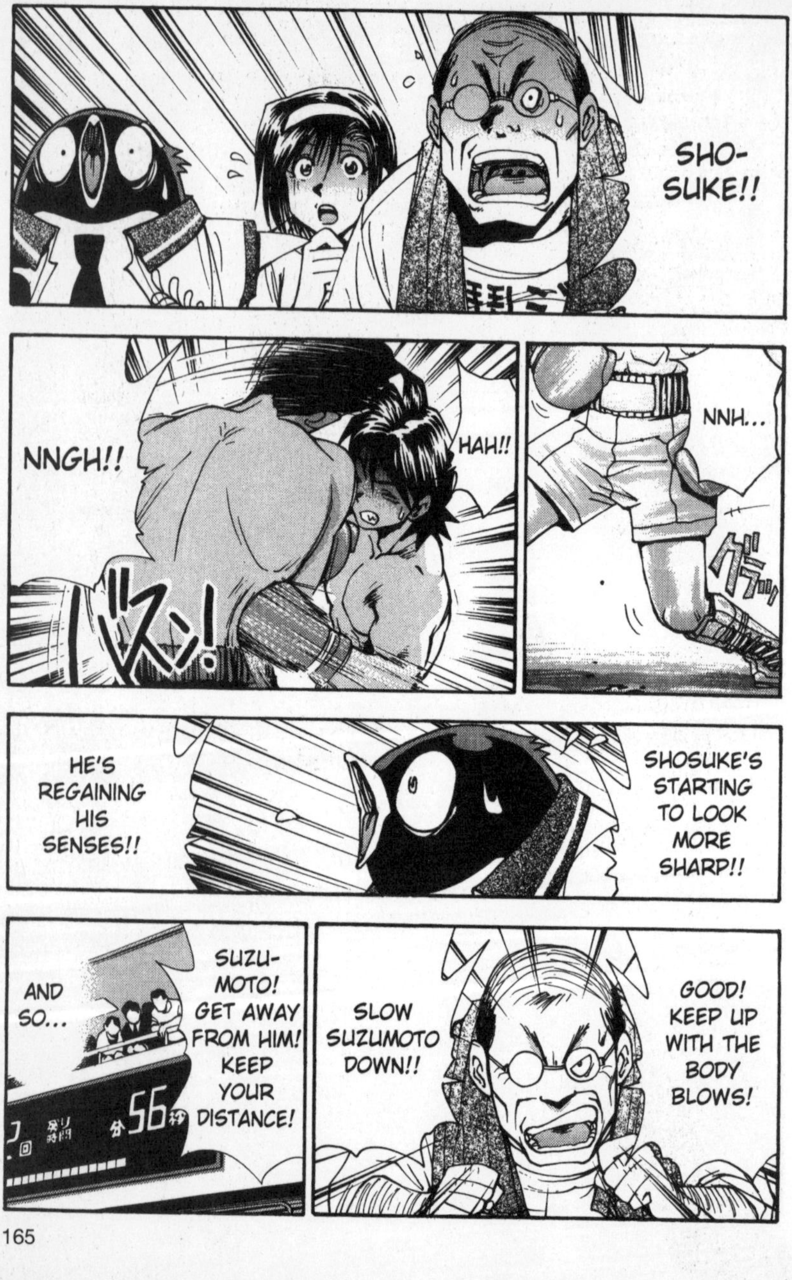
SHO-SUKE!!
NNH...
グラッ
HAH!!
NNGH!!
SHOSUKE'S STARTING TO LOOK MORE SHARP!!
HE'S REGAINING HIS SENSES!!
GOOD! KEEP UP WITH THE BODY BLOWS!
SLOW SUZUMOTO DOWN!!
SUZU-MOTO! GET AWAY FROM HIM! KEEP YOUR DISTANCE!
AND SO...

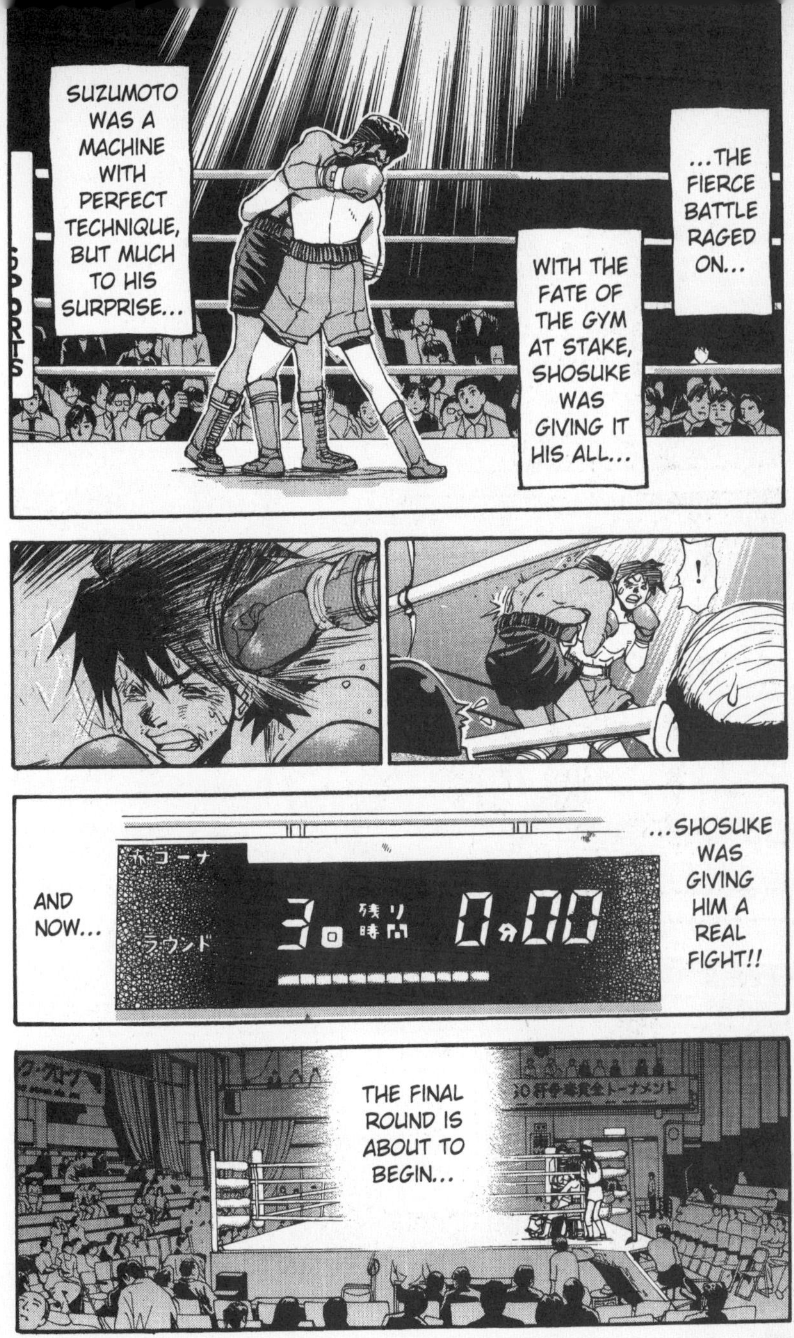
...THE FIERCE BATTLE RAGED ON...
WITH THE FATE OF THE GYM AT STAKE, SHOSUKE WAS GIVING IT HIS ALL...
SUZUMOTO WAS A MACHINE WITH PERFECT TECHNIQUE, BUT MUCH TO HIS SURPRISE...
SPORTS
!
...SHOSUKE WAS GIVING HIM A REAL FIGHT!!
AND NOW...
3回 ラウンド
残り時間 0分00
THE FINAL ROUND IS ABOUT TO BEGIN...

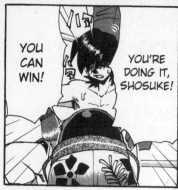

YOU'RE DOING GREAT, SHO-SUKE!!
SHO-SUKE!!
YOU'RE DOING IT, SHOSUKE!
YOU CAN WIN!
KEEP AT HIM, KID
TAKE A LOOK AT SUZU-MOTO OVER THERE!
HUH?
ALL THOSE BODY BLOWS ARE GETTING TO HIM! HE'S EX-HAUSTED!
YOU'RE BEATING HIM WITH YOUR TOUGH-NESS!
BOXING
THIS IS THE FINAL ROUND!
FROM HERE ON OUT, **FORGET** STRAT-EGY.
ラウンド 4回
残り時間 3

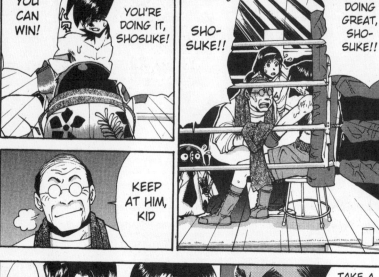

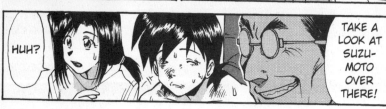

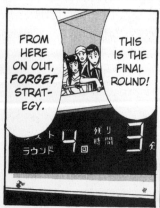

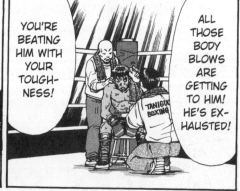

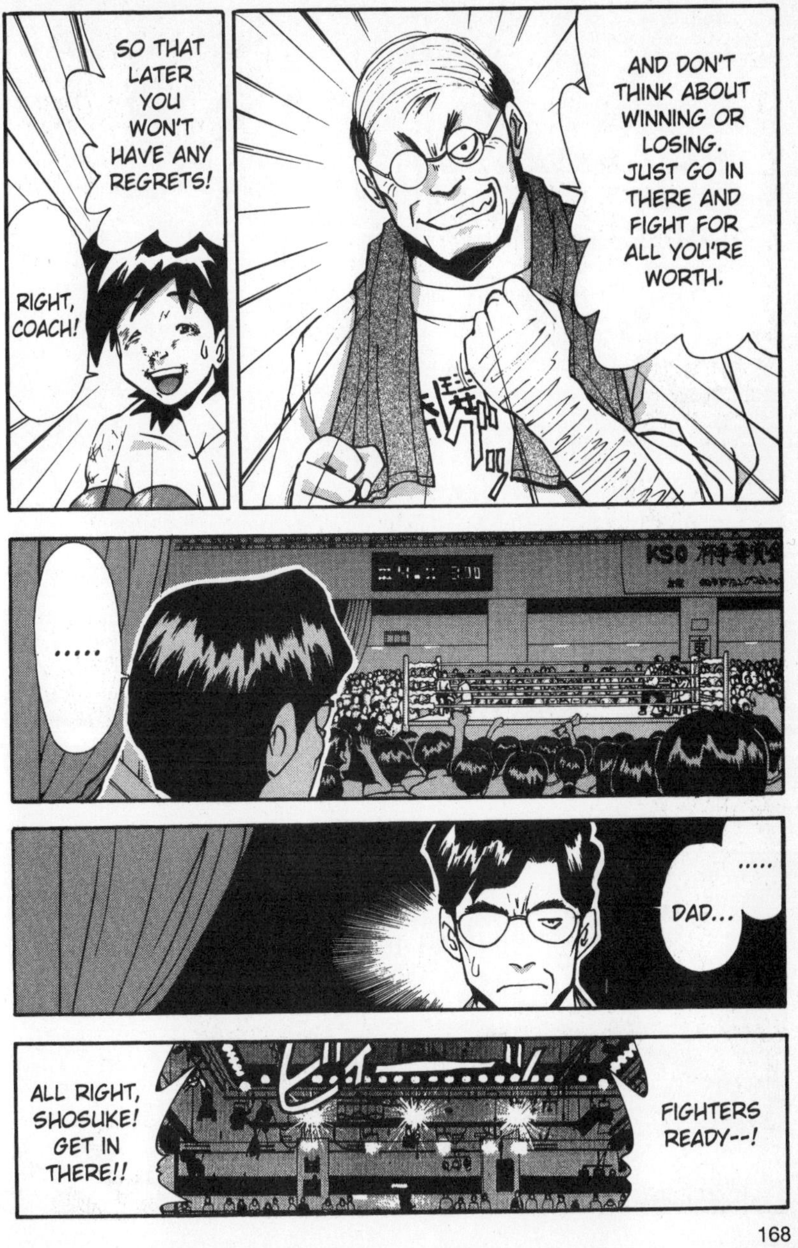
AND DON'T THINK ABOUT WINNING OR LOSING. JUST GO IN THERE AND FIGHT FOR ALL YOU'RE WORTH.
SO THAT LATER YOU WON'T HAVE ANY REGRETS!
RIGHT, COACH!
.....
.....
DAD...
FIGHTERS READY--!
ALL RIGHT, SHOSUKE! GET IN THERE!!

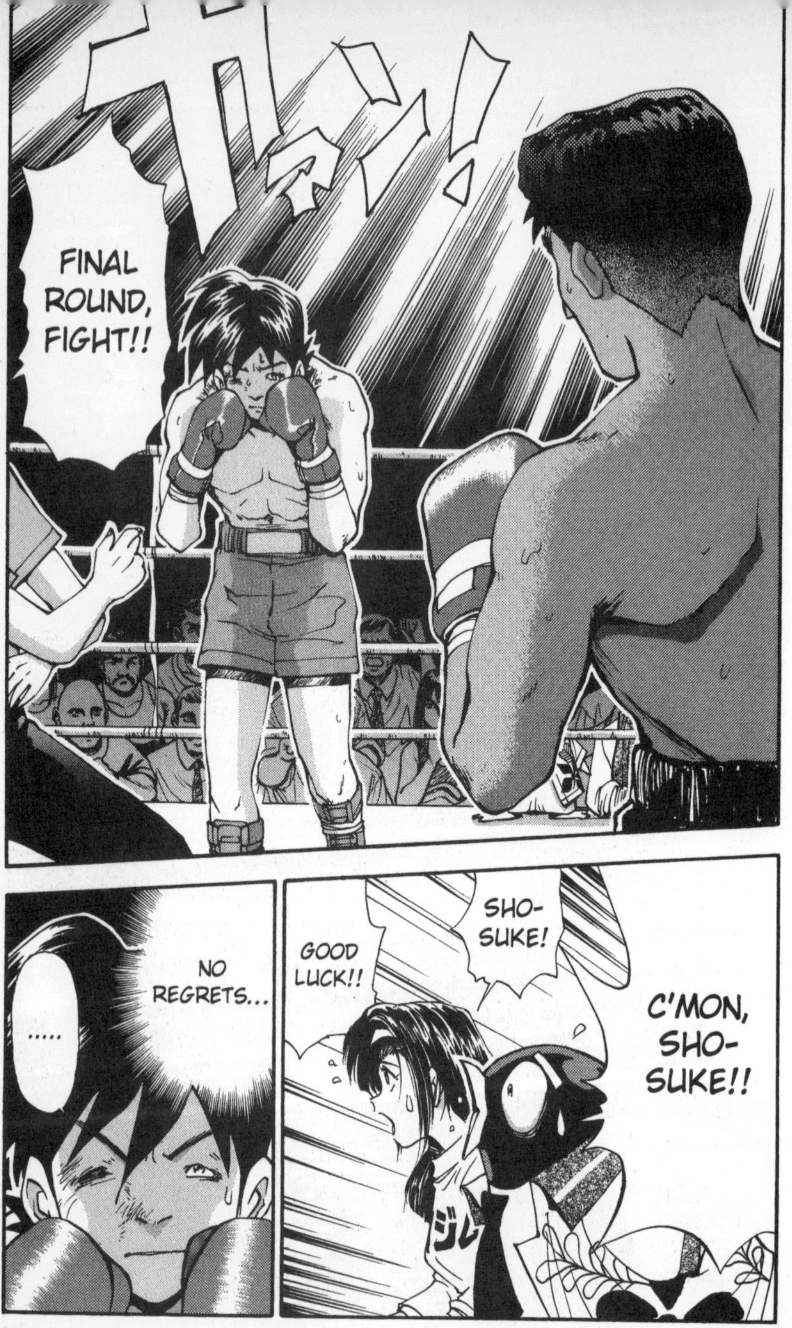

FINAL ROUND, FIGHT!!
C'MON, SHO-SUKE!!
SHO-SUKE!
GOOD LUCK!!
NO REGRETS...
.....

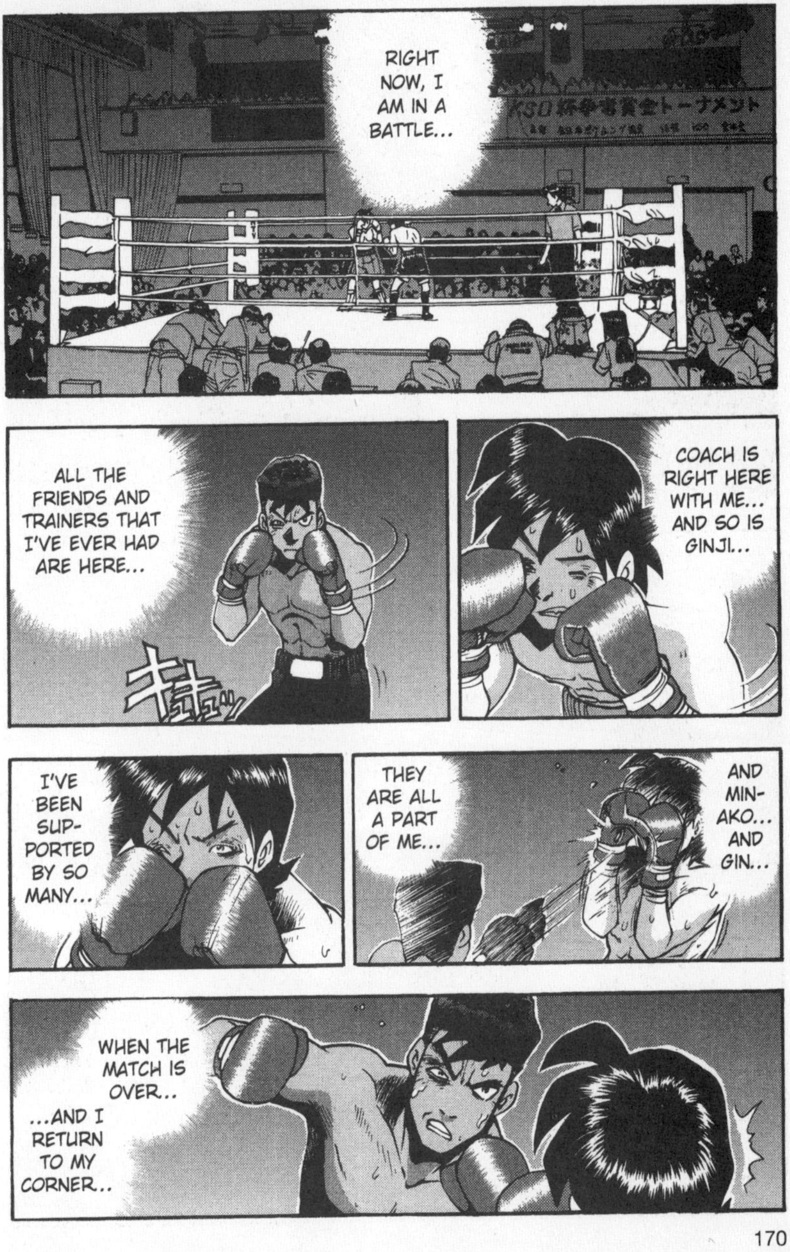
RIGHT NOW, I AM IN A BATTLE...
COACH IS RIGHT HERE WITH ME... AND SO IS GINJI...
ALL THE FRIENDS AND TRAINERS THAT I'VE EVER HAD ARE HERE...
AND MIN-AKO... AND GIN...
THEY ARE ALL A PART OF ME...
I'VE BEEN SUP-PORTED BY SO MANY...
WHEN THE MATCH IS OVER...
...AND I RETURN TO MY CORNER...

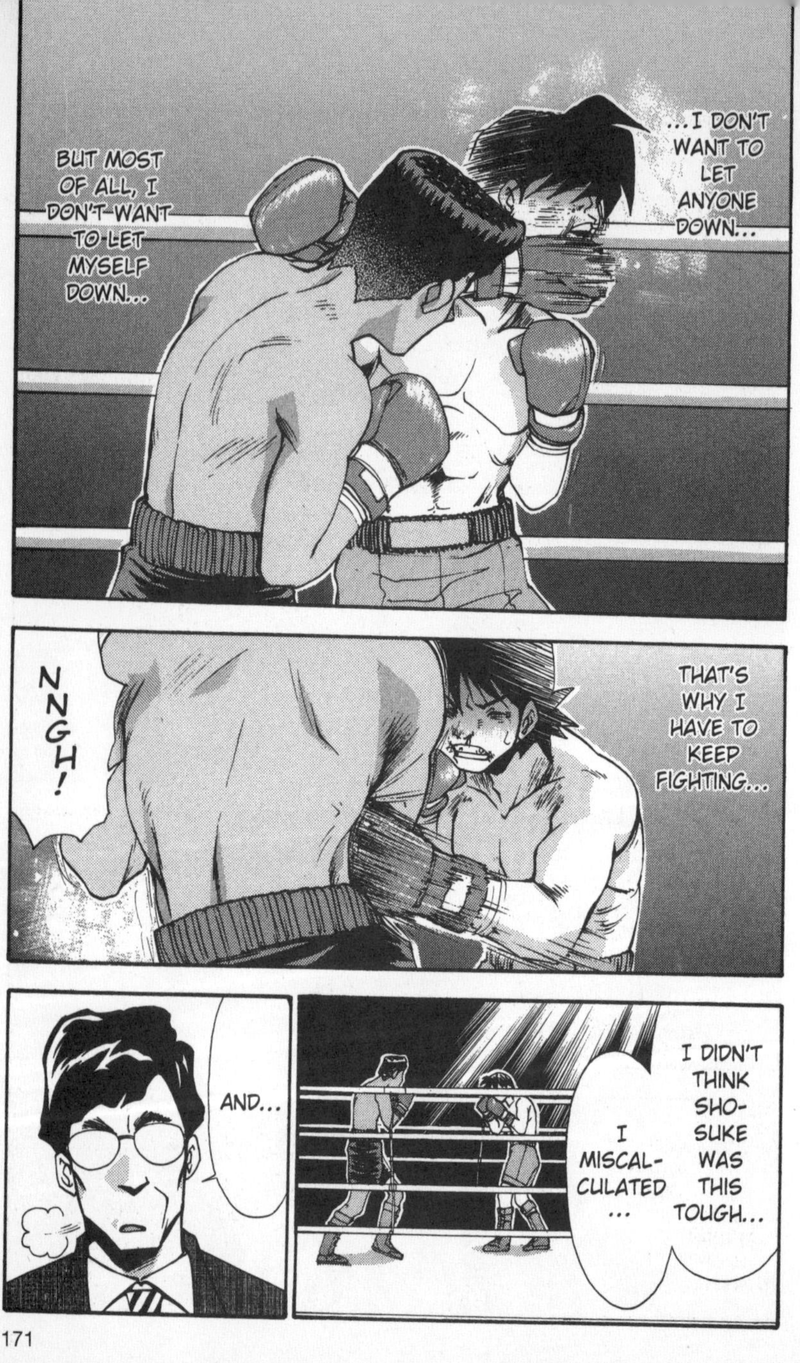
...I DON'T WANT TO LET ANYONE DOWN...
BUT MOST OF ALL, I DON'T WANT TO LET MYSELF DOWN...
THAT'S WHY I HAVE TO KEEP FIGHTING...
NNGH!
I DIDN'T THINK SHO-SUKE WAS THIS TOUGH...
I MISCAL-CULATED...
AND...

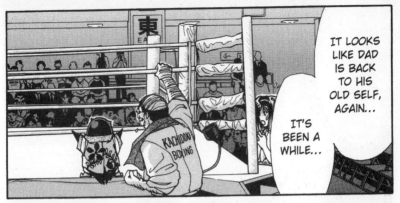

IT LOOKS LIKE DAD IS BACK TO HIS OLD SELF, AGAIN...

IT'S BEEN A WHILE...

.....

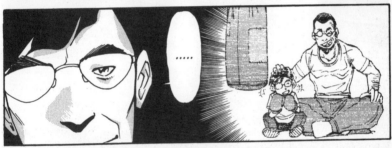

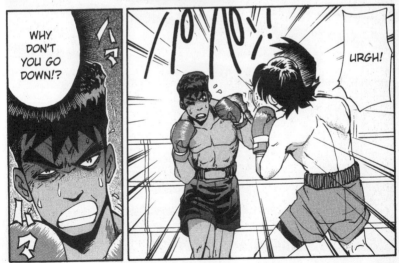

WHY DON'T YOU GO DOWN!?

URGH!

172

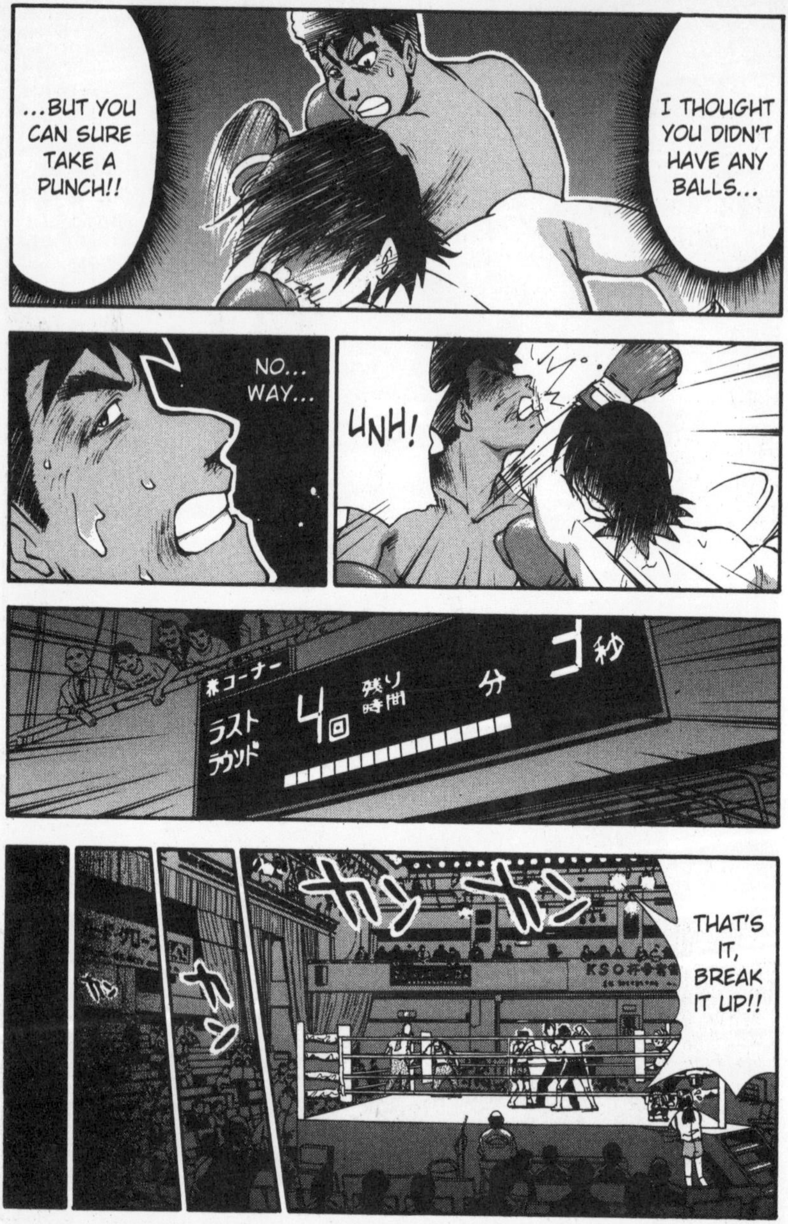
I THOUGHT YOU DIDN'T HAVE ANY BALLS...
...BUT YOU CAN SURE TAKE A PUNCH!!
UNH!
NO... WAY...
コーナー
ラスト ラウンド
4回
残り時間
分
秒
THAT'S IT, BREAK IT UP!!
カーン カーン
カン

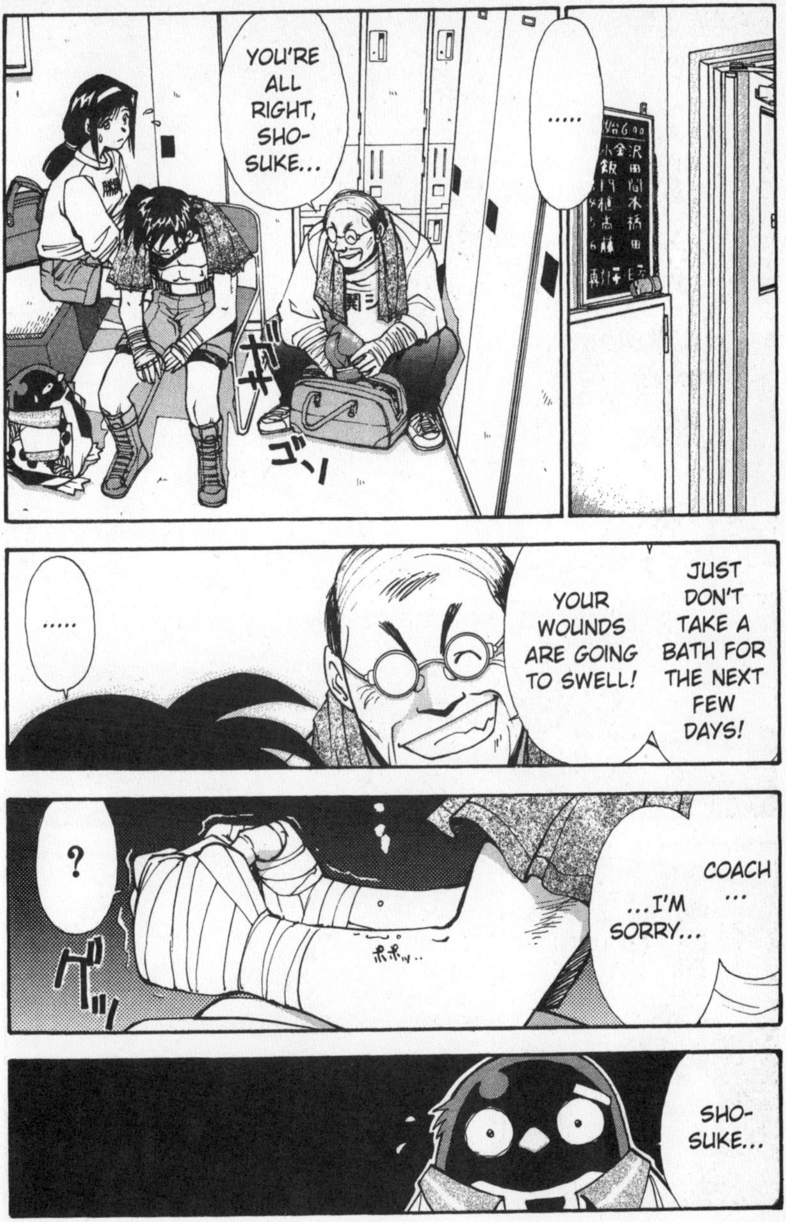
.....
YOU'RE ALL RIGHT, SHO-SUKE...
JUST DON'T TAKE A BATH FOR THE NEXT FEW DAYS!
YOUR WOUNDS ARE GOING TO SWELL!
.....
COACH...
...I'M SORRY...
?
SHO-SUKE...

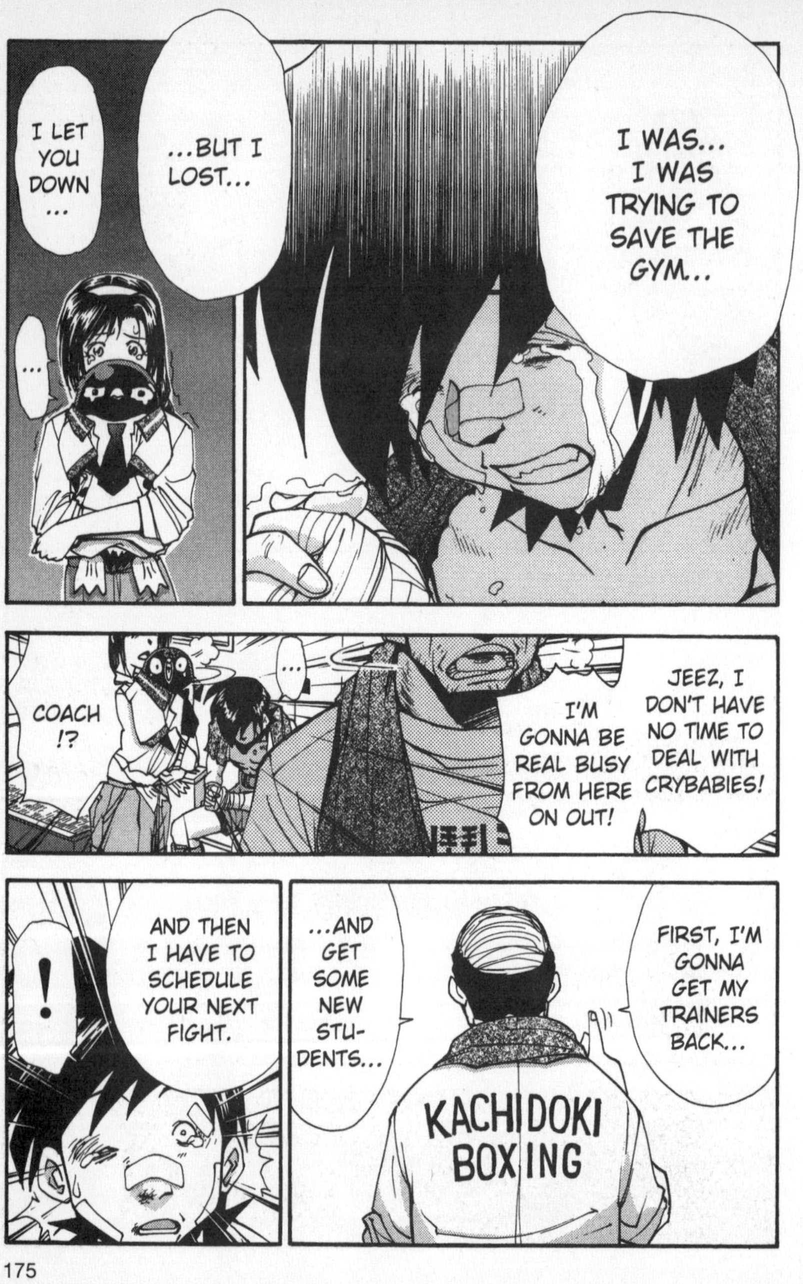
I WAS... I WAS TRYING TO SAVE THE GYM...
...BUT I LOST...
I LET YOU DOWN ...
...
JEEZ, I DON'T HAVE NO TIME TO DEAL WITH CRYBABIES!
I'M GONNA BE REAL BUSY FROM HERE ON OUT!
...
COACH !?
FIRST, I'M GONNA GET MY TRAINERS BACK...
...AND GET SOME NEW STU-DENTS...
KACHIDOKI BOXING
AND THEN I HAVE TO SCHEDULE YOUR NEXT FIGHT.
!

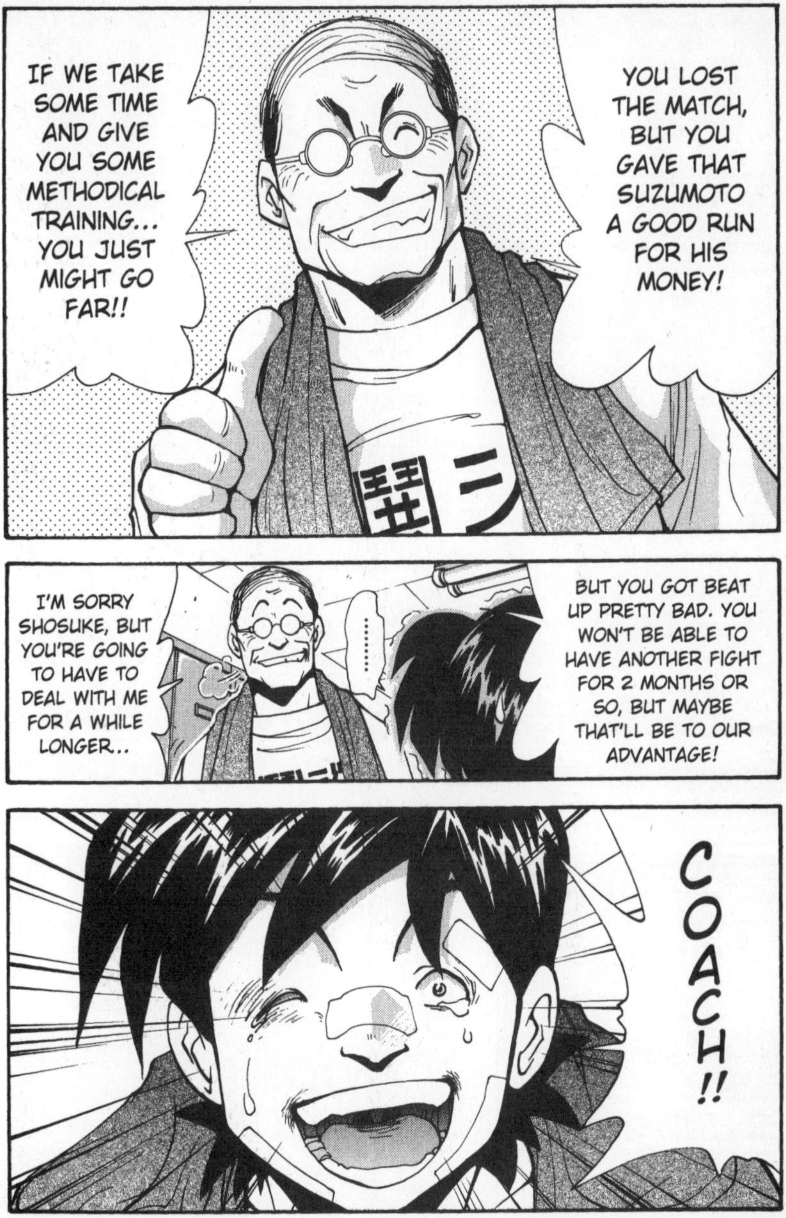
YOU LOST THE MATCH, BUT YOU GAVE THAT SUZUMOTO A GOOD RUN FOR HIS MONEY!
IF WE TAKE SOME TIME AND GIVE YOU SOME METHODICAL TRAINING... YOU JUST MIGHT GO FAR!!
BUT YOU GOT BEAT UP PRETTY BAD. YOU WON'T BE ABLE TO HAVE ANOTHER FIGHT FOR 2 MONTHS OR SO, BUT MAYBE THAT'LL BE TO OUR ADVANTAGE!
......
I'M SORRY SHOSUKE, BUT YOU'RE GOING TO HAVE TO DEAL WITH ME FOR A WHILE LONGER..
COACH!!

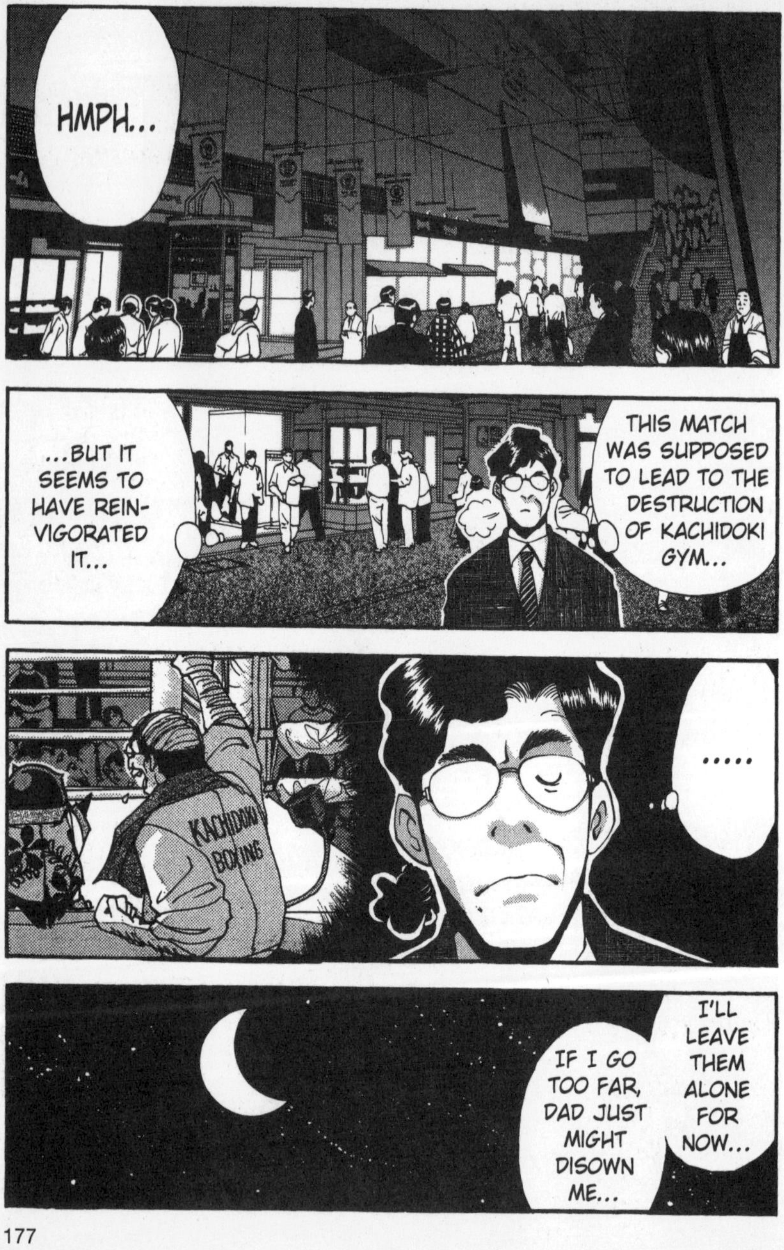
HMPH...
THIS MATCH WAS SUPPOSED TO LEAD TO THE DESTRUCTION OF KACHIDOKI GYM...
...BUT IT SEEMS TO HAVE REIN-VIGORATED IT...
.....
KACHIDOKI BOXING
I'LL LEAVE THEM ALONE FOR NOW...
IF I GO TOO FAR, DAD JUST MIGHT DISOWN ME...

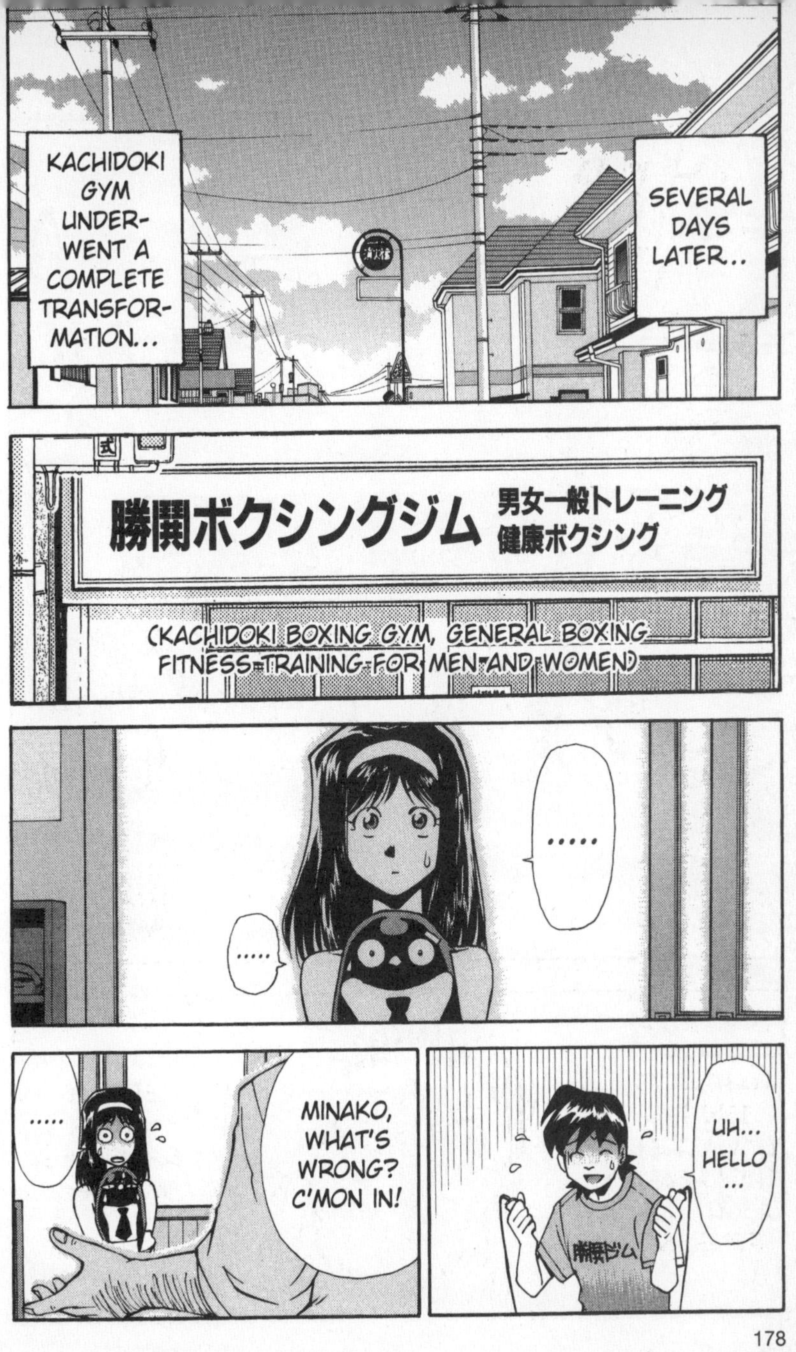
SEVERAL DAYS LATER...
KACHIDOKI GYM UNDER-WENT A COMPLETE TRANSFOR-MATION...
勝関ボクシングジム
男女一般トレーニング
健康ボクシング
(KACHIDOKI BOXING GYM, GENERAL BOXING FITNESS TRAINING FOR MEN AND WOMEN)
.....
.....
UH... HELLO ...
勝関ジム
MINAKO, WHAT'S WRONG? C'MON IN!
.....

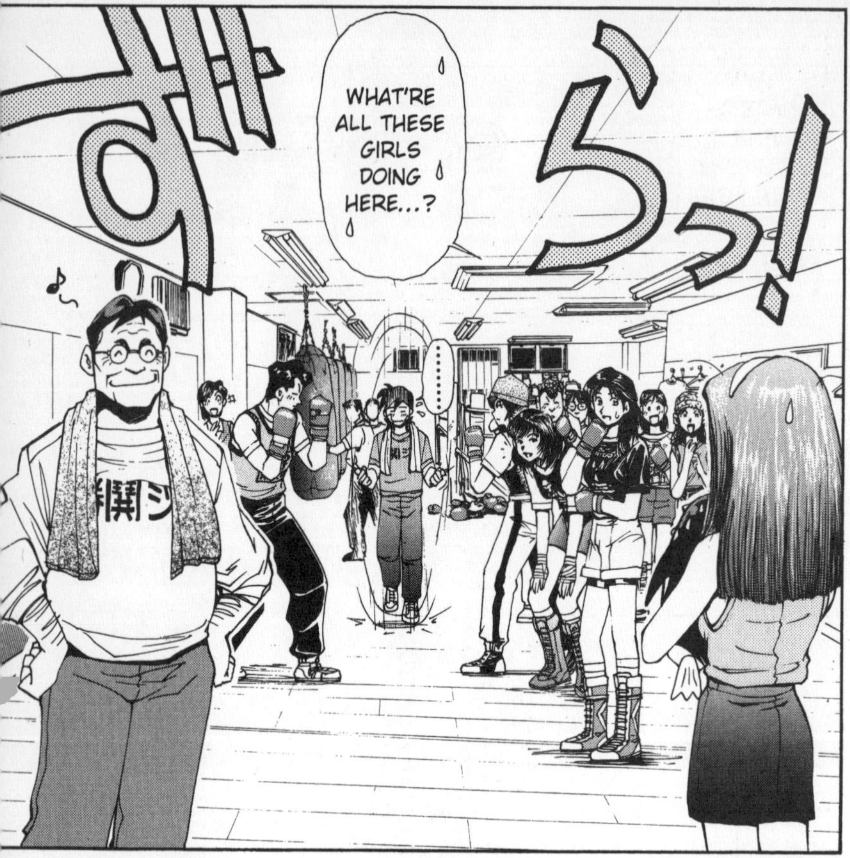
WHAT'RE ALL THESE GIRLS DOING HERE...?
......

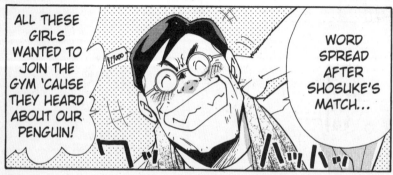

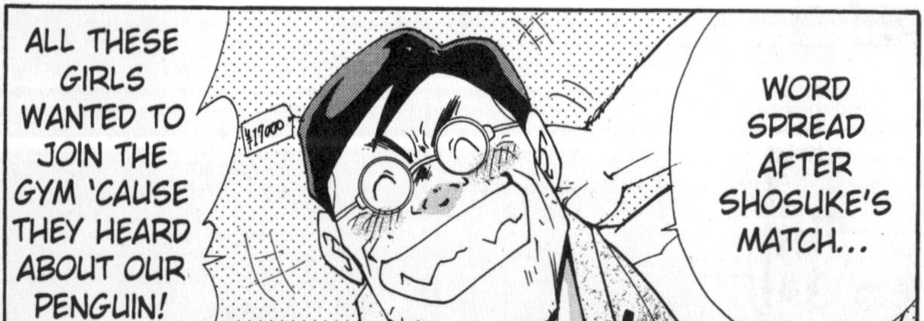
WORD SPREAD AFTER SHOSUKE'S MATCH...
ALL THESE GIRLS WANTED TO JOIN THE GYM 'CAUSE THEY HEARD ABOUT OUR PENGUIN!
ハッハッ

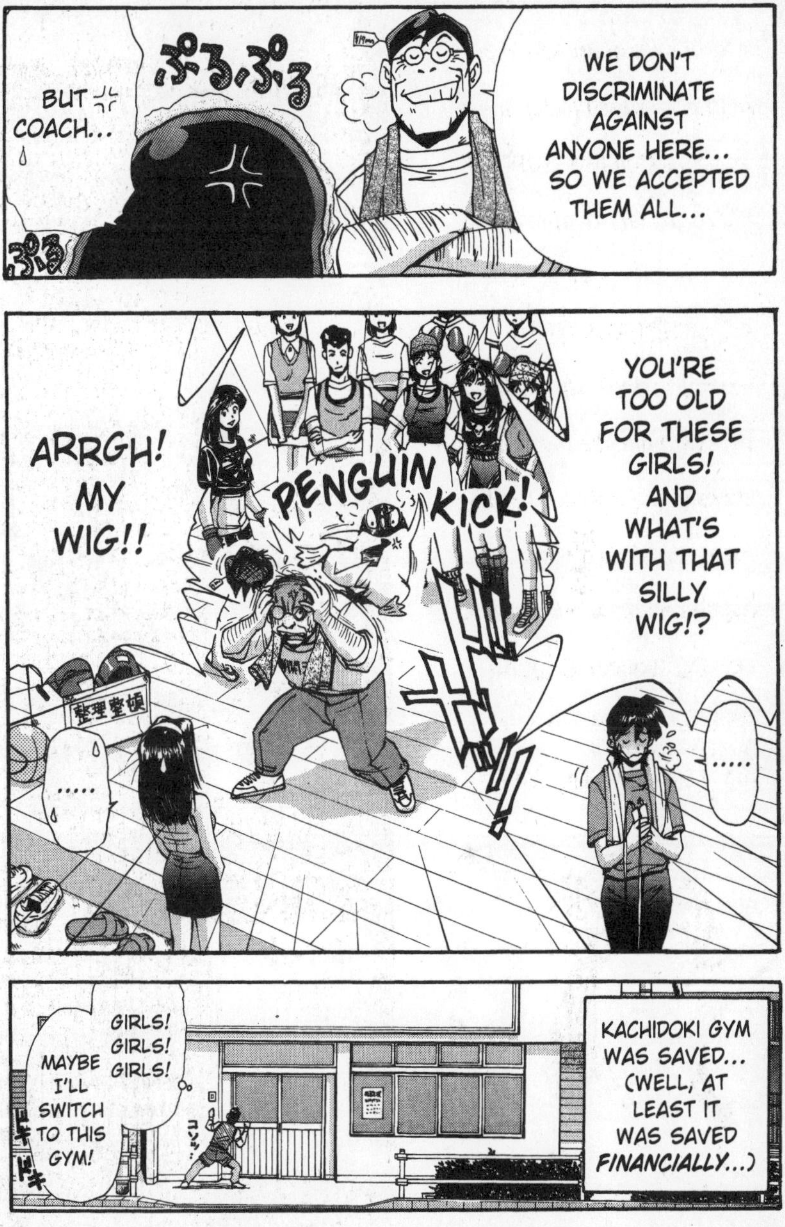
WE DON'T DISCRIMINATE AGAINST ANYONE HERE... SO WE ACCEPTED THEM ALL...
ぷるぷる
BUT COACH...
ぷる
YOU'RE TOO OLD FOR THESE GIRLS! AND WHAT'S WITH THAT SILLY WIG!?
PENGUIN KICK!
ARRGH! MY WIG!!
.....
整理整頓
.....
KACHIDOKI GYM WAS SAVED... (WELL, AT LEAST IT WAS SAVED *FINANCIALLY*...)
GIRLS! GIRLS! GIRLS!
MAYBE I'LL SWITCH TO THIS GYM!
ドキドキ

*W*ithin the context of TUXEDO GIN, the cry of an Adelie penguin is rendered in Japanese as something like "KUWAA!" We've chosen to represent it here, where it's been translated, as "SQUAWKK!" Actually, the cry of an Adelie penguin sounds more like a series of clicks and gargles. But who wants to see Gin-chan attacking someone with his patented "High Voltage Fury Jab From Hell" while he's screaming "KLIK KLIK KLIK KLIK!?"

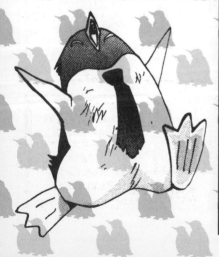

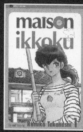
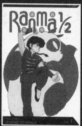
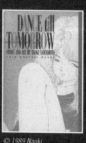

Glossary of SOUND EFFECTS, SIGNS, and other Miscellaneous Notes

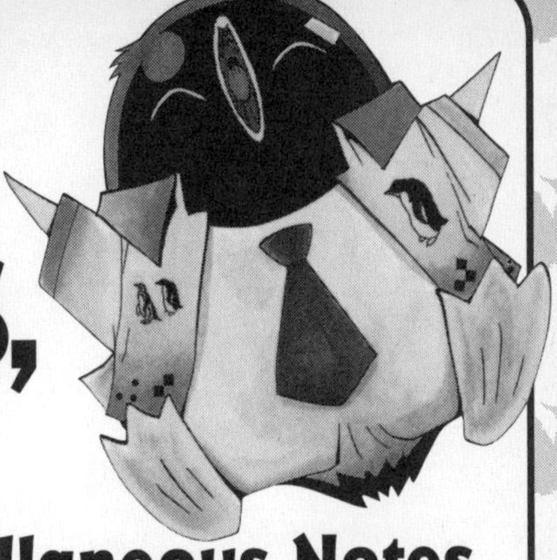

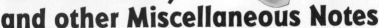

Each entry includes: the location, indicated by page number and panel number (so 3.1 means page 3, panel number 1); the phonetic romanization of the original Japanese; and our English "translation" – we offer as close an English equivalent as we can.

6.1	*CHUN CHUN: birds chirping*
	Sign: Oshokuji Dokoro Kaoru (Restaurant Kaoru)
7.2	*DARA DARA DARARI: sweating*
7.3	*GARA: sliding door*
7.5	*GABA: getting up*
8.1	*GORON: rolling over*
8.3	*PIKU PIKU: twitching*
	HARAHERI HERIHARA: going in and out of consciousness
9.1	*NGOO: snoring*
12.2	*KURU: turning around*
12.3	*SAWA: putting hand on Minako*
12.4	*GOKU: gulp*
13.1	*FUFUFU: heh heh heh*
14.3	*POTSUN: fwump*
15.1	*BOOO: spaced out*
15.2	*ZUUUN: depression*
15.3	*WAOOO: howling.*
16.1	*GORON: bottle rolling*
16.3	*UII: drunk*
16.6	*GOKU GOKU GOKU: gulp gulp gulp*
17.1	*DON: eruption*
17.1	*PUHAA!!: drunken breath*
17.2	*YORO: losing balance*
17.2	*KURA: dizziness*
17.3	*SUTEEEN: falling over*
17. 4	*TSUKA TSUKA: footsteps*
17.4	*PUSU PUSU PUSU: burning up*
17.6	*MUWAA: slowly getting up*
18.2	*GOSO GOSO: rustle rustle*
18.3	*YOTTO: lifting something heavy*
18.5	*JIWA: tearing up*
18.6	*DONGARA GASHAAN: crash bang*
18.6	*KUWA!: squawk!*
18.7	*DOTA DOTA DOTA: running*
19.1	*PUHA!: drunk breath*
19.1	*GARA: sliding door rattle*
19.3	*HIKU: hiccup*

19.3 *YURARI YURARI: swaying back and forth*
19.4 *BAN: bam*
20.1 *KUDO KUDO KUDO KUDO: boring long lecture*
20.1 *YURA YURA: swaying back and forth*
20.2 *HIC: drunk*
20.2 *NIKO: smile*
21.1 *GAGAAAN!: shock*
21.2 *KORON: fwump*
21.3 *FURA: weak hand*
22.3 *SUU SUU: sleeping*
25.1 *Tag on Cigar: Vahana [a play on Havanna]*
26.3 *GARA: sliding door*
26.4 *DA: dash*
27.1 *DOKA: crash*
27.2 *KII: break squeal*
27.3 *DO DO DO: idling engine*
27.4 *YURA: slowly stands up*
BOTO BOTO: dripping blood
27.5 *VUOOON: bike engine*
28.2 *PETA PETA: webbed feet flapping*
29.3 *JIIIII: glare*
30.1 *GARA: sliding door rattle*
30.2 *SHIIIIN: silence*
31.1 *ZUUUN: deep in thought*
31.2 *AUU: arrgh!*
32.1 *SUU: door opens*
32.3 *BATA BATA: running*
32.4 *POTA POTA: sweat dripping*
33.2 *DOYA DOYA DOYA: crowd noise*
33.3 *GACHA GACHA: unlocking door*
33.4 *GARA: rattle*
35.3 *MURI MURI MURI: moving Ginji around*
35.4 *GAAAN: shock fx*
35.6 *BUCHI: snap*
35.7 *BUGYURU: circulation increasing*
35.7 *DEKO: vein popping*
36.1 *BAKON: punch*
36.2 *BACHI BACHI BACHI BACHI BACHI: slapping*
36.2 *KISHAAA: crash*
36.3 *GO: blunt hit*
36.4 *GATA GATA GATA: trembling*
37.2 *DADADADADA: running*
37.3 *PETA PETA PETA: webbed feet flapping*
38.1 *GYA GYA: skidding*
38.1 *BA: jumping out of way*
38.3 *SUTATAN!: quick step*
38.5 *GA: tripping*
38.6 *DOKA: crash*
39.2 *YORO YORO: swaying back and forth*
39.3 *TSURU: slip*
39.4 *DOKA DOKA: falling clatter commotion*
RURURURU: sliding across floor
40.1 *KUEE: squawk!!*
40.3 *DAN: jump*
40.4 *TSURURURURU: sliding*
40.5 *DOGA: landing on Ginji*
41.1 *TSURURURU: sliding*
41.4 *BAKIIN: crash shatter*
41.5 *HYUU: wind*

Glossary of SOUND EFFECTS, SIGNS, and other Miscellaneous Notes

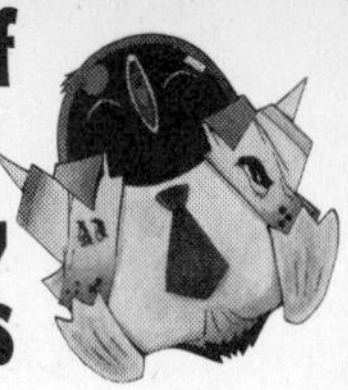

42.1	*GOOOOO: falling*
42.6	*DOBOON: splash*
43.1	*ZAZA: waves*
43.2	*BASHA!: splash*
43.3	*BASU: something hitting Musashi*
43.4	*GASHI: bite*
43.4	*BASU BASU: punching*
43.4	*GYUN: swimming*
43.4	*GUO: attacking*
49.3	*PITA: stops*
49.3	*TOCO TOCO TOCO: walks over*
49.5	*PA PA: waves flag*
49.6	*PATA PAPATA: waves flag*
49.7	*PAPATA: waves flag*
49.8	*PATA PAPATA: waves flag*
50.1	*DAKI!: hug*
50.2	*PIIN: idea pops*
50.2	*HA: gasp*
50.4	*GYUN: stare*
51.1	*JIIII: glare*
51.3	*GATA: gets up suddenly*
51.4	*KACHA KACHA: plate rustling*
52.2	*HAA: sigh*
52.4	*BASHA BASHA: splash*
52.5	*ZABU ZABU: walking in water*
53.5	*TOSU: fwump*
54.1	*GABA: gets up*
55.3	*PIKU: anger*
55.4	*DOGO: bam!*
55.5	*KAKE KAKE KAKE: sound of pushups*
56.3	*GARA: sliding door.*
56.4	*BORO: feeling injured*
57.1	*ZUKIN ZUKIN: throb throb*
57.4	*UUN ITEE: groan ouch!*
58.1	*BOSU: beating*
58.2	*KA: swip!*
58.4	*BASHI BASHI BASHI: beating*
58.5	*GOGOGOGO: anger*
58.6	*BASHI BASHI: beating*
59.1	*SHUN: slump*
59.2	*HAHAHA: laugh*
59.5	*BATTARI: falls down*
59.5	*PIKU PIKU: twitch twitch*
60.1	*SUU: writing with marker*
61.1	*BACHIIN!: smack*
61.3	*YURA: stagger*
61.4	*BASHI BASHI BASHI: beating*
62.3	*JIIIIN: getting emotional*
62.4	*BIKUN: startled*
62.5	*TON TON TON: coming upstairs*
62.6	*GARA: sliding door opens*
63.5	*writing: Ginji buji (Ginji's okay)*
64.1	*ZUGATAN: falling over*
64.3	*UU: crying*
64.3	*CHAN CHAN: goofy music*

65.1	*UOOOO: crowd goes wild*
65.2	*UOOO: penguins cheering*
	GU: clench
	PORO PORO: tears dripping
65.3	*WAAAA: crowd cheering*
	DOYA DOYA DOYA: penguins swarming
	PETA PETS: flippers flapping
67.3	*TSUUU: bloody nose*
68.1	*JYA: standing in place*
69.1	*GABA: getting up fast*
69.3	*JIIIN: waking up*
69.4	*CHUN CHUN: birds chirping*
69.4	*PATA: falling onto floor*
70.1	*BOOO: spaced out*
70.1	*MOGO MOGO: sleepily moving mouth*
71.3	*HAAAA: sigh*
71.3	*GORON: lying down*
72.4	*PATAM: slam*
73.1	*GOOOO: roll*
	DA GA DA: klak klak tump
44.2	*PUKAA: floating*
46.3	*PAFU: fwump*
49.1	*GARA: door rattles open*
49.2	*JYA: standing in place*
73.3	*GOOOO: roll*
73.4	*SHUGOGOOO: roll*
74.1	*BA: jumps*
74.2	*GYUN: getting air*
74.2	*HO HO HO: huf huf huf*
74.3	*DOOON: crash*
74.4	*KARA KARA: wheels spinning.*
75.2	*GAAAN: shock*
77.1	*sign: Kachidoki Boxing Gym Danjo Ippan Training Kenko Boxing (Kachidoki Boxing Gym, General Boxing Fitness Training for Men and Women)*
77.2	*CHIRI CHIRI: hair standing on end*
77.2	*DOKI DOKI: ba-bump ba-bump*
77.4	*SOO: sneak*
78.1	*DOYON: gloom*
78.2	*YURAA: slowly standing up*
78.3	*PA: lights turn on*
78.4	*GAAAAN: shock*
78.5	*BOOOO: spaced out.*
79.3	*KURA: losing balance*
79.3	*YORORO: falling down*
79.4	*TOSU: sitting down.*
79.4	*HAAAA: deep breath*
82.1	*BAN: slam*
82.2	*UU UUU: getting emotional*
84.1	*BIKU: startled*
84.4	*HAA HAA: heavy breathing*
85.1	*GAKU: slump*
85.2	*SHIIIIN: silence*
86.1	*ZUPAAN: kick*
86.4	*GYU: fitting gloves on*
86.5	*GUGU: fits other glove on*
87.1	*PYON: hop*
87.2	*KUI KUI: waving leg*

Glossary of SOUND EFFECTS, SIGNS, and other Miscellaneous Notes

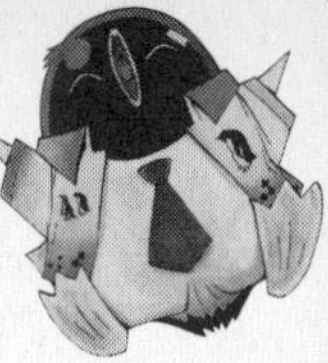

87.3	BITA: falls over
87.3	HAU: oof
87.6	BAAN: boxing stance
91.3	NGOO: snoring
91.5	CHOTTO KOFUKU: a little happy
93.2	AU!: Hey!
96.1	sign: Kachidoki Boxing
96.1	KA: sunlight
96.3	PON: solitude
96.4	FUU: sigh
96.4	GARA: sliding door
97.1	BIKU: startled
97.1	PIKAA: shine
97.3	TOTETETE: shuf shuf shuf
97.4	TOTETETETE: shuf shuf shuf
98.1	MUUU: using strength
98.1	GYU: wringing out
98.2	GYU: being squeezed by all of Minako's dialogue balloons.
98.3	HAA HAA HAA: huf huf huf
98.3	TOTETETETE: shuf shuf shuf
100.2	HIEE: gasp
100.3	EHHEN: ahem
102.1	UHAHAHAHAHA: ha ha ha ha
102.3	BISHI: swip
103.3	GA: bump
103.4	DA: runs
103.6	BECHI: softer sounding bump
104.1	GARA: sliding door
104.4	PASHI: fwip
105.2	B class fighter: In Japan, pro boxers are divided into three classes. Matches for Class A fighters last 8 rounds or more, Class B fighters have 6 round matches, and Class C matches are 4 rounds.
106.1	KUWA: squawk
	BIBI: stands up
106.2	SHIIIIN: silence
108.2	sign: Kachidoki Boxing Gym Danjo Ippan Training Kenko Boxing (Kachidoki Boxing Gym, General Boxing Fitness Training for Men and Women)
109.1	JIII: glare
109.5	GYU: stands firm
109.6	GIN: glare
109.7	PYON!: jump
110.1	SUPAPAPAN: bwapwapwap
110.2	GISHI GISHI: creak creak
110.2	SUTA: fwump
112.2	SOOOOO: sneaking a peak
112.3	SA: sneak sneak
112.3	TOKO TOKO: waddle waddle
112.4	KOSO: sneaking

112.4 NYU: extends neck
112.6 HYOKO!: peek!
113.2 CHON: touches gloves
113.4 PASHI: bap
114.1 DON: bam
115.5 BATAN: door shuts
116.4 IRA IRA: irritated
116.5 KURU!: turns around
117.1 SHIN: silence
117.7 GYU: clenches fist
118.2 DA: dash
118.3 GURU: turns around
119.1 DA: run
119.2 BA: lunge
119.3 PYON: jumps
119.4 GYUN: rushes forward
119.4 BA: shifts position
119.5 SUKA: swings arm in air
120.1 SUPAN: punch
120.2 BOSU: hits ground
121.5 DON: bwap
122.3 SHIN: silence
122.5 SUKU: stands up
122.7 GU: clench
125.1 GAPO: crack
125.1 GUSHU: crack
125.2 GO GO: gulp gulp
125.3 DADAN!: slamming down glasses
125.5 GABA: brings head up
128.1 HA HA HA: huf huf huf
128.3 GASA GASA: rustle rustle
128.4 TA TA: jogging
129.1 PETA PETA PETA: penguin feet flapping
129.1 TA TA TA TA: jogging
129.2 PETA PETA PETA PETA PETA: flap flap flap
129.3 GA: clench
130~131.1 UZAZAZAZAZA: swarm
130~131.2 DADADADA: running
130~131.2 WARA WARA WARA: swarming
132.2 GON!: bam
133.1 ZUKIN ZUKIN: throb throb
133.3 KURA GURA: disoriented
134.1 PEKORI: bow
134.2 TA TA TA: running
134.5 SHU: punching air
135.2 SHU SHU KYU KYU: swip swip squeak squeak
135.3 SHU SHU: swings arms
135.5 GO: bump
135.5 HAA HAA: huf huf
136.2 BIKUN: startled
136.4 GATA: getting up
136.4 BASU: hits gloves together
137.5 PETA PETA PETA: webbed feet walking
138.1 DOWA: crowd reaction
KUWAA!: squawk!
139.1 DOYA DOYA DOYA: crowd being loud
WAAA: crowd being loud
139.2 YAJI YAJI YAJI WAA: crowd noise
DOYA DOYA DOYA: crowd noise
142.1 GOGOGOGOGOGO : anger
142.2 PURU PURU: trembling in anger
142.3 KAAAAN: bell
143.1 DA: dash

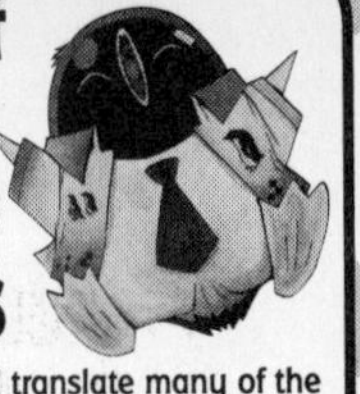

Glossary of SOUND EFFECTS, SIGNS, and other Miscellaneous Notes

In order to leave the artwork as close to the original as possible, we didn't retouch and translate many of the sound effects and signs contained within this manga. However, we wouldn't want you to miss anything, so we've included a glossary of sound effects and other things not translated or retouched.

The Glossary begins on page 182.

143.4 *SHU: swing*
143.4 *SU: dodge*
144.1 *WAAAAA: crowd going wild*
144.3 *BAN BAN: bam bam*
146.1 *HAA... HAA... HAA...: huf huf huf*
147.3 *HAA HAA: huf huf*
147.5 *PAPAPAN: pow pow pow*
149.2 *KAAAAN: bell*
149.4 *MOMI MOMI MOMI: massage fx*
149.4 *KUUUUU: crying*
151.2 *PON: hand on shoulder*
151.3 *PU: laughing*
152.4 *KAAAN: bell*
153.5 *ZUI: rushes forward*
154.1 *ZUPAAAN!: kapow*
154.2 *KYU: fwip*
154.4 *GU: grab*
154.5 *GA: snatch*
155.1 *SU: fwip*
155.5 *WAAAA: crowd goes wild*
156.1 *GA: bwap*
157.2 *GYUBA: holds stance*
157.6 *DAN!: lunge*
158.1 *BA: jumps*
159.1 *BASUN!: punch*
160.1 *BAKUN!: bam!*
161.4 *GYU: grip*
162.2 *WAAAA: crowd*
162.4 *BOOO: dazed*
163.1 *POKEEEE: dazed*
163.3 *KYUBA: lunge*
165.2 *GURA: leg giving out*
165.3 *BASUN: punch*
167.2 *HAA HAA: huf huf*
168.1 *GU: clenches fist.*
168.5 *BEEEEEE: beeeep*
169.1 *KAAAAN!: bell*
170.3 *KYU KYU: fwip fwip*
172.3 *PAPAN: jabs*
172.4 *HAA HAA: huf huf*
173.5 *KAN KAN KAN KAN: klang klang klang*
174.2 *GASA GOSO: rustle rustle*
174.4 *GU: clench*
179.1 *ZURA: Surprise! Look at all the people fx.*
179.2 *WAHAHA: ha ha ha*
180.1 *PURU PURU: Trembling in anger*
180.2 *DOKA!: Kick*
180.3 *KOSO: sneaking around*
180.3 *DOKI DOKI: heart beating*

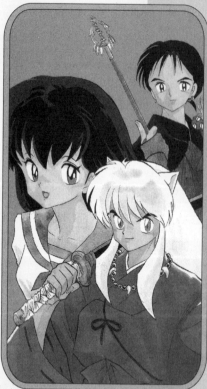

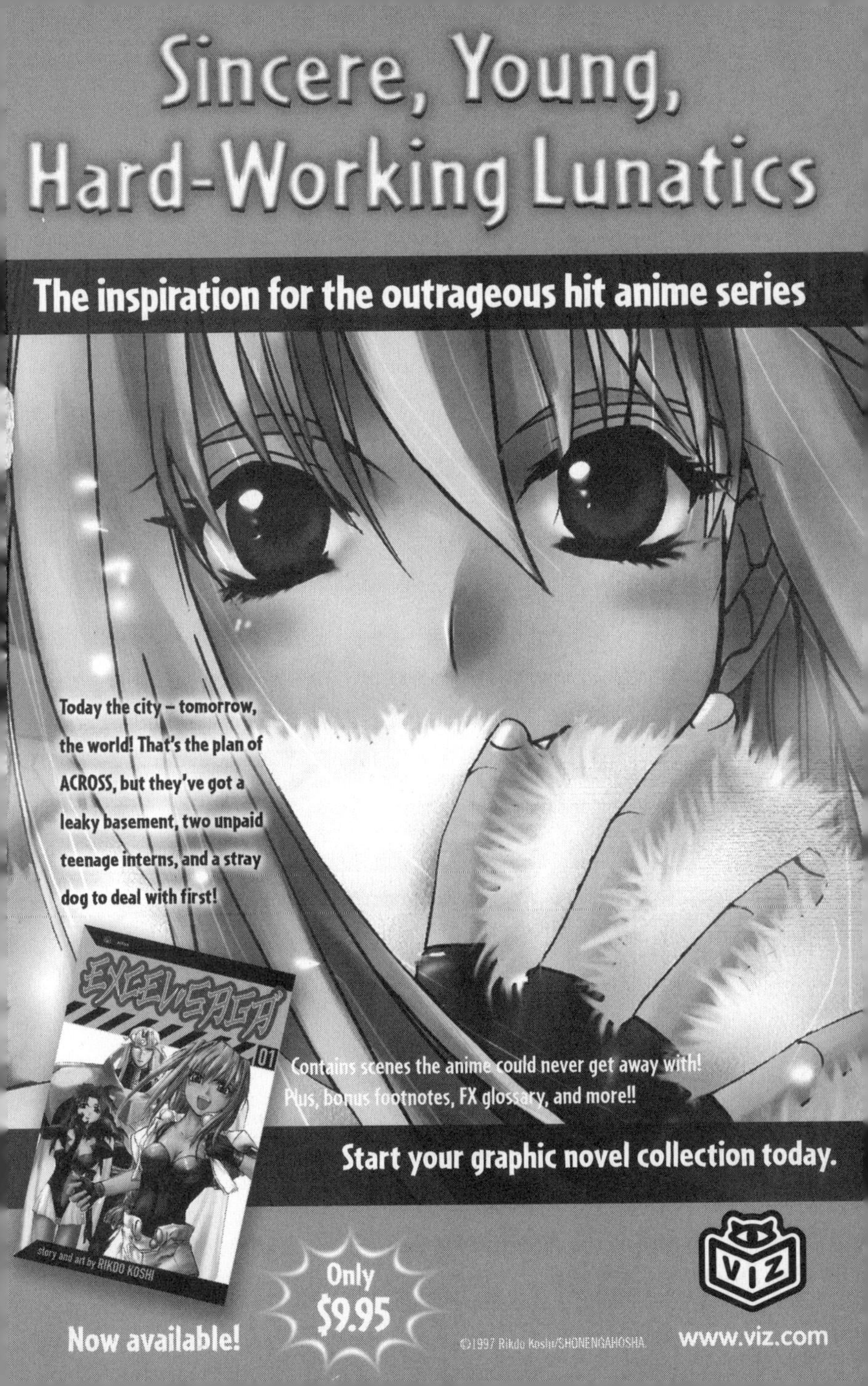
Sincere, Young, Hard-Working Lunatics
The inspiration for the outrageous hit anime series
Today the city – tomorrow, the world! That's the plan of ACROSS, but they've got a leaky basement, two unpaid teenage interns, and a stray dog to deal with first!
EXCEL♥SAGA
01
story and art by RIKDO KOSHI
Contains scenes the anime could never get away with!
Plus, bonus footnotes, FX glossary, and more!!
Start your graphic novel collection today.
VIZ
Only $9.95
Now available!
©1997 Rikdo Koshi/SHONENGAHOSHA.
www.viz.com

COMPLETE OUR SURVEY AND LET US KNOW WHAT YOU THINK!

☐ Please check here if you DO NOT wish to receive information or future offers from VIZ

Name: _____

Address: _____

City: _____ **State:** _____ **Zip:** _____

E-mail: _____

☐ Male ☐ Female **Date of Birth** (mm/dd/yyyy): ___ / ___ / ___   (Under 13? Parental consent required)

What race/ethnicity do you consider yourself? (please check one)

☐ Asian/Pacific Islander ☐ Black/African American ☐ Hispanic/Latino

☐ Native American/Alaskan Native ☐ White/Caucasian ☐ Other: _____

What VIZ product did you purchase? (check all that apply and indicate title purchased)

☐ DVD/VHS _____

☐ Graphic Novel _____

☐ Magazines _____

☐ Merchandise _____

Reason for purchase: (check all that apply)

☐ Special offer ☐ Favorite title ☐ Gift

☐ Recommendation ☐ Other _____

Where did you make your purchase? (please check one)

☐ Comic store ☐ Bookstore ☐ Mass/Grocery Store

☐ Newsstand ☐ Video/Video Game Store ☐ Other: _____

☐ Online (site: _____)

What other VIZ properties have you purchased/own? _____

_____

How many anime and/or manga titles have you purchased in the last year? How many were VIZ titles? (please check one from each column)

ANIME
- [ ] None
- [ ] 1-4
- [ ] 5-10
- [ ] 11+

MANGA
- [ ] None
- [ ] 1-4
- [ ] 5-10
- [ ] 11+

VIZ
- [ ] None
- [ ] 1-4
- [ ] 5-10
- [ ] 11+

I find the pricing of VIZ products to be: (please check one)

- [ ] Cheap
- [ ] Reasonable
- [ ] Expensive

What genre of manga and anime would you like to see from VIZ? (please check two)

- [ ] Adventure
- [ ] Comic Strip
- [ ] Detective
- [ ] Fighting
- [ ] Horror
- [ ] Romance
- [ ] Sci-Fi/Fantasy
- [ ] Sports

What do you think of VIZ's new look?

- [ ] Love It
- [ ] It's OK
- [ ] Hate It
- [ ] Didn't Notice
- [ ] No Opinion

THANK YOU! Please send the completed form to:

NJW Research
42 Catharine St.
Poughkeepsie, NY 12601

D0920093

All information provided will be used for internal purposes only. We promise not to sell or otherwise divulge your information.